DARWINIAN
NATURAL RIGHT

SUNY Series in Philosophy and Biology
David Edward Shaner, Editor

DARWINIAN NATURAL RIGHT

The Biological Ethics of Human Nature

Larry Arnhart

State University
of New York Press

Published by
State University of New York Press

© 1998 State University of New York

For information, address State University of New York Press,
90 State Street, Suite 700, Albany, NY 12207

Production by Bernadine Dawes • Marketing by Dana Yanulavich

Library of Congress Cataloging-in-Publication Data

Arnhart, Larry, 1949–
    Darwinian natural right : the biological ethics of human nature /
Larry Arnhart.
        p.   cm. — (SUNY series in philosophy and biology.)
    Includes bibliographical references and index.
    ISBN 0-7914-3693-4 (alk. paper). — ISBN 0-7914-3694-2 (pbk. :
alk. paper)
    1. Ethics, Evolutionary. I. Title. II. Series.
BJ1311.A66   1998
171'.7—dc21   97-49287
                                                         CIP

1 2 3 4 5 6 7 8 9 10

For Susan
My wife and my friend

Ius naturalis est, quod natura omnia animalia docuit.
Natural right is that which nature has taught all animals.
—Justinian, *Institutes*

Contents

Abbreviations

In my references to Aristotle's texts, I use the standard Bekker page numbers, and I employ the following abbreviations.

De Anima	*DA*
De Caelo	*DC*
Eudemian Ethics	*EE*
Generation of Animals	*GA*
History of Animals	*HA*
Magna Moralia	*MM*
On Memory	*Mem*
Metaphysics	*Meta*
The Movement of Animals	*MA*
Nicomachean Ethics	*NE*
Parts of Animals	*PA*
Poetics	*Poet*
Physics	*Phy*
Politics	*Pol*
Rhetoric	*Rh*

Acknowledgments

I could not have written this book without the intellectual inspiration and personal encouragement provided by Roger Masters of Dartmouth College. Although he does not agree with all of my arguments, his brilliant work in applying biological reasoning to issues in political philosophy has been a model for me to imitate.

I began working on this book during the academic year of 1988-1989, which I spent at Stanford University. This year of research was supported by a grant from the National Endowment for the Humanities and a sabbatical leave from Northern Illinois University. During that year, the faculty in the Program in Human Biology at Stanford were gracious in allowing me to attend some of their classes.

In 1992, a research grant from the Earhart Foundation allowed me to continue my work. In 1996, some of my final revisions of the book were done while attending the Summer Institute on human biology at Dartmouth College, which was directed by Roger Masters and Robert Perlman. This Institute was organized by the Gruter Institute for Law and Behavioral Research and sponsored by the National Science Foundation and the National Endowment for the Humanities.

Some of the ideas in this book were first worked out in courses that I have taught in the Department of Political Science at NIU as part of the program in "Politics and the Life Sciences." I am particularly grateful to Andrea Bonnicksen, James Schubert, and Gary Glenn for supporting these courses.

Gary Johnson and other members of the Association for Politics and the Life Sciences have offered comments and criticisms to help me think through my arguments.

As with much of my work, I have been forced to sharpen my reasoning in this book in response to the insightful questions of Rick Sorenson. Many of his questions were formulated during symposia on his porch in Worcester, Massachusetts. His friendship has sustained me for more than twenty-five years.

My greatest debt, however, is to my wife Susan. I could not have finished this book without her intellectual and emotional companionship. Many of the ideas in this book were first formulated in conversations with her. For example, many of her thoughts about psychopathy have entered chapter 8. And much of my thinking in comparing the positions of Aristotle, Hobbes, Kant, and Darwin shows the influence of her insights.

ARISTOTLE, DARWIN, AND NATURAL RIGHT

> The difference between Plato and Aristotle is that Aristotle
> believes that biology, as a mediation between knowledge of
> the inanimate and knowledge of man, is available.
> —Leo Strauss, *On Tyranny*

AN INTELLECTUAL JOURNEY

The ultimate aim of politics is to form the character of human beings to promote some conception of the best life. This must be so, because every political debate depends fundamentally on opinions about what is good and bad, just and unjust. The moral opinions that drive political controversy are ultimately opinions about the best way of life for human beings, about how human beings must live to satisfy their natural desires. Consequently, the greatest questions of politics concern the problem of how to shape the moral character of human beings to conform to a naturally good way of life.

Although differing opinions of the best way of life create great diversity in the political experience of human beings, there is a regularity in those moral opinions that expresses a universal human nature. For example, every political regime must provide somehow for family life, because the dependence of the young on adult care is an enduring feature of human nature. Every political regime must also have some hierarchy of dominance in which some individuals will have higher social status than others, because the competition for social rank is another enduring feature of human nature. There is great variability, however, in the particular expressions of these universal tendencies, and therefore prudence is required in judging what is appropriate for the circumstances of particular individuals and particular societies. Satisfying the natural human desires requires moral character. Parents must have the moral character that inclines them to properly nurture the moral character of children. And those who desire high social rank must have the moral character that inclines them to satisfy their desire for preeminence without tyrannizing over others.

1

As a college student in the late 1960s, I found that this view of politics as a character-forming activity rooted in human nature was best developed by Aristotle. In his *Nicomachean Ethics* and *Politics*, he argues that the aim of politics is to shape moral character to satisfy the natural desires of human beings. In the *Ethics*, he studies the moral and intellectual virtues necessary for human flourishing or happiness. In the *Politics*, he shows how the social and governmental structures of various political regimes can foster or impede the virtues of human character. Judging human virtues and political regimes cannot be determined by universal rules, he insists, because the diversity in the individual and social circumstances of life requires prudence or practical wisdom, which cannot be reduced to abstract rules. Nevertheless, human nature does provide a universal standard of judgment: human beings are by nature social and political animals who use their natural capacity for speech to deliberate about the conditions of their social and political life. Therefore, we can judge political communities by how well they conform to the nature of human beings as political animals and rational animals.

Despite the important differences between Aristotle's Greek *polis* and the modern liberal democratic state, the writings of Harry Jaffa (1965, 1973, 1975) convinced me that the Lockean notion of natural rights as adopted by American political thinkers like Thomas Jefferson and Abraham Lincoln appeals to natural justice as rooted in human nature, which thus resembles Aristotle's conception of natural right. When Jefferson and Lincoln spoke of human beings as endowed by nature with a moral sense that distinguishes right and wrong, they manifested an Aristotelian tradition of ethical naturalism that supports the idea of natural rights in American political thought.

As I continued my reading of Aristotle in college and in graduate school in the early 1970s, I began to look at some of his biological writings. Although I noticed that political scientists who read Aristotle almost never read his biological works, it appeared to me that his view of human beings as political and rational animals was rooted somehow in his biological understanding of human nature. I noticed that in the *Ethics* he compares human beings with other animals, particularly in explaining the biological basis of parent-child bonding. And I saw in the *Politics* that in explaining the political nature of human beings, he compares them with other political animals such as the social insects.

Recently, some of the scholars studying Aristotle have come to recognize the importance of Aristotle's biology for all of his philosophic writing (Nussbaum 1978; Gotthelf and Lennox 1987). Some of this new scholarship now suggests that for Aristotle, "ethics and politics are in a way biological sciences" (Salkever 1990, 115). And at the same time, some biologists have shown new respect for Aristotle's contributions to the history of biology. "All of biology," one biologist has declared, "is a footnote to Aristotle" (Moore 1993, 33).

In 1978, I read a conference paper by Roger Masters entitled "Classical Political Philosophy and Contemporary Biology." (A revised version of this paper was eventually published in 1987 with the title, "Evolutionary Biology and Natural Right.") Masters argued that Aristotle's political thought rested on a biological understanding of human nature that was essentially compatible with modern Darwinian theories of social behavior. Masters saw a biological approach to politics in Aristotle's claims that human beings are by nature political animals, that their political nature shows an ambivalent combination of individualistic competition and social cooperation, and that the full development of human moral and political capacities requires a complex interaction of nature and nurture. On each of these points, Masters thought that modern Darwinian biology could confirm Aristotle's insights. Even more surprising to me, however, was Masters's contention that Aristotle's understanding of "natural right" as resting on a teleological understanding of human nature could also be compatible with modern biological science.

According to the ancient Greek notion of "natural right," which appears in Aristotle's writings, human beings, like all natural beings, have natural ends, so that whatever fulfills those natural ends is naturally good or right for them. For example, if human beings are inclined by nature to live in political communities, if that is one of their natural ends, then political life is right by nature for them, and whatever hinders their living as political animals is contrary to nature. But this depends on a teleological conception of nature—the idea that nature acts for the sake of ends. Leo Strauss, a political scientist who had taught Masters at the University of Chicago, argued that insofar as modern science had apparently refuted the ancient teleological conception of the universe, modern science had thereby refuted natural right.

Strauss thought this created a dilemma. Either we try to develop a nonteleological science of human life by explaining human action as governed by purely mechanistic laws, or we try to maintain a dualistic separation between a nonteleological natural science and a teleological science of human life. Strauss thought neither alternative was intellectually satisfying. Mechanistic explanations of human action cannot account adequately for human ends. But to insist on the absolute separation of natural science and the science of human life is intellectually incoherent (Strauss 1953, 7–8).

I was impressed, however, by Masters's argument, in response to Strauss, that Aristotle's teleological conception of nature was based primarily on his biology rather than his physics, and even if modern physics seems to deny teleology, modern biology does not. Although modern physicists try to explain inanimate nature without reference to ends, modern biologists must explain animate nature as serving certain ends. The growth of plants and animals to maturity, for example, or the striving of animals to satisfy their needs implies natural ends or goals that become part of any full biological explanation. Consequently, Aristotle's understanding of natural right as resting on a biological conception of natural teleology might be fundamentally compatible with modern biological science.

The arguments of Masters led me to read Darwin to see if his account of human nature would support Aristotle's idea of natural right. I saw that like Aristotle Darwin claimed that human beings are by nature social animals—coming together first in families and then in larger social communities. He also agreed with Aristotle in deriving morality from human nature. From David Hume, Darwin adopted the idea that morality was founded on a natural moral sense, and he explained this moral sense as a natural adaptation of human beings shaped by their evolutionary history. I wondered, however, whether Hume's idea of the moral sense was consistent with Aristotle's position.

In 1988, I read an article by Alaisdair MacIntyre on Hume that convinced me that Hume was closer to Aristotle than I had previously believed (MacIntyre 1959). MacIntyre persuaded me that, in contrast to Immanuel Kant's dualistic separation between morality and nature, Hume's idea of the moral sense as rooted in natural human desires belonged to a tradition of ethical naturalism begun by Aristotle. This thought was strengthened by my reading of Robert McShea's book, *Morality and Human Nature* (1990). Not only did McShea defend Hume's rooting of morality in the natural passions or sentiments that typically constitute human nature, McShea suggested that this view of morality could be founded on a Darwinian explanation of human nature as shaped by natural selection.

I began to see a tradition of ethical naturalism that included Aristotle's idea of natural right, Hume's idea of the natural moral sense, and Darwin's idea of the moral sense as shaped by natural selection. I found confirmation for this thought in 1993, in the work of James Q. Wilson. In his Presidential Address to the American Political Science Association and in his book, *The Moral Sense*, Wilson surveyed the contemporary research in the social sciences supporting the existence of a natural moral sense, and he concluded that this research sustained the ethical naturalism of Aristotle, Hume, and Darwin in rooting human morality in the biological nature of human beings (Wilson 1993a, 1993b).

I began to suspect that some human desires were universal because they expressed natural propensities of human biology. This thought was confirmed by my reading of Donald Brown's *Human Universals* (1991) and some of Edward O. Wilson's books. Brown challenged the assumption of cultural relativism among anthropologists by showing that the anthropological evidence indicated the existence of hundreds of universal behavioral traits found in some form in all or most societies. Brown's suggestion that many of these human universals were biological was sustained by Edward Wilson's sociobiological theory of human nature. In his recent intellectual autobiography, *Naturalist* (1994), Wilson summarizes his Darwinian view of human nature:

> Human beings inherit a propensity to acquire behavior and social structures, a propensity that is shared by enough people to be called human nature. The defining traits include division of labor between the sexes, bonding between parents and children, heightened altruism toward closest kin, incest avoidance, other forms of ethical behavior, suspicion of strangers, tribalism, dominance orders within groups, male dominance overall, and territorial aggression over limiting resources. Although people have free will and the choice to turn in many directions, the channels of their psychological development are nevertheless—however much we might wish otherwise—cut more deeply by the genes in certain directions than in others. So while cultures vary greatly, they inevitably converge toward these traits. The Manhattanite and New Guinea highlander have been separated by 50,000 years of history but still understand each other, for the elementary reason that their common humanity is preserved in the genes they share from their common ancestry. (1994, 332–33)

Since the human traits considered by Wilson—such as parental care, familial attachment, sexual division of labor, and male dominance—are included in Aristotle's account of human nature, it seemed to me that, despite the differences between Darwin's biology and Aristotle's biology, a Darwinian science of social behavior might support Aristotle's ethical naturalism.

TEN PROPOSITIONS

I am now prepared to defend what I will call "Darwinian natural right." It combines ideas from the classic texts of Aristotle, Hume, and Darwin as well as the contemporary work of political scientists like Masters, McShea, and James Q. Wilson, and biologists like Edward Wilson. I can state my position in ten propositions.

1. The good is the desirable, because all animals capable of voluntary movement pursue the satisfaction of their desires as guided by their information about the world.

2. Only human beings, however, can pursue happiness as a deliberate conception of the fullest satisfaction of their desires over a whole life, because only they have the cognitive capacities for reason and language that allow them to formulate a plan of life, so that they can judge present actions in the light of past experience and future expectations.

3. Human beings are by nature social and political animals, because the species-specific behavioral repertoire of *Homo sapiens* includes inborn desires and cognitive capacities that are fulfilled in social and political life.

4. The fulfillment of these natural potentials requires social learning and moral habituation; and although the specific content of this learning and habituation will vary according to the social and physical circumstances of each human group, the natural repertoire of desires and cognitive capacities will structure this variability.

5. We can judge divergent ways of life by how well they nurture the natural desires and cognitive capacities of human beings in different circumstances, but deciding what should be done in particular cases requires prudential judgments that respect the social practices of the group.

6. Rather than identifying morality with altruistic selflessness, we should see that human beings are moved by self-love, and as social animals they are

moved to love others with whom they are bonded as extensions of themselves.

7. Two of the primary forms of human sociality are the familial bond between parents and children and the conjugal bond between husband and wife.

8. Human beings have a natural moral sense that emerges as a joint product of moral emotions such as sympathy and anger and moral principles such as kinship and reciprocity.

9. Modern Darwinian biology supports this understanding of the ethical and social nature of human beings by showing how it could have arisen by natural selection through evolutionary history.

10. Consequently, a Darwinian understanding of human nature supports a modern version of Aristotelian natural right.

SEVEN OBJECTIONS

My Aristotelian and Darwinian conception of natural right, as summarized in the foregoing ten propositions, is subject to at least seven major objections.

1. *The fact-value dichotomy.* The most common objection to any ethical naturalism is that moral values cannot be derived from natural facts. This argument is attributed to David Hume, who is said to have shown that there must be a radical separation between questions of what *is* or *is not* the case, which belong to the realm of nature, and questions of what *ought* or *ought not* to be done, which belong to the realm of morality. Because of this dichotomy, it is a logical fallacy to infer a moral *ought* from a natural *is*.

If there is a universal human nature that includes certain desires, those natural desires will influence human action. And therefore, an Aristotelian or Darwinian science of human nature might help us to explain human action as a product of those natural desires. But if there is an unbridgeable gap between facts and values, *is* and *ought*, then this science of human nature could not support human ethics. From the fact that human beings have a natural desire to do something, it does not follow that they *ought* to do it. On the contrary, it might seem that what makes human beings uniquely moral animals is that they can choose to resist those natural desires that violate standards of moral duty.

As human beings, it often seems, we are naturally selfish animals. We are naturally inclined to lie, steal, and even kill to satisfy our selfish desires while exploiting our fellow human beings. But we can learn to restrain our egoistic desires when they violate our moral duties to others. And since the preservation of social order requires that people respect their social duties, every society must enforce some rules of social cooperation. Although some people obey those rules only when they fear being punished if they don't, other people obey because they have a sense of conscience, so that they feel guilty when they act contrary to their moral duty. But in any case, doing one's moral duty means resisting rather than conforming to one's human nature.

Natural science can describe the way things *are*, but it cannot prescribe the way things *ought* to be. A Darwinian science of human nature might describe the biological factors influencing human motivation, but it could not prescribe norms of proper human conduct without invoking moral standards that transcend the facts of human biology. For example, it would be proper for biologists to investigate the biological psychology of human sexuality, but for them to infer from the biological facts of human sexual motivation that some kinds of sexual conduct were morally better or worse than others would be fallacious.

If we accept the radical separation of natural facts and moral values, an Aristotelian or Darwinian conception of ethical naturalism must be rejected as a fallacious attempt to deduce moral conclusions from factual premises.

2. Human freedom. Separating nature and morality, natural law and moral law, would seem to be necessary to secure the moral freedom of human beings. Unlike other animals, human beings are moral beings because they have the freedom to act outside the laws of nature that govern animal behavior. If human behavior were as completely determined by the laws of nature as animal behavior, then human beings would not have "free will," and we could not hold them morally responsible for their actions.

A second objection to ethical naturalism rooted in human biology, therefore, is that it denies human freedom by explaining human action as determined by the same natural laws that govern other animals. A biological science of human nature cannot explain human morality if morality presupposes a human freedom from nature that sets human beings apart from the animal world.

3. Human learning. Human morality transcends animal nature because human beings have a freedom that other animals lack. The reason for that uniquely human freedom is that while animal behavior is mostly instinctive, human behavior is mostly learned. In contrast to the fixity of animal instinct, the flexibility of human learning gives human beings a freedom of choice that allows them to act as moral agents. This thought would support a third objection to Aristotelian or Darwinian ethical naturalism: human morality is not biologically determined, and therefore it cannot be explained as a product of natural laws, because it arises from human learning rather than from animal instinct.

4. Human culture. As an expression of the uniquely human capacity for learning, human beings are the only cultural animals. Whatever human beings learn they can share with one another through language and other forms of symbolism, and this collection of social symbols can be passed from one generation to another as the cultural tradition of a social group. Language, ideas, artifacts, and patterns of customary behavior—anything that can have symbolic meaning for human beings—can become parts of a culture. Human societies differ from one another insofar as they create different cultural traditions.

If moral norms are largely products of culture, and if culture is largely a social invention that is not determined by nature, this would suggest a fourth objection to ethical naturalism: any attempt to derive ethics from human nature must fail if ethics is shaped more by culture than by nature.

If ethics were rooted in a universal human nature, we would expect ethical norms to be universal. The radical differences in ethical norms as they emerge in different cultures indicates that ethics is more cultural than natural, and thus there is no universal morality because cultures are radically diverse. While a naturalist explanation of morality would assume a moral universalism founded on the unity of human nature, a culturalist explanation of morality would assume a moral relativism founded on the diversity of cultural traditions.

5. Impermanent species. Cultural diversity is not the only source of ethical relativity. Although the ethical naturalist assumes an unchanging human nature, Darwin's theory of evolution asserts that the human species—like all species—is changeable. Contrary to Aristotle's assumption that species are eternal and unchanging, which was commonly accepted prior to Darwin's work, Darwin claimed that all species have evolved from ancestral species, and all present species will evolve over time, with some old species becoming extinct and new species emerging in their place.

Consequently, as a fifth objection to ethical naturalism, it would seem that ethical principles rooted in the nature of the human species must be changeable if we accept the Darwinian teaching that all species are changeable. An ethical naturalism founded on Aristotle's assumption that species are eternal would have to deny Darwin's evolutionary account of species. If so, then the Aristotelian naturalist cannot also be a Darwinian.

6. The problem of teleology. The Aristotelian naturalist might also have to defend a teleological conception of nature against Darwin's denial of teleology, which would be another point of conflict between Aristotelian naturalism and Darwinian naturalism. Aristotle's appeal to nature as a source of moral norms requires a teleological conception of nature as directed to the fulfillment of final ends. All natural beings aim at natural ends, goals, or purposes. Consequently, the natural good for each being is to attain its natural end. The natural good for human beings is to fully develop those natural ends that are distinctively human. So, for example, political life is naturally good for human beings, because as political animals they find their end or goal *(telos)* in political life.

Modern science, however, including Darwinian biology, denies this ancient teleological conception of the universe. According to modern science, nature is governed solely by material or mechanical laws that act without aim or purpose. According to modern Darwinian biology, the evolution of species is determined by forces of blind necessity and historical contingency that lack any cosmic purpose. Any appearance of purposefulness in nature, it would seem, is an illusion of human yearnings for cosmic norms to support human morality. Therefore, a sixth objection to a Darwinian conception of Aristotelian natural right is that Darwinian biology denies the natural teleology that supports natural right.

7. Religious transcendence. Nature would be purposeful, and there would be cosmic support for human morality, if human beings were created in the image of God. If human beings were endowed by their Creator with a moral dignity that set them apart from the rest of nature, then obeying the moral law sanctioned by God would fulfill their true nature and thus satisfy their deepest longings. It is not clear, however, that an Aristotelian or Darwinian conception of natural right allows for such religious belief. Far from sustaining a religious view of the world, Darwinism seems to claim that we can explain the appearance of design in nature without any need for invoking a Divine Creator. Therefore, as a final objection to the attempt to root ethics in the biology of human nature, it could be argued that a Darwinian explanation of nature denies any appeal to God as the transcendent ground of morality.

These seven objections rest on seven antithetical dichotomies: (1) biological facts versus moral values, (2) biological determinism versus human freedom, (3) biological instinct versus social learning, (4) biological universality versus cultural relativity, (5) Aristotelian fixity versus Darwinian flux, (6) biological mechanism versus human purposefulness, and (7) natural morality versus religious morality.

I will argue that these are false dichotomies. (1) If the human good is what is desirable for human beings, then the facts concerning the natural human desires do imply ethical conclusions. (2) A biological explanation of human nature does not deny human freedom if we define that freedom as the capacity for deliberation and choice based on one's own desires. (3) The human ability for learning by experience extends the animal instincts for learning through the uniquely human capacity for language and other symbolism. (4) The life of any human community reflects a complex interaction between nature and culture, between the natural desires and capacities that characterize the human species and the historical or ecological circumstances that characterize particular social traditions, so that we need to understand both the circumstantial variations and the human universals expressed in particular societies. (5) Despite the mutability of species in evolutionary time, the patterns of speciation are stable enough over long periods of time to justify our apprehension of natural kinds as enduring features of the world. (6) Although Darwinian theory denies the cosmic teleology of natural theology or mystical vitalism, Darwinian biology recognizes the immanent teleology—the goal-directed character—of living beings, which is the only kind of teleology required for Aristotelian naturalism. (7) Darwinian natural right confirms the moral teaching of religion, at least so far as religious morality is rooted in human nature.

I have not mentioned one fundamental objection to my argument in this book—namely, the objection that Darwin's theory of evolution is not true. Although I recognize that there is plenty of room for controversy in determining the exact mechanisms of evolutionary change, the arguments—

from "scientific creationists" and others—for completely rejecting Darwin's theory of evolution seem implausible to me. But developing a general defense of Darwin's theory would require a book unto itself, and others have already done that better than I could. The arguments against Darwin have been summarized by Henry Morris (1985) and Philip Johnson (1991), and Ronald Numbers (1992) has written a good history of "scientific creationism." The case in defense of Darwin, which I find persuasive, has been well stated by Douglas Futuyma (1983), Philip Kitcher (1982), Timothy Goldsmith (1991), and Monroe Strickberger (1996). The most common reason for doubting Darwin's theory is that the complexity of the living world—as illustrated by complex organs such as the eye—manifests a design that implies a Divine Designer, because such complexity of design cannot be explained as the product of Darwinian evolution. Richard Dawkins (1986, 1996) has shown, however, that in fact Darwin's theory of evolution was the first scientific theory to explain how complex adaptations like the eye could be built up by small steps through natural selection working on random variations. Creationists like to cite the criticisms of Darwinian "gradualism" and "adaptationism" by biologists such as Stephen Jay Gould, Richard Lewontin, and Niles Eldridge as evidence that Darwinian theory has been refuted (Eldridge and Gould 1972; Gould 1989; Gould and Lewontin 1979). But Dawkins (1986, 223–52; 1996, 105–7) and Ernst Mayr (1988) have shown that the valid points made by these critics are fully compatible with modern Darwinian theory. The flaws in the argumentation of Gould and Lewontin are so serious that their work is now studied by rhetorical theorists as a model of sophistical rhetoric in science (Bazerman 1993; Borgia 1994; Charney 1993; Coyne and Charlesworth 1997; Wright 1990). In explaining order in the organic world, structuralist biologists like Gould emphasize formal causes, while adaptationist biologists like Dawkins emphasize functional causes. For a full explanation, we need to see the partial truth in both sides of this debate (Amundson 1996).

In this book, I will speak of natural selection as the primary force in evolutionary change, because I agree with Darwin that natural selection is "the main but not the exclusive means of modification" (Darwin 1936a, 367). Other mechanisms and contingent events are often crucial for evolutionary history. For example, the mass extinction of dinosaurs and many other species about sixty-five million years ago might have been caused by the catastrophic impact of a meteor, which would not be explained by natural selection. Yet it is still true, even for those scientists like Gould who emphasize evolutionary mechanisms other than natural selection, that natural selection is the primary cause shaping evolutionary adaptation (Gould 1997a, 1997b).

AN OVERVIEW OF THE BOOK

This book develops my arguments for my ten propositions and my replies to the seven objections. In chapter 2, I defend my proposition that the good is the desirable. I show that the combination of reason and desire in human action manifests a normative structure found in all voluntary animal movement. I also claim that there are at least twenty natural desires that are universal to all human societies, and therefore the satisfaction of these natural desires constitutes a universal standard for judging social practices as either fulfilling or frustrating human nature, although prudence is required in judging what is practicable within the limits of particular social and physical circumstances.

As political animals, human beings satisfy their desires in social and political groups. But it has become common for social scientists in the Hobbesian tradition to assume that the political order of human life is not a natural expression of human biology but an artificial construction of human culture. In chapter 3, I argue against this Hobbesian dichotomy between biology and culture; and I defend Aristotle's claim that human politics is rooted in human biology.

Just as Hobbesian social scientists assume that culture transcends biology, they also assume that human freedom transcends the laws of nature, and consequently human morality transcends natural facts. In chapter 4, I show that these are false dichotomies. There is no absolute separation between natural facts and moral values, because human morality is derived from a natural moral sense. And there is no absolute separation between nature and freedom, because human freedom manifests a natural human capacity for deliberate choice in satisfying natural desires according to some plan of a whole life well lived.

In the central chapters of the book, I provide some illustrations of how Darwinian natural right distinguishes between those social relationships that are according to nature and those that are contrary to nature. In chapter 5,

I contend that the familial bonding of parents and children is a biological bond that satisfies the natural desire for parental care. In chapter 6, I contend that the conjugal bonding of husband and wife is a biological bond that satisfies the natural desires for mating, parenting, and a sexual division of labor based on the natural complementarity of male and female. Utopian communities that try to abolish familial and conjugal bonding must fail, I argue, because the emotional cost from frustrated desires is unbearable for most people.

In these central chapters, I maintain that there are natural differences between men and women based on their biological nature: typically (on average) men are more dominant, and women are more nurturant. Female nurturance sustains the social order of familial life, while male dominance sustains the social order of political life. Although this is denied by those feminists who believe that all sex differences in behavior are arbitrary constructions of culture, I argue that feminist criticisms of cultural practices that oppress women contradict cultural relativism. A coherent and cogent feminism must appeal, I claim, to an ethical naturalism that draws its norms from a universal human nature. In chapter 6, I offer female circumcision (clitoridectomy and infibulation) as an example of a custom injuring women that can be condemned because it unnecessarily frustrates natural human desires.

In contrast to familial and conjugal bonds as conforming to human nature, I turn in chapter 7 to slavery as an example of a social relationship that is contrary to human nature. I survey the history of the debate over slavery to show that although slavery arises from the natural desire of the master to exploit the slave, slavery frustrates the natural human desire to be free from exploitation, which expresses the moral sense rooted in human biology.

While arguing for a natural moral sense, I concede that some human beings apparently have no moral sense. Psychopaths, for example, seem to lack the social emotions necessary for a moral sense, which allows them to act as social predators unrestrained by any sense of guilt or shame. In chapter 8, I examine some modern studies of psychopaths, and I conclude that they suffer from some abnormality of the brain, so that they lack the social emotions necessary to live successfully as social animals. For that reason, I suggest, we must treat them as moral strangers.

In defending natural right as founded on human biology, I assume the reality of natural kinds and natural ends, because I assume that human beings exist as a distinct species, and I assume that their species-specific nature inclines them to certain ends or goals. In chapter 9, I show that Darwinian biology affirms the existence of natural kinds and natural ends. Although species are not eternal, they are real for as long as they exist. And although Darwinian science denies any cosmic teleology for nature as a whole, Darwinism affirms the teleology of living beings as directed to ends or goals.

Finally, in chapter 10, I respond to the objection that Darwinian natural right cannot support morality if it cannot accept a religious belief in God as the transcendent source of moral law. I argue that since the moral sense arises from natural human experience, religious belief is not essential, although it can reinforce the dictates of nature. Moreover, I contend that even in the Mosaic law of the Bible and in the Christian theology of Thomas Aquinas, one can see a recognition of the natural self-sufficiency of morality based on human nature as aiming towards the earthly happiness of human beings. I conclude by showing that although the natural human desire to understand is sometimes taken as a sign of the supernatural origin of the human soul, this intellectual desire can be explained as a product of purely natural evolutionary causes.

CHAPTER 2

DESIRE AND REASON

The good is the desirable. Consequently, the human good is both variable and universal. The human good is variable insofar as what is desirable for human beings varies according to individual temperament, individual history, social custom, and particular circumstances. The human good is universal insofar as there are universal human desires rooted in human nature. There are at least twenty human desires that are universal because they are part of the biological nature of human beings as manifested in all societies throughout human history. The universality of these natural desires supports universal standards of moral judgment, so that we can judge societies as better or worse depending upon how well they satisfy those natural desires. The variability of human life, however, requires prudence or practical judgment in deciding what is desirable for particular individuals in particular conditions. In this chapter, I argue that this view of the good as the desirable can be grounded on a biological understanding of human nature as developed by Aristotle and Charles Darwin.

In defending this Aristotelian and Darwinian ethics as rooted in nature and prudence, I reject all forms of relativism and dogmatism. I reject cultural relativism, which asserts that ethics is a purely cultural invention that varies arbitrarily from one culture to another, because while I recognize the importance of social learning and custom in moral development, I believe that natural human desires are universal and therefore limit the variability of cultural practices. I reject historicist relativism, which asserts that ethics is a purely historical invention that varies radically from one historical epoch to another, because while I recognize the importance of historical traditions, I believe that natural human desires constitute the unchanging ground of ethics throughout human history. I reject skeptical and solipsistic relativism, which asserts that there are no standards of ethical judgment beyond the impulses of unique individuals, because while I recognize the importance of individual diversity, I believe there are regularities in human desires that manifest a human nature typical of the human species. I also reject rationalist dogmatism, which asserts that ethics rests on the logical imperatives of pure reason, because while I recognize the importance of

17

human reason in judging how best to satisfy human desires, I believe that the motivational foundation of ethics is not the logic of abstract reason but the satisfaction of natural desires. And I reject religious dogmatism, which asserts that ethics can only be rooted in transcendent laws of a divine power, because while I recognize that religious ethics can reinforce natural ethics, I believe that ethics as founded on natural desires exists independently of any belief in a divine power.

THE NATURE OF DESIRE

In their voluntary activity, animals move to satisfy their desires in the light of their information about opportunities and threats in their particular circumstances. This does not mean, of course, that the good is whatever an animal happens to desire at any moment, because an animal can mistakenly desire what in fact is not truly desirable. Furthermore, what is desirable differs for each kind of animal, because each species has its own natural range of desires. Consequently, the good is not the same for all, because what is desirable varies according to the nature of each species.

Like other animals, we human beings move to satisfy our desires in the light of our information about the world. We have a natural range of desires that we share as members of the human species and that distinguishes us from other animals. Our human pattern of desires includes appetitive desires such as hunger and sexual lust, social desires such as anger, love, and honor, and intellectual desires such as curiosity and wonder.

We differ from other animals in that our uniquely human capacities for language and deliberation allow us to gather and assess information about the past, the present, and the projected future so that we can consciously formulate long-term plans of action. Through these cognitive capacities as developed in mature adults, we can conceive of our desires as organized into a coherent order for the fullest satisfaction over a complete life, and we can then judge our conduct as good or bad according to whether it promotes or impedes our pursuit of happiness so conceived. We need good habits of choice so that we desire what is truly desirable. We also need prudential judgment to decide what should be done in particular cases, and prudence requires not only a general knowledge of human desires but also a specific knowledge of the people involved and a shrewd perception of what is practically achievable in the given circumstances.

In the striving for a good human life, reason and desire are mutually dependent. Without reason, we could not intelligently manage our desires for their full satisfaction. Without desire, our reason would lack any power to move us to think or act rationally. Even the most abstract activities of reason depend on desires such as curiosity or wonder to motivate and guide our thoughts. "Thought by itself moves nothing," Aristotle explains, because any human action that is deliberately chosen requires a union of reason and desire. A deliberate choice manifests either "desiring reason" or "reasoning desire" (*NE* 1139a36–b6).

I will use the English word "desire" to translate the Greek word *orexis*. Aristotle coined the Greek noun *orexis* from the Greek verb *orego*, which means "to reach out." *Orexis* is the soul's "reaching out" for something in the world. For Aristotle, it is a general term for all kinds of longing or striving, including physical appetites, social emotions, and intellectual yearnings (*DA* 433a9–b31). I use the word "desire" in the same way as a general term for all kinds of psychic impulse or inclination. With that sense in mind, I will defend an ethics of desire: the good is the desirable, and reason judges how best to satisfy the desires.

Sometimes desires are consciously apprehended, but not always. Like other animals, human beings often do not have full conscious awareness of the desires that move them. But to the extent to which they are conscious of their desires, human beings can make prudent judgments about their conduct.

This view of ethics as arising from reason and desire—ethics as rooted in natural human desires, as requiring habits of right desire, and as guided by prudential reasoning in judging the contingencies of action—was originally developed by Aristotle in his ethical and biological writings (Richardson 1992). But other philosophers in the tradition of ethical naturalism, such as David Hume, have defended a similar understanding. Just as Aristotle declared that "thought by itself moves nothing," Hume declared that "reason alone can never be a motive to any action of the will" (1888, 413).

As explained by John Bricke (1996), Hume advances a "conativist" theory of ethics that is similar to the view I will defend in this book. According to this theory, a reason for action is a complex psychological state in which the conative component (a desire) plays the primary role, and the cognitive component (a belief) plays the secondary role. To have a desire is to have a propensity toward, or an aversion against, some kind of conduct. To have a belief is to have some informational representation of the world. A desire is some need one wants to be satisfied. A belief is some proposition one holds to be true. Desire is the primary cause of action because it sets the goals of action. Belief is the secondary cause of action because it provides information relevant to the goals set by desire. Belief can provide instrumental information by determining the means available for the desired ends. Or belief can provide constitutive information by determining whether some possible object of action conforms to the desired ends. Thus, the cause of an action combines a conative state of desire and a cognitive state of belief. "An agent must both set requirements for the world (by having desires), and (by having suitably related beliefs) attempt to meet requirements set by the world" (Bricke 1996, 28). Yet desires are primary because satisfying them is the ultimate motivation to which reason is subordinated.

I agree with Adam Smith in recognizing the importance of reason in formulating general rules of morality from our experience of some forms of conduct as pleasing and others as displeasing, and yet reason alone could never render any object either pleasing or displeasing for its own sake, because "nothing can be agreeable or disagreeable for its own sake, which is not rendered such by immediate sense and feeling" (Smith 1982, 320).

Consider, for example, the action of a parent in seeking medical treatment for a child. As a parent, my parental desire to care for my child's well-being is a primary cause of my parental conduct because it sets the goal. In pursuing that goal, my beliefs about what is essential to my child's well-being and about the best means to that goal will decisively shape my parental conduct: believing good health to be one element of my child's well-being and believing that a certain kind of medical treatment would promote my child's health will contribute to my resolve to seek such treatment. But still my desire to care for my child is the ultimate motivating force for that conduct.

Charles Darwin's biological explanation of the natural moral sense showed how parental desires and other natural desires could have arisen as an evolutionary adaptation for human beings. Recent advances in evolutionary theories of human nature have given more support to the conclusion that natural ethics as founded on natural desires can be explained ultimately as a product of natural selection. In this book, I will argue that Darwinian explanations of the natural moral sense support an Aristotelian ethics of desire.

THE NORMATIVE STRUCTURE OF ANIMAL MOVEMENT

To be or not to be? That is the question. Or, at least, that is the question for all animals, if not for all living organisms. An animal lives only so long as it sustains its life through satisfying its desires. When it fails to do this, it dies. When it fails to do this well, it suffers. Its natural desires are determined by the specific kind of animal that it is. To live every animal must act, either consciously or unconsciously, to achieve the goals set by its nature. An animal either succeeds or fails in this, and its relative success or failure will decide whether it lives or dies and whether its life is satisfying or not.

This is not true for inanimate entities. We might explain a thunderstorm, for instance, as a physical and chemical system that sustains itself for a period of time and then dissipates, but we could not properly speak of its relative success or failure in achieving its goals. In all animal behavior, by contrast, there are natural goals, which are standards of achievement that we can identify as "values" or "goods." If we define "value" or "good" in relational terms as whatever satisfies a desire, then all animals have "values" because they all have natural desires that they strive to satisfy as they gather information about their world. This would include human beings, who are unique only in the complexity of their desires and the complexity of the information they gather to satisfy their desires (Binswanger 1990, 1992; Herrick 1956; Polanyi and Prosch 1975).

The natural history of value arises from the normative structure of animal movement as the interaction of three functions: knowing, desiring, and evaluating. The modern biology of animal behavior—particularly in the field of "cognitive ethology"—would confirm this analysis as developed by Aristotle in *The Movement of Animals* (Lear 1988; Nussbaum 1978; Nussbaum 1986, 264-89). In their intentional behavior, animals gather information *(knowing)* related to their needs *(desiring)* and then act according to their assessment of the information in relation to their needs *(evaluating)* (Bennett 1991; Mason 1982). Consequently, the biological explanation of animal behavior requires teleological or functional concepts. Animals act in a goal-directed manner to satisfy their natural needs based on their information about the changing environments in which they live. Animal movement is thus inherently normative or value-laden insofar as animals cannot live without choosing between alternative courses of action as more or less desirable.

We commonly explain human action as the product of desires and beliefs, because we assume people choose those actions that they believe will satisfy their desires. The economic theory of rational choice applies the same explanatory principle: human behavior is explained as the product of preferences (desires) and expectations (beliefs) (Rosenberg 1992, 118–24). There is some evidence that the economic models of goal-directed behavior that have been developed to explain human behavior can apply just as well to the behavior of other animals, which may be a product of evolutionary pressures that favored adaptive behavior (Real 1991).

Under the influence of Aristotle's biology, Thomas Aquinas concluded that, although only human beings act from "free" judgment, other animals act from an "estimative" judgment about what will satisfy their desires. All animals have a natural capacity for practical judgment that shows a "participation in prudence and reason" and a "likeness of moral good" (*Summa Theologica* I, q. 83, a. 1; q. 96, a. 1; I–II, q. 11, a. 2; q. 24, a. 4; q. 40, a. 3).

I realize that some Cartesian philosophers and behaviorist psychologists would deny that animals have any consciousness and would assert that all animal movement can be explained as the behavior of mindless machines. I agree, however, with Donald Griffin (1991) in dismissing such an absolute denial of animal consciousness as implausible. Since we have direct experience of our own consciousness, and since we can assume our consciousness arises somehow from our nervous system, it seems unreasonably dogmatic to deny that any other animals with nervous systems can have consciousness, particularly when it is difficult to explain some of the behavior of other animals without invoking their beliefs and desires. I concede, nonetheless, that merely anecdotal evidence of animal consciousness unconstrained by logical analysis and empirical testing is insufficient (Beer 1991; Bennett 1991). A good example of cognitive ethology disciplined by rigorous analysis and testing is the work of Cheney and Seyfarth (1990) on primate intelligence. I would adopt Frans de Waal's principle of "evolutionary parsimony" as the basis for a "critical anthropomorphism": if species closely related by evolutionary descent engage in similar behavior, we should assume similar mental processes unless we have some reason to doubt this. So if a nonhuman animal closely related to human beings performs a behavior that we would explain as intentional when done by a human being, we should assume it is intentional for the nonhuman animal unless proven otherwise (de Waal 1996, 64–65).

The normative structure of animal movement is manifest in the functional organization of the nervous system as designed by natural selection. Consider, for example, the following passage from a textbook by Neil Carlson on physiological psychology:

> The brain is the organ that moves the muscles. That may sound a bit simplistic, but ultimately, movement—or more accurately, behavior—is the primary function of the nervous system. In order to make useful movements, the brain must know what is happening outside, in the environment. Thus, the body contains cells that are specialized for detecting environmental events and others that are specialized for producing movements. Of course, complex animals such as ourselves do not react automatically to events in our environment; our brains are flexible enough so that we behave in different ways, according to present circumstances and those we experienced in the past. Besides perceiving and acting, we can remember and decide. All these abilities are made possible by the billions of cells found in the nervous system. (Carlson 1991, 20)

Don't we see in the "useful movements" of animals, including human movement, that animals judge something good insofar as it is desirable, and desirable insofar as it is good? Does it not seem absurd to imagine otherwise—that something could be good for an animal although utterly undesirable, or something could be desirable although utterly bad? This explains why the biology of human nature necessarily has moral implications, as indicated by the moral passions stirred by debates in human biology. If we find that we are naturally inclined to something or adapted for something, then we believe this helps us to know what is good for us.

This does not mean identifying the human good with momentary or capricious impulses: we sometimes get what we think we desire only to discover it is not desirable. This common human experience of being mistaken about our desires and then regretting our mistakes confirms the reality of our basic desires as a part of our nature that cannot be willfully disregarded. To live well, we must perceive what it is we truly desire, we must order our often conflicting desires into a coherent pattern, and we must decide how best to use the resources provided by our physical and social circumstances for satisfying our desires. All of this requires habituation and thought over a whole lifetime. Other animals cannot do this to the same degree, because they lack the cognitive capacities—particularly those in the human neocortex—for planning and deliberation.

The human ordering of natural desires over a complete life identifies human morality as different from, even though rooted in, animal movement. What we desire is a life planned to achieve the fullest satisfaction of our desires and the fullest development of our capacities over a whole life, which is what Aristotle calls *eudaimonia*, "happiness" or "flourishing." Neither nonhuman animals nor human children can enjoy happiness in this sense, because they lack the ability to organize their desires to conform to a conception of a whole life well lived. By nature human beings desire external goods (such as wealth), bodily goods (such as health, sensual pleasures, and beauty), and psychic goods (such as love, friendship, honor, and thinking). To pursue these goods in the right order, to the right degree, at the right time to avoid contradiction requires good habits of choice—the moral and intellectual virtues that Aristotle examines in the *Ethics*. Although there are analogies between these human virtues and the behavioral patterns of other animals, only human beings have the cognitive capacities for conceptual abstraction and symbolic communication, which Aristotle identifies as *logos*, and these cognitive capacities allow human beings to become moral agents who judge present actions in the light of past and future to conform to some enduring standard of a good life.

Despite the distinctively human character of moral judgment, moral conduct is the human expression of a goal-directed striving shared with other animals. Looking at those animals closest to human beings in evolutionary history, we can see the desires and capacities from which morality emerged among our prehistoric human ancestors. Even apparently simple animals display the complex normative structure of animal movement in the interplay of knowing, desiring, and evaluating.

Consider hermit crabs, for example. These small crustaceans occupy the empty shells of dead snails. They are most easily seen in tidal pools along ocean coastlines. Their shells protect them from predators, reduce their physiological stress, and promote their reproductive success. Some shells are better than others in satisfying these desires, and as the animals grow they need to move to larger shells. Finding the right shell means the difference between life and death, or at least the difference between being cramped or cozy in one's portable domicile.

A hermit crab will carefully inspect a new shell to assess its weight, size, and structure. Even after moving into a new shell, the animal will continue to test the shell for suitability, and it will sometimes decide to move back into the old shell. Biologists who study this animal have discovered a complex pattern of behavior by which it evaluates the quality of a shell to decide how well it satisfies the animal's desires (Elwood and Neil 1992).

The process of evaluation becomes even more intricate when hermit crabs fight over shells. Then they must assess not only the relative value of their shells but also the size, strength, and resoluteness of their opponents. This competition often displays a hierarchy in which the most dominant crab gets first choice of a shell. If the dominant crab moves into a new shell, the old shell is occupied by a less dominant crab, which creates another vacancy for a third crab, and so on down the hierarchy. Sociologists who study the social structure of "vacancy chains," in which resources are passed from one individual to another down a social hierarchy, have discovered remarkable similarities between hermit crabs occupying vacant shells left behind by more dominant crabs and human beings occupying jobs and houses left vacant by those of higher status (Chase 1991; Chase and DeWitt 1988).

Despite the greater complexity of the human situation, hermit crabs are like human beings and other animals in that their behavior conforms to the same normative structure: they have natural desires, they have natural capacities for gathering information relevant to their desires, and they are naturally inclined to do whatever seems to satisfy their desires according to their evaluation of the information.

Among human beings the process of evaluation is often a social activity in which the individual members of a group express diverse opinions and try to agree on what would be best for the whole group. This might appear to distinguish human ethics from animal movement. Such striving for social consensus on a course of action is not, however, uniquely human.

We know, for instance, that honey bees go through a complex decision-making process when they need to select a new nest site. Foragers who have located food (nectar or pollen), water for cooling the hive, or materials for repairing the hive engage in a symbolic dance inside the hive

that conveys information about the direction, the distance, and the desirability of whatever they have found. When the population of the hive
becomes too large, roughly half of the hive will leave the nest as a swarm
seeking to colonize a new nest; and the same dance language will be used
to decide on the best site (Gould 1993; Gould and Gould 1988; Seeley
1985; Winston 1987). Although Aristotle observed bees dancing and seemed
to recognize this as some form of communication (HA 624a35–b12), the
symbolism of the dance was only recently worked out by Karl von Frisch
(1967).

Hundreds of bee scouts look for cavities in trees, bushes, and rocks that
might be good sites for a new nest. They must consider many distinct
qualities in evaluating a nest site—such as the volume of the cavity, its
dryness, freedom from drafts, the size and location of the entrance, and
distance from the parent nest. A scout may spend more than an hour inspecting one cavity. When the scouts return to the swarm, the vigor of
their dances signifies the quality of the cavities.

Not only does each scout advertise her site, she also attends the dances
for the other sites; and after inspecting the alternatives promoted with the
most vigorous dances, she can be convinced to dance for a site other than
the one she initially represented. Two dozen or more sites will be considered at the start. Over a period of days, the best sites win increasing support
until the scouts agree on one site as the best. In some cases, however, the
scouts are divided into irreconcilable factions; and if no site is finally accepted, the swarm will form a nest in the open and eventually be destroyed
by predators or the weather. Some biologists interpret this process of evaluation as indicating the democratic character of honey-bee politics, because
diverse preferences are weighed until a consensus forms (Gould and Gould
1988, 26–28, 51–53, 65–67, 86–99, 122).

Another important activity for honey bees is searching for nectar, pollen, and water. The success of a colony depends on distributing foragers in
a manner that reflects the desirability of the foraging sites for the colony.
Thomas Seeley has summarized many years of biological research on how
this is done.

> The employed foragers compete with one another for recruits from the
> pool of unemployed foragers. This competition is, however, "friendly" in
> that each forager honestly adjusts the strength of her waggle dance signal

in relation to the desirability of her food source. Desirability reflects both the profitability of the source and the colony's need for its commodity (nectar, pollen, or water). Because the unemployed foragers respond essentially at random to the employed forager's recruitment signals, recruitment is strongest to the most desirable sites. And because the employed foragers decide honestly whether or not to abandon a forage site, abandonment is strongest from the least desirable sites. The net result is an increase in the foragers at the most desirable sites and a decrease at the least desirable sites. (Seeley 1995, 259)

Like hermit crabs, honey bees thus demonstrate the normative structure of animal behavior even for animals with simple nervous systems: they are naturally adapted to gather and evaluate information as they make vital decisions that aim at the most desirable outcomes. Honey bees also show us that some nonhuman animals can use complex systems of communication to make decisions as a group, so that their behavioral evaluations emerge from social agreement. Sometimes the process fails, they cannot agree, and they die prematurely. Nature endows them with motivating desires and cognitive capacities but does not guarantee their success, which depends on hospitable circumstances and intelligent action. As with human beings, nature does not always provide these animals with what they need to fully actualize their natural ends.

Many animals actualize their natural potentials only within social groups. Indeed, there may be no animal that is completely solitary throughout its entire life. In the most complex forms of animal societies, there is a division of labor in which different individuals performing different tasks collaborate in common endeavors. The hives of bees and other social insects show this social coordination through a division of tasks with a degree of complexity approaching that of human communities. Aristotle even identifies the social insects as political animals (*HA* 487b31–88a14, 588a13–89a10, 623b1–29b4; Arnhart 1990). For such animals, as for human beings, living in political communities is natural because it satisfies their natural desires and conforms to their natural capacities. That social and political life is *good* for them is a *fact* of their nature, because such a life is suited for the kind of animals they are.

Despite the similarities between a bee hive and a human community, the intricacy of the human brain and nervous system permits a flexibility in human social evaluation far beyond that of the social insects. To find a

comparable level of social intelligence, we must look at our primate relatives, and particularly chimpanzees (Goodall 1986; Wrangham et al. 1994).

Frans de Waal has shown that chimpanzees and other primates display
a "sense of social regularity," a respect for rules and norms that would seem
to manifest the rudimentary origins of the moral sense that has been more
fully developed by human beings (de Waal 1996, 89–97). Like inanimate
objects, animals follow *descriptive rules* of typical behavior. For example,
stones tend to fall to the earth under the influence of gravity, and mammalian mothers tend to protect their young. Unlike inanimate objects, however, animals also follow *prescriptive rules* of behavior as conforming to social
expectations. So, for example, in social groups of mammalian animals, the
adult members must learn how to handle infants to avoid provoking a
mother's aggression when she perceives her infants are being threatened.
Mothers thus enforce social rules about how their infants *ought* to be treated
by punishing those who violate the rules. Juvenile primates often get into
trouble when they handle infants before they have learned the rules of
maternal protectiveness.

In general, de Waal argues, animals create prescriptive rules whenever
they develop social expectations about how members of the group ought to
behave and then enforce these expectations through reward and punishment.
Such rules can arise as social conventions sanctioned by the community
and maintained by social learning. De Waal has shown by his experimental
observations that different species of primates can be distinguished by their
social conventions. Among chimpanzees, dominant males are expected to
share food with those who beg for it, and those who do not share induce
protest from their group. By contrast, rhesus macaques do not expect sharing, and therefore dominant males are not punished when they refuse to
share their food. Even among chimpanzees, however, the sharing of food
by dominant individuals seems to be far more common among captive
chimpanzees than among wild chimpanzees, and therefore this social rule
might be a social convention that develops only in the circumstances of
captivity where chimpanzees are forced to live together in confined conditions. In any case, chimpanzees illustrate how the intensively social desires
of some animals incline them to develop and obey normative rules of social
behavior that foreshadow human morality as rooted in the social desires of
human beings.

TWENTY NATURAL DESIRES

If the good is the desirable, then human ethics is natural insofar as it satisfies natural human desires. There are at least twenty natural desires that are manifested in diverse ways in all human societies throughout history: a complete life, parental care, sexual identity, sexual mating, familial bonding, friendship, social ranking, justice as reciprocity, political rule, war, health, beauty, wealth, speech, practical habituation, practical reasoning, practical arts, aesthetic pleasure, religious understanding, and intellectual understanding. Actually, it might be more precise to say that these are twenty general categories of desire, each of which might include many particular desires. My descriptions here of these twenty natural desires will be deliberately vague, because I want to leave room for variability in the specification and direction of these desires in particular circumstances. So, for example, I will speak in vague terms here of sexual mating and familial bonding as natural desires, but in chapters 5 and 6 I will consider the diverse expressions of these desires in the variable social and physical conditions of human life.

I call these desires *natural* because they are so deeply rooted in human nature that they will manifest themselves in some manner across history in every human society. But there are many more desires that might be called *arbitrary* because they arise not from a universal human nature but from individual or social preferences. Arbitrary desires direct or specify the natural desires. So, for example, while the desire to speak is natural, the desire to speak a particular language is arbitrary and depends on the circumstances of the individual who needs to join a particular linguistic community. While the desires for sexual mating and familial bonding are natural, the desire for a "bride price," in which the groom or his kin give money or goods to the bride's kin, is a socially arbitrary desire common in many societies but not all. While the desire for aesthetic pleasure is natural, the desire for a particular style of art might be largely an arbitrary preference arising from someone's personal or social history. Clearly distinguishing natural desires and arbitrary desires allows us to judge arbitrary desires by how well they serve natural desires.

I will elaborate my understanding of some of these desires later in this book. Here I will only sketch them briefly. My selection of the twenty desires that I identify as natural and universal is based on various kinds of evidence. Donald Brown, in his *Human Universals* (1991), and Irenäus Eibl-Eibesfeldt, in his *Human Ethology* (1989), have surveyed the anthropological and biological research showing that there are hundreds of human universals, which include the twenty desires on my list. Anthropologists such as Carol and Melvin Ember (1993) and sociologists such as Joseph Lopreato (1984) confirm the universality of these twenty desires. Psychologists who study the psychology of motivation would recognize these twenty desires as manifesting the basic motives for human action (McClelland 1985). When Aristotle, in the *Nicomachean Ethics* and the *Rhetoric*, reviews the common opinions of human beings about what is desirable in life, he includes the twenty desires on my list. When an Aristotelian scholar like Martha Nussbaum (1992) describes "the basic human functions" that support universal norms of moral judgment, she includes the desires on my list. Furthermore, scholarly collections of "great ideas" in Western thought, such as the *Great Treasury of Western Thought* edited by Mortimer Adler and Charles Van Doren (1977), invariably include these twenty desires as prominent topics of human concern. Thus, some contemporary social scientific research and some classic texts of philosophy and literature confirm the universality of these twenty desires as rooted in human nature. Moreover, I believe our commonsense experience of the world would suggest that these twenty desires are indeed universal features of the human condition. As I present these twenty desires here in this section, I offer only very general explanations for why I think these desires are natural. In later chapters, I will elaborate my arguments and evidence for the naturalness of some of these desires. Parental care, for example, is one of these desires, and chapter 5 is devoted entirely to this desire.

Despite the uncertainty in reconstructing the evolutionary history of human ancestors, there is evidence for believing that this pattern of twenty desires developed in the Paleolithic environment of our hunting-gathering ancestors, the evolutionary environment in which human nature was shaped by natural selection (Campbell 1985; Klein 1989; Lewin 1993). The evidence of human paleontology suggests, for example, that parental care of children was as important for Paleolithic hunter-gatherers as it is for modern human beings. The same could be said about all of the natural desires.

In the case of each desire, I speak of what human beings "generally" desire, because I am speaking of general tendencies or proclivities that are true for all societies but not for all individuals in all circumstances. There can be individual exceptions for every natural desire. A few individuals might have little or no sex drive, for example. There is great fluctuation in sexual interest across the human life span. And in extreme cases of physical deprivation and suffering, all people might find their sexual appetite suppressed by other appetites. But this does not deny the fact that the desire for sexual pleasure is a natural desire for most sexually mature people under the normal conditions of life, which is why every human society must have rules for the proper expression of this desire.

1. *A complete life.* Human beings generally desire life. Like other animals, they pass through a life cycle from birth to maturity to death. Every human society is organized to manage the changing desires associated with this life cycle, which passes through distinct stages such as infancy, juvenility, adolescence, adulthood, and old age. Children, adults, and the old have different desires, and to satisfy those desires they must fill different roles in society. Although human beings will risk their lives for a good cause, they generally agree that to be fully happy one must live out one's natural life span.

2. *Parental care.* Human beings generally desire to care for children. Human life would be impossible without parental care of the young. A large portion of the activity and resources of every human society is devoted to parental care and familial life generally. Children desire the care of adults. And although parental caregiving is onerous, most human adults desire to provide such care. Human beings desire to care for those children to whom they have some special bond—either those to whom they are biologically related or those to whom they have developed some adoptive attachment.

3. *Sexual identity.* Human beings generally desire to identify themselves as male or female. Sex is the single most important characteristic of personal identity. It is the first thing we notice about a person and the last thing we forget. In all human societies, sex terminology is fundamentally dualistic. Male and female are the basic sexes. Others are either a combination of the basic sexes (hermaphrodites) or a crossover from one to the other (men who act as women or women who act as men). All human societies have some sexual division of labor. And although different societies assign somewhat different sex roles, there are some recurrent differences that manifest a universal bipolarity in the pattern of human desires. For

example, women in general (on average) tend to be more nurturant as manifested in a greater propensity to care for children, and men in general (on average) tend to be more dominant as manifested in a greater propensity to seek high-status positions. Yet while this average difference is true for most men and women, for some it is not: some women have "manly" desires, and some men have "womanly" desires.

4. Sexual mating. Human beings generally desire sexual coupling. In every human society, there is intense interest in sexuality, and social regulation is needed to manage the conflicts created by sexual competition. Incest avoidance, for example, is universal. Incest between mother and son is so rare as to be almost inconceivable for most people, although incest between father and daughter is a more common problem. In comparison with women, men, on average, tend to be more violent in their sexual jealousy and more promiscuous in their sexual interests. One indication of the tendency of men to promiscuity is that in every society the customers for prostitutes are almost always men. On average, men desire to mate with young beautiful women, while women desire to mate with men who have social resources and high status. Most men restrain their restless and thus disruptive desire for promiscuous mating to satisfy their desire for monogamous fidelity and parental care.

5. Familial bonding. Human beings generally desire to live in families. Despite the variability in patterns of familial life across different societies, a mother with her children is the universal core of the family. As centered on the mother-child bond, the extended structure of the family usually includes men who are involved, either directly or indirectly, in helping to care for the children. Across all societies, there is some arrangement for marriage as a publicly recognized right of sexual access to a reproductively mature woman. And in every society, kinship is one of the most important social relationships, although the precise structure of kinship ties is somewhat variable.

6. Friendship. Human beings generally desire friendship. They seek social relationships of mutual affection and respect based on shared interests and cooperative endeavors. Although sexual partners and family members can be friends, friendship in itself is a social bond of reciprocal attachment that does not derive from sexual mating or familial bonding. Human beings can have intense and enduring friendships with only a few people, because such friendships require shared experiences over a long period of life.

7. *Social ranking.* Human beings generally desire social recognition through comparative ranking. Their esteem for themselves requires the esteem of others whose judgments they respect. Human beings attain social recognition through status, prestige, fame, or honor within the groups to which they belong. Although some societies are much less hierarchical than others, all societies have some distinctions of rank based on age, sex, kinship, and other forms of ascribed and achieved statuses. As I have already indicated, men generally (on average) have a stronger desire for dominance in social hierarchies than do women.

8. *Justice as reciprocity.* Human beings generally desire reciprocity in their social dealings. A natural sense of justice as reciprocity arises from the human tendency to answer in kind—returning benefit for benefit and injury for injury. This tendency to reciprocity is enforced by moral passions found in most human beings: they are inclined to feel gratitude, love, and benevolence in return for benefits conferred on them; they are inclined to feel anger, hatred, and malevolence in return for injuries inflicted on them; and they are inclined to feel guilt, shame, and regret for their violations of their reciprocal obligations to others. Although some human beings do not feel these moral passions very strongly, and a few do not feel them at all, such people are treated as moral deviants by their fellow human beings. In modern psychological research, those people who lack any moral passions are recognized as psychopaths.

9. *Political rule.* Human beings generally desire political organization. Human beings are by nature political animals, because they naturally live in social systems that require (at least occasionally) central coordination. In some primitive human communities, such as hunter-gatherer bands, this centralized coordination of society is informal and episodic. In other larger and more complex communities, such as bureaucratic states, this centralized coordination is formal and enduring. Political life cannot be completely autocratic, because no single human being can rule absolutely without some support from others. Nor can it be completely democratic, because all members of a community cannot rule as equals in every decision. Consequently, every political community is a de facto oligarchy. Human politics is also a sphere for male dominance. No political community has ever been matriarchal. Even though women often exercise great power in other areas of life, and even though many women often enter the political sphere, the public arenas of political life are generally dominated by men. In the political

history of England, for example, one of the greatest monarchs and one of the greatest prime ministers have been women. And yet both Queen Elizabeth I and Margaret Thatcher led governments dominated by men.

10. War. Human beings generally desire war when it seems to advance their group in conflicts with other groups. Human beings divide themselves into ethnic and territorial groups, and they tend to be more cooperative with those people who belong to their own group than with those outside their group. So when the competition between communities becomes severe, violent conflict is likely. Human beings desire war when fear, interest, or honor move them to fight for their community against opposing communities. War shows the best and the worst of human nature. War manifests the brutal cruelty of human beings in fighting those they regard as enemies. Yet war also manifests the moral sociality of human beings in fighting courageously for their community. War is an instrument of politics, and like political rule generally, warfare is a predominantly male activity.

11. Health. Human beings generally desire to live healthy lives. Their physical appetites drive them to eat, sleep, and find shelter. Every human society must provide for such bodily needs. Every society attempts to heal the sick through medicine and other means. Much of the daily routine of life is devoted to satisfying the physical desires that sustain a healthy life.

12. Beauty. Human beings generally desire beauty in the human body. Everywhere human beings distinguish beauty and ugliness in bodily appearance. They esteem the bodily signs of health and vigor. They adorn their bodies for pleasing display. Men tend to prefer women whose physical appearance shows signs of youthful nubility.

13. Wealth. Human beings generally desire the wealth necessary for a flourishing life. To satisfy this desire, every society has concepts of property that distinguish what is owned by an individual or a group from what is owned by others. Wealth is desired to equip oneself and one's family and friends for a good life. Wealth is also desired as a display of status or prestige.

14. Speech. Human beings generally desire to speak. Children are naturally adapted to learn their native language. Through language human beings think about and discuss themselves and their world. Through the linguistic capacity for conceiving abstractions, they can judge good and bad, true and false. The social activity of human beings depends on the manipulation of these verbal abstractions. Speech is a tool for persuasion, the primary means by which human beings negotiate the terms of their social life with one another. Rhetoric, poetry, storytelling, gossip—these and other arts of speech bind people together and drive them apart.

15. *Practical habituation.* Human beings generally desire to manage their appetites and passions by habituation. Parents and other adults form the character of the young by habituating them to resist momentary impulses to self-gratification for the sake of their long-range satisfaction. Even as adults, human beings must acquire and maintain those habits of good conduct that allow them to organize their often conflicting desires into some coherent pattern over a whole life. Because of the diversity of temperaments, different individuals need different kinds of habituation that moderate the weaknesses and foster the strengths to which they are inclined by temperament.

16. *Practical reasoning.* Human beings generally desire to manage their appetites and passions by deliberation. Unlike other animals, human adults have the rational capacity to deliberate about what a whole life well lived might be and then to organize their actions to conform to that deliberate conception of a good life. Such deliberation requires prudence or practical wisdom in judging what is best for particular people in particular circumstances. The variability in individual temperaments, individual history, and social conditions makes it impossible to formulate general rules to decide what should be done in every case. Consequently, prudence requires not only a general understanding of human nature but also a particular insight into the unique circumstances of a given case. Such understanding and insight comes only from a lifetime of practical experience and shrewd reflection on that experience. Prudence is required at all levels of social life. The success of parental care depends on parental prudence. The success of political rule depends on political prudence.

17. *Practical arts.* Human beings generally desire craftsmanship. Every human society depends on making and using tools to manipulate natural resources for human benefit. Some of the basic tools—such as cutters, pounders, levers, containers, and weapons such as projectiles—are universal. Some tools are made in uniform patterns of artistic style. As naturally adapted for craftsmanship, human beings enjoy producing and seeing products of practical skill.

18. *Aesthetic pleasure.* Human beings generally desire aesthetic pleasure

through artistic products and natural environments. In every society, human beings take pleasure in artistic activities such as singing, dancing, playing musical instruments, forming language into poetic patterns, telling stories, carving, painting, and decorating objects. They also take pleasure in natural landscapes that resemble the savannas where the human species evolved. Although human beings are flexible enough to live in urban environments, they try to recreate the natural environments of their evolutionary history as hunter-gatherers through parklike landscapes, gardening, and the company of animals.

19. Religious understanding. Human beings generally desire to understand the world through supernatural revelation. In every society, belief in the power of divinity satisfies the natural human yearning to make sense of things. Driven to fear and despair by their natural experience of pain and death, many human beings imagine themselves surrounded by supernatural forces that determine their fate. Driven to hope and pride by their feeling of divine inspiration, many human beings imagine that their natural existence can be redeemed by supernatural intervention.

20. Intellectual understanding. Human beings generally desire to understand the world through natural reason. Some human beings satisfy their natural human yearning to make sense of things through their intellectual understanding of nature. This study of nature by natural human reason alone is fulfilled in the life of philosophy or science.

I will argue that these twenty natural desires are universally found in all human societies, that they have evolved by natural selection over four million years of human evolutionary history to become components of the species-specific nature of human beings, that they are based in the physiological mechanisms of the brain, and that they direct and limit the social variability of human beings as adapted to diverse ecological circumstances.

NURTURING NATURE

In calling these twenty desires "natural," I do not mean to imply that they arise spontaneously in all human beings without any cultivation by habit or learning. "Nature" has many different meanings. I assume a complex conception of nature as both original potential and developed potential. While we commonly separate nature and nurture or nature and art, animal nature—including human nature—must be nurtured if it is to reach its natural completion. This ambiguity is evident in the linguistic history of "nature" and related words (Cropsey 1977; Klein 1985; Lewis 1967). We say the nature of something is its original or innate condition, what it is if nothing is done to it. Yet we also say the nature of something is its characteristic or normal state when it has developed its mature form. Understanding nature as original potential may require a sharp distinction between nature and art; understanding nature as developed potential may require conceiving of art as sometimes the completion or imitation of nature. A body healing itself on its own is natural in the first sense. A body healing itself with the aid of the medical art is natural in the second sense.

According to the first sense, our nature is what we are at birth—our original potentialities or inclinations—before any habituation or learning. According to the second sense, however, we could say that our nature is to become a rational, ethical, and political animal as the completion of our inborn inclinations, social habits, and individual judgments. In the pursuit of their natural ends, all animals seek the conditions that will satisfy their desires as guided by their information about environmental threats and opportunities. For some animals this requires extensive learning and habituation, so that their nature is fulfilled through art. As human beings, we differ only in the complexity of our desires and in our unique capacity for deliberately acting in the light of some conception of a whole life well lived as the fullest and most coherent satisfaction of our desires.

We often assume that human beings are unique in their dependence on nurture and artifice for the full development of their nature. But our experience with domestic pets should teach us that this cannot be true. To explain the character and behavior of dogs, for example, we must consider the interaction of innate dispositions and early learning experiences. Each breed of dog has its distinctive behavioral propensities, but the characteristic behavior of any particular dog will express the complex interaction between the individual temperament of the dog and its early social environment of rearing (Scott and Fuller 1965; Serpell and Jagoe 1995).

Similarly, monkeys and apes are by nature such intensely social animals that their natural development depends on social learning. Wolfgang Köhler, in his classic book, *The Mentality of Apes*, concluded that because social experience was so important for stimulating the natural capacities of chimpanzees, "it is hardly an exaggeration to say that a chimpanzee kept in solitude is not a real chimpanzee at all" (1927, 282). Harry Harlow's famous laboratory experiments with rhesus monkeys deprived of maternal bonding demonstrated how social deprivation impeded the emotional growth of such animals (1986). Jane Goodall's observations of wild chimpanzees have shown the same social needs. To satisfy their natural desires, chimpanzees must acquire social habits and social intelligence. They must learn first from their mothers and then from other members of their community an intricate repertoire of social skills. "The infant is not born with built-in responses that will dictate his behavior in complex social situations," Goodall explains, "he learns by trial and error, social facilitation, observation and imitation, and practice" (1986, 568). Frans de Waal (1996) has shown that chimpanzee groups depend upon a "sense of social regularity"—rules of social behavior enforced by rewards and punishments—that must be learned by young chimpanzees as part of their socialization into a group.

Many social scientists assume that human biology is largely irrelevant to human social behavior, because they believe that human social life arises from a uniquely human openness to nurture or culture that transcends biological nature. Consequently, the critics of Darwinian explanations of human social behavior insist that "we know of no relevant constraints placed on social processes by human biology" (Allen et al. 1978, 290). Yet if human morality is rooted in natural biological inclinations, and if human freedom is freedom within nature rather than freedom from nature, then the moral freedom that human beings exercise through nurture or culture is biologically natural.

Many social scientists have adopted John Locke's idea that at birth the human mind is a tabula rasa or "white paper" that "receives any characters" (Locke 1959, 1:48, 1:87, 1:121). In the absence of innate principles, the mind receives whatever experience and custom write onto it. This would seem to support cultural relativism. Moral principles cannot be naturally innate, Locke argues, if we see that there is hardly any moral norm that has not been violated by some society somewhere in the world. For example, parental care for children might seem to be one moral principle that has been naturally imprinted on the mind. Yet the customary practice of infanticide in some societies shows that even parental care is not a natural moral principle, and thus custom is "a greater power than nature" (Locke 1959, 1:69–88).

Locke is mistaken, however, in his assumption that since the innate or the natural must be universal and invariant, any diversity or flexibility in human behavior must be purely cultural or customary. Modern biology shows that innate traits in most cases are not absolutely fixed, because the observed phenotype emerges from the interaction of inborn potential, developmental history, and the external environment. The human brain and human behavior arise from a complex interplay of natural inclination, individual experience, and social learning (Brauth, Hall, and Dooling 1991; Kandel 1991; Kandel and Jessel 1991). This modern biological account of the interaction of nature and nurture conforms more to Aristotle's understanding of human nature than to Locke's view of the mind as a blank slate.

Aristotle believes that what is naturally right varies according to the variable circumstances of particular individuals and particular communities. This does not dictate moral relativism, however, because for any given set of circumstances, there are naturally better and worse ways to satisfy the natural desires of human beings (*NE* 1103a14–27, 1107a1–7, 1134b18–35a5, 1137b11–32, 1140a24–45a2; *Pol* 1256a20–b7, 1288b10–89a25; *Rh* 1360b4–66a23; Mulhern 1972). Parental care for children, for example, is so deeply rooted in human biology that although its expression will vary according to individual temperament and social conditions, any attempt to abolish parent-child bonding (as suggested in Plato's *Republic*) would be contrary to human nature (*HA* 588b24–89a10; *NE* 1161b16–62a28, 1168a22–27; *Pol* 1261b16–62b37). I will elaborate this point in chapter 5.

David Hume shows that while there is great diversity in the physical world as well as the moral world, in both worlds the diversity is naturally regular. "There is a general course of nature in human actions as well as in the operations of the sun and the climate" (1888, 402). Just as different kinds of trees regularly produce different kinds of fruit in different regions of the world, so do differences in sex, age, and social conditions regularly produce differences in human behavior. If a traveler told us of a country in the Arctic where all the fruits ripen in the winter and wither in the summer, we would not believe him, because this would violate the regularities of physical nature. Nor would we believe him if he told us of a people who lived by the principles of Plato's *Republic* or Hobbes's *Leviathan*, because this would violate "the necessary and uniform principles of human nature" (1888, 402).

If one examines carefully the apparent diversity of morals across cultures,

Hume contends, one sees that "the principles upon which men reason in morals are always the same, though the conclusions which they draw are often very different" (1902, 335–36). People are often mistaken in their moral reasoning, but since the fundamental principles of morality are uniform, erroneous conclusions can be corrected by better reasoning and wider experience. For instance, in societies like Athens, parents could be motivated by their love of children to commit infanticide if they lacked the resources to care for children properly (1902, 334). Contrary to Locke, Hume believes the practice of infanticide in circumstances where caring for the child is difficult does not deny the naturalness of parental affection (1888, 483–84, 486, 570–73; 1902, 189–92, 201–8, 295–311). Hume would agree with Darwin that parental love and all other moral sentiments are natural to human beings although their full development requires cultivation by "habit, example, instruction, and reflection" (Darwin 1936b, 494).

Locke is wrong in inferring that infanticide shows parental care to be purely a product of culture rather than nature. Infanticide tends to occur only in specific circumstances: the infant is deformed, or there is not enough food to feed the infant, or the paternity of the infant is uncertain (Daly and Wilson 1988; Eibl-Eibesfeldt 1989, 186–201; Scrimshaw 1984). Children older than one month are rarely killed, because by then the mother's bond to the child is usually strong. Parents in desperate circumstances may have to kill one infant to preserve another infant or even to preserve themselves. Parental love is natural, but it must compete with other natural sentiments, and this competition forces parents to make tragic choices when their physical and social resources are scarce.

Like human beings, some other animals practice infanticide and abortion in some circumstances (Hausfater and Hrdy 1984). This does not deny the naturalness of parental care for these animals. Rather, it shows the natural variability of animal behavior in adapting to variable circumstances. Behavioral ecologists apply Darwinian theory in explaining such behavioral plasticity as biologically natural (Krebs and Davies 1993). Natural selection can favor individual behavioral differences in a species, and these individual differences can be caused either by genetic differences or by mechanisms of phenotypic plasticity such that a single genotype produces behavioral differences in different environments (Kagan 1994; Wilson 1994). Behavioral ecologists reject the assumption of Locke and many social scientists that nature must be invariable in all circumstances.

For any organism the transformation of genotype into phenotype depends upon its unique developmental history (Lewontin 1992; Oyama 1985). Every biological trait—morphological, physiological, or behavioral—emerges from the interaction of genetic endowment and environmental conditions. Some biological traits are environmentally stable in that they are not much affected by environmental variations, but others are environmentally flexible in that they are much affected by environmental variations. Examples of environmentally stable traits are morphological traits such as the color of eyes, physiological traits such as the maintenance of body temperature, and behavioral traits such as eating. Examples of environmentally flexible traits are morphological traits such as body weight, physiological traits such as acquired immune reactions, and behavioral traits such as nut-cracking among chimpanzees. Although we might speak of environmentally stable traits as "innate" and environmentally flexible traits as "acquired," these are only the extreme ends of a continuum of biological traits that all require some combination of innate and acquired factors.

Since the instinctive behavior of animals ranges from the extremely stable to the extremely flexible, it is a mistake to assume that all instinctive behavior is completely fixed, and all learned behavior is completely flexible. We know, for example, that monkeys raised in extreme environments of social isolation cannot as adults display the sexual and parental behavior typical for monkeys (Harlow 1986). But it would be mistaken to conclude from this that sexual and parental behavior is not instinctive for monkeys. Instead, we should conclude that the sexual and parental behavior typical for monkeys can emerge only within a limited range of social environments similar to the environments that were typical for their evolutionary ancestors.

Animal behavior manifests great phenotypic variability, particularly for those animals with complex nervous systems, so that animals are endowed by nature with the capacity to change their behavior in response to changing circumstances (Gordon 1992; Real 1994). Behavioral ecologists have found that animals in complex societies must weigh social and ecological variables as they make decisions about their lives (Emlen and Wrege 1994; Harcourt and de Waal 1992; Masters 1994c). Social intelligence is particularly important for primates (Byrne and Whiten 1988; Seyfarth and Cheney 1994). Some nonhuman primates display cultural variation between groups that reflects the unique social history of each group (Dunbar 1988; Goodall

1986; McGrew 1992; Wrangham et al. 1994). So it seems that human beings are not the only cultural animals.

Sociobiology, particularly as developed by Edward O. Wilson (1975), has been perceived by its critics as attempting to explain human social behavior as controlled mostly by genetic inheritance, which seems to ignore the complexity and flexibility of human behavior as a purely phenotypic response to variable environments (Kitcher 1985). Behavioral ecology, however, is concerned precisely with such adaptive responses to environmental conditions. Even some of the critics of sociobiology have conceded that human sociobiology would be defensible if it were transformed into human behavioral ecology (Kitcher 1990).

Rather than trying to choose between nature and nurture as the predominant influence on human behavior, the human behavioral ecologist studies the complex interaction of nature and nurture by considering how social and ecological factors influence behavioral flexibility both within and between populations (Borgerhoff Mulder 1991; Crook 1989; Winterhalder and Smith 1992). As a product of Darwinian evolution, human nature should manifest some general propensities that were adaptive in human evolutionary history. Yet the individual expression of those propensities will vary according to individual temperament and in response to the social and physical circumstances of the individual.

Critics of sociobiology such as Stephen Jay Gould often insist on a false dichotomy—biological potentiality versus biological determinism—that ignores the importance of biological propensity. "My criticism of Wilson," Gould explains, "does not invoke a nonbiological 'environmentalism': it merely pits the concept of biological potentiality—a brain capable of the full range of human behaviors and rigidly predisposed toward none—against the idea of biological determinism—specific genes for specific behavior" (1977, 257–58). Explaining human social behavior through biological determinism is utterly implausible if that means claiming that specific genes determine specific behavior with no flexibility. Therefore, Gould insists, we must accept the only alternative idea—"biological potentiality—a brain capable of the full range of human behaviors and rigidly predisposed toward none." But Gould uses the word "rigidly" here to obscure a third alternative: the idea of biological predisposition or propensity as something more than a mere potentiality and yet something less than a rigid determinism.

With respect to sexual mating, for example, human beings have a biological potentiality for a wide range of behaviors—including celibacy, promiscuity, monogamy, polygyny, and polyandry. Gould would have a strong argument in claiming that there are no specific genes that absolutely determine or "rigidly" predispose us to one of these behaviors. But he would be wrong to assume from this that we have an indifferent potentiality for any of these. Although we have a potential for choosing complete celibacy, most human beings find this too difficult because it denies our strong propensity or desire for sexual mating. Promiscuity is easier because it caters to our sexual propensities. Polyandrous marriage (one wife with several husbands) seems to be a very weak potentiality for human beings because the intense sexual jealousy of males incline them against it. In contrast to polyandry, monogamous mating has been universal to all human societies and polygynous mating (one husband with several wives) has been common, because they satisfy biological desires. In chapters 5 and 6, I will argue that this pattern of social behavior reflects the biological nature of human mating. An understanding of biological propensities or desires can explain why celibacy is difficult, promiscuity is easy, polyandry is rare, monogamy is universal, and polygyny is common, although none of these behaviors is "rigidly" determined by specific genes. Our nature predisposes us to favor some behavior over others, although the specific expression of our behavior will reflect the variable conditions of physical environment, social circumstances, and individual temperament.

The influence of parenting on children manifests the complex interplay of nature and nurture. Traditionally, many psychologists have assumed that the effects of parental care on children show that environmental socialization is more important than innate temperament in human development. This assumption seems dubious, however, in the face of recent research in behavioral genetics, based largely on adoption and twin studies, that indicates how the natural temperament of the child shapes the social environment. Aristotle (*GA* 767b24–69b31; *NE* 1144b1–5) and Darwin (1936b, 413–15) believe that much of the variability in the mental dispositions of human beings and other animals arises from traits inherited at birth that guide development to adulthood. This seems to be confirmed by the evidence in behavioral genetics that genetic propensities explain much of the variation in human behavioral traits (Bouchard et al. 1990; Lykken 1995; Plomin, DeFries, and McClearn 1990; Plomin, Owen, and McGuffin 1994).

Human variability in personality arises from individual differences in the neurochemical mechanisms that mediate perception and behavior, and to some degree these temperamental differences are inherited (Kagan 1994; Masters 1993, 81–83, 122–23). A child's natural propensities foster psychological differences indirectly by influencing the environment of the child. Children with different temperaments evoke different responses from their parents. As children grow older, they have increasing power to modify or select their environments to conform to their individual temperament. Successful parenting is not the imposition of external norms on the child but the cultivation of the child's innate potential. Therefore, we should think of the development of children under parental care as expressing not "nature versus nurture" but "nature through nurture" or the "nature of nurture" (Plomin and Bergeman 1991; Scarr 1992).

The regularity in the patterns of parental care across cultures manifests inborn inclinations shaped by natural selection in evolutionary history. The variability in those patterns manifests the flexibility of human social behavior as shaped by individual experience and social learning. Like other animals, human beings display innate potentialities and propensities that are neither absolutely fixed nor absolutely malleable. For the full development of human beings, nature must be nurtured.

FOUR SOURCES OF MORAL DISAGREEMENT

If the good is the desirable, and if there is a natural pattern of desires for human beings that includes the twenty desires I have just specified, why do human beings fall into moral conflict? The pervasiveness of moral disagreement is the one fact most often cited by proponents of moral relativism who believe there are no natural, universal standards for resolving moral debate. It does not follow, however, from the fact of moral controversy that there are no natural standards for moral judgment. There are four sources of moral disagreement: fallible beliefs about circumstances, fallible beliefs about desires, variable circumstances, and variable desires. Consequently, as Aristotle often insists, ethics is not a science like mathematics in which one properly seeks certainty and precision. Because of its uncertainty and imprecision, ethics requires the sort of practical judgment rooted in experience that cannot be reduced to abstract rules. But still, the ultimate standard for ethics is the pattern of natural desires that distinguishes human nature.

1. Fallible beliefs about circumstances. Moral judgment is often uncertain and imprecise because our knowledge of the circumstances of action is uncertain and imprecise. We often disagree about moral questions, even when we agree in our principles, because we have differing views of the relevant circumstances. In fact, much of our moral reasoning is devoted to gathering and assessing the facts pertinent to our practical decisions.

2. Fallible beliefs about desires. We are often unsure about what we truly desire. Even when we think we know what we desire at some particular moment, it is not always clear whether satisfying that momentary desire will impede the satisfaction of a more important desire in the future. Much of our moral deliberation with ourselves and with others requires reasoning about the consistency or contradiction of diverse desires over a complete life. Furthermore, we often disagree about whether individually or socially arbitrary desires properly specify our natural desires. For example, as we shall see in chapter 6, some women in some societies believe that to satisfy their natural desires for marriage and having children they must have their genitals mutilated—clitorises cut off and vaginas sewn up—but this customary desire for genital mutilation can be criticized as founded on mistaken beliefs that frustrate the natural desires of both women and men.

3. Variable circumstances. The variability in the practical circumstances that distinguish one individual from another and one society from another dictates variability in our moral judgments. Although the pattern of natural human desires is universal, satisfying those desires in different individual and social circumstances requires different patterns of conduct appropriate to the circumstances.

4. Variable desires. There is both normal and abnormal variation in human desires. The normal variation arises from age, sexual identity, and individual temperament. Natural human diversity is such that the young do not have exactly the same desires as the old, men do not have exactly the same desires as women, and individuals with one temperament do not have exactly the same desires as those with another temperament. The abnormal variation in desires arises from abnormality in innate dispositions or in social circumstances. So, for example, while human beings are normally social animals with social desires that incline them to feel the pleasures and pains of those close to them, we shall see in chapter 8 that a few human beings are psychopaths, who lack the social desires that normally characterize human beings as social animals. And sometimes abnormal social circumstances such as the custom of female genital mutilation promote arbitrary desires that frustrate natural desires.

PRUDENCE

Because of these four sources of moral uncertainty and imprecision, morality depends on the exercise of what Aristotle identified as prudence. Prudence is the practical wisdom for judging correctly how to satisfy the variable desires of human beings in the variable circumstances of action. We need prudence to judge the appropriate expression of each desire as varying according to the social and physical conditions of particular individuals in particular societies. We also need prudence to judge how best to resolve conflicts among the natural desires. In my Aristotelian emphasis on prudence, I reject the common assumption of many contemporary philosophers that the purpose of moral philosophy is to find universal normative principles—Kantian, utilitarian, or whatever—to resolve all moral conflicts in some abstract way. Like Aristotle, I believe that moral judgment lacks the precision and certainty of mathematics or formal logic because of the contingency of moral circumstances. In many cases, moral problems produce tragic conflicts that cannot be perfectly resolved by appeal to universal, formal rules.

Modern moral philosophers often assume that morality comes primarily from learning and following explicit norms stated as definitions and rules. For example, one might learn the definition for "lie" and then learn the rule that lying is wrong. Aristotle would reject such a view because it fails to recognize that moral virtues are forms of social habituation that depend ultimately on the intellectual virtue of prudence, which cannot be reduced to rules and definitions. Prudence is a form of practical knowledge that one acquires by learning how to successfully manage one's individual and social life. The virtue of honesty, for example, comes from learning how to tell the truth to the right people at the right time and in the right way. In many cases, the demands of politeness, friendship, privacy, self-interest, or just joking playfulness require that we not tell the whole truth. Knowing when, where, and with whom one should be completely truthful comes from practical social experience that cannot be reduced to rules and definitions (*NE* 1127a14–28b9). Recently, philosophers such as Owen Flanagan (1996) and Paul Churchland (1995, 1996) have defended this Aristotelian understanding of morality as based on prudence.

To illustrate the character of prudence in moral life, much of my writing in this book will be devoted to historical cases of moral conflict in particular circumstances. In my chapter on slavery, for example, I consider the conflict between the master's natural desire to exploit slaves and the slave's natural desire to resist exploitation. I argue, in agreement with Thomas Jefferson and Abraham Lincoln, that although slavery is wrong because it denies the natural sense of justice as reciprocity, the American founders exercised prudence in looking for ways to abolish slavery gradually in the hope of avoiding the civil war and racial conflict that would ensue from immediate abolition. Similarly, in my chapter on men and women, I speak about female circumcision as frustrating the natural desires of women and men, but I suggest that prudence might require that this practice cannot be immediately abolished in those societies where it is a long-established custom. Such prudent respect for local customs and historical conditions is necessary to accommodate the ecological variability of human social life. Prudent judgment is rooted in human ecology.

In response to any notion of natural right or natural law as founded on human nature, a common criticism is that this promotes a moral absolutism that fails to respect the contingency of moral reasoning in concrete circumstances. But this criticism has no application to an Aristotelian understanding of ethics as based on prudence. For human beings, Aristotle insisted, "although there is something that is just by nature, all is variable" (*NE* 1134b29–30). The natural desires of human beings constitute a universal norm for morality and politics, but there are no universal rules for what should be done in particular circumstances. Since the practical situations faced by human beings are infinite, deciding what is best in any concrete situation is a matter of practical judgment or prudence (*NE* 1138b18–39b14, 1140a24–45a11). This often requires not only choosing between bad and good, but also choosing between incompatible goods or between a lesser evil and a greater evil. Sometimes the prudent person must tolerate an evil if the attempt to abolish the evil would produce an even greater evil. Sometimes prudence means choosing the less bad as good. Rather than denying natural right, this understanding of prudence presupposes it. To rank conflicting goods or to distinguish lesser and greater evils presumes a general standard of what is good for human beings as satisfying their natural desires. But while this general standard guides decisions, it cannot determine them in particular cases except as informed by a practical understanding of the given circumstances.

The need for prudence is a consequence of human biology in at least two respects. First, the variation in human moral experience that makes prudence necessary manifests a general variability in all biological phenomena, and particularly in animal behavior. All plants and animals are naturally adapted in various ways for flexible responses to the changing ecological circumstances in which they find themselves. Human beings and many other animals are naturally adapted for complex social behavior through which they adjust themselves to the fluctuating conditions of their social and physical ecology. Human ethics is part of human ecology, because human communities develop those standards of right and wrong conduct that seem to satisfy human desires within the ecological conditions of each community. Prudence emerges as the practical wisdom that human beings develop as they judge the relative success or failure of various ethical expectations in various ecological conditions. From this point of view, ethics could be seen as a part of human ecology (Andrewartha and Birch 1984, 435–57; Arnhart 1996; Flanagan 1996). Much of what Aristotle says about the diversity of political regimes as adapted to diverse social and physical circumstances could be identified as human ecology (*Pol* 1256a20–b7, 1288b10–89a25).

A second biological explanation for the importance of prudence is that it emerges from the neural structure of the brain. As Paul Churchland (1995, 1996) has argued, moral reasoning is an activity of the brain, and much of what we now know about how the brain works through networks of synaptic connections among neurons would support Aristotle's understanding of moral reasoning as prudence or practical wisdom. The brain represents the world primarily not through rules that can be verbally stated as principles, but through prototypes that allow for judgments that cannot be expressed as verbal principles. For example, our brains can recognize and discriminate sensations of color and taste in ways that we could never express in verbal principles. Similarly, we can recognize faces and the facial expression of emotions even when we cannot translate these into verbal statements. It seems that the brain uses a prototypic image of an angry face to recognize the visible expression of anger without being able to formulate rules for distinguishing anger from other facial expressions.

Churchland has argued that a similar kind of activity seems to occur when we engage in moral judgments. Like other social animals, our brains have been shaped by natural selection to recognize and respond to social signals so that we can successfully navigate our way through the social environment. Our practical experience of the social world gives us prototypes of moral phenomena such as honesty, love, sympathy, cruelty, and unfairness. Acquiring and applying such moral prototypes in our social lives is a practical skill that cannot be translated into verbal rules, although we may sometimes formulate some rules as rough abridgments of our practical experience. In contrast to the modern view of morality as the learning of abstract rules, Aristotle's view of morality as founded on practical habituation and practical judgment conforms to the way the mind works. Prudence is a natural human capacity, Churchland concludes, because it is an activity of that most important organ of our body—the brain.

Aristotle believed that prudence is required not just in judging what is good for oneself and one's family and friends. Prudence is also required in judging what is good for the larger community to which one belongs, because human beings are by nature political animals.

CHAPTER 3

POLITICAL ANIMALS

Are human beings by nature political animals, as Aristotle claimed? Or was Thomas Hobbes warranted in denying Aristotle's claim and asserting that political order is an utterly artificial human construction? Is political life rooted somehow in biological nature? Or does politics require a human conquest of nature?

The positions of Aristotle and Hobbes represent two fundamental alternatives in political science and the social sciences generally. Hobbes assumes a radical separation between animal societies as founded on natural instinct and human societies as founded on social learning. Human beings cannot be political animals by nature, Hobbes believes, because "man is made fit for society not by nature but by education" (*De Cive*, chap. 1). This supports the modern notion of culture as the uniquely human realm of social learning through which human beings express their rational humanity by transcending their natural animality. This concept of culture as separated from nature has become dubious, however, in the face of mounting evidence in the biological sciences that some nonhuman animals (such as chimpanzees) have capacities for learning and teaching that allow for cultural traditions, and therefore the Hobbesian antithesis between instinct (or nature) as completely fixed and learning (or nurture) as completely flexible is false.

Unlike Hobbes, Aristotle sees no unbridgeable gulf between animal instinct and human learning. Rather, like many biologists today, he believes almost all animals have some natural instincts for social learning, and some are intelligent enough to live as social and political animals. What distinguishes human beings is that they are *more* political than other animals because of the human biological capacity for language, which allows human beings to organize communal life around shared verbal concepts of expediency and justice. Aristotle's position would thus support the recent revival of Darwinian social theory by rooting political science in biological science.

In this chapter, I will argue that Aristotle was correct, and that modern biology does indeed sustain his biological account of political animals. I

51

begin by comparing Aristotle's political biology with modern biological theories of social behavior. I then defend Aristotle's position against six criticisms made by Hobbes. I conclude by showing how an Aristotelian understanding of political animals leads us away from the modern Hobbesian dichotomy of nature and culture, and I suggest redefining culture as a completion and expression of nature.

ANTS, BEES, AND OTHER POLITICAL ANIMALS

According to Aristotle, some animals are solitary and others gregarious. Of the gregarious animals, some are political. Some of the political animals have leaders, but others do not. The distinguishing characteristic of the political animals is that they cooperate for some common work or function *(koinon ergon)*. Humans, bees, ants, wasps, and cranes are all political animals in this sense (*HA* 488a7–14).

Human beings are more political, however, than these animals because of the uniquely human capacity for speech *(logos)*. Other animals can share their perceptions of pleasure and pain. But human beings can use speech to share their conceptions of the advantageous, the just, and the good (*Pol* 1253a1–18). Human beings are the most political animals, it seems, because through speech human beings cooperate for common ends in ways that are more complex, more flexible, and more extensive than is possible for other political animals. Through speech human beings can deliberate about the "common advantage" *(koinon sumpheron)* as the criterion of justice (*Rh* 1362a15–63b5). A just political community can be judged to be one that serves the common advantage of all its members, as contrasted with an unjust political community that serves only the private advantage of its ruling group (*NE* 1160a13–14, *Pol* 1279a17–19).

Aristotle explains that political life satisfies various natural human impulses (*Pol* 1253a30–31, 1278b17–31). Human beings desire to live together even when they do not need mutual aid. They are brought together for the common advantage insofar as communal life satisfies their natural needs for moral and intellectual development. They also come together merely to preserve their lives because most human beings find a natural sweetness in simply being alive.

Furthermore, all social cooperation ultimately arises as an extension of the natural impulses to sexual coupling and parental care of the young. Some animals provide little care for their offspring. But the more social and more intelligent animals care for the complete development of their young. Human beings and the other political animals are characterized by the great duration and intensity of parental care, which includes not only feeding and protecting the young but also passing on the habits and knowledge required for living in groups with complex social structures (*HA* 588b23–89a9; *GA* 753a8–14; *NE* 1155a1–33, 1159a27–37, 1160b23–62a29).

While the strongest bonds of common advantage arise among individuals related by kinship, other social bonds arise from mutualism and reciprocity. Sometimes individuals cooperate because it is mutually beneficial. At other times individuals cooperate in helping others with the expectation of some reciprocal return in the future. Social conflict occurs when people think these relationships of mutual benefit and reciprocal exchange have not been maintained (*NE* 1132b33–33a5, 1155b34, 1159b25–62a34; *Pol* 1270b21–23, 1281b26–31, 1318b10–19a6). The social norms of mutual aid and reciprocal cooperation are enforced by moral passions and the concern for reputation (*Rh* 1361a25–61b2, 1364b37–65a10, 1366a34–68a27, 1371a7–23, 1380b35–82a18, 1383b11–85a15; Arnhart 1981, 102–5, 120–21, 114–34).

Although human beings display a complexity in their social bonding through nepotism, mutualism, and reciprocity that indicates the unique complexity of human speech and cognition, Aristotle believes other animals show traces of all the psychic dispositions and capacities that are more clearly manifested in human beings (*HA* 588a15–89a10). He sees evidence in nonhuman animals of memory *(mnesis)*, thought *(dianoia)*, judgment *(sunesis)*, art *(techne)*, and prudence *(phronesis)*, so that some animals develop social behavior through habituation and learning (*HA* 589a10–633b9; *PA* 648a6–8, 650b24–26, 686a24–87a23).

While Aristotle generally denies that nonhuman animals have "intellect" *(nous)*, he indicates that even something like intellect might be found in some animals, particularly if "imagination" *(phantasia)* is considered "some kind of *noesis*" (*DA* 433a10–11, *HA* 610b22, *PA* 656a6–8, *NE* 1178b22–33). And while he generally asserts that "speech" *(logos)* and "language" *(dialektos)* are uniquely human, he recognizes the powers of other animals for communication (*DA* 420b5–21a7; *HA* 488a30–35, 504b1–6, 535a28–36b24, 608a10–18; *PA* 659b28–60b11, 664a18–65a6; *GA* 786b6–88a32).

Some birds teach their young to sing, and the languages they teach differ in different localities in a manner comparable to the diversity of human languages, which suggests that among birds "language is not natural in the same way as voice but can be trained" (*HA* 536b18–20).

In his biology of social behavior, Aristotle does not separate animal instinct and human learning. In varying degrees, all social animals have natural instincts for social learning. Of course, in the capacity for learning, human beings far surpass other animals. Still, it is as true for nonhuman animals as it is for human beings that social life emerges as a joint product of nature and nurture.

Just as some birds are predisposed by nature to sing, human beings are predisposed by nature to speak; and yet, in both cases, a natural predisposition is fulfilled through social learning. Here nature and art are not antithetical but cooperative, Aristotle believes, because "generally art in some cases completes what nature cannot carry out to an end, in others, it imitates nature" (*Phy* 199a16–17). In the same way, Aristotle can say that political life is by nature for human beings while acknowledging that the establishment and maintenance of political order depends on the statesman's art (*Pol* 1253a29–31, 1325b33–26a6). Political life is natural for human beings because it promotes their natural ends and because it arises, at least in part, from their natural potentials, although the completion of those natural ends and potentials requires habituation and learning (Depew 1995; Miller 1989, 1995).

Much of the learning necessary for the social life of animals comes from parents teaching their young. But much is also learned from the competition and cooperation of individuals in the wider community. Some political animals—such as bees, wasps, cranes, and humans—distinguish between leaders and followers (*HA* 488a8–14, 553a26–54b26, 614b19–26, 623b26–29a30). Leaders can help a community by directing it to its common ends, but leaders can also harm a community when they lead factions that divide it (*HA* 553b15–19, 615b17–18, 625a1–26b15). The most successful individuals are those who have the intelligence to maneuver their way through the complex social interplay of conflicts and confluences of interest.

Darwinian biologists might wonder why Aristotle does not recognize the social intelligence of those animals most closely related to human beings—the apes. It is remarkable, however, that although Aristotle does not specifically identify them as political animals, he believes that apes belong to intermediate species close to human beings in that they "share in the nature of both man and the quadrupeds" (*HA* 502a16). From his anatomical comparisons, which included dissections of monkeys and apes, he concluded that in their feet, legs, hands, face, teeth, and internal parts, the apes are manlike (*HA* 502a17–b27; *PA* 689b1–35).

In 1699, Edward Tyson, an English doctor, wrote a book on the anatomy of a chimpanzee, which began with an extended analysis of Aristotle's study of monkeys and apes. Concluding like Aristotle that this ape was halfway between a monkey and a human, Tyson showed resemblances to a monkey in thirty-four characteristics and resemblances to a human in forty-seven characteristics. In the brain, "the seat of the soul itself," he saw a surprisingly close resemblance to human beings (Tyson 1699, 3–15, 54–57, 92–95). Tyson's book has been praised by Darwinians like Thomas Huxley as "the first account of a man-like ape which has any pretensions to scientific accuracy and completeness" (1894b, 7:11). Modern primatologists commonly cite the book as the first rigorous work in their field.

Not only Aristotle's study of primates but also many other points of his biology have been confirmed by modern biological research, despite the fact that he had no theory of the evolutionary origin of species. One prominent biologist has even declared, "All of biology is a footnote to Aristotle" (Moore 1993, 33). If we recognize that Aristotle uses the term "political animal" in a broad sense corresponding to our use of the term "social animal," we can see that the modern biology of social behavior largely supports his political naturalism.

Like Aristotle, Darwin was fascinated by the complex social life of some insects (1936a, 193–202). Today entomologists distinguish various levels of sociality among insects from the solitary to the eusocial, depending on whether they display one or more of three traits—cooperative care of the young, reproductive division of labor, and overlap between generations so that offspring assist parents (Wheeler 1928; Wilson 1971). The eusocial insects, which possess all three traits, include ants, bees, and wasps. These animals display many forms of complex social behavior: child care, eugenics, class structures, social division of labor, fighting over social dominance, group hunting, warfare, slavery, agriculture, animal husbandry, and the second most complex language in the animal world.

In explaining the natural causes of social cooperation, not only among insects but also among birds and mammals, Darwinian biologists have developed evolutionary theories supporting Aristotle's insight that social bonding arises from nepotism, mutualism, and reciprocity. "The feeling of pleasure from society," Darwin believed, "is probably an extension of the parental or filial affections, since the social instinct seems to be developed by the young remaining for a long time with the parents" (1936b, 478). Ethologists have shown the importance of parental care, especially for primates, as the root of all social bonding (Eibl-Eibesfeldt 1989; Kano 1992; Goodall 1986; Wilson 1975, chap. 16). Through the concepts of "kin selection" and "inclusive fitness," biologists can also explain why some animals in some circumstances are inclined to help not only their own offspring but also the offspring of close relatives (Hamilton 1964). Through the concepts of "reciprocal altruism" (Trivers 1971) and "indirect reciprocity" (Alexander 1987), biologists explain how it might be advantageous for animals to help even non-kin if there is some expectation of reciprocity. When the advantages of cooperation are direct and immediate for the cooperating individuals, we could call this "mutualism" (Corning 1983, 84–88, 103–20, 254–58).

Darwinian biologists understand, however, that because of human speech and cognition, the patterns of human nepotism, mutualism, and reciprocity are more complex and more extensive than those of other animals. Compared with other primates, for example, human beings are unique in maintaining lifelong relationships with dispersing offspring of both sexes (Rodseth et al. 1991). Symbolic communication and conceptual abstraction allow human beings to sustain relationships in the absence of face-to-face proximity. Similarly, although other animals show some sense of social reciprocity, only human beings can translate their expectations of reciprocity into formal rules and institutions (Boehm 1992; Goodall 1983; Scott 1989; de Waal 1991). Just as Aristotle said, human deliberation about the common advantage of the community makes human beings more political than other political animals.

Nevertheless, the special character of human politics cannot rest on any sharp separation of human learning from animal instinct. The Hobbesian nature-nurture dichotomy, which assumes an antithesis between fixed instinct and flexible learning, is untenable. All animal behavior arises from the interaction of genetic predispositions and environmental circumstances

(Marler and Terrace 1984; Brauth et al. 1991). The nervous system mediates behavior, and learning alters the structure and function of the nervous system at all levels (Black 1991; Diamond 1988; Rakic 1991). Rather than separating instinct and learning, we might more properly say that animal behavior depends on "instincts for learning" (Gould and Marler 1984).

Humans learning to speak and birds learning to sing illustrate the natural instincts for learning (Baker and Cunningham 1985; Catchpole and Slater 1995; Kuhl 1991; Marler 1991a, 1991b). Both humans and birds are inclined by nature to learn particular kinds of verbal signals in particular ways at particular periods in their lives. But exactly what they learn will depend upon their social training. Those deprived of the proper social training will not communicate in the normal way. And just as humans learn diverse languages, birds learn diverse dialects. This was seen by Aristotle, and it was confirmed by Darwin (1936b, 462–63, 704–14), who presented this as evidence that "an instinctive tendency to acquire an art is not peculiar to man." Recent research in linguistics and neurology has shown how the human instinct to learn language has been shaped by natural selection and rooted in specific neural networks of the brain (Hauser 1996; Pinker 1994; Pinker and Bloom 1990).

We often assume that human beings are unique in their dependence on nurture and artifice for the full development of their nature. That is not true. Chimpanzees, for example, acquire habits and skills that vary from one community to another. Tool use is highly variable. In some chimpanzee communities, mothers teach their children how to crack nuts using stones suitable as anvils and hammers; in other communities, this is not done, although both the nuts and the stones are easily available (Boesch and Boesch 1989; Boesch 1991; Goodall 1986, 560–64; McGrew 1992). In some groups, chimpanzees have learned to eat plants containing drugs to treat parasites and disease (Gibbons 1992b; Nishida 1990; Rodriguez and Wrangham 1993). This supports Aristotle's claim that some nonhuman animals have discovered the medicinal use of drugs (*HA* 611b21–12a8).

As I have already argued in chapter 2, some primates are by nature such intensely social animals that their natural development depends on social learning. For example, whether a young male succeeds in rising to the top of the dominance hierarchy will depend on how well he has learned the tricks of clever maneuvering within an intricate social network. The success of a chimpanzee in the dominance hierarchy is never merely a consequence of superior physical strength, although that is important. Rather, a combination of innate dispositions, acquired skills, and advantageous opportunities allow only a few individuals to become an alpha male (or alpha female). The dominant male chimpanzee must move adroitly in dealing both with other adult males who could take his position and with the rest of the community influenced by his leadership, which requires shrewdness in the formation of coalitions and alliances (Harcourt 1992; Harcourt and de Waal 1992). Primatologist Frans de Waal interprets his observations of such political behavior among chimpanzees as Darwinian corroboration for Aristotle: "When Aristotle referred to man as a political animal, he could not know just how near the mark he was. Our political activity seems to be a part of the evolutionary heritage we share with our close relatives" (1982, 211).

THE HOBBESIAN CRITIQUE

According to James Mackintosh, in his *Dissertation on the Progress of Ethical Philosophy* (1836), all of the fundamental controversies in modern ethical philosophy were initiated by Hobbes. In criticizing Hobbes's claim that human beings are by nature asocial and amoral beings, Mackintosh argued that human beings are endowed by nature with a moral sense that approves certain actions without regard to their consequences, although the essential tendency of such actions is to promote the common advantage or general happiness. When Darwin developed his theory of human sociality and morality, he was decisively influenced by Mackintosh's book (Darwin 1987, 537–38, 558, 563–64, 587–89, 618–29; 1936b, 471–95). He went beyond Mackintosh, however, in showing how the moral sense could have arisen in human nature as a product of natural selection.

Darwin agreed with Immanuel Kant and other writers "who maintain that of all the differences between man and the lower animals, the moral sense or conscience is by far the most important"; but unlike Kant and others, Darwin believed human morality could be studied "exclusively from the side of natural history." His general claim was that any social animal with natural capacities for speech and reasoning comparable to those of human beings would develop a moral sense (1936b, 471–72). This has led one Darwinian scholar to conclude: "Aristotle believed that men were by nature moral creatures. Darwin demonstrated it" (Richards 1987, 612).

Darwin's ethical naturalism revived an Aristotelian tradition that Hobbes had challenged in his denial that human beings were by nature political animals. Against Aristotle Hobbes contended, in both *De Cive* (chap. 5, par. 5) and the *Leviathan* (chap. 17), that there were six differences between social animals (like bees and ants) and human beings. (1) Unlike social animals, human beings compete for honor and prestige. (2) Among social animals, there is no conflict between the private good and the common good, as there is among human beings, because the natural appetites of the social animals incline them as individuals to do what is good for all. (3) Social animals lack reason, which human beings use to criticize the administration of common business and thus create civil conflict. (4) Social animals lack the art of words, which human beings use to argue about what is good and evil and thus fall into sedition and war. (5) Social animals do not distinguish between injury (breach of covenant) and damage; and therefore, unlike human beings, they are not offended with one another as long as their physical appetites are satisfied. In these five respects, uniquely human attributes create social conflicts not found among the social animals. A sixth difference between human beings and social animals, according to Hobbes, follows as a consequence of the other five. (6) "Lastly, the agreement of these creatures is natural; that of men, is by covenant only, which is artificial: and therefore it is no wonder if there be somewhat else required, besides covenant, to make their agreement constant and lasting; which is a common power, to keep them in awe, and to direct their actions to the common benefit" (*Leviathan*, chap. 17).

Hobbes's six arguments presuppose two fundamental premises (compare *De Homine*, chap. 10). First, among the naturally social animals, social cooperation is completely harmonious because there are no conflicts of interest to create competition. Second, nature and instinct are necessarily antithetical to artifice and learning, so that social order cannot be natural or instinctive if it depends in any way on artificial or learned activity. Darwinian biologists would deny both premises.

Hobbes's first premise might be supported by the idea advanced by some biologists that an insect colony is a "superorganism": the individual insects cooperate for the good of the whole colony like the cells in a single organism (Wheeler 1939; Wilson 1971, chap. 16; Seeley 1989, 1995). There is growing evidence, however, that this analogy does not hold for many species of social insects that show severe conflicts of interest within a colony. One should expect conflicts of reproductive interests in social insects because, unlike the somatic cells in a single organism, the members of a social insect colony do not possess identical genomes.

If the workers of a colony cannot reproduce, and if the colony has only one queen at a time, which is typically the case for many species of social insects, it may serve the reproductive fitness of all members to act for the reproductive efficiency of the whole colony. Yet for those species in which these conditions are not always or usually satisfied, reproductive competition between individual insects can create aggressive encounters and dominance hierarchies. There are many possible lines of conflict: between colonies, between queens, between workers, or between queens and workers (Brockmann 1984; Cole 1988; Hölldobler and Wilson 1990, 209–26; Jeanne 1991). Although kinship supports cooperation within colonies of social insects, kin conflict arises whenever groups of relatives have conflicting interests (Bourke and Frank 1995, 200–257). Among many species of ants, bees, and wasps, queens are equally related to their sons and daughters, while workers are more related to their sisters than to their brothers. Consequently, the reproductive interests of the queen incline her to produce equal numbers of male and female offspring, while the reproductive interests of the workers incline them to allocate resources to favor the production of females over males. As one might predict, social insect workers sometimes kill the male larvae laid by their queen (Seger 1996; Sundstrom et al. 1996).

Consider the eusocial paper wasps of the genus *Polistes* (Reeve 1991; Roseler 1991). Although the workers are generally sterile, they are potentially fertile; and when conditions permit them to lay eggs, they compete with the queen for reproductive opportunities. Queens also compete with one another. A queen can found a new colony by herself, or she can jointly found a colony with another queen, or she can usurp control of a colony founded by another queen. Aggressive encounters between queens can create dominance hierarchies. Consequently, *Polistes* societies manifest a shifting balance of cooperation and competition that emerges from the opportunistic behavior of individuals seeking to promote their selfish interests. Moreover, the *Polistes* social system varies in response to local ecological conditions as each colony adapts to its peculiar circumstances. The architecture of the nest, for example, is highly variable. One biologist describes the social wasps in the following way: "Intelligent, adaptable ecological generalists and skilled makers of artifice, they are, above all, political animals . . . for whom the tension between cooperation and self-aggrandizement is the overriding condition of daily life" (Seger 1991, 804).

Not only is Hobbes wrong in assuming that insect societies are free of conflict, he is also wrong in assuming that these societies arise by natural instinct without individual learning. In a social insect colony, no two individuals are the same in their behavior over their lifetimes. The individuality of each insect reflects individual history as well as innate predispositions. Some biologists would argue that "how an individual colony member behaves is influenced by many factors, including its genetic makeup, trophic history, age, experience, social environment, and external environment" (Jeanne 1991, 390). Ants reared in isolation during sensitive periods in which they normally would learn their social behavior cannot perform that behavior when returned to the colony (Jaisson, Fresneau, and Lachaud 1988). Behavioral flexibility in individual ants allows them to adjust their division of labor in response to the changing needs of the colony (Bourke and Franks 1995, 425–28; Gordon 1991, 1992). Like other social animals, the social insect's natural potential for social life cannot be fully actualized without social learning and habituation: its nature must be nurtured (Papaj and Lewis 1993).

Although the capacities of the social insects for learning are impressive considering their simple nervous system, they obviously fall far short of the intelligence displayed by mammals in their social behavior (Gould 1984; Hölldobler and Wilson 1990, 365–70; Wilson 1971, 215–24). As I have already argued, some mammals, and particularly the higher primates, show a social intelligence that suggests they are the political animals closest to human beings.

Viewed in the light of modern biological and anthropological theories of the origins of social cooperation, Hobbes's insistence that human political order is utterly artificial is partially correct and partially incorrect. As Roger Masters (1989, 150–212; 1996, 109–132) has argued, Hobbes is at least partially correct insofar as the emergence of large-scale states with centralized governments and bureaucracies depends upon peculiarities of human history that cannot be completely rooted in their natural sociality. For most of their evolutionary history, human beings have lived in small hunter-gatherer bands of fifty to one hundred individuals bound together by ties of kinship and reciprocity in face-to-face relationships. Living in such groups is natural for human beings because it arises from bonds of kinship and reciprocity that belong to a natural repertoire of social behavior that human beings share with other social mammals and particularly primates. Hobbes is wrong, therefore, in denying the natural sociality of human beings. But he is right in seeing that the emergence of centralized states with huge populations cannot be derived completely from natural sociality.

Modern states arose for the first time in human history about ten thousand years ago in various parts of the world (such as Egypt, Mesopotamia, India, and Mesoamerica). The most likely explanation for this would have to combine many factors, which have been surveyed by Masters. When large populations of people began to rely on agricultural production and animal husbandry, centralized states became beneficial in managing complex economic and technological practices (such as irrigation systems) that supported this new way of life. War, conquest, and the need for defense against external attacks made large military bureaucracies advantageous. At the same time, the appearance of popular leaders skilled in coordinating military activity and economic development would enhance the growth of states. But the emergence of such large states created opportunities for cheaters or "free riders" to accept the benefits (peace and prosperity) without bearing the costs (taxes, military service, obedience to the law), and as growing numbers of people became cheaters, states would collapse into disorder. To prevent such a collapse, political subjects would find it beneficial to establish sovereign rulers capable of enforcing obedience from all, and political rulers would find it beneficial to provide such enforcement if they were rewarded with the power, prestige, and wealth that might accompany public office. Such a mutually beneficial arrangement between subjects and rulers might constitute a Hobbesian "social contract" that would depend on human language and social tradition. In contrast to nonhuman primates, who must live in small groups based on personal contact and social grooming, human beings can use language to formulate and enforce social norms to coordinate huge groups of individuals who cannot know one another by direct acquaintance (Dunbar 1993).

Hobbes was right, therefore, about centralized states being a uniquely human contrivance, because they require human speech and long-range calculation. And yet, it is as true for human beings as for other primates that social regularity arises as "order without law": most disputes are resolved through informal social norms based on nepotism, mutualism, and reciprocity (Boehm 1983; Ellickson 1991; Goodall 1983; de Waal 1991). Hobbes concedes that even in the state of nature prior to formal government, there was social order from "the government of small families, the concord whereof dependeth on natural lust" (*Leviathan*, chap. 13). Furthermore, most of Hobbes's "laws of nature," which dictate the establishment of government, reflect the natural inclinations to mutualism and reciprocity that human beings share with other primates (*Leviathan*, chaps. 14–15).

Observers such as Jane Goodall and Frans de Waal have found that chimpanzee communities need a stable dominance hierarchy, in which the alpha male assumes the role of an impartial mediator in settling conflicts (Boehm 1992; Goodall 1986; de Waal 1982, 1986, 1996). The highest-ranking males intervene in conflicts to support the underdog. De Waal describes this as something like a "social contract" in which the group selects and supports a leader based on his effectiveness in protecting the weak against the strong and thus securing the peace and order of the community. He sees this as a move from despotic dominance to leadership in which those of high status must serve the community, which is a likely source of the "egalitarian ethos" that emerged early in hominoid evolution (de Waal 1996, 125–32). This indicates that, contrary to Hobbes, human beings are not the only animals who need "a common power, to keep them in awe, and to direct their actions to the common benefit."

These biological roots for human politics were important to Richard Cumberland, who in 1672 wrote the first defense of Aristotle's understanding of political animals against Hobbes's critique. Cumberland argued that all the natural causes that incline animals to social cooperation—such as parental care, mutual aid, and reciprocal exchange—are just as strong in human beings as they are in some other animals. He saw the distinctly human capacities for speech and reason as the natural instruments by which human beings become more political than the other political animals (Cumberland 1727, chap. 2). From his survey of comparative anatomy, which indicated that monkeys and apes made "the nearest approaches to human sagacity and passions," Cumberland concluded that the size and complexity of the human brain and nervous system show that human beings are formed by nature for the rational organization of social cooperation to serve the common advantage (1727, 143–59). Recent biological research supports this by showing how human neural structures allow cognitive and linguistic capacities acting on social emotions to create a natural moral sense (Lieberman 1991; MacLean 1990).

THE NATURE OF CULTURE

In the modern history of the social sciences, the Hobbesian dichotomy of nature and artifice became a dichotomy of nature and culture. Alfred Kroeber's essay of 1917, "The Superorganic," is a classic statement of the concept of culture as adopted by anthropologists. Kroeber insists there is an "abyss," an "eternal chasm," between the organic and the cultural. To the organic realm belong heredity and instinct, which human beings share with other animals. To the cultural realm belong tradition and learning, which are uniquely human. Culture, Kroeber declares, is "the thing in man that is supra-animal" (1917, 205). He even goes so far as to claim that the "so-called social insects" such as bees and ants are not really social animals at all, because they lack the capacity for social learning that is possessed only by human beings (1917, 176–77). In a later essay, he acknowledges the high intelligence of the nonhuman primates but insists on the "total absence of culture" among them (1928, 340). In the early decades of the twentieth century, social scientists who adopted this concept of culture opposed any attempt to apply Darwinian theories of human nature to the social sciences (Degler 1991). Similarly, against the recent revival of Darwinian social theory, opponents have appealed to the concept of culture (Sahlins 1976).

Kroeber claimed that his distinction between animal instinct and human culture had found its "most complete and most compact" expression in Aristotle's declaration, "Man is a political animal" (1917, 180). Significantly, Kroeber omitted the phrase "by nature," and he ignored the reference to other political animals. Almost invariably, when social scientists quote Aristotle's remark, they make the same changes as Kroeber to preserve the presumed dichotomy of nature and culture, biology and politics.

The ultimate source of this radical separation of nature and culture is not Aristotle but Hobbes. Despite the monism of Hobbes's materialism, his political teaching presupposes a dualistic opposition between animal nature and human will: in creating political order, human beings transcend and conquer nature (Strauss 1952, 7–9, 168–70). This dualism was explicitly developed by Immanuel Kant, who originally formulated the modern concept of culture (1983; 1987, secs. 83–84). Culture is that uniquely human realm of artifice in which human beings escape their natural animality to express their rational humanity as the only beings who have a "supersensible faculty" for moral freedom. Through culture, human beings free themselves from the laws of nature. Although culture has become a vague concept in the social sciences, it retains all of the central features prescribed by Kant. (1) Culture is uniquely human. (2) It is uniquely human because only human beings have the understanding and the will to set purposes for themselves by free choice. (3) Culture is an autonomous human artifice that transcends nature. (4) Culture is the necessary condition for forming moral values.

This understanding of culture entered English anthropology in 1871, when Edward Tylor in *Primitive Culture* defined culture as "that complex whole which includes knowledge, belief, art, law, morals, custom, and any other capabilities and habits acquired by man as a member of society" (1871, 1:1). Now textbooks on "cultural" anthropology can begin with Tylor's definition as having "established culture as a separate field for investigation that could be studied apart from psychology or biology, since cultural phenomena were believed to have their own laws" (Barnouw 1978, 4).

Beyond anthropology, this concept of culture supports the common view of the "social sciences" in general as separated from the "natural sciences." The "sciences of the spirit" *(Geisteswissenschaften)* must be separated from the "sciences of nature" *(Naturwissenschaften)*. This same separation supports the idea of history as the human transcendence of nature. Thus, Alexandre Kojève, speaking for Hegel, can say, "[T]he Aristotelian system explains man's biological existence but not his truly human—i.e., historical—existence" (1969, 115).

Darwin's argument for the continuity between human beings and other animals denies the concept of culture by denying the dichotomies on which it rests: biology versus culture, nature versus nurture, instinct versus learning, animality versus humanity, facts versus values. Some Darwinians, however, have tried to accommodate the concept of culture as a uniquely human realm of activity that transcends biology. Thomas Huxley, in his famous lecture entitled "Evolution and Ethics," implicitly rejected Darwin's ethical naturalism by denying that ethics could be "applied natural history" (1894a, 74), because Huxley had adopted the Kantian concept of culture (Paradis 1989). Interpreting Darwin's "struggle for existence" as a Hobbesian war of all against all, so that there was no natural ground for social cooperation or moral concern, Huxley concluded that "the thief and the murderer follow nature just as much as the philanthropist." Social progress could arise, therefore, only from a checking of the "cosmic process" by the "ethical process," and thus building "an artificial world within the cosmos." "The ethical progress of society depends, not on imitating the cosmic process, still less in running away from it, but in combating it," which would "set man to subdue nature to his higher ends" (1894a, 80–83). In recent years, some Darwinians have followed Huxley's lead in arguing that morality requires a human conquest of nature. George Williams, for example, hopes that morality as a cultural invention can provide "the humane artifice that can save humanity from human nature" (1989, 213).

Other Darwinians, however, have denied this claim that morality must be a cultural construction with no roots in biological nature. Adhering to Darwin's original position, they have argued for investigating the "natural history of value," in which "value" would be understood as the satisfaction of animal desires (Herrick 1956, 136–57). To some extent, this satisfaction of natural desires is controlled by rigid instincts; but many animals, to varying degrees, satisfy their desires through social learning and flexible behavior. In the complexity of their learning and behavior, human beings differ in degree but not in kind from other animals.

Against Williams's claim that human beings are naturally amoral or immoral, Frans de Waal has argued that this view of human beings as innately depraved is rooted in a Calvinist doctrine of original sin that is not supported by the biological evidence. Comparing human beings with other primates who show the precursors of human moral dispositions indicates that morality is rooted in biological nature.

> Evolution has produced the requisites for morality: a tendency to develop social norms and enforce them, the capacities of empathy and sympathy, mutual aid and a sense of fairness, the mechanisms of conflict resolution, and so on. Evolution also has produced the unalterable needs and desires of our species: the need of the young for care, a desire for high status, the need to belong to a group, and so forth. (De Waal 1996, 39)

Huxley and Williams assume that morality depends on a uniquely human capacity for culture that transcends biology. But de Waal argues that chimpanzees and other primates have some capacity for culture. John Bonner, in *The Evolution of Culture in Animals*, defines culture as "the transfer of information by behavioral means, most particularly by the process of teaching and learning," in contrast to "the transmission of genetic information passed by the direct inheritance of genes from one generation to the next" (1980, 10). This corresponds to Kroeber's distinction between the cultural and the organic, but unlike Kroeber Bonner surveys the evidence that some nonhuman animals exhibit cultural behavior.

Recently, some primatologists have shown that if one applies to the study of chimpanzee communities the techniques of cultural anthropology for studying human communities, one discovers evidence of cultural diversity among chimpanzees. For example, there is great variation from one chimpanzee group to another in tool use, botanical knowledge, and hunting techniques (Boesch 1991; Caro and Hauser 1992; McGrew 1992; Nishida 1987; Peterson and Goodall 1993; Wrangham et al. 1994). If one compares studies of chimpanzee groups in different environments—such as Frans de Waal's (1982) study of a captive group of chimpanzees in a Dutch zoo and Jane Goodall's (1986) study of a wild group of chimpanzees in the Gombe National Park of Tanzania—it becomes evident that each chimpanzee group has a social history that distinguishes it from other groups. Each group has developed a distinct history as unique individuals have adapted to the social and physical circumstances of the group. Like human beings and other primates, chimpanzees are cultural and historical animals.

This evidence supports Bonner in rejecting the traditional dichotomy of biology and culture. "Culture, as I have defined it, is a property achieved by living organisms. Therefore in this sense it is as biological as any other function of an organism, for instance, respiration or locomotion. Since I am stressing the way information is transmitted, we could call one *cultural evolution* and the other *genetical evolution* with the understanding that they are both biological in the sense they both involve living organisms" (Bonner 1980, 10–11). If culture is the flow of information between animals about their physical environment and their social relationships, then human culture differs from nonhuman culture only in the degree to which human language extends and formalizes this flow of social information (Quiatt and Reynolds 1993).

The evidence that some nonhuman animals have natural capacities for social learning that support what look like cultural traditions forces us to redefine both nature and culture. However we define them, we need to see them not as antithetical, but as complementary.

If we define culture in a broad sense as the transfer of information by social learning as opposed to the transfer of information by genetic inheritance, then we would have to conclude, as Bonner does, that human culture differs in degree but not in kind from culture in other animals, because human culture is more complex. If we define culture in a narrow sense so that it depends on symbolic language, we could plausibly argue that culture as symbolism is uniquely human, and therefore human societies in this respect differ in kind and not just in degree from other animal societies (Lieberman 1991; Noble and Davidson 1991). This latter position would be controversial, however, among cognitive ethologists like Donald Griffin (1984, 1992) who believe some nonhuman animals are capable even of symbolic language. The broad definition would conform to Aristotle's occasional remarks about the animal capacities for learning and teaching that even include something like language. The narrow definition would conform to Aristotle's more central claim that although other animals can learn and teach, only human beings have symbolic speech *(logos* or *dialektos)*.

If culture is defined broadly, it is clearly natural for human beings because it is a natural attribute shared with other cultural animals. But even if we adopt the narrow definition of culture as linguistic symbolism unique to human beings, we need not conceive of culture as transcending nature. Every animal species is unique in its behavioral repertoire for adapting to variable ecological circumstances, and human beings may be unique in that cultural symbolism is a crucial part of their natural repertoire for behavioral adaptation. Culture is natural for human beings because through culture they develop their natural capacities and satisfy their natural desires.

CHAPTER 4

THE HUMAN NATURE OF
MORALITY AND FREEDOM

My argument in this book for Darwinian natural right is not only Darwinian but also Aristotelian and Humean. My position is Aristotelian in that I agree with Aristotle that human beings are by nature social and political animals. It is Humean in that I agree with David Hume that human beings are by nature endowed with a moral sense. And it is Darwinian in that I agree with Charles Darwin that human sociality and morality are rooted in human biology.

Most social scientists, however, assume that such a political naturalism grounded in Darwinian biology is refuted by three objections. First, Darwinian naturalism ignores the radical separation between *is* and *ought* by deducing moral values from biological facts. Second, it promotes a biological determinism that denies the human freedom presupposed by morality and law. Third, it fails to recognize that human morality and politics are products of social learning rather than biological instincts. I have already responded to the third objection in chapter 2 by arguing that nature versus nurture is a false dichotomy. In this chapter, I will argue that the other two objections also rest on false dichotomies: facts versus values and nature versus freedom.

NATURAL MORALITY

One of the most pervasive assumptions in the social sciences is that there is an unbridgeable gap between *is* and *ought*. This is often called "Hume's law" to indicate that Hume was the first to discover it. Because of this separation between judgments of fact and judgments of value, it is thought, scientific objectivity in the social sciences dictates moral relativism (Brecht 1959). Consequently, one of the most common objections to any Darwinian theory of human morality as rooted in human nature is that this fallaciously infers moral values from natural facts (Kitcher 1985). Even many of those who propose Darwinian theories of ethics accept the fact-value dichotomy: "[T]he very last thing the Darwinian wants to do is break Hume's law by denying that there is a genuine 'is/ought' distinction" (Ruse 1986, 251).

I would argue, however, that far from separating facts and values, Hume showed how moral judgments could be grounded in certain facts of human nature. This explains why Darwin and the new Darwinian political theorists can incorporate Hume's theory of the moral sense into their evolutionary account of human morality.

The common interpretation of Hume as having separated *is* and *ought* depends on only one paragraph in his *Treatise of Human Nature* (1888, 469–70). Some Hume scholars have shown that if one considers carefully both the textual and historical contexts of this paragraph, one sees that the common interpretation is wrong (Buckle 1991, 282–84; Capaldi 1966, 1989; Martin 1991). The textual context makes clear that Hume's claim is that moral distinctions are derived not from pure reason alone but from a moral sense. The historical context makes clear that Hume is restating Francis Hutcheson's criticisms of some early modern rationalists such as Samuel Clarke and William Wollaston, who believed that moral distinctions could be derived from abstract reasoning about structures in the universe that were completely independent of human nature.

Far from denying that moral judgments are judgments of fact, Hume claims that moral judgments are accurate when they correctly report what our moral sentiments would be in a given set of circumstances. Moral judgments do not have *cosmic objectivity* in the sense of conforming to structures that exist totally independently of human beings. Yet neither do moral judgments have only *emotive subjectivity* in the sense of expressing purely personal feelings. Rather, as Nicholas Capaldi (1989) has argued, moral judgments for Hume have *intersubjective objectivity* in that they are factual judgments about the species-typical pattern of moral sentiments in specified circumstances.

Hume compares moral judgments to judgments of secondary qualities such as colors (1888, 469; 1985, 233–34). My judgment that this tomato is red is true if the object is so constituted as to induce the impression of red in normally sighted human beings viewing it under standard conditions. Similarly, my judgment that this person is morally praiseworthy is true if the person's conduct is such as to induce the sentiment of approbation in normal human beings under standard conditions. Just as an object can *appear* red to me when in fact it is not, so a person can *appear* praiseworthy to me when in fact he is not. The moral judgment whether some conduct would give to a normal spectator under standard conditions a moral sentiment of approbation is, Hume insists, "a plain matter of fact" (1902, 289). The moral sentiment itself, however, is a feeling or passion rooted in human nature that cannot be produced by reason alone.

When Hume declares that "reason is, and ought only to be the slave of the passions" (1888, 415), he is not promoting emotivist irrationalism. As the context of this remark makes clear, he believes that reason can *direct* action but not *motivate* it: "[T]he impulse arises not from reason, but is only directed by it" (1888, 414). When our passions are accompanied by false judgments, reason can properly correct them. "The moment we perceive the falsehood of any supposition, or the insufficiency of any means our passions yield to our reason" (1888, 416). "Reason and judgment may, indeed, be the mediate cause of an action, by prompting, or by directing a passion" (1888, 462). Consequently, "reason and sentiment concur in almost all moral determinations and conclusions" (1902, 172). For example, reason might instruct us as to how justice could be useful to society, but this alone would not produce any moral approbation for justice unless we felt a sentiment of concern for the happiness of society (1902, 285–87).

Hume suggests that his science of human nature could be rooted ultimately in biological sciences such as anatomy and physiology (1888, 7, 13, 190, 212, 248, 275–76, 340–41; 1902, 10), because "the lives of men depend upon the same laws as the lives of all other animals" (1985, 582). Some recent research in neurobiology seems to confirm Hume's argument that reason and emotion are distinct and yet complementary causes of human behavior, because rational conduct must be guided by emotional assessments that enforce a system of preferences. If this is so, then Kant's conception of ethical rationality as utterly free from emotion is impossible (Damasio 1994). As Aristotle saw, the emotions are essential to good reasoning because they contain judgments about the world as it relates to our lives (Arnhart 1981, 111–34).

Aristotle agrees with Hume about the primacy of desire or passion in motivating human action. "Thought by itself moves nothing," Aristotle believes, although reason can guide the desires that do move us. Desire always moves us, but thought never moves us without desire (*DA* 433a10–31; Richardson 1992). Deliberate choice *(proairesis),* therefore, requires a conjunction of desire and reason into "desiring thought" or "thinking desire"

(*NE* 1139a36–b6). Aristotle's insistence that only desire can motivate moral action was often cited with approval by the moral-sense philosophers (Barratt 1869, 20, 97, 192, 197).

Like Hume, Aristotle also believes that the passions manifest a natural moral sense, which is particularly evident in moral passions such as anger and indignation (Arnhart 1981, 102–5, 114–34). Aristotle identifies the moral passions as praiseworthy states of character. Although they are not "virtues in the strict sense," because they do not arise by deliberate choice, they are the natural dispositions to morality that become moral virtues through the cultivation of proper habituation and prudential judgment (*EE* 1233b16–34b11; *NE* 1144b1–18). Cicero restates Aristotle's position in explaining that all animals act according to nature in satisfying their natural desires, and human beings act according to their distinctively human nature in satisfying their "primary natural desires" through the moral and intellectual virtues (Cicero, *De Finibus* 2.33–41, 2.107–10, 3.16–22; 5.17–20, 5.24–72). Thus, Aristotle recognizes, but does not elaborate, the psychological basis of ethics in the moral passions that is elaborated by David Hume and other philosophers like Adam Smith who argued for the existence of a moral sense (Berns 1994).

Hume's moral sense is rooted in the natural social affections of human beings. In rejecting the "selfish system of morals" of Hobbes and Locke, who deny the natural sociality of human beings and argue that moral inclinations are utterly artificial products of a social contract, Hume insists that although the progress of the moral sentiments does require "the artifice of politicians," this political artifice succeeds only with the support of nature. If human beings were utterly selfish and solitary in their nature, they could never develop the social sentiments necessary for moral life. "The utmost politicians can perform, is, to extend the natural sentiments beyond their original bounds; but still nature must furnish the materials, and give us some notion of moral distinctions" (1888, 295–96, 500, 619–20; 1902, 214–15, 296–97).

Aristotle believes that the natural sociality of human beings and other political animals is an extension of parent-child bonding. The various forms of friendly feeling that unite human beings as individuals, as fellow citizens, and as members of the human species, radiate out from the natural affection between parents and offspring that human beings share with other animals whose offspring require intensive and prolonged parental care (*GA* 753a8–

14; *HA* 612b18–20b9; *NE* 1155a1–33, 1159a27–37, 1160b23–62a29; *Rh* 1371b13–26). "Consequently, in the household are first found the origins and springs of friendship, of polity, and of justice" (*EE* 1242b1–2). Insofar as justice coincides with friendship, the claims of justice vary in proportion to the nearness of attachments (*NE* 1155a16–29, 1159b25–60a8, 1165a14–36). One's obligations are stronger to closer relatives than to more distant ones, and stronger to close friends and fellow citizens than to strangers, although some friendly feeling is possible toward all members of one's species. There can be a kind of sympathy among animals of the same species, and this is especially true for human beings, so that "we praise those who love their fellow human beings" (*NE* 1155a20–21). Still, the humanitarianism of human beings will always be difficult to cultivate and almost always weaker than their egoism, their nepotism, and their patriotism.

Similarly, Hume regards the dependence of offspring on parental care as the natural root of human sociality and morality (1888, 483–86, 570–73; 1902, 189–90, 192, 201–8, 240, 295–311). The natural moral sentiments that bind people in families can expand to embrace larger groups. Then, gradually, through the experience of mutual intercourse between societies, the boundaries of justice can enlarge as people discover the utility of extended social interdependence. This "natural progress of human sentiments" depends upon a natural sympathy or "sentiment of humanity," a concern for the welfare of one's fellow human beings that extends in principle to all members of the human species. Of course, the concern for strangers will almost always be weaker than the concern for oneself and one's immediate family and friends, but the affection of humanity is strong enough to constitute the universal principle of morality. It is the "internal sense or feeling, which nature has made universal in the whole species" (1902, 169–73, 192, 218–29, 268–78).

If we accept the common view of Hume as having argued that we cannot infer what *ought* to be from what *is* the case, then it would seem that he contradicts himself by deriving morality from the natural inclinations of human beings. The contradiction disappears, however, once we see that the dichotomy between *is* and *ought* falsely attributed to Hume was actually first formulated by Immanuel Kant, who used it as an argument against the kind of ethical naturalism developed by Hume! Furthermore, once this point is understood, it becomes clear that while the proponents of Darwinian naturalism are Humeans, their critics are Kantians.

As opposed to Hume, Kant is a radical dualist who separates reality into two metaphysical realms. According to Kant, judging what *is* the case belongs to the "phenomenal" realm of nature, but judging what *ought* to be belongs to the "noumenal" realm of freedom (Kant 1956, 4–5, 18, 30–31, 99, 163–64; 1959, 4, 30, 44–45, 67–74, 80; 1965, 465, 472–79, 526; 1987, 286–87). (The distinction in English between *is* and *ought* corresponds to Kant's distinction in German between *sein* and *sollen*.) For Kant, the natural world is governed by causal laws that can be understood by natural science; and in this world there can be no free will, because every event must be determined by a causal mechanism. By contrast, in our moral experience, we praise and blame people in accordance with a moral law that transcends nature and is thus unknowable by natural science; and in this world we must assume free will, because moral judgment would be impossible unless we assumed that people were capable of freely choosing to obey or disobey the moral law. As moral agents, we obey categorical imperatives of what *ought* to be, but this *ought* expresses a moral necessity that has no place in nature. "When we have the course of nature alone in view, '*ought*' has no meaning whatsoever" (Kant 1965, 473). As moral agents, human beings transcend the realm of nature and enter a realm of freedom that belongs to them as rational beings not governed by the laws of nature.

Kant's separation of *is* and *ought* treats morality as an autonomous realm of human experience governed by its own internal logic with no reference to anything in human nature such as natural desires or interests. He does this because he accepts the Hobbesian view of human nature. Since human beings are by nature asocial, selfish animals, they cannot live together in peace unless they conquer their natural inclinations by willing submission to moral rules devised by reason to pacify their conflicts (Kant 1970, 1987, 317–21; Simpson 1986).

When Darwin develops his evolutionary theory of morality, he adopts a Humean naturalism rather than a Kantian dualism. Darwin believes that his theory of evolution by natural selection will provide a biological explanation for what Hume, Adam Smith, and other Scottish moral philosophers identify as the moral sense (1936b, 471–513, 911–19; 1987, 537, 558, 563–64, 619–29). When he begins his account of the moral sense in *The Descent of Man*, he quotes a passage from Kant's *Critique of Practical Reason* about how the word *ought* is one of the noblest traits of human beings. But in the immediately following passage of Kant's book, Kant says this experience of the moral *ought* shows us "man as belonging to two worlds" (Kant 1956, 90). Darwin, however, denies this dualism and thus departs from Kant by indicating that he will approach morality "exclusively from the side of natural history" (Darwin 1936b, 471).

Darwin sees that one of the central characteristics of the human species is the duration and intensity of child care. For that reason alone human beings must be by nature social animals. The reproductive fitness of human beings requires strong attachments between infants and parents and within kin groups. Darwin believes this natural bonding of parents and children is the foundation of all social bonding and of the moral sense. "The feeling of pleasure from society is probably an extension of the parental or filial affections, since the social instinct seems to be developed by the young remaining for a long time with their parents; and this extension may be attributed in part to habit, but chiefly to natural selection" (1936b, 478). For Darwin this supports Hume's claim about the moral emotions of sympathy and benevolence as the basis for social cooperation (1936b, 479–87).

Darwin also believes natural selection would favor mutuality and reciprocity as grounds for cooperation. Animals with the sociality and the intelligence of human beings recognize that social cooperation can be mutually beneficial for all participants. They can also recognize that being benevolent to others can benefit oneself in the long run if one's benevolence is likely to be reciprocated (1936b, 443–44, 472, 479, 499).

Like Hume, Darwin explains human morality as emerging from the complex cooperation within groups competing with other groups, and thus only gradually and with great difficulty does human moral concern expand to include those outside one's own group. Throughout human history, justice has meant helping one's friends and harming one's enemies. Yet Darwin also agrees with Hume in claiming that as human beings are united into ever larger communities, their natural sympathy and benevolence can to some extent embrace all members of the human species (1936b, 480–81, 491–95).

Human beings are moral animals, Darwin explains, because they have the cognitive capacity to compare their desires or passions and judge that some are more important or enduring than others. As social animals, they feel concern for the good of others, and they feel regret when they allow their selfish passions to impede the satisfaction of their social passions. The word *ought*, Darwin concludes, signifies the consciousness that since some passions are more persistent than others, one cannot be fully happy if one does not satisfy those stronger passions (1936b, 480–87).

Darwin develops a theory of how human morality could have emerged through four overlapping stages. First, *social instincts* would have led human ancestors to feel sympathy for others in their group, which would promote a tendency to mutual aid. Second, the development of the *intellectual faculties* would allow early human ancestors to perceive the conflicts between instinctive desires, so that they could feel dissatisfaction at having yielded to a momentarily strong desire (like fleeing from injury) in violation of some more enduring social instinct (like defending one's group). Third, the acquisition of *language* would permit the expression of social opinions about good and bad, just and unjust, so that primitive human beings would respond to praise and blame in satisfying their social instincts. Fourth, the capacity for *habit* would allow individual conduct to conform to social opinions through acquired dispositions. An additional factor stressed by Darwin is *tribal warfare*, which would favor the intellectual and moral capacities that allow individuals to cooperate within groups to compete with other groups. "Ultimately our moral sense or conscience becomes a highly complex sentiment—originating in the social instincts, largely guided by the approbation of our fellow-men, ruled by reason, self-interest, and in later times by deep religious feelings, and confirmed by instruction and habit" (1936b, 500).

Many species of animals have social instincts, and clearly human beings are also social animals. Like Aristotle, Darwin believes human sociality arises as an extension of the bonds between parents and children. The duration and complexity of child care among human beings exceeds that of any other species. The earliest human societies, as among those savage societies that have survived into recent history, were probably loosely organized bands of families united for common defense against competing tribes. Throughout most of human history, the social instincts within a tribe never extended beyond the tribe.

The moral propensity to act for the good of one's group might seem to contradict natural selection. For example, courageous individuals naturally inclined to sacrifice their lives in defense of their community might often leave fewer offspring than cowardly individuals. Darwin believed, however, that in the competition between groups those with the more courageous members would often prevail (1936b, 443–44, 497–98, 500). Not only courage but other moral dispositions to social cooperation might strengthen one group against others. Although many evolutionary biologists regard this appeal to group selection as one of Darwin's regrettable mistakes (Dawkins 1976; Williams 1966), some recent research—as surveyed by David Sloan Wilson and Elliott Sober (1994)—suggests that Darwin was correct. Although natural selection can act within a group to favor selfish individuals over others, it can also act between groups to favor groups of altruists over others. Group selection occurs in those circumstances where selection between groups is stronger than selection within groups. In such cases, groups can be the evolutionary "vehicles" for genes as the evolutionary "replicators" (Eibl-Eibesfeldt 1989, 90–103; Sober 1993, 88–117; Wilson 1983; Wilson and Sober 1994). Throughout most of human evolutionary history, human beings lived in hunter-gatherer groups that enforced an egalitarian cooperativeness within the group. Those individuals who acted for selfish interests contrary to the interests of the group were punished. In such circumstances, natural selection could work at the level of the group to favor cooperative dispositions such that individuals would act for the good of their group in competition with other groups (Boehm 1997).

As soon as Darwin published his naturalistic theory of morality in *The Descent of Man*, he was attacked by St. George Mivart (1871). Mivart insisted on a Kantian separation between nature and morality. Although the human body could be explained as a natural product of biological evolution, Mivart contended, the human soul was a supernatural product of divine creation. And as an expression of the soul's transcendence of nature, human morality manifested a uniquely human freedom from natural causality.

Thomas Huxley (1871) immediately defended Darwin's ethical naturalism against Mivart's dualist critique, but Huxley moved later in his life—particularly in his famous lecture "Evolution and Ethics" (1894a)—toward a dualistic theory of ethics that Mivart (1893) recognized as his own. Huxley adopted the Hobbesian-Kantian view that since human beings in their natural state were selfish and asocial, the moral improvement of humanity required a self-abnegating denial of human nature (1894a, 31, 44–45, 59, 68, 75–77, 81–85). Because of the "moral indifference of nature," one could never derive moral values from natural facts. "The thief and the murderer follow nature just as much as the philanthropist" (1894, 59, 80). More recently, in the continuing debate over the ethical implications of Darwinian biology, biologists such as David Lack (1957), John Eccles (1989), Gunther Stent (1978), and George Williams (1989, 1993) have adopted Huxley's Kantian claim that ethics cannot be rooted in human nature because of the un-bridgeable gulf between the selfishness of our natural inclinations and the selflessness of our moral duties.

This Kantian opposition between natural selfishness and moral selfless-ness shows the theological influence of Augustinian asceticism. For August-ine (*City of God* 5.12–13, 5.20, 8.8, 14.13, 14.28), no act is truly virtuous if it is rooted in self-love, but since self-love is natural to human beings in their "fallen" state, true virtue requires a transcendence of nature through grace. By contrast, Aristotle believed that since the final end of ethics is happiness understood as the fullest satisfaction of natural human desires, living virtuously expresses one's natural self-love (*NE* 1168a28–1169b2). From Aristotle's sensible perspective, the Kantian view of morality as ut-terly selfless makes it impossible to explain what motive anyone would have to be moral. Thomas Aquinas follows Aristotle in teaching that by nature our love of others is an extension of our self-love, and thus we should love those nearest to us—our family, friends, and fellow citizens—more than strangers (*Summa Theologica* II–II, q. 26, a. 4–8; q. 31, a. 3). Aristotle and Aquinas would disagree with those sociobiologists who iden-tify morality with altruism and then define altruism as selfless behavior (Chandler 1991; Dawkins 1976, 215; Wilson 1975, 578).

Political scientists such as Robert McShea, Roger Masters, and James Q. Wilson defend a naturalistic theory of ethics similar to that proposed by Hume and Darwin. They argue that contemporary biological theories for explaining social behavior confirm Darwin's view of sociality and morality as rooted in sympathy, mutuality, and reciprocity. The theory of "inclusive fitness" (Hamilton 1964) explains how natural selection could favor caring not only for ourselves and our offspring but also for our close kin. The theory of "reciprocal altruism" (Trivers 1971, 1985; Alexander 1987; Axelrod 1984; de Waal 1992) explains how natural selection would favor our helping others and gaining a reputation for being helpful if that in-creases the probability that others will help us in the future. Some theorists have extended this idea of reciprocity through formal models of game theory in which cooperation could emerge among egoists through a strategy of "tit for tat" (Axelrod 1984).

De Waal (1996) has shown that food sharing among chimpanzees follows a reciprocal pattern that has long been thought to characterize early human evolution. Among most primates, food sharing is restricted to mothers sharing with their offspring. But de Waal has revealed, through carefully controlled experiments with captive chimpanzees, that chimpanzees share food according to a rule of tit for tat. Those generous in sharing their food on one day are most likely to receive food from others on another day, while those who are stingy are most likely to provoke rejection whenever they beg food from others. Moreover, while the dominant males of most other primates take food from subordinates, dominant chimpanzee males often share with subordinates. In fact, the dominance of chimpanzee males seems to depend on their generosity in distributing food to other members of their group. Chimpanzee fighting also manifests a reciprocal pattern. When A helps B in a fight, B is more likely to help A in a future fight. But if A often helps others fighting against B, then B is likely to do the same against A. De Waal believes this chimpanzee tendency to retaliation in enforcing reciprocity in food sharing and fighting could be the evolutionary basis for the human tendency to revenge. The human sense of vengeance—the desire to get even—is the earliest and deepest expression of the human sense of justice.

Furthermore, James Q. Wilson (1993a, 1993b) argues that natural selection may have promoted a generalized psychological propensity to "attachment" or "affiliation." What he calls "affiliation" corresponds to what Aristotle calls "friendship" *(philia):* a natural drive to social bonding diversely expressed as sexual, familial, companionate, political, or philanthropic attachments (*NE* 1155a1–1172a15). Wilson believes the human sentiments of sympathy and benevolence, which throughout most of human evolutionary history would have enhanced reproductive fitness by inclining human parents to care for their young, can now be extended to people who are not offspring or even to nonhuman animals. In thus affirming the social dispositions of human beings as rooted in biological nature, Wilson belongs to that growing number of social scientists who argue for going "beyond self-interest" in recognizing the importance of trust and mutual aid in sustaining social order (Frank 1988; Mansbridge 1990; Ridley 1997).

A Darwinian theory of human nature can support the conclusion that human beings have been shaped by natural selection to have the moral reasoning and the moral sentiments that promote reciprocity as a foundation of social life. For example, it is clear that human ancestors were naturally adapted to seek energy-rich foods through hunting or scavenging for meat and gathering plants. Such a foraging strategy would have favored complex forms of social intelligence to secure cooperation based on reciprocity. As one biological anthropologist explains, "[I]t required the capacity to cooperate with others (for instance, to communicate about who should run ahead of a hunted zebra and who behind), to defer gratification (to save food until it could be brought to an agreed site for all to share) and both to determine one's fair portion and to ensure that it was received" (Milton 1993, 92).

De Waal (1996) concludes that Darwinian biology can explain morality as rooted in nature. Although human beings are the only moral beings in the strict sense, at least insofar as morality requires deliberation of the sort that is uniquely human, other animals do have many of the emotional dispositions and cognitive abilities that support human morality. Other animals—and particularly chimpanzees—show sympathy, reciprocity, the establishment of prescriptive social rules, and the concern for reconciling conflicts to preserve social order, which are all necessary for the evolution of human morality.

Is such naturalistic reasoning about ethics fallacious in moving from *is* to *ought*? If we agree with Kant that the "moral ought" belongs to an utterly autonomous realm of human experience that transcends the natural world, then we would have to say that any move from human nature to human morality is mistaken. But if we agree with Hume that moral obligation is grounded in natural human sentiments or desires, then we would have to say that human morality must be rooted in human nature.

"Value for humans," McShea claims, "arises out of and is validated by their species-specific feeling pattern" (1978, 659). Parenthood is a human value because human beings have a strong feeling for parental caregiving. Friendship is a human value because human beings have a strong feeling for their friends. Courage in war is a human value because human beings have a strong feeling for patriotic loyalty. Such values are natural to human beings, because such feelings arise from what Hume called "the original fabric and formation of the human mind, which is naturally adapted to receive them" (1902, 172). Pure reason alone cannot create values because it cannot create feelings. Reason can, however, elicit, direct, and organize feelings to ensure their fullest satisfaction over a complete life. Indeed, what distinguishes human morality from the behavior of other animals is the cognitive capacity of human beings for reflecting on their present feelings in the light of past experiences and future expectations. Nevertheless, as Frans de Waal (1996) has shown, even chimpanzees obey prescriptive rules of social behavior when they learn that conformity to social expectations is necessary if they are to successfully navigate their way in their social group.

For McShea (1990), the species-typical feelings or desires, which emerged from human evolution to become embedded in the genetic structure of human nature, constitute a universal pattern of motivation for human beings. The good for human beings is the satisfaction of their desires, doing what they feel like doing, doing what they want to do. This is difficult because to do what we want to do, we must know what we really want to do, and then we must know how to get what we want in particular circumstances. Since our natural desires are not reducible to one another, and since they often conflict, their satisfaction over a whole life requires good habits of choice and prudent judgment. What we ultimately seek in all of our action, but never fully attain, is what Hume called "the state of calm passion," in which each desire is muted to allow for all the others (1888, 417–22, 437, 583; 1902, 239–40). In some cases, the diversity of desires produces tragic conflicts that cannot be fully resolved. Managing such irresolvable conflicts is the work of prudence.

In this view of morality, ethical naturalists make no mistake in moving from *is* to *ought*, McShea explains, as long as they "limit themselves to the assertion that for a particular intelligent species certain feelings are predictably aroused by certain facts and that the experience of such feelings is the only basis on which we can make evaluative judgments" (1990, 226). "Values are prescriptive, imply obligation, because we feel that they do. The fact of obligation is nothing more nor less than the feeling of obligation" (1990, 235). Roger Masters (1992, 300–302; 1993, 115–16) endorses McShea's Humean naturalism and sees it as compatible with both Aristotelian and Darwinian naturalism in basing morality on the natural human desires. Likewise, James Q. Wilson (1993a, 237–40) adopts the Humean argument for morality as grounded on sentiment or feeling in developing his own theory of the natural moral sense. Evidence from neurology, behavioral biology, and the social sciences supports this belief that there is a natural sense of justice that arises in the human brain from the interaction of reason and emotion (Damasio 1994; Masters and Gruter 1992).

I appeal to this natural moral sense in defending a naturalistic ethics based on my claim that the good is the desirable. George Edward Moore would object that this claim rests on an ambiguous use of the word "desirable" that is common to those who mistakenly try to define "good" in natural terms, which he called the "naturalistic fallacy" (Moore 1968). From the fact that something is "desirable" in the sense that it "can be desired," it does not follow, Moore argued, that it is "desirable" in the sense that it "ought to be desired." Surely, what people actually *can* and *do* desire is not always what they *ought* to desire. Assertions about what people *can* and *do* desire are *descriptive* statements of *fact*, Moore insisted, but assertions about what people *ought* to desire are *prescriptive* statements of *value*. Falsely assuming that we can derive prescriptions of human morality from descriptions of human nature is the "naturalistic fallacy."

Earlier, however, in chapter 2, I have indicated that what is "desirable" for human beings is whatever promotes their human flourishing. What human beings happen to desire at any moment is not always desirable, therefore, insofar as it does not always promote their flourishing. The common experience of regretting what we have done reminds us that we often mistakenly desire what is not truly desirable: for example, we might discover that satisfying some present desire impedes the satisfaction of some future desire; or we might find that in pursuing some narrowly selfish desires, we have failed to cultivate those social bonds of affection and cooperation that we need to satisfy our social desires. Learning how to manage our desires over a complete life in a manner that is appropriate for our individual and social circumstances requires proper habituation and prudent reflection.

Moore's worry about the "naturalistic fallacy" presumes Kant's separation between factual judgments of what *is* the case and normative judgments of what *ought* to be the case. But this verbal distinction cannot be maintained in moral practice, because every normative judgment presupposes a factual judgment about the satisfaction of human desires as a *reason* for the normative judgment. If "we ought to be just" is an example of a normative judgment, then we could ask, "Why ought we to be just?" If the answer is "because it is right for us to be just," this would still beg the question of why this is right for us. Eventually, we must answer that "we ought to be just because justice satisfies some of our deepest desires and thus contributes to our happiness." A Kantian separation between *is* and *ought* would render all normative judgments impotent, because we would have no factual reasons to obey them.

NATURAL FREEDOM

Kant's primary argument for a radical separation of the natural *is* and the moral *ought*, which would make ethical naturalism indefensible, was that such a separation was a necessary condition for the freedom of the will that must be assumed in all moral judgment (Kant 1965, 409–15, 464–79). For morality to be possible, moral agents must be able to transcend nature through "free will." Those who accept Kant's dualism must conclude that biology and the natural sciences in general have nothing to contribute to our understanding of morality, because morality is an utterly autonomous realm that transcends nature (Stent 1978).

In contrast to this Kantian notion of moral freedom as freedom *from* nature, the ethical naturalist would argue that our moral experience requires a notion of moral freedom as freedom *within* nature. For Aristotle, Hume, and Darwin, the uniqueness of human beings as moral agents requires not a free will that transcends nature but a natural capacity to deliberate about one's desires.

Aristotle accounts for moral responsibility with no reference to a "free will" acting outside the order of nature. Some scholars believe the idea of "free will" was not even discussed by anyone until Augustine first formulated it as a tenet of his theology (Augustine 1964; Arendt 1978), although some early Christian theologians interpreted Aristotle's idea of "deliberate choice" (*proairesis*) as "free will" (Pelikan 1993, 129–31, 144, 159–60, 283, 323). In Kant's commentary on the biblical account of Creation in the book of Genesis, he developed the modern concept of culture as a uniquely human expression of freedom from nature that manifests the moral dignity of human beings as created "in the image of God" (Kant 1983). Contemporary "creationist" critics of Darwinian biology advance the same dualistic claim for human culture as transcending biological nature (Morris 1985, 178–208). If Kant's notion of "free will" as transcending nature is a postulate of his religious faith, and is therefore a part of his project "to deny *knowledge*, in order to make room for *faith*" (Kant 1965, 29), as I believe it is, then such an idea cannot be derived from natural reason and natural human experience without the aid of divine revelation.

Aristotle believes we hold people responsible for their actions when they act voluntarily and deliberately (*NE* 1109b30–1115a3; *Rh* 1368b27–1369a7). They act voluntarily when they act knowingly and without external force to satisfy their desires. They act with "deliberate choice" *(proairesis)* when, having weighed one desire against another in the light of past experience and future expectations, they choose that course of action likely to satisfy their desires harmoniously over a complete life. Such deliberation is required for "virtue in the strict sense," although most human beings most of the time act by impulse and habit with little or no deliberation (*NE* 1116b23–1117a9, 1144b1–21, 1150a9–16, 1151a11–28, 1179b5–30).

Children and other animals are capable of voluntary action. But only mature human adults have the cognitive capacity for deliberate choice. Thus, for Aristotle, being morally responsible is not being free of one's natural desires. Rather, to be responsible one must organize and manage one's desires through habituation and reflection to conform to some conception of a whole life well lived. One must do this to attain happiness, which is the ultimate end of all human action.

Similarly, Hume believes success in our pursuit of happiness requires a "general calm determination of the passions, founded on some distant view or reflection" (1888, 417–19, 437, 583; 1902, 239–40). Rather than acting on the passion of the moment, we can pause while we imagine other passions that we have felt in the past or are likely to feel in the future. Unlike other animals, who act to satisfy whatever desire is stirred by their immediate circumstances, we are moral beings because we can reflect on our desires as experienced over a whole life and weigh what we want now against what we might want in the future. Thus our freedom comes from our ability to delay, to reflect, and then to choose between alternative courses of action based on their distant consequences.

Hume rejects the contrast between free will and determinism as a false dichotomy (1888, 399–412; 1902, 80–103). Moral freedom should be identified not as the absence of determinism but as a certain kind of determinism. We are free when our actions are determined by our deliberate choices. In contrast to Kant, Hume doubts that we ever have any real experience of people acting outside the laws of nature. Moral judgment assumes a regular and predictable connection between what people desire and what they do. To hold people responsible for their actions, we must assume that their beliefs and desires causally determine their actions.

Darwin agrees that "every action whatever is the effect of a motive," and therefore he doubts the existence of "free will" (1987, 526–27, 536–37, 606–8). Our motives arise from a complex interaction of innate temperament, individual experience, social learning, and external conditions. Still, although we are not absolutely free of the causal regularities of nature, Darwin believes, we are morally responsible for our actions because of our uniquely human capacity for reflecting on our motives and circumstances and acting in the light of those reflections. "A moral being is one who is capable of reflecting on his past actions and their motives—of approving of some and disapproving of others; and the fact that man is the one being who certainly deserves this designation is the greatest of all distinctions between him and the lower animals" (1936b, 912).

Neuroscientists appear close to explaining the neural basis for voluntary action and moral deliberation. Animals with sufficiently large and complex frontal lobes are capable of voluntary action, in the sense that they can learn to adapt their behavior to changing environmental circumstances. Because human beings have larger and more complex frontal lobes than other animals, human beings can use images and words to compare alternative courses of action through mental trial and error and then choose between them, a capacity for rational choice that can be impaired by damage to the frontal lobes (Luria 1980, 257–327; Passingham 1993, 1–12, 222–61; Damasio 1994; Damasio, Grabowski, Frank, Galaburda, and Damasio 1994; Duncan 1995).

It might seem, however, that such scientific advances in the biological psychology of human action challenge any notion of moral responsibility (E. O. Wilson 1978, 71–78). For instance, some scientists claim that the inclination to violent criminality is somehow rooted in the neurophysiological constitution of the criminal. This has led some legal scholars to conclude that holding criminals responsible for their crimes is unscientific (Jeffery 1994). If so, this would confirm the common fear that biological explanations of human behavior promote a reductionistic determinism.

Roger Masters and James Q. Wilson agree that biological factors influence criminal behavior, because they believe the distinctive character traits of violent criminals—such as impulsiveness and lack of empathy—are to some extent biological (Masters 1994a, 1994b; Wilson 1991, 1993a; Wilson and Herrnstein 1985). For example, the tendency to certain kinds of impulsive violence seems to be associated with low levels of serotonin (a neurotransmitter). The importance of serotonin for human behavior is indicated by the success of Prozac (fluoxetine) as a popular antidepressant drug that raises the level of serotonin (Jacobs 1994; Kramer 1993). The tendency to violence seems to increase when a deficiency in serotonin is combined with hypoglycemia and alcoholism (Virkkunen et al. 1987; Virkkunen et al. 1989). To the extent that these factors are influenced by genetic endowment, it would seem that some people are naturally more susceptible to criminal violence than others.

Masters and Wilson insist, however, that such biological explanations of human behavior do not deny human freedom. They argue that the biological mechanisms governing human behavior—such as the serotonergic system—are too complex to be explained in a simple, reductionistic manner (Tork 1990; Yuwiler, Brammer, and Yuwiler 1994). Genetic propensities interact with individual experience, social learning, and the physical environment. There is some evidence, for example, that social interaction may induce higher levels of serotonin in those individuals who attain high social status (Raleigh and McGuire 1994; Madsen 1985, 1986; Tiger 1992, 248–59).

Alcoholism displays the same causal complexity. Although there probably is some genetic factor influencing alcoholism, the influence is slight in comparison with individual motivation and social circumstances. Some research suggests that people become alcoholics when they are motivated to acquire the habit of drinking alcohol, and therefore they give up their alcoholism when they are sufficiently motivated to change their habits, although as the habit of heavy drinking becomes stronger, the motivation to change must also become stronger to succeed (Fingarette 1988a, 1988b; Bower 1988a, 1988b). The body of an alcoholic might be abnormal in the way it metabolizes alcohol, but the metabolic process does not itself force the alcoholic to introduce alcohol into his body. The neurophysiological reactions to alcohol occur only after the alcoholic chooses to drink. This sustains Aristotle's claim that alcoholics can be held responsible for their drinking, and punished for their conduct while intoxicated, because the *habit* of drinking excessively results from often *choosing* to drink excessively (*NE* 1113b22–14a30).

Knowing that some people have a biological propensity to alcoholism or any other disruptive behavior does not lessen their moral responsibility. On the contrary, Masters (1994b) and Wilson (1991) insist, such knowledge enhances their responsibility to control their bad propensities through medical treatment or proper habituation. If we discover that people inclined to low serotonergic functioning and hypoglycemia become dangerously impulsive when they drink alcohol, we could require them to refrain from drinking. Even so resolute a libertarian as John Stuart Mill would support this: "The making himself drunk, in a person whom drunkenness excites to do harm to others, is a crime against others" (Mill 1956, 119). If we could identify children who are most at risk for becoming criminals as adults, we could look for ways to alter their childhood environment to promote those moral habits that would protect them against criminality. Knowledge of how good and bad character traits emerge from the complex interaction of nature and nurture enhances our moral freedom.

CONCLUSION

The new Darwinian naturalism in political theory challenges the dichotomies that have traditionally separated the social sciences from the natural sciences. There is no absolute gap between *is* and *ought* if human morality is founded on a natural moral sense. There is no absolute gap between nature and freedom if human freedom expresses a natural human capacity for deliberate choice. And there is no absolute gap between nature and nurture if habituation and learning fulfill the natural propensities of human beings. If the new Darwinian naturalists succeed in defending these conclusions, the science of social and political order could become once again—as it was for Aristotle, Hume, and Darwin—the science of human nature. One important part of that science would be the study of the natural bonding between parents and children.

CHAPTER 5

PARENT AND CHILD

We all began our lives in the body of a woman. When we emerged from our mother's womb, we were completely dependent for many years on the intensive caregiving of our parents or other adults who assumed parental responsibilities. Although other mammals display a similar pattern of parental care for their young, human young depend on adult care for a longer period and for more complex social learning than is the case for any other animals. In previous chapters, I have indicated the importance of parental care as a foundation of Darwinian natural right. In this chapter, I will elaborate some of the evidence and arguments for parental care as a natural desire.

As we have seen, Aristotle and Darwin believed that parental care for the young was the natural root for all other social bonds. In this chapter, I will argue that parent-child bonding is the primary natural bond for human beings, and although we should expect the specific patterns of child-care to vary from one family to another and from one society to another, we can judge some ways of caring for children as better than others in conforming to the natural desires and capacities of parents and children. The desire of children for parental care and the desire of adults to give such care often conflict with other human desires, and consequently difficult adjustments must be made to mediate these conflicts. Any attempt to simply eliminate these conflicts, however, by breaking the parent-child bond will be unbearably frustrating for most people. This becomes clear when we consider those utopian social experiments in which this bond is prohibited. The evidence from these utopian communes as well as other biological and anthropological evidence suggest that the parent-child bond must hold a central place in the organization of human desires. I shall also argue that although both mothers and fathers are important for child-care, mothers tend to have a stronger parenting desire than do fathers.

PLATO'S SECOND WAVE

In Plato's *Republic*, Socrates describes a perfectly just city. Assuming that justice requires that each person performs the job for which that person is best fitted by nature, Socrates sketches a city in which the social division of labor would conform to the natural desires and capacities of human beings. In this city, the naturally superior men and women would rule together as equals. In book 5 of the *Republic*, Socrates admits that three requirements for his city are so shocking that they will provoke scorn and laughter. He speaks of them as "three waves" that might sweep away his proposal. First, the men and women suited for military service must have the same education and training, including nude gymnastic exercising for men and women together, so that they learn to rid themselves of any sense of sexual shame. Second, the male and female rulers must live communally, which requires abolishing the family and private property. Third, the highest positions of rule must be held by philosophers.

Consider the second wave. Socrates' fundamental premise is that justice requires the social division of labor to conform to natural human differences—each person doing what he or she is best adapted for by nature. Since men and women are obviously different in their nature, it might seem that a natural division of labor would require men and women to do different things in the just city. Socrates argues, however, that this reasoning is fallacious. Natural differences demand differences in social activity only if the natural differences are relevant to the activity. That some men are bald and others hairy is a natural difference, but it does not follow that bald men make good doctors and hairy men good shoemakers, because baldness and hair are not relevant to medical practice or shoemaking. Similarly, the natural differences between men and women are largely irrelevant to any social activity.

The only important sexual difference, according to Socrates, is that "the female bears and the male mounts" (454d). Yet it does not follow from this natural difference that men are naturally more fit to rule in a just city than women are. It is by nature that women become pregnant, but it is not by nature that they must bear the responsibilities of family life that interfere with the activities of ruling. If the private family were abolished, and the rearing and education of children became a communal activity, women would be free to show their natural equality with men in their desire and their ability to rule. Although nature dictates that women do all the *bearing* of children, nature does not dictate that women do all the *nursing* and *parenting* of children. If nursing and parenting children were done communally, then women would be free to do almost everything men do.

Some scholars, like Natalie Harris Bluestone, believe that Plato's Socrates stated all the basic arguments for complete sexual equality that would later be developed by feminists. Other scholars, like Leo Strauss, believe that Plato actually intended to show the foolishness of trying to abolish the family to achieve sexual equality. According to Strauss, the *Republic* asserts that "justice is full dedication to the common good; it demands that one withhold nothing of his own from his city; it demands therefore by itself absolute communism" (1977, 73). Strauss concludes that the just city so conceived is impossible because it is against nature. "The just city is against nature because the equality of the sexes and absolute communism are against nature" (1977, 127). Furthermore, he insists, Plato intended that careful readers would see that his just city is impossible because it is unnatural, and therefore the *Republic* is actually an implicit critique of utopian idealism. Bluestone points out, however, that Plato's Socrates declares his proposals to be "according to nature" (*Republic* 456b–c). She believes Socrates is right about this: since men and women are by nature identical in everything except their reproductive organs, any sexual differences in the social division of labor—such as women handling most of the child-care—must be conventional rather than natural and therefore open to change.

I shall argue that trying to abolish the bonding between parents and children in favor of a completely communal system of child-care is indeed "against nature." I agree with Bluestone that something approximating Plato's proposal is *possible* in certain kinds of utopian communities. Yet I disagree with her insofar as I think most people would find such communities unbearable because they frustrate some of the strongest natural desires. Human nature is flexible enough to allow some people in special circumstances to abolish familial attachments, but it is not so flexible as to permit this to happen without great emotional cost.

I also disagree with Bluestone's claim that the natural differences between men and women in their reproductive capacities are irrelevant to their behavior with children. These differences are relevant to family life because the nature of *most* women inclines them to have stronger parenting desires than do *most* men, although *some* men will have stronger parenting desires than do *some* women. Furthermore, there tend to be natural differences in kind as well as degree: mothers are not fathers. I believe that the biological and the anthropological evidence for sexual differences shows this.

Bluestone points to the Israeli kibbutz as the best modern example of Platonic communism. "Like Plato," she observes, "the original founders of the kibbutz movement sought to eliminate sex differences, traditional family arrangements, and property ownership for the good of the whole" (1987, 172). Another scholar, Theodor Gomperz (1905, 3:123), suggests that the best example of Platonic communism is the nineteenth-century "Perfectionist" community founded by John Humphrey Noyes in Oneida, New York. Both examples, however, show the severe cost of Plato's "second wave" in frustrating natural human desires.

RELIGIOUS COMMUNISM IN THE ONEIDA COMMUNITY

When John Humphrey Noyes, in his *History of American Socialisms*, surveyed the hundreds of socialist communities established in America, he saw one idea diversely expressed: "the enlargement of home—the extension of family union beyond the little man-and-wife circle to large corporations" (1870, 23). In the most successful communities, such as those of the Shakers, he discerned two principles: religion and the abolition of the family. It seemed that socialist communities without religious devotion that preserved familial attachments would inevitably have their communal spirit broken up by selfishness. Only through religious dedication and the weakening of familial bonds could a socialist community become like one large family with the selfish interests of each person subordinated to the communal interests of all.

The Shakers avoided the social divisiveness that comes from sexual bonding and parental care of the young by practicing complete celibacy. Noyes himself had found another solution to the same problem when he established "Bible Communism" in the Oneida Community in central New York State in 1849. As an alternative to celibacy, Noyes preached "free love" or "complex marriage." As "Perfectionists," the Christians at Oneida thought they were establishing heaven on earth in fulfillment of biblical prophecies. Except for a few personal items, they shared all their property. And under the system of "complex marriage" or "pantogamy," each adult was married to all the others, and the children were reared in common. This prohibited both exclusive sexual bonding between one man and one woman and exclusive familial bonding between parents and their children.

Adults who wished to have sexual relations could do so only if this were approved by Noyes and a Committee of Elders who carefully supervised all sexual pairing. The men, however, were expected to practice "male continence": Noyes claimed that men could learn how to have sexual intercourse with orgasmic pleasure but without ejaculation.

The procreation of children also required the explicit approval of Noyes and the Elders, who ensured that the number of children would not grow too large for the community to support. Mothers cared for their young until they were weaned, but then the children lived in the "Children's House" under communal supervision. Children were permitted to visit their mothers no more than two hours a week, but even those brief visits would be denied if the children showed too much attachment to their mothers. Like all other behavior, this was regulated by a system of "mutual criticism," in which complaints about any member were made in public meetings where those accused were expected to confess all sins and promise to reform.

Noyes believed the difference between Heaven and the world was "that in one reigns the *we-spirit,* and in the other the *I-spirit,*" and "from *we* comes *ours,* and from the *we-spirit* comes universal community of interests" (1853, 30–31). He thought this communal spirit could be achieved in sexual life by recognizing that although sexual union is natural to human beings, restricting sexual union to pairs is not. He saw two natural desires expressed in sexuality—the "amative" desire for sexual union and the "propagative" desire for producing children (1853, 42–47). "Male continence" permitted a clear separation of the two, because men and women could have sexual union without producing children. And "complex marriage" would allow the amative desire to extend beyond any pair to encompass the whole community. The communal rearing of children would satisfy the propagative desire while relieving the mothers of the exclusive burdens of child-care placed on them by the traditional family.

The Oneida Community liberated women by freeing them to take on any task for which they were suited. They participated equally with the men in community meetings. If they bore a child, they did so only by their free consent. And once the child was weaned, the community assumed full responsibility for the child's rearing so that mothers were not the primary caretakers of their children.

The Oneida Community was often disrupted, however, by the "sin" of "partiality" or "special love," which was any bond of affection that excluded others and thus subverted the communal spirit. The most common expression of "partiality" was the attachment of mothers to their children. When the superintendent of the Children's House complained of "motherly interferences," the newspaper of the Oneida Community warned: "We had better abandon our system altogether and put the children all under their parents again, than have it half-and-half-Community government checked by parental partiality" (Robertson 1970, 317).

One of Noyes's own children—Pierrepont Noyes—described in his autobiography the difficulty that his mother had in controlling her "parental partiality" for him. During his weekly visits, his mother was often intensely affectionate.

> A child avid for play forgets easily; but whenever, as I played on the floor, she bent over me, her dark eyes appealing, and asked, "Darling, do you love me?" I always melted. My marbles and blocks were forgotten. I would reach up and put my arms about her neck. I remember how tightly she held me and how long, as though she would never let me go. (Noyes 1937, 67)

The superintendent of the Children's House often punished Pierrepont by forbidding his weekly visit to his mother's room. The child's emotional dependence on his mother was condemned as showing the "sin" of "stickiness," and his mother was condemned for her "idolatry."

When it was noticed that some of the little girls had become attached to their dolls, this also was criticized. One girl confessed to the Community: "I have had a great deal of trouble with my doll, because when I play with her, I get silly and frivolous, and then I have to be criticized" (Robertson 1970, 331). One woman later wrote of her memory of how the Community decided to destroy the dolls: "[W]e all formed a circle around the large stove, each girl carrying on her arm her long-cherished favorite, and marching in time to a song; as we came opposite the stove-door, we threw our dolls into the angry-looking flames, and saw them perish before our eyes" (Robertson 1970, 333).

The Oneida Community survived in its purity for thirty years, from 1849 to 1879, beginning fewer than one hundred members and ending with more than three hundred. In 1879, Noyes left Oneida, and "complex marriage" was abandoned. Although it was a successful experiment in many respects, the collapse of the experiment in 1879 had many causes. One of the primary causes was the difficulty in maintaining the system of "complex marriage" (Klaw 1993; Muncy 1974, 192–96; Robertson 1972, 14–21, 91–92, 130, 142–43, 153–65). John Noyes's control of the mating system was criticized as autocratic. Some of the men resented Noyes's authority as "first husband" to initiate the young virgins into sexual maturity. Many of the younger members of the community desired a monogamous system. "Special love" was never fully eliminated. In fact, many of the controversies in the late 1870s arose from John Noyes's fatherly devotion to his firstborn son, Theodore. Noyes wanted Theodore to take his place as leader of the community.

The Oneida experiment shows that under special circumstances—a small community bound together by religious fervor under the persuasive authority of a talented leader—something like Platonic communism can be achieved: people can sacrifice their desires for private property and familial bonding as impediments to the communal spirit of the whole group. But Oneida also shows that this will be felt as a *sacrifice*, and the first generation of children who have grown up within the community will as adults find the sacrifice of private family life too great to bear. The attachment between parent and child—and especially between mother and child—is too important to the natural organization of human desires to be suppressed without creating an emotional cost that will be unendurable for most people. It should also be noted that giving up private property seemed to be easier than giving up private families. A similar experiment in communal living— but without the religious element—was attempted in the Israeli kibbutzim, and the results were the same: the natural human desires for familial ties eventually asserted themselves.

SECULAR COMMUNISM IN THE KIBBUTZ

In 1949, anthropologist George Murdock, drawing evidence from the 250 human societies represented in the Cross-Cultural Survey project at Yale University, concluded that the nuclear family was the basic unit of all human society. "Whatever larger familial forms may exist, and to whatever extent the greater unit may assume some of the burdens of the lesser, the nuclear family is always recognizable and always has its distinctive and vital functions—sexual, economic, reproductive, and educational" (Murdock 1949, 3). But in 1954, Melford Spiro, another anthropologist, argued that the experience of the kibbutz in Israel showed that the nuclear family was not universal. Of the four functions said by Murdock to define the nuclear family, the economic and educational functions had been given over in the kibbutz to the community as a whole. "The kibbutz can function without the family," Spiro claimed, "because it functions as if it, itself, were a family; and it can so function because its members perceive each other as kin, in the psychological implications of that term" (1954, 845).

In 1979, however, Spiro reported that the kibbutz had changed. He said that when he had begun studying the kibbutz in 1951, he had accepted the common assumption of social scientists "that human beings have no nature—or . . . that human nature is culturally constituted and, therefore, culturally relative" (1979, xv). When he returned to the kibbutz in 1975, he found that this social and economic revolution in human nature had succeeded in every area of life except one. Over the years the women in the kibbutz had demanded a return to traditional family roles in which mothers cared for their own children. It now seemed to Spiro, contrary to his earlier acceptance of cultural relativism, that in this one area of life—the attachment of mothers to their children and the differentiation of sex roles that arises from this attachment—nature had triumphed over culture; or, to put the point more accurately, nature favored the rebirth of some old cultural practices that the new culture could not suppress.

From the earliest foundings in 1910, the kibbutzim in Israeli have grown to include more than one hundred thousand individuals in over 240 communities, each separate kibbutz having 250 to 400 members. Despite their present diversity, most of the original kibbutzim were intended to be radical experiments in communism that would transform Jewish culture. The original Jewish settlers had been accustomed to living in communities that were urban, commercial, capitalist, and religious, as well as centered on patriarchal families with close ties between parents and children. By contrast, the community of the kibbutz would be rural, agricultural, socialist, and secular, with communal child-care that would break the particular ties between parents and children. Just as all property, except for a few personal items, would be owned in common, so would the children be managed as belonging to the whole community. As a result, every person would be economically, socially, and politically equal.

To ensure sexual equality, women were to be freed from their traditional role as primary caretakers of the children, so that the women would be the same as the men, and all men and women would be assigned to those social roles for which they were best suited without regard to sexual identity (Tiger and Shepher 1975, 29–30). Two to six weeks after birth, infants were put in communal nurseries, and then their entire care and education would be communal. In most of the early kibbutzim, children lived in dormitories under the care of trained nurses and teachers, so that the children would not even be permitted to sleep in their parents' apartments. All of the household chores that traditionally were done by women—such as cooking, cleaning, and laundering—were done communally.

In 1950, a kibbutz journal proclaimed the achievement of sexual equality:

> We have given her [the woman] equal rights; we have emancipated her
> from the economic yoke [of domestic service]; we have emancipated her
> from the burden of rearing children; we have emancipated her from de-
> pendency on the husband, her provider and commander; we have given
> her a new society; we have broken the shackles that chained her hands.
> (Spiro 1979, 6)

The "burden of rearing children" was considered the root of what was called "the biological tragedy of women." As a result of the mammalian reproductive system, females bear children, and usually the mothers become the primary caretakers of the children, which seems to confine women to low-status domestic work, while leaving men free for high-status economic and political activity outside the home. Consequently, it seemed that if women were to live the same lives as men, the women must be liberated from their "biological tragedy."

Although the communal care of the children appeared to work in the early years, gradually mothers demanded more time with their children, and now the special bonding between parents and children has reappeared in most kibbutzim. Studies of the kibbutzim suggest that even in the early years, when children were not permitted to live with their parents, the primary attachment-figures for the children were their parents, particularly their mothers (Bowlby 1982, 316–18).

Initially small deviations from communal norms have grown into a major revival of familial autonomy (Tiger and Shepher 1975, 66–67). For example, when one man returning from World War II brought back an electric tea kettle, he was ordered to turn over the kettle to his kibbutz. When he refused, others acquired kettles, and soon families were having afternoon tea ceremonies, with cakes and cookies, in their apartments. For the first time, families were gathering for a small meal in their own apartments rather than the communal dining halls. Mothers wanted a special time every morning when they could visit their children. Then they wanted to be in the Children's House every evening to put the children to bed. Finally, some mothers wanted their children to sleep every night at home in the family apartment. Now, in most kibbutzim, the private family centered on parent-child attachments has become the basic social unit for rearing the children, although most of the other social, economic, and political activities of the kibbutz remain communal.

The older women of the founding generation and the men resisted these changes as a betrayal of the ideological ideals of the kibbutz. The demand for restoring family autonomy came from the "sabra" females— the young women who had grown up in the kibbutz. These women insisted that it was "against nature" to separate mothers from their children. This was surprising because the rearing of the young in the kibbutz was designed to eliminate traditional notions of motherhood and sexual differences.

Since the founders of the kibbutz agreed with Plato's Socrates in claiming that the only natural sexual differences were in anatomy, they believed that sexual behavior and sexual psychology were cultural constructions that could be changed by changing the culture (Spiro 1979, 97–100). They taught their children that sexual differences were unimportant. In the children's houses, boys and girls used the same toilets, showered in one shower room, and slept in the same bedrooms. It was assumed that in such circumstances the children would grow up with no sense of sexual shame. (Is this Plato's "first wave"?) This worked until the children reached puberty. Then suddenly the girls felt intensely uncomfortable when the boys saw them naked. In high school, the boys and girls agreed to shower at different times. Finally, in response to the demands of the girls, the high school authorities began establishing sexually segregated bathrooms and bedrooms. A sense of sexual modesty had asserted itself in opposition to the social environment, which suggested that this was natural and not merely cultural.

Contrary to what they were taught in the kibbutz, the children exhibited sexual differences in behavior that prefigured those they would later exhibit as adults (Spiro 1979, 79–96). For example, in the fantasy play of the children, girls were more likely than boys to enact the role of a parenting mother. Boys showed more conflict and aggressive behavior than girls. The environment of social learning in the kibbutz had been designed to discourage such differences between girls and boys.

The kibbutz looks like the most radical attempt in modern history to achieve a secular communist society that would abolish private property and private families and promote sexual, social, economic, and political equality. It has achieved some of these goals, but the most obvious failure is that the bond between parent and child has reasserted itself as the primary unit of social life. The best explanation for this is that the human desires associated with parent-child attachment, and particularly the desires of women to care for their children, are too deeply rooted in human nature to be suppressed for long.

There are various objections to this conclusion, all of which assume that cultural prejudices favoring private families and maternal care of the young somehow obstructed the success of the kibbutz (Beit-Hallahmi 1981; Brandow 1979; Tiger and Shepher 1975, 263–69). Perhaps the experiment of the revolution in the kibbutz did not go far enough in changing traditional attitudes about family life and gender. Or perhaps the founders of the kibbutz never completely escaped the attitudes that were instilled in them as children, so that they unconsciously fostered traditional attitudes that subverted their social reforms. Or perhaps the familial and patriarchal attitudes of Israeli society exerted an external influence on the kibbutz that could not be resisted.

The difficulty with these objections is that they do not explain why the kibbutz was so successful in all of its other radical reforms that also run contrary to Jewish traditions—such as abolishing private property. Why is parent-child bonding so much more difficult to abolish than any other cultural practice? It's hard to imagine any human beings trying harder than the founders of the kibbutz to abolish the family. Their failure suggests that something very powerful in human nature was resisting them. Of course, how we care for children is influenced by social learning. But why is it so difficult for parents to learn that children should be cared for communally? And why is it so easy for parents to learn to feel a deep attachment to their own children?

Accepting mother-infant bonding as natural does not mean, as many of the founders of the kibbutz seemed to believe, rejecting sexual equality as unnatural. As Spiro has suggested, sexual equality can have at least two meanings: equality as identity or equality as equivalence (Spiro 1979, 7–9, 20–21, 44–60, 109–10). In its early history, the kibbutz movement was devoted to sexual equality as sexual identity: men and women were equal only if they were identical in all important attributes. To be equal to men, women must be like men in every important respect. By this standard the sexual differentiation that arose in the later history of the kibbutz meant a loss of sexual equality.

But by the second meaning of equality, we could say that men and women can still be equal even when they tend to be different in their natural desires as long as their differences have *equal worth*. Antoinette Brown Blackwell, an American feminist of the nineteenth century, could deny Darwin's claim that women are intellectually *inferior* to men, even as she affirmed that as placental mammals women would naturally tend to be more nurturant than men, because she could argue that men and women are by nature "true equivalents—equals but not identicals" (1875, 11).

Viewing maternal care as rooted in natural desires that arise from the mammalian biology of human beings could explain the behavior of women in the kibbutz. This was the final conclusion of Lionel Tiger and Joseph Shepher in their extensive study of women's changing role in the kibbutz. Mammalian young need social interactions with a primary caretaker for their physical and emotional health, and most mammalian mothers desire to provide such care. Of course, this remains true as a general tendency even though *some* men have a stronger desire for providing "maternal" care than *some* women. "If the predisposition of mothers to be with their off-spring is a positive attraction, not a negative retreat, it is because of our mammalian and primate origins and the long, formative hunting-gathering period of our evolutionary past" (Tiger and Shepher 1975, 276).

The history both of the Oneida Community and of the kibbutz indicates that in special circumstances—religious or ideological devotion to communism within small cohesive groups—the parent-child bond can be broken for a generation or more. Yet this history also indicates that this suppression of parenting desires in the social organization of desires is so emotionally devastating (especially to mothers) that it becomes unbearable.

Furthermore, to attempt to abolish familial bonding in large societies that lack the communal intensity of Oneida or the kibbutz would be disastrous.

FOUR BIOLOGICAL CAUSES

It is easy to understand Aristotle's opposition to Plato's proposal for abolishing the family, because Aristotle saw the social nature of human beings as rooted largely in the human desire for intensive and prolonged care of the young. On this point, Aristotle anticipated Darwin, who suggested: "The feeling of pleasure from society is probably an extension of the parental or filial affections, since the social instinct seems to be developed by the young remaining for a long time with their parents; and this extension may be attributed in part to habit, but chiefly to natural selection" (1936b, 478). Similarly, Aristotle in the *History of Animals* (588b30–589a3) observes: "Some animals, just like plants, complete the reproduction of their progeny according to the seasons. Others trouble themselves about the feeding of the young, but whenever this is completed, they separate themselves and have nothing more in common with them. Still others who are more intelligent *[sunetotera]* and share in memory live for a longer time and in a more political manner with their offspring." In the *Generation of Animals* (753a8–14) he explains: "It would seem that nature wishes to provide for a sensation of attentive care *[aisthesis epimeletikes]* for the offspring. In the lower animals nature implants this only until birth; in others, there is care for the complete development of the offspring; and among the more intelligent animals *[phronimotera]*, there is care for its upbringing. Among those who share in the greatest intelligence, there arises intimacy and friendship even towards the completely grown offspring, as among human beings and some quadrupeds." The parental affection of mothers tends to be greater, however, than that of fathers, both because mothers must invest more effort in pregnancy and childbirth, and because they are more certain of their parentage (*NE* 1161b16–29, 1166a1–9, 1168a20–21).

Aristotle refers repeatedly to maternal love for children as the model for, and natural origin of, all forms of love, friendship, and affiliative behavior (*NE* 1159a27–37, 1161b16–28, 1162a16–28, 1166a1–10, 1168a19–27). In speaking of the affection between friends of the highest sort, those whose friendship is founded on a mutual respect for one another's good character, Aristotle uses the Greek verb *stergein*, which normally refers to a mother's love for her children (*NE* 1157a12, 1168a8). Maternal care for children becomes a natural disposition to caregiving that can expand to unite spouses, unrelated associates, fellow citizens, and even all human beings. The inclination to feel some affection for all members of the human species—*philanthropos*—grows out of the affection of parents for children (*NE* 1155a16–29).

Modern Darwinian biology can support Aristotle's claim that human sociality is rooted in the natural bonding of mother and child. But first we need to see that Darwinian explanations of animal behavior are complex in that there are at least four levels of analysis (Tinbergen 1963): (1) functional causes, (2) phylogenetic causes, (3) developmental causes, and (4) immediate causes. Although biological explanations of human nature are often criticized for being crudely "reductionistic" in their "genetic determinism," this criticism is unreasonable, because it ignores the complexity of biological explanations that must account for many levels of causality. As biologist Timothy Goldsmith observes, "nothing of importance in biology can be said to have but a single cause" (1991, 8).

Consider, for example, how Darwinian biologists might explain why some male birds sing in the spring (Catchpole and Slater 1995; Hauser 1996; Welty and Baptista 1988). At the level of functional causes, we could say that the evolutionary function of male songs as a product of natural selection is to attract mates and defend territories in the spring. At the level of phylogenetic causes, we could say that modern song birds with complex songs have evolved from ancestral species of birds with simpler calls and songs. At the level of developmental causes, we could say that young male birds in their early growth develop neural structures that allow them to learn to sing by listening to the singing of other birds of their species. Finally, at the level of immediate causes, we could say that birds sing when hormonal changes in the spring stimulate the song control centers of the brain, which are thus primed to sing in response to springtime conditions. It is possible that each of these four explanations is true, because they correspond to four distinct levels of biological explanation: immediate circumstances, the developmental history of the organism, the phylogenetic history of the species, and ultimate adaptive functions. These same four levels of explanation apply to parent–child bonding (Daly and Wilson 1995).

1. *Functional causes.* The function of parental care for animals is to protect and nurture offspring that could not survive or grow to maturity without such care (Clutton-Brock 1991). Throughout the history of the human species, infants have survived and grown only with the help of adults who were willing to feed, protect, and educate them for many years. If we accept Darwin's theory of evolution by natural selection, which favors those functional adaptations that promoted survival and reproduction in evolutionary history, it would seem likely, therefore, that the desire to care for children is a natural adaptation for human beings.

Some biologists, using concepts from the mathematics of population biology, would explain the importance of child-care for human beings by saying that we are extreme "*K*-strategists" rather than "*r*-strategists" (Daly and Wilson 1983; Pianka 1970; Wilson 1975). In nature there is a trade-off between parental nurture and fecundity, so that some organisms produce many offspring but invest little energy in each (*r*-strategy), while others produce fewer offspring but invest more energy in each (*K*-strategy), a difference in reproductive strategies recognized by Aristotle (*HA* 570b30–32; *GA* 755a21–36). Compared with most other animals, human beings have moved far in the second direction by producing a small number of offspring and then nurturing each one intensively for a long period. Typically, human parents remain attached to their children for their entire lives. And although the attachment of mothers may tend to be greater, fathers are usually integrated into those lifelong bonds in a manner that is unique to human beings.

Among most mammals, when the young have been weaned, and thus have reached the end of their infant nursing period, they develop quickly to puberty and adulthood. Primates and some social carnivores, by contrast, have an extended period of juvenility between weaning and puberty. This juvenile stage of development is adaptive for human beings and other primates because it allows more time for social learning, one of the primary features of primate life as shaped by natural selection. The evolutionary success of human beings depends largely on a human pattern of development that delays puberty and thus extends the time in which juveniles can learn from adults (Bogin 1988, 1990).

John Paul Scott (1989), an ethologist, explains the development of social systems among animals as the evolution of caregiving. Animal mating provides an opportunity for social organization to emerge through "extension of function, from self-care to care of fertilized eggs, from this to the care of the resulting offspring, from this to the care of related adults, and also to adult mates that are not genetically related but become related to offspring that are produced" (1989, 140). The ultimate extension of caregiving would be to unrelated children and adults. Among human beings this is facilitated by language, which, as Aristotle says (*Pol* 1253a15–18), allows human beings to form households and political communities through shared conceptions of the common interest. While sociobiologists commonly speak of animal social behavior as either "selfish" or "altruistic," Scott suggests avoiding the confusing connotations of such language by speaking rather of "epimeletic behavior," which he defines as "giving care or attention to other members of the same species" (1989, 134). Aristotle uses the Greek word *epimeletikos* in exactly the same sense when he speaks of human social behavior as a development of the "attentive caregiving" displayed by social animals (*GA* 753a8).

As we have seen, both Aristotle and Darwin believed there were sexual differences in the natural propensities to caregiving: women tend to have a stronger parenting desire than do men, both because women typically devote more effort to their children than do men, and because women typically are more certain of their maternity than men are of their paternity (*HA* 608a35–b2; *NE* 1161b16–29, 1166a1–9, 1168a20–21; *EE* 1241b7–9). Some modern Darwinian theories of reproductive strategies as functional adaptations shaped by natural selection would support this (Daly and Wilson 1983, 1995; Symons 1979). According to a theory of parental investment developed by Robert Trivers (1972, 1985), the sex with the lesser parental investment will aggressively compete for and promiscuously court the other sex. Among mammals, the female's investment of energy in an egg exceeds the male's investment in a sperm. This creates an evolutionary pathway to ever greater nurturance by the female. Because the egg is less mobile than the sperm, with the evolution of internal fertilization, the fertilization is more likely to occur in the body of the female. Subsequent evolutionary developments—gestation, placentation, and lactation—increase the mother's investment in nurturing the young (Trevathan 1987). The father's investment, by contrast, may be nothing more than his act of fertilization. Furthermore, a mammalian mother is almost always certain of which offspring are hers, while a father is often uncertain of which offspring are his. Men can be cuckolded; women cannot. For these reasons, according to Trivers, we might expect natural selection to favor males who are promiscuous and females who are coy, so that males would compete with other males for sexual access to females, and females would compete with one another for resources to support their offspring. While the females cared for the offspring, the males would look for new mating opportunities.

There are circumstances, however, where natural selection would favor males caring for their offspring as promoting their reproductive fitness. Among a few species, such as water bugs, sea horses, and some birds, the male invests more in caring for offspring than does the female, and as parental investment theory would predict, the females compete with one another in courting males who are relatively coy (Clutton-Brock 1991; Trivers 1985). This reversal in the typical courtship roles can even occur within the same species in response to changing ecological circumstances. Such a reversal of roles has been observed among some insects: when the male's parental investment becomes greater relative to the female's, promiscuous females compete sexually for the parental resources of coy males (Gwynne and Simmons 1990). Among primates and other mammals, whenever males are relatively confident of their paternity, and the mothers alone cannot easily provide for the needs of the offspring, it may be in the reproductive interests of males to help their mates in caring for the young (Hrdy 1981, 1986; Kleiman and Malcolm 1981). This is commonly true for human beings (Lamb et al. 1987).

At the level of functional causes, therefore, we can explain human parental care as a functional adaptation for nurturing and protecting offspring that could not survive and flourish without such care.

2. Phylogenetic causes. Although Aristotle had no theory of the evolution of species from ancestral species, he would have agreed with Darwin's claim that the human desire to care for children was rooted in natural dispositions shared with other animals. Aristotle saw that the more intelligent and more political animals tended to display intensive and prolonged child-care (*HA* 588b24–89a10, 608a10–20b9; *GA* 753a7–17). He thought that among birds biparental care was associated with a capacity for communication comparable to human language (*HA* 504b1–6, 535a28–36b24). He spoke repeatedly of the shrewd plotting and prudent calculations required of animals that care for their young. They must gather food, deceive predators, defend territories, build nests, and teach the young what they need to learn to survive and reproduce. Darwin went beyond Aristotle, however, in explaining how parental care emerged through evolutionary history by natural selection.

From a survey of the phylogenetic history of parental care among all animals, the only general explanation is that parental care tends to arise when the benefits of such care for the offspring exceed the costs for the parents (Clutton-Brock 1991). Parental care is most highly developed in situations where eggs or young face harsh environments or severe competition from other animals. Parental care is rare among invertebrates. Among the few invertebrates and reptiles that do care for eggs or young, usually the female provides the care with no help from the male. By contrast, among those fish that care for eggs or young, it is common for only the males to show parental care. Typically for these fish the eggs are fertilized externally, and the males defend territories or nests where the females lay their eggs. Although there are some exceptions, exclusively male care among these animals is associated with external fertilization; and exclusively female care is associated with internal fertilization. All birds and mammals fertilize their eggs internally. But while male care is rare among mammals, it is common among birds. Birds are unique among vertebrates in that biparental care occurs in more than 90 percent of the species, which seems to be related to the fact that most birds are monogamous. All mammalian females care for their young, but in only a few mammalian species do males provide any direct care. Male parental care in some form is common, however, among carnivores and primates. Among these mammals, biparental care is usually associated with monogamy.

This connection between biparental care and monogamy would seem to confirm Trivers's theory of parental investment: if mating is monogamous, males are more likely to care for the offspring because they are more confident of their paternity. Among mammals, maternity is usually far more certain than paternity. Female mammals can normally know which offspring are theirs. But males can never be completely certain about which offspring are theirs. Since natural selection would seem to favor individuals caring for their own offspring rather than the offspring of others, we would expect mothers to generally invest more in caring for offspring than do fathers. We would also expect that male care of offspring would arise only among species that exhibit monogamous or one-male mating systems where males are sure of their paternity. In fact, for mammals the most common and most intensive male care of offspring is among monogamous primates.

There are exceptions to this pattern, however, which suggest that paternity certainty cannot fully explain paternal care among primates (Smuts 1985; Smuts and Gubernick 1992). For instance, gibbons are monogamous, but the males do not provide direct care for the young. Furthermore, among many primate species that show mating in one-male groups, the males do not care for the young, although their paternity certainty is high. On the other hand, among some primate species in which females mate promiscuously with more than one male, some males care for infants, although their paternity certainty is low.

Among some primates—such as olive baboons and savanna baboons—males and females form "friendships" with one another: individuals unrelated by kinship can develop a special relationship in that they spend much of their time together, they groom one another, and they help one another in various ways (Smuts 1985; Strum 1987). Males will care for the infants of their female friends, even when the infants are unrelated to the males. One possible Darwinian explanation for this is that such males increase their chances of mating with a female in the future by caring for her infants. This would be a form of "sexual selection" in which females prefer to mate with their male friends who have cared for the females' infants in the past (Smuts and Gubernick 1992).

Even where males care for infants with a high probability of paternity, the probability of paternity could be not a cause of the male child-care, as Trivers assumes, but a side effect of male-female friendships. If males who care for infants increase their chances of mating with the infants' mothers, then eventually the males will be caring for infants who are their own offspring. Furthermore, not only can males who care for infants be rewarded with increased mating opportunities with the mother, they can be rewarded in other ways. For example, mothers can intervene in fights over status to secure the status of their favored males (Smuts 1985; Smuts and Gubernick 1992).

This could explain the emergence of male child-care in human evolution. It is often assumed by those who adopt the "paternity certainty" theory that a monogamous mating system had to be established before males would care for offspring. An alternative explanation would be that male care for infants evolved initially as an expression of male friendship for the mothers, which would be favored by sexual selection because females would prefer to mate with male friends who had nurtured the females' offspring, and eventually males would be caring for offspring that were highly likely to be their own. Of course, all else being equal, we would expect males to be more inclined to care for their own offspring than for the offspring of other males, and thus the emergence of pair-bonded mating systems in human evolution would promote paternal care by increasing the confidence of fathers in their paternity.

While the evolutionary basis for paternal care among human beings thus remains in doubt, there is little doubt as to the evolutionary necessity for maternal care. Among those animals most closely related to human beings—chimpanzees and bonobos (pygmy chimpanzees)—the importance of mother-infant bonding is clear. Inadequate maternal care or the loss of the mother creates physical and psychological problems for the infant that can lead to death (Kano 1992; Goodall 1986, 101–4, 203–6, 376–86, 568–69). Although all mammalian infants depend on adult care, primate infants are more helpless than the infants of other species. One of the prominent features of primate evolution is the large brain. Because of the limits on the size of newborn brains imposed by the birth canal of the mother, chimpanzee infants are born with brains that are only about half the size of adult brains, so that the brain must double in size during the first year of life, which makes the newborn chimpanzee infant far more helpless than other mammalian infants.

Human evolution continued this trend even farther: while the hominid brain evolved to become ever larger, the evolution of bipedalism required anatomical changes that limited the size of the female's birth canal and thus limited the size of the newborn's brain (Trevathan 1987). Consequently, a human infant at birth now has a brain that is only one-fourth the size of an adult brain, which means that a human infant is even more helpless for a longer time than is a chimpanzee infant. Thus, human beings are born in a state of helplessness that demands intensive caretaking by mothers and, to some extent in some circumstances, by fathers as well.

At the level of phylogenetic causes, therefore, human parental care can be explained as the consequence of an evolutionary trend among closely related primate species toward producing offspring that require extensive adult care.

3. Developmental causes. Both Aristotle and Darwin believed that there was a natural human instinct to care for one's offspring, and although this instinct would generally be found in both mothers and fathers, mothers would tend to be somewhat more nurturant than fathers. If this were true, we would expect that the normal development of human beings would produce neuroendocrine systems that would incline adults to care for children, while inclining women somewhat more strongly than men to give such care. We would also expect that children would be naturally inclined to elicit parental care. There is now substantial evidence from the biological study of human development to confirm these expectations.

The development of parent-child bonding in human beings and other primates manifests a natural instinct for learning that depends on the interaction of nature and nurture. Although parental care is a natural adaptation shaped by natural selection, the bonding of parent and child must be learned in a social environment similar to the typical environments of human evolutionary history, in which a child was surrounded by mother, father, siblings, and other relatives. Children in socially deprived environments without normal social interaction are at risk for developing disruptive patterns of social behavior.

John Bowlby (1982), in his comprehensive survey of the evidence for attachment behavior in human beings, has shown that parent-child bonding is a natural instinct that follows a pattern similar to that found in other animals with parental care. From birth, infants are naturally inclined to make contact with their mothers through head turning, sucking, grasping, clinging, and reaching. During the early months of life, infants communicate with their mothers through crying, babbling, and smiling. By the end of the first year, infants typically display the behavior of attachment toward their mothers or mother surrogates. They cry when mother leaves, and they greet her return with delight. When they are sick or alarmed, they seek mother's protection and comfort. With mother as a base of operations, they explore their environment and regularly return to her for reassurance before resuming their exploration.

As Bowlby indicates, mothers are not the only attachment-figures for children. Although mothers are often the primary objects of attachment, any adult—such as a father, a grandparent, an older sibling, or an adoptive parent—can become the attachment-figure if that person cares for a child in a "mothering" fashion. A child can feel some attachment to more than one adult, but there seems to be a natural inclination for a child to direct the strongest attachment to one person.

As environmentally flexible instincts for learning, a child's desire for adult care and a parent's desire to care for children do not emerge in a rigidly stereotyped fashion, because the development of these desires depends upon a social environment of interaction between parents, children, and other relatives, which is the kind of environment that was typical for human ancestors in evolutionary history. In atypical environments where children may be deprived of nurturing social contact, parent-child bonding may not develop in its naturally adaptive form.

Harry Harlow's famous experiments with rhesus monkeys reared in social isolation showed that the higher primates cannot develop their natural behavioral instincts if they are deprived of their normal social environments (Harlow 1986). Even when infant monkeys have their physical needs for food, water, and shelter satisfied, they cannot grow into normal adults if they cannot attach themselves to a mother or mother surrogate. Harlow put infant monkeys in cages where they had no contact with their mothers or any other monkeys. He constructed dummies to serve as surrogate mothers, and he found that monkey infants preferred those dummies that were made of soft, warm cloth to those made of wire mesh.

The infants cuddled with the cloth mothers and became attached to them just as they would to real mothers. Using their cloth mothers as a safe base of operations, infants would explore novel objects in their cages and then return to their mothers before resuming their exploration. If the surrogate mothers were removed, infants would scream and freeze in a crouched position, too terrified to explore the cage. Many psychologists have assumed that animals became attached to their parents only as a source of food, and therefore they would have no need for parents if their physical needs were satisfied. Harlow showed, on the contrary, that the emotional security of a monkey requires the "contact comfort" that can only come from attachment to a real mother or a cloth mother that has the soft and warm qualities of a mother.

Harlow also showed, however, that even a cloth mother cannot completely replace a real mother in nurturing the growth of an infant monkey into a normal adult. His experiments with monkeys raised from birth in social isolation confirmed the experience of zookeepers with mammals caged in solitude: sexual mating and parental care require social learning. Monkeys who have grown up without the social experience of contact with their mothers or other monkeys do not as adults know how to breed or how to care for young. None of Harlow's isolated males could inseminate a female, because they apparently had never learned what to do. Some of the isolated females were inseminated by experienced males. But these "motherless mothers" did not know how to care for their children. Some were abusive mothers who attacked and even killed their children. Others were indifferent mothers who refused to feed or otherwise care for their young. The only adequate mothers were those who had had some social contact in their first year of life with other monkeys. So it seemed that a monkey's instincts for sexual mating and parental care can only develop through social learning in contact with its mother and other young monkeys during its first year of life.

Harlow was surprised, however, to observe that although female monkeys reared in social isolation became abusive or indifferent mothers in their treatment of their first offspring, they became adequate mothers with their second or third offspring (Harlow 1986). It seemed that mothers could overcome the effects of isolated rearing by learning enough from social contact with their first child to become good mothers with subsequent children.

Monkeys, human beings, and other primates have been shaped by natural selection with instincts for social learning rather than rigidly fixed patterns of behavior. The advantage of this learned flexibility in their behavior is that they can adapt to changing social environments. The disadvantage is that in a socially deprived environment where they cannot learn normal social behavior through parental care, they cannot as adults live as healthy social animals. For such animals, therefore, parental care of infants is essential not only for satisfying their physical needs, but also for nurturing their emotional and intellectual development as animals who must learn to live in complex social environments.

Like other animals whose normal development depends on parental care, human beings are naturally disposed to care for their children. If this were not so, it would be hard to explain why most parents normally sacrifice so much of their time and energy in nurturing their children. Yet this would still be hard to explain if children were not naturally inclined to elicit caretaking behavior from their parents. From birth the brains of human infants are adapted for social attachment to a caretaker. If that need for attachment to an adequate caretaker is frustrated, this can disrupt the normal development of the neural and hormonal systems. Research in neurology has shown that just as sensory deprivation early in life can distort the areas of the brain devoted to sensory perception, so can social deprivation early in life damage areas of the brain in ways that will interfere with the normal social development of the adult (Carlson and Earls 1997; Kandel and Jessell 1991; Kraemer 1992). It is not surprising, therefore, that infants are equipped with complex desires and capacities that foster social interaction with caregivers.

From birth, infants have the natural desires and capacities of social animals. Even before birth a fetus is socially as well as physically attached to the mother. Experimental studies suggest that probably because of their pre-natal experience in hearing their mothers' voices, newborns prefer their mothers' voices to other female voices, and they prefer female voices to male voices (Field 1990; Jacobs and Raleigh 1992). From an early age, infants can recognize, display, and imitate the seven facial expressions found universally among human beings that signify anger, fear, happiness, sad-ness, surprise, interest, and disgust.

Infants are also endowed by nature with moral emotions. Darwin (1877) thought he saw signs of sympathy in infants as young as six months and signs of a moral sense in infants as young as thirteen months. Recent re-search on child development indicates that within the first two years of life infants show empathy, shame, and guilt, which provide the emotional basis for a natural moral sense (Damon 1988; Wilson 1993b). Of course, this natural moral sense has to be cultivated by social experience and particu-larly by the work of parents who enforce their moral expectations. Even when young children are free from adult supervision, they learn in playing with one another that they need to accept principles of sharing to settle conflicts, principles such as equality, merit, benevolence, and reciprocity. Equality means distributing equal shares to all. Merit means giving special rewards for hard work or for doing something that deserves praise. Be-nevolence means helping those who are somehow disadvantaged. Reci-procity means treating others as they have treated us. Children express their natural sociality in their desire to play with one another, and they discover that they must conform to the group's demand for reciprocity to satisfy that desire for social play. Frans de Waal (1996) has observed that infant chim-panzees undergo a similar period of socialization as they learn the social expectations of their group.

By contrast to the natural sociality of normal human children, autistic children seem to be born with some neurobiological deficiency such that they lack the desire for social affiliation. Consequently, autistic children develop into asocial adults who withdraw into a largely solitary existence with little social contact (Grossman, Carter, and Volkmar 1997).

4. Immediate causes. Parent-child bonding, I have argued, has a *functional cause* in that it has been favored by natural selection as serving the survival and reproductive success of human beings. Parental care has a *phylogenetic cause* in that it has emerged from an evolutionary history that human beings share with other primates and other mammals. Parental care has a *developmental cause* in that the desire to care for children emerges as an outcome of the normal development of children into adults.

Yet this still does not fully explain the natural basis for the immediate motivations that cause the attachment of parents and children. Parents do not care for their children because they have consciously calculated that this promotes their reproductive fitness. Parents care for their children because they have a strong desire to do so, and the pleasure that comes from satisfying that desire compensates for the pain that often accompanies child-rearing. I would argue, however, that this desire to care for children is a natural desire that has been favored by natural selection as one of the psychic mechanisms that move human beings to act in ways that generally foster reproductive success. Even without any conscious calculation of the benefits for survival and reproduction, the desire for food moves animals to eat, the desire for sexual pleasure moves them to copulate, and the desire to care for their offspring moves them to secure their reproductive investment in progeny.

The desire to care for children, like all natural desires, is rooted in the hormonal and neural systems of the human body. We know that the body has psychic mechanisms that make some behaviors pleasurable and others painful. And although we do not know enough about these mechanisms to understand precisely how they influence social attachment, we can detect a few of the biochemical factors related to parental behavior. For example, various hormones act on those parts of the central nervous system of mammalian females that mediate maternal behavior (Panksepp, Siviy, and Normansell 1985; Rosenblatt 1992). Those hormonal factors do not act alone, however, because they interact with other factors in the body and with conditions in the social environment. For example, exposure to young and the experience of parental care can alter the brain's sensitivity to hormones that promote parental behavior. In the emergence of this behavior in mammals, there is no strict separation between nature and nurture. Rather, mammals are inclined by their nature to learn from their social experience how to care for offspring.

Recent scientific research shows that parent-child bonding is one expression of the many social desires supported by neurobiological mechanisms for affiliation (Carter, Lederhendler, and Kirkpatrick 1997). Although the neurobiology of social attachment is too complex to be reduced to two chemicals, oxytocin and vasopressin are particularly important (Carter et al. 1992; Carter et al. 1997; Insel, Young, and Wang 1997; Witt 1997). These chemicals are nine-amino-acid peptides with similar molecular structures. They are produced in the hypothalamus of the brain and found only in mammals. They are associated with many activities related to social bonding and reproduction: copulation, pair bonding, uterine contractions, lactation, maternal care, and paternal care (Insel 1992a). It is likely that oxytocin as found in mammals evolved from mesotocin as found in amphibians, reptiles, and birds (Moore 1992). Like oxytocin, mesotocin controls reproductive behaviors, and it differs from oxytocin in only one of its nine amino acids. Similarly, it is likely that vasopressin in mammals evolved from vasotocin in amphibians, reptiles, and birds, since these two peptides also resemble one another in their molecular structure and in their regulation of reproductive behaviors.

While it is difficult to study directly the action of these and related hormones in human beings, studies of some nonhuman mammals have shown the importance of this hormonal system for social bonding. Prairie voles, for example, brown rodents common in the American midwest, differ from most other rodents in that they form monogamous pair bonds, and both parents care for the young. Studies indicate that their monogamous bonding and biparental care is associated with oxytocin and vasopressin (Carter et al. 1992; Carter and Getz 1993; Insel 1992b; Insel and Hulihan 1995; Panksepp 1992; Winslow et al. 1993). The sexual and social interaction between male and female prairie voles stimulates the production of oxytocin and vasopressin, which act on their brains to facilitate social bonding between the two individuals. Once pair-bonded the male and female guard one another and defend a territory. Oxytocin promotes the female's care of her offspring and bonding to her mate, while vasopressin promotes the male's paternal care and pair-bonding.

Oddly enough, the social monogamy of prairie voles does not ensure sexual exclusivity. Females socially bonded to a male sometimes copulate with unfamiliar males, and consequently monogamous males sometimes rear pups that are not their own. Like some human beings, these animals combine monogamous mating with occasional philandering.

From this and other manifestations of the influence of oxytocin, Thomas Insel, a leading researcher on this subject, concludes that oxytocin "influences the motivational or affective properties of social interaction. More specifically, one might hypothesize that this peptide makes social contact rewarding, thereby permitting an asocial species to become social for the elaboration of parental and reproductive behaviors" (1992b, 26). Insel concedes, however, that if this hormone influences social attachments among human beings, its effects are surely influenced by the complex activities of the human cerebral cortex (Insel and Carter 1995).

Just as is the case for maternal behavior, hormonal changes influence paternal behavior among birds and mammals (Brown 1985). But for paternal as well as maternal behavior, the hormonal effects depend on how they interact with many other factors such as the reproductive strategy typical of the species, the previous mating experience of the individual animal, and external stimuli from the mate and from the eggs or young. The hormonal influence on paternal behavior varies both between and within species. The one general principle is that whenever males become closely associated with young—through attachment to a territory, a nest, or a monogamous mate—those males show greater hormonal responses to young than males not associated with young.

Human fathers tend to be more involved in caring for their offspring than the males of other mammalian species. Yet the degree of paternal care varies according to the immediate factors of individual motivation and social ecology. For example, in polygynous societies, and in conditions where men must be engaged in warfare for long periods, men are unlikely to devote much attention to child-care. In monogamous societies without much warfare, fathers are more likely to invest in child-care, but only if their economic activity does not take them away from home (Lamb et al. 1985; Lamb et al. 1987; West and Konner 1976). Among the Aka Pygmies, who live in the tropical forests of Central Africa, fathers provide more direct care of infants than has been reported for any other human group (Hewlett 1992). Since the Aka hold no territory, Aka fathers do not need to engage in warfare that would take them away from home. Their most important economic activity—hunting with nets for small animals—requires the cooperation of husbands and wives. In such circumstances, fathers are inclined to help the mothers in caring for the children as part of the reciprocal relationships that develop within the family.

THE HUMAN ECOLOGY OF PARENTAL INVESTMENT

If human beings tend to have a natural desire to care for children, as I have argued, it might seem strange that in modern industrialized societies, people tend to have small families. One might expect that the increasing economic resources in such societies would allow people to satisfy their desire for children by having large families. The fact that the people in industrialized societies tend to have fewer children than those in less-developed societies, which social scientists have called "the demographic transition," might seem to deny my claim about parenting as a natural desire. And yet I would see this as a natural expression of the prudent flexibility of human beings in adapting their parental desires to changing ecological circumstances.

Jane Lancaster (1997), an anthropologist who applies a Darwinian theory of human nature to explain cultural behavior, has shown that an evolutionary theory of parental investment can explain the cultural variation in parental behavior. From the point of view of Darwinian theory, human parental investment in children is neither genetically fixed nor culturally arbitrary. Parental investment is not genetically fixed, because the human desire for parental care manifests itself in variable ways in response to the variable ecological conditions of the physical and social environment. And yet parental investment is not culturally arbitrary, because its variability follows a predictable pattern as human beings strive to satisfy their natural desire for parenting in diverse circumstances. As Aristotle would say, parental care of children is natural, but prudence dictates that the best way to satisfy that natural desire varies to conform to the conditions in which human beings happen to find themselves.

Patterns of parental investment emerge from a series of decisions involving trade-offs that all animals (including human beings) must make (either consciously or unconsciously) over the course of their life history

(Hill 1993; Trivers 1972). These trade-offs require allocating scarce resources (such as time, energy, and risk) between competing activities. The first trade-off is between *somatic effort* (investing resources in the growth and development of the individual animal) and *reproductive effort* (investing resources in the individual animal's offspring). The second trade-off is between two forms of reproductive effort—*mating effort* (investing resources in the search for mates) and *parental investment* (investing resources in the care of offspring). The third trade-off is between two forms of parental investment: one stresses the *quantity* of offspring (investing in a large number of offspring but with each receiving little investment), and another stresses the *quality* of offspring (investing in a lesser number of offspring but with each receiving more investment). All animals must make such choices (consciously or unconsciously), and whether one choice is better or worse than another depends on the variable ecological conditions of their lives (Emlen 1995).

Like other animals, Lancaster argues, all human beings must decide (consciously or unconsciously) how much to invest in themselves as compared with their children, because producing and caring for children is costly. All human beings who decide to reproduce must then decide how much to invest in finding mates as compared with investing in the children produced by mating, because directing resources to finding new mates can mean decreasing the resources available for the children produced through earlier mating. All human beings who decide to invest care in their children must then decide whether to divide their resources among many children or concentrate their resources on a few children, because children typically consume more parental resources than they produce, and therefore any increase in the quantity of children requires some reduction in the quality of the resources available for each child.

The differences in how people make these decisions manifest the complex interactions of differences in individual temperament, individual history, sexual identity, and social history. Although most human beings will become parents at some time in their lives, a few will never become parents, either because they lacked the opportunity (through infertility or failure to find a mate), or because by temperament and circumstances their parental desire was weak in comparison with other desires. Men will tend (on average) to invest somewhat more in mating effort and somewhat less in parental care than do women, because while a man can impregnate many women, women cannot be impregnated more than ten to twenty times in their lives. Yet despite this difference in tendency between men and women, most men desire the social stability that comes from mating with one woman or a few women and then investing great paternal care in the children produced.

The choices human beings make about parental investment will also reflect social history, because the likelihood that one choice is better than another in satisfying the natural desire for parental care will depend on social conditions that determine the costs and benefits of alternative reproductive strategies. One example of social variability in parental investment explained by Lancaster concerns the choice between the quantity and quality of children. As a general rule, animals in good condition (having good health, plentiful physical resources, or high social status) tend to produce more offspring than animals in bad condition. This seems to have been true for human beings throughout most of their history: the healthier, wealthier, and more powerful people have tended to have more children that survive to adulthood. But now a new pattern has emerged. People in modern, industrialized societies tend to produce fewer children on average than people in the less developed societies. In the most economically developed societies of the world today, the average fertility rate has dropped to about two children for each family.

Lancaster has shown that one can explain this in Darwinian terms. In the developed societies, the economic and social success of children depends ever more on their educational training so that as adults they can compete for jobs that require special skills. Consequently, rearing successful children in such societies requires that parents make increasingly costlier investments in the education of their children. And as the *cost* of children has thus *increased*, the *quantity* of children demanded by parents has *decreased*, because parents now express their natural desire for parenting successful children by investing more resources in fewer children, thereby choosing *quality* over *quantity* in their children. Even if this is only part of the explanation for small families in modern societies, this illustrates the kind of decisions that parents make as they adjust their patterns of parental investment to conform to the ecological circumstances in which they find themselves. A natural human desire for parental care will be culturally variable because of the variability of the social and physical conditions of parental care.

INFANTICIDE, ADOPTION, AND SEXUAL BONDING

If caring for children is a natural desire, why do some parents abuse and even kill their children? If human beings prefer to care for their own off-spring rather than the offspring of strangers, why is adoption so common? And why are human beings inclined to separate sexuality from reproduction?

Philosophers such as John Locke (1959, 1:75–76) have cited the practice of infanticide as evidence for the claim that morality cannot be rooted in human nature. If there is any naturally innate moral principle, parental care for children would seem to be the most obvious example. But the fact that some parents prefer to kill their children suggests, Locke asserted, that parental care is not natural to human beings. Some historians have even argued that the love of children is a recent invention of modern European culture, because throughout history the abuse of children was considered normal (de Mause 1974). If this were so, then caring for children would seem to be not a natural desire but a purely artificial product of cultural learning.

Contrary to this conclusion, however, some historians have shown that there is plenty of historical evidence that most parents have always been concerned with the proper rearing of their children (Mount 1982; Pollock 1983). Furthermore, Martin Daly and Margo Wilson (1988) have shown from their study of the anthropological record of infanticide that most parents are not inclined to kill their children except in extreme circumstances. Typically, there are three conditions in which infanticide is most likely to occur. Either the infant is born in poor health. Or the parents lack the material resources to care for the infant. Or there is some doubt about the paternity of the infant. For most mothers killing a child is a painful action done only in harsh circumstances.

Yet even if caring for one's own children can be explained as a natural desire that has been favored by natural selection, it might seem that the common practice of adoption, in which people choose to care for children who are not biologically related to them, must be purely cultural and not natural. Cuckoos lay their eggs in the nests of other birds, many of whom will incubate the cuckoo eggs and care for the cuckoo hatchlings as their own. Some birds have evolved to resist such parasitism. American robins, for example, reject the eggs deposited in their nests by cowbirds. By comparison, human beings are peculiar. Unlike cuckoos, we usually desire to rear our own children. But unlike robins, we sometimes adopt children who are not our own. That peculiar pattern of behavior can be explained, however, as a product of natural desires shaped by natural selection (Silk 1990).

In those societies where adoption is most prevalent—such as the societies of Oceania and in the North American arctic regions—natural parents are reluctant to give up their children. They do so typically only when they cannot care for their children properly, and the adoptive parents are generally related by kinship to the natural parents. Sometimes adoption establishes reciprocal alliances between families that exchange children.

In modern industrial societies, adoptions do not show the same patterns of nepotism and reciprocity manifest in traditional societies. In North America and Western Europe, adoptive parents rarely have any kinship relation to their adoptive children. Still, since the most common reason for adoption seems to be the infertility of the adoptive parents, it appears that for most people biological parenthood is preferred over adoption.

A Darwinian explanation for this would be that natural selection has favored a natural desire to care for children that can lead people to adoption when they cannot have children of their own. In the circumstances of human evolutionary history, the desire to care for children would have almost always induced human beings to care for their own children or for children of close relatives, which would have increased their reproductive fitness. But once thus established by natural selection, this desire could be extended in some cases to facilitate caring for the children of strangers (Silk 1990).

Adoption also occurs among some nonhuman primates (Galdikas and Vasey 1991; Goodall 1986; Jolly 1985). In most cases, the adoptive parents are biologically related to the infants; but in some cases, they are not. Barbara Smuts (1985) observed among savannah baboons that when a mother rejected an infant, or when a mother died and left an infant, sometimes the infant was adopted by a male who had been a close companion of the mother, although he was not biologically related to the infant. The adoptive male would carry, groom, and protect the infant.

Of course, the parenting desire can be overridden by other natural desires. Human beings can even pursue their sexual desires with no connection to reproduction. This separation of sexuality from reproduction is not unique to human beings. Many mammalian females copulate when they are not ovulating. Some primates—particularly, bonobos (pygmy chimpanzees)—use sexual behavior for social communication and social bonding (Kano 1992; de Waal 1989; de Waal and Lanting 1997; Wrangham 1993). Bonobos engage in sexual interaction—copulation, noncopulatory mounting, manual genital massage, and genito-genital rubbing between females—to establish social relationships, to release tension in potentially aggressive situations, and to restore social bonding after aggression has occurred. Natural selection has favored the desire for sexual pleasure as serving social functions beyond reproduction.

Nevertheless, sexual intercourse does often lead to the production of children who could not survive or develop into normal adults without parental care. I have argued in this chapter that natural selection has shaped human nature so that children have a natural desire for parental care, and adults have a natural desire to provide such care. This natural bonding of parent and child will disrupt any community based on the goal of communal sharing in which all members are equally attached to all others, because parents and children will form special attachments. Any attempt to abolish such attachments between parents and children, as in the Oneida Community or in the kibbutzim, must fail because it goes against human nature. Rather than attacking parent-child bonding, any stable community must be rooted in this bond as the natural foundation of human sociality. Parents caring for their children is a fundamental norm of Darwinian natural right.

There are natural differences, however, at least on average, between maternal care and paternal care—both differences in degree and differences in kind. This must be so insofar as men and women are not identical on average in their natural propensities.

CHAPTER 6

MAN AND WOMAN

Men and women are different by nature. The natural pattern of desires typical for men is not the same as that typical for women. Men typically have a stronger desire for sexual promiscuity, while women typically have a stronger desire for intimate companionship. Men typically have a stronger desire for dominance, while women typically have a stronger desire for nurturance. Men typically desire the solidarity of comradeship, while women typically desire the solidarity of kinship. Because of their typical desires, the distinctive virtue of men is courage, while the distinctive virtue of women is sympathy.

These natural differences are typical or average, but many individuals are exceptions. On the average men are taller than women, although some women are taller than some men. Similarly, on the average men's desires differ from women's, although some men are more feminine in their desires than some women, just as some women are more masculine in their desires than some men.

Even typical men and typical women differ only in degree. The typical man has the dispositions of the typical woman but to a lesser degree, just as the typical woman has the dispositions of the typical man but to a lesser degree. Every normal human being displays some combination of male and female traits.

Although the differences between men and women often produce conflict, there is a natural complementarity between the typically masculine and the typically feminine desires of human nature. The fullest expression of human sociality comes from the balanced combination of sexuality and intimacy, dominance and nurturance, comradeship and kinship, courage and sympathy.

In our daily experience, most of us most of the time accept the differences between men and women as manifestations of human nature. In our intellectual discussions, however, we often assume that the differences in the typical social behavior of men and women are not natural but purely cultural. There are no natural differences in the psychological dispositions of men and women, according to this view, but social expectations that

123

male and female behavior should be different create differences through social learning that are based only in arbitrary cultural traditions. Some feminists would argue that, since these cultural traditions are often oppressive to women, to justify these traditions as grounded in biological nature is unfair to women. Only by recognizing that all sex differences in behavior are arbitrary cultural constructions, these feminists would claim, can we liberate women from traditional practices that harm them.

In this chapter, I will argue that there are differences between men and women in their natural desires that have been shaped by natural selection, because these natural differences enhanced survival and reproduction in human evolutionary history. Although social learning either intensifies or diminishes the natural propensities for men and women to behave differently, which creates diversity across cultures in the patterns of sex differences, the natural propensities limit and direct cultures to produce a universal pattern of male and female differences.

I will also argue that far from promoting the oppression of women by men, this grasp of the natural basis of sex differences in human biology allows us to recognize and condemn cultural practices that frustrate the natural desires of women. If the social relationships of men and women were arbitrary constructions of culture, we would have no natural standard for judging these relationships as beneficial or harmful, and thus we could not reform the cultural constructions of sexual identity to promote the happiness of men and women through cooperative relationships of mutual dependence. I will consider female circumcision (clitoridectomy and infibulation) as an illustration of a custom that can be condemned because it frustrates natural human desires for health and sexual pleasure. The feminist attack on cultural practices like this that harm women requires an understanding of male and female natures as complementary expressions of the human nature that has emerged from human evolutionary history. Feminism can be grounded in an ethical naturalism that looks to natural human desires as the norm for moral reform.

FEMINIST NATURALISM

In *The Descent of Man, and Selection in Relation to Sex*, first published in 1871, Charles Darwin offered an evolutionary theory of the natural differences between men and women. He believed that women had evolved to be nurturant caregivers, while men had evolved to be aggressive hunters, so that men and women would tend to have different desires and capacities conforming to their different roles in the sexual division of labor. He concluded that as a result of these natural differences, women were intellectually inferior but morally superior to men. "The average standard of mental power in man must be above that of women," and thus "man has ultimately become superior to woman," which he thought explained the fact that most eminent artists and scientists were men. Nevertheless, women were naturally superior to men in their moral dispositions, because the "maternal instincts" of women inclined them to "greater tenderness and less selfishness" than men. "Man is the rival of other men; he delights in competition, and this leads to ambition which passes too easily into selfishness" (1871, 2:326–28).

A few years later, in 1875, Antoinette Brown Blackwell responded with the first feminist criticism of Darwin in her book, *The Sexes Throughout Nature*. She argued that Darwin's evidence did not support his conclusion about the intellectual inferiority of women. Instead, the correct inference from the biological facts would be that the sexes are "true equivalents—equals but not identicals" in all physical and mental powers (1875, 11). She charged that Darwin's interpretation of the evidence had been distorted by his "male standpoint," and that "only a woman can approach the subject from a feminine standpoint" (1875, 17, 22). The ultimate arbiter between these conflicting standpoints, she insisted, would be the facts of nature as known by science:

> It is to the most rigid scientific methods of investigation that we must undoubtedly look for a final and authoritative decision as to woman's legitimate nature and functions. Whether we approve or disapprove, we must be content, on this basis, to settle all questions of fact pertaining to the feminine economy. . . . In physiology, in psychology, in politics, in all forms of social life, it is to Nature as umpire—to Nature interpreted by scientific methods, that we most confidently appeal. (1875, 231–32)

Blackwell's feminist argument rested, therefore, on a modern scientific version of Aristotelian naturalism: the ultimate norms for human life arise from a rational study of human nature, and the proper social status of women will depend upon what we know about their nature.

Throughout the modern history of feminism from the Renaissance to Mary Wollstonecraft to John Stuart Mill to the present, the fundamental appeal has been to a naturalistic argument: women are not naturally inferior to men, and therefore the oppression of women is a product of history rather than nature, which means that the unfair treatment of women can be ended, or at least moderated, through historical change (Lerner 1986, 6–10). Since natural science—and particularly biology—has become the authoritative source for knowledge about human nature, modern feminists like Blackwell have sought biological support for the natural equality of women and men.

This explains why the resurgence of feminism in the 1960s and 1970s renewed the feminist challenge to the "male standpoint" in Darwinian biology. Feminists criticized the assumption that "Man the Hunter" had been the prime mover in human evolution, which seemed to denigrate the contributions of women to the evolution of human nature in ways that implicitly legitimated male dominance as natural. Female primatologists— Jeanne Altmann, Sarah Blaffer Hrdy, Jane Goodall, Barbara Smuts, Shirley Strum, Adrienne Zihlman, and others—showed that the lives of female primates were more complex and more important for primate evolution than many male scientists had thought. Louis Leakey, after achieving fame for his studies of the human fossil record in East Africa, chose three women to study the three species of great apes—Jane Goodall (chimpanzees), Dian Fossey (gorillas), and Biruté Galdikas (orangutans)—because he thought the nurturant nature of women would make them more patient and perceptive in direct observation of animal behavior than men would be. Some feminists believe the success of these three women confirms the scientific value of "the feminine emphasis upon individuality, relationships, and empathy" (Montgomery 1991, 128). All of this confirms Blackwell's defense of the "feminine standpoint" in natural science and her claim that men and women were naturally equivalent, even if not identical, in their moral and intellectual capacities as products of evolution.

Far from justifying the subordination of women to men, recognizing natural sexual differences helps us to appreciate the need for restraining the predatory proclivities of men and promoting the civilizing prudence of women. As Susan Okin (1990) has indicated in a survey of what feminists have said about what it means to "think like a woman," there is no commonly accepted feminist position that would deny natural differences in the psychology of men and women. Some feminists argue that the liberation of women will come when women can celebrate their feminine ways of thinking (Noddings 1990; Jaggar 1990). Rather than denigrating the typically female experience of mothering, and insisting that women must think and act like men, these feminists defend women's experience as fostering a "different voice"—to use Carol Gilligan's (1982) famous phrase—that is *neither inferior nor superior* to the typically male voice but *only different*. The female voice speaks of an ethic of care and love that binds people together in a web of concrete relationships. The male voice speaks of an ethic of rights and justice that adjudicates conflicts between competing individuals through abstract rules. One example of this difference is in the American legal profession: the ever-increasing number of women in law schools and legal practice sometimes find themselves uncomfortable with the men's view of law as a competitive game with winners and losers as decided by impersonal rules, a view that is not so much incorrect as it is incomplete (Jack and Jack 1988). The work of Deborah Tannen, a sociolinguist, suggests that this difference in "voices" is literally a difference in conversational styles, in which men reflect their view of life as "a contest, a struggle to preserve independence and avoid failure," while women reflect their view of life as "a community, a struggle to preserve intimacy and avoid isolation" (1990, 25). As is the case for Gilligan, Tannen believes men and women have something to learn from each other: "Many women could learn from men to accept some conflict and difference without seeing it as a threat to intimacy, and many men could learn from women to accept interdependence without seeing it as a threat to their freedom" (1990, 294).

Feminists can argue that the natural inclination of women to parental care cultivates their mental powers. Sara Ruddick (1980, 1989), for instance, reflects on "maternal thinking" as a way of thinking about nature. Although the particular circumstances of child-care vary according to the cultural context, Ruddick believes that all children have natural needs that make universal demands on the adults caring for them. All children need help to survive, to grow, and to enter a social group. All children express these needs in different ways, however, because they are born with natural temperaments that distinguish them as individuals. To satisfy children's needs for preservation, growth, and social acceptance, mothers must protect, nurture, and train their children in some manner that conforms to the nature of each child. "A child leans out of a high-rise window to drop a balloon full of water on a passerby. She must be hauled in from the window (preservation) and taught not to endanger innocent people (training), and the method used must not endanger her self-respect or confidence (nurturance)" (Ruddick 1989, 23). Interpreting each of these demands and weighing them when they conflict pose difficult questions. To formulate and answer such questions mothers must think. And insofar as the physical, emotional, and intellectual needs and powers of their children are given by nature, mothers thinking about their children are thinking about nature.

Ruddick's argument has a long lineage in the history of feminism that stretches back to Mary Wollstonecraft's *Vindication of the Rights of Woman*, which was first published in 1792. Far from being a mindless activity, rearing children, Wollstonecraft believed, demands careful thinking if it is to be done well. Allowing women to develop their minds as freely as men would therefore make them better mothers. "As the care of children in their infancy is one of the grand duties annexed to the female character by nature, this duty would afford many forcible arguments for strengthening the female understanding, if it were properly considered" (1983, 265).

Alison Jaggar, in *Feminist Politics and Human Nature* (1983), has shown that all forms of feminist theory, like political philosophy generally, rest upon some conception of human nature and of women's nature as an expression of that universal nature. Jaggar herself appeals to certain biological facts of human nature in criticizing "the liberal assumption that human individuals are essentially solitary, with needs and interests that are separate from if not in opposition to those of other individuals." She explains:

> As soon as one takes into account the facts of human biology, especially reproductive biology, it becomes obvious that the assumption of individual self-sufficiency is impossible. Human infants resemble the young of many species in being born helpless, but they differ from all other species in requiring a uniquely long period of dependence on adult care. This care could not be provided by a single adult; in order to raise enough children to continue the species, humans must live in social groups where individuals share resources with the young and the temporarily disabled. Human interdependence is thus necessitated by human biology, and the assumption of individual self-sufficiency is plausible only if one ignores human biology. (1983, 40–41)

Thus, Jaggar employs an Aristotelian understanding of human biology—a teleological conception of human beings as striving to satisfy their species-specific desires—to support "human interdependence" as a principle for feminist political theory.

Jaggar also follows Aristotle in invoking his principle that justice requires treating like cases alike and different cases differently. Insofar as women and men are naturally alike, they should be treated alike. Insofar as they are naturally different, they should be treated differently. Of course, distinguishing the natural likenesses and the natural differences—not only with respect to men and women but also with respect to different women in different circumstances—is a crucial issue for feminist debate (Jaggar 1990). In any case, as Aristotle saw, human nature is so complex that the full range of human desires and powers comes into view only by considering both men and women, with the thought that women's experience may reveal possibilities obscured by men's experience. "The concept of women's standpoint," Jaggar explains, "asserts that women's social position offers them access to aspects or areas of reality that are not easily accessible to men. The standpoint of women reveals more of the universe, human and non-human, than does the standpoint of men" (1983, 384–85). Although she departs from Aristotle when she asserts that the female standpoint is *superior* to the male standpoint, she agrees with him in stressing parent-child bonding as part of the naturally social nature of human beings.

THE BIOLOGY OF SEX DIFFERENCES

This difference between "the standpoint of women" and "the standpoint of men" reflects biological differences. Aristotle, from his study of embryological development and the early growth of animals, concluded that gonadal activity differentiates not only the anatomy of male and female animals but also their psychological dispositions. Modern biology seems to confirm Aristotle's position (Arnhart 1994).

There are sexual differences in the central nervous system of mammals (particularly in the hypothalamus) that are probably related in complex ways to sexual differences in social behavior (Breedlove 1992; Hampson and Kimura 1992; Kimura 1992, 1996; LeVay 1993; MacLusky and Naftolin 1981). Among rodents there are clear differences between males and females in their nervous system that strongly control differences in their social behavior. Among primates there are similar differences, but they are neither as clear nor as strong as they are for rodents. Moreover, the plasticity of the brain and nervous system in response to social experience makes it difficult to determine the relative contributions of genetic factors and environmental factors in creating these sexual differences. We know, for example, that among some mammalian animals the experience of nursing and parenting changes the circuitry of the brain. And although there seem to be differences in the brains of heterosexual and homosexual human beings, it is not clear whether this neural difference creates differences in behavior, or whether different behavior creates different patterns in the brain (Einstein 1997; LeVay 1993).

As with other sexual differences, the intrinsic pattern for organizing the central nervous system is female, with departure to the male pattern resulting from the action of testicular hormones (principally testosterone) in early development. The brain and neural system of adult mammals respond to fluctuations in hormone levels with sexually differentiated behavior.

Most of the evidence for these conclusions comes from experiments with nonhuman mammals, because it is not usually permissible to subject human beings to the same genetic and hormonal experiments that are conducted on other animals. Yet there have been "experiments of nature" in which through abnormalities in the endocrine system before or shortly after birth, genetic females undergo hormonal masculinization, or genetic males do not (Ellis 1982, 1986; Hunter 1995; Imperato-McGinley et al. 1979; LeVay 1993; Money and Ehrhardt 1972). Consequently, genetic males who appear at birth to be girls and are reared as girls can experience masculinization at puberty. Or genetic females exposed to androgenic hormones during their prenatal development can seem unusually "tomboyish," although they have been reared as girls.

The development of sexual identity depends critically on the environment of early rearing: those children who are raised as boys will tend to conform to the social expectations for boys, and those raised as girls will tend to conform to the social expectations for girls. But it is a mistake to infer from this that sexual identity is purely a social construction—a product of nurture rather than nature. This mistake is evident in a famous case of sex reassignment. This case has often been cited as evidence that infants are sexually neutral at birth, and that gender identity is determined by the social environment. In 1973, doctors reported the case of a genetic (XY) male who had been successfully reared as a girl. Born a normal male, the patient's penis had been accidentally cut off when he was eight months old. Assuming that individuals have no sexual identity at birth, and assuming also that it would be easier to surgically transform ambiguous genitals to look like a vagina than to reconstruct a penis, the doctors convinced the parents of the patient to rear him as a girl and never tell him he had been born a boy. Initially, the reports indicated complete success as the parents reared this child as a normal girl. This case was often cited in textbooks to show that nature puts no limit on the construction of gender by social rearing. In 1997, however, it was reported that this individual had decided at the age of fourteen to live as a male, and at age twenty-five he had married a woman and adopted her children. Beginning when he was very young, he did not feel right being a girl. He felt that his parents and the doctors were forcing him to deny his deep desire to be male. His social environment identified him as a girl, but his emotional constitution identified him as a boy. His genetic endowment and his prenatal experience in being exposed to masculinizing hormones in the womb had given him a male brain predisposed to male desires (Angier 1997; Diamond and Sigmundson 1997).

If there are biological mechanisms favoring such differences in the psychic propensities of males and females, the ultimate cause might be a simple fact about sexual reproduction denoted by the term "anisogamy": the sex cells or "gametes" are unequal, the female's eggs being much larger than the male's sperms. Masculinity and femininity might have evolved from this mere difference in size (Daly and Wilson 1983; Dawkins 1976; Symons 1979; Trivers 1972, 1985). Applying Aristotle's matter-form distinction, we could say that although female and male each contribute one half of the chromosomal "form" of the zygote, the female contributes almost all of the "matter," because the cytoplasm of the egg provides the material for the early differentiation and growth of the zygote. Thus, the female's investment of energy in an egg is much greater than the male's investment in a sperm. This creates an evolutionary pathway to ever-greater nurturance by the female. Because the egg is less mobile than the sperm, with the evolution of internal fertilization, the fertilization is more likely to occur in the body of the female. Subsequent evolutionary developments—gestation, placentation, and lactation—increase the mother's investment in nurturing the young. By contrast, the male invests so little in any one act of fertilization that in many cases he maximizes his reproductive success by competing with other males in trying to inseminate as many females as possible. This creates a difference in the reproductive strategies of males and females. Males compete with one another for sexual access to females. Females compete with one another for resources to support their offspring.

MATING DESIRES

Although human fathers commonly invest much care in their children, the *minimum* parental investment of a woman is much greater than the *minimum* parental investment of a man. Throughout evolutionary history, women had to invest in each offspring at least nine months of pregnancy and many months if not years of nursing and caring for the infant, while men could potentially impregnate many women without any additional investment in the children born. Men can increase the number of their offspring by promiscuous mating, but women cannot. If Trivers (1972, 1985) is right in his Darwinian theory of mating strategies as determined by parental investment, we should expect that women will typically be more selective than men in choosing mates, and women will typically desire mates with resources that can support her and her children. But even if men in general tend to be more sexually promiscuous than women, we would expect that women would be promiscuous when such behavior was beneficial to them. We would also expect that although men would be promiscuous with short-term mates, men would be more selective in their choice of long-term mates with whom they wanted to share parental responsibilities.

Darwinian theory predicts that these and other sexual strategies for mating would evolve as components of human psychology to the extent that they fostered survival and reproduction in human evolutionary history. Since all of us are descendents of evolutionary ancestors who were successful in surviving and reproducing, we can predict that we have inherited the mating desires that made our ancestors successful. Of course, there is no need for these Darwinian desires to be based on conscious calculations of reproductive success. When human beings feel sexual and romantic desires, they are often not thinking consciously about their genetic interests in offspring. Yet Darwin's theory of evolution would predict that in evolutionary history those sexual and romantic desires that made some human beings more reproductively successful than others would be favored by natural selection, and consequently propensities to have such desires would be inherited by descendents like us as part of our evolved psychological nature.

Recently, some psychologists and anthropologists have tested this Darwinian view of human mating desires by studying the attitudes and behavior of people concerning sex and marriage in different societies to see if the Darwinian predictions hold true. For example, psychologist David Buss and his colleagues have surveyed the mating preferences of more than ten thousand people in thirty-seven countries on six continents and five islands. Contrary to the common view that mating preferences vary arbitrarily across cultures, they found a universal pattern of mating desires that conforms to the Darwinian theory of human mating strategies (Buss 1989, 1994a, 1994b).

In all thirty-seven countries, Buss found that men prefer to mate with women who are young and physically attractive, while women prefer to mate with men who have economic resources and high social status. Since the reproductive success of a man depends predominantly on the fertility of his mate, Darwinian theory correctly predicts that the physical cues to fertility in women—such as youth, smooth skin, regular facial features, and good body tone—are sexually attractive to men around the world. Since the reproductive success of a women depends predominantly on the ability and willingness of her mate to invest resources in her and her children, Darwinian theory correctly predicts that the social cues to such resources in men—such as wealth, status, older age, and ambition—are sexually attractive to women around the world.

Buss found that both men and women distinguish between short-term mates and long-term mates (Buss 1994a, 1994b). In comparison with women, men typically have a stronger desire for short-term mates, desire a greater number of mates, and desire sexual intercourse after a shorter period of acquaintance. Men find promiscuity desirable in a short-term mate but undesirable in a long-term mate. Women find promiscuity undesirable in both contexts. Women are more selective than men in their choice of even short-term mates, because women often use short-term mating as a way of assessing men who might become long-term mates in the future. Men seek long-term mates who are likely to be sexually faithful to them. Women seek long-term mates who are likely to provide resources for themselves and their children.

These natural desires for mating create universal patterns of marriage and divorce. The anthropological evidence suggests that human beings prefer monogamous marriages (Fisher 1992). Most human beings marry one person at a time. Although many societies have permitted polygamous marriage, most marriages are monogamous even in these societies. Most men are not wealthy enough to marry more than one woman at a time, and the sexual jealousy of co-wives often makes polygynous marriages unstable. The polyandrous marriage of one women to more than one husband is extremely rare, because the sexual jealousy of co-husbands is too intense to permit this in normal circumstances.

Yet although they prefer to marry one person at a time, human beings do not typically mate with a single person for an entire lifetime. Divorce is a human universal found in all societies. In the most extensive anthropological study of cross-cultural patterns of divorce, Laura Betzig (1989) compared the causes of divorce in 160 societies, and she found that they conformed to the predictions of Darwinian theory. The most common causes were infidelity and infertility, both of which hinder the reproductive function of marriage. The other common causes of divorce—sexual withdrawal, lack of economic support, conflict among multiple wives, and cruelty—can all be explained as factors that would impede the reproductive success of a spouse in the environments of evolutionary history.

Anthropologist Helen Fisher has argued that the cross-cultural data on divorce and remarriage show several patterns that can be explained through a Darwinian understanding of human mating desires (Fisher 1992, 1995). Men and women tend to divorce during the early part of their reproductive careers—in their twenties and early thirties. Most divorced people who are still at an age to reproduce remarry. Divorce is highest among couples who have produced no children or only one. The more children a couple produces the less likely they are to divorce. The older the spouses are and the longer they remain married the less likely they are to divorce. Fisher explains these patterns as manifesting a human reproductive strategy of serial pair-bonding. Human beings tend to form pair bonds that last long enough to rear their young during the years of infancy when children are most in need of care by both parents. But when the children no longer need the care of both parents, divorce is more common. As couples grow older and have more children, they develop ties of stable attachment that can last for the rest of their lives.

Although divorce is universal, the rate of divorce varies greatly according to the social and economic circumstances of a society. In agrarian societies, for example, husbands and wives are often so economically dependent on one another that divorce is rare. In industrialized and urban societies, the economic independence of individuals makes it easier for them to divorce their spouses. In societies with governmental programs supporting single mothers and their children, it is easier for women with infant children to divorce their husbands, because the governmental welfare system can take the place of paternal resources in supporting the children. In a welfare state, the government becomes a surrogate husband for divorced mothers. Thus, the reproductive strategies of human beings are flexible enough to change in response to changing physical, economic, and social conditions.

This flexibility is limited, however, by the natural desires for mating and parenting that characterize most men and most women. Human beings naturally desire to mate. Although a few human beings never mate, most will have at least one mate during their lives, and some will have more than one. Some of these matings will produce children, and the care of the children will strengthen the conjugal bond of the parents. Eventually, most human beings settle into a stable marriage that satisfies their natural desires for mating and parenting within the stable order of familial bonding. Of course, in some circumstances legitimized extramarital relations can be compatible with social stability, and some promiscuity is inevitable in most circumstances. Yet completely random and unregulated promiscuity is unbearable for human beings. Consequently, one paramount moral standard for judging any society is its success or failure in satisfying the natural desires for stable sexual bonding.

Satisfying the natural mating desires is difficult because the desires often conflict with one another both within individuals and between individuals. The typically male desire for mating with a variety of sexual partners contradicts the typically female desire for mating with one partner in a stable relationship of intimacy. A society could satisfy the male desire for variety by establishing a mating system of complete promiscuity. But unlike some other animals, such as chimpanzees, human beings have never been able to organize stable societies based on unregulated promiscuity. Although human societies have accommodated promiscuity within certain limits, and although divorce is universal, every human society prescribes some form of marriage as a social, economic, and sexual bond between husband and wife.

Donald Symons, in his book, *The Evolution of Human Sexuality* (1979), argues that the conflict between the male desire for sexual variety and the female desire for conjugal intimacy is a product of evolution, because in evolutionary history the desire for variety was adaptive for men but not for women. Therefore, the institution of marriage, he believes, is an unnatural constraint on male desires imposed by women to satisfy female desires. I believe Symons is wrong, however, because I agree with Joseph Carroll (1995), who argues that despite the conflict between male and female desires, there is a fundamental complementarity in their desires that supports the stable arrangements of family life. Even Symons implicitly recognizes this complementarity in a few passages of his book. "The desire for sexual variety," he writes, "dooms most human males to a lifetime of unfulfilled longing; when the desire can be satisfied easily, as among many homosexual men, it often frustrates the satisfaction of other desires, such as those for intimacy and security" (1979, 228). His point about homosexual males is that, unlike heterosexual males, they do not have to limit their desire for variety to accommodate the female desire for stable intimacy, and consequently homosexual males can pursue among themselves a life of unlimited promiscuity. But Symons notices that in contrast to lesbians, who are just like heterosexual women in their desire for stable companionship, homosexual males who try to live a life of indiscriminate sexual indulgence seem unfulfilled. Ultimately, monogamous fidelity is more satisfying even for homosexual males. Some homosexuals argue for legalizing homosexual marriages as a way of providing social encouragement for homosexual monogamy, even as they concede that monogamous commitment is usually easier for lesbians than for male homosexuals (LeVay 1996, 149–61; Sullivan 1995, 13–18, 108–10, 180, 202).

As Symons indicates, men have desires for intimacy and security that are frustrated when they yield completely to their desire for sexual variety. Therefore, as Carroll argues, the long-run satisfaction of male desires requires that men subordinate their momentary desires for promiscuous gratification to their enduring desires for secure attachments to a wife and children. Indeed, as Darwin saw, establishing harmony in our desires by restraining the momentary desires to promote the enduring desires constitutes our moral life. Marriage often seems undesirable to men because it requires that they restrain their indiscriminate sexual desires, but marriage is ultimately desirable for most men because it satisfies their deeper desires for conjugal stability and parental care.

If marriage did not satisfy male desires, it would not be a universal practice of all societies. If most men found the institution of marriage ultimately unsatisfactory, they would have abolished it long ago. They have always had the power to do so, because every human society has been ruled by men.

MALE DOMINANCE AND MALE VULNERABILITY

Aristotle believes that among human beings, as well as some other animals, the male is by nature "more hegemonic"—more inclined to rule or dominate—than the female (*GA* 608a8–b18, *Pol* 1259b1–2). The male's spirited love of dominance is manifested in the family, in politics, and in war. In the family, some husbands show a tyrannical inclination to impose their authority over everything in the household (*NE* 1160b36–37). In politics, the love of rule leads some men to the tyrannical belief that the best human life would be to have "authority over everything" (*Pol* 1325a35–36). In war, the manly courage of the warrior-citizen facing death in battle epitomizes virtue as virility in asserting one's group against competing groups (*NE* 1115a6–1117b21).

Darwin explained the natural inclination of males to dominance as a product of evolutionary history in which natural selection worked through male competition both between and within tribal groups of males. He observed that "from the remotest times successful tribes have supplanted other tribes," and he inferred that such tribal competition would favor improvements in the intellectual and moral faculties of human beings. Those tribes whose members were morally disposed to be "faithful to their comrades" would prevail. "A tribe including many members who, from possessing in a high degree the spirit of patriotism, fidelity, obedience, courage, and sympathy, were always ready to give aid to each other and to sacrifice themselves for the common good, would be victorious over most other tribes; and this would be natural selection" (1871, 1:158–66). To the extent that "sympathy, fidelity, and courage" were inherited dispositions, they would become part of the innate constitution of males. At the same

time, the competition between males within each tribe for access to females would favor those males with the "courage and pugnacity" to drive
away their rivals, and because of the reproductive success of the dominant
males, the disposition to aggressive dominance would be passed on to their
male offspring (1871, 2:257–58).

If Aristotle and Darwin are correct about the desire for dominance
being naturally stronger in men than in women, then male dominance
should be a human universal rooted in human nature. In fact, there is much
anthropological and biological evidence that that is the case. Steven Goldberg
has surveyed much of that evidence in his book, *Why Men Rule: A Theory
of Male Dominance* (1993), which is a revised version of *The Inevitability of
Patriarchy* (1973). Although Goldberg's book is controversial, his great
achievement is in examining all the supposed examples of matriarchal societies and showing that they were not really matriarchies at all.

Goldberg argues that male dominance is a universal feature of every
human society, and that this results from physiological differences between
men and women. Typically male desires incline most men towards dominance, while typically female desires incline most women towards
nurturance. Consequently, in every society, the overwhelming number of
high-status positions in hierarchies are filled by men. Of course, some women
have a desire for dominance that is stronger than that of some men, and
therefore some women rise to the top of social hierarchies. But since men
on average have a stronger desire for dominance, the number of women in
the highest positions of leadership has never surpassed about 7 percent in
any society. Margaret Thatcher of Great Britain, Indira Gandhi of India,
and Benazir Bhutto of Pakistan are examples of politically dominant women
in recent history, because each of them became prime minister in a parlia-
mentary government. Yet the political success of these women as individuals does not change the fact that the political hierarchies of England, India,
and Pakistan are generally dominated by men.

Goldberg emphasizes, however, that the greater dominance of men
does not imply greater competence. There is no reason to believe that men
are generally better qualified to lead a society than are women. Yet because
men are generally more inclined than are women to sacrifice other desires
to satisfy their desire for dominance, men tend to rise to the top of all social
hierarchies.

Although the male desire for dominance is universal, Goldberg argues, how that desire is expressed in different societies depends upon socially determined standards of dominance. For example, while physical aggression is often associated with male dominance, that is not always the case. Physical aggression is only a means to an end, and men will employ other means to dominance if necessary. In Japan, men once sought dominance through militaristic violence, because that was the culturally prescribed route to dominance, but now Japanese men seek dominance through economic success, which conforms to a new culturally defined standard of dominance.

Goldberg concedes that his argument would be refuted if there were clear evidence of at least one society in which most of the highest positions of leadership were not held by men. It has often been asserted that there have been matriarchal societies in which women ruled over men, or egalitarian societies in which women and men ruled as equals. Goldberg shows, however, that a careful examination of the evidence does not support this interpretation of the societies in question (Goldberg 1993, 231–47). For example, the Iroquois people may have had the least patriarchal society that has ever existed. Lewis Henry Morgan's famous account of the high status of women in Iroquois society led Friedrich Engels, Karl Marx's collaborator, to infer that in the earliest hunter-gatherer societies, women were equal or even superior to men in status and power. Morgan himself, however, indicated that although Iroquois women helped to select the male leaders, women were not permitted to hold leadership positions in the hierarchy. Describing "the absence of equality in the sexes," Morgan observed that "the Indian regarded woman as the inferior, the dependent, and the servant of man" (1851, 324). According to a recent anthropological history of the Iroquois, "Iroquoian women had a dominant voice in all matters concerning the welfare of their community, although public business and dealings were conducted by male spokesmen" (Trigger 1985, 89).

From such anthropological evidence that male dominance of the highest positions of leadership is universal, Goldberg infers that there must be some universal cause rooted in human biology. It seems implausible that the *variable* factors of cultural learning could explain this *universal* pattern. To say that culture is the cause of universal male dominance begs the obvious question: Why does every culture teach male dominance? If male dominance were culturally arbitrary, we would expect that some cultures would teach female dominance. When all cultures reinforce—to varying degrees— a universal pattern of human desires, we must suspect there is some universal propensity in human nature that produces this outcome in diverse cultural environments.

Goldberg argues that there is a universal propensity to male dominance based in some neuroendocrinological factors that differentiate males and females: normal males have a central nervous system that is structured to respond to testosterone and other biochemical substances with a tendency to dominance behavior. Goldberg offers two kinds of evidence for this conclusion. First, he surveys some studies of human physiology suggesting that hormonal masculinization of the central nervous system during fetal development promotes male dominance behavior. Second, he surveys studies of nonhuman mammals indicating that testosterone is associated with male dominance and aggression as controlled by parts of the male brain that have been masculinized during fetal development. Although such research is controversial, there is growing evidence that male and female brains are different, and that these differences support different patterns of desire (Hampson and Kimura 1992; Kimura 1992, 1996; LeVay 1993).

Men tend to have higher levels of testosterone than women do, and these elevated levels of testosterone seem to promote the male desire for dominance—the desire to enhance one's status over other people (Mazur and Booth 1997). Among a few nonhuman species, such as spotted hyenas and bonobos, the females tend to be more dominant than the males (de Waal and Lanting 1997). One possible explanation for this among spotted hyenas is that females secrete more of certain testosterone-related hormones than males do (Monahan and Glickman 1992, 264).

Among primates, male dominance is associated with physiological changes that influence mood and general health. For example, primatologist Robert Sapolsky (1988, 1992) has discovered that among wild baboons in Africa the level of stress hormones is low in dominant males but high in subordinate males. As a result, low-ranking males show signs of emotional distress and physical disability. Scientists have also discovered that dominant human males tend to have high levels of whole-blood serotonin (Madsen 1985, 1986). As Howard Bloom (1995) has argued, such physiological factors associated with social ranking could explain the vigorous elation of high-ranking men and the moody depression of low-ranking men. For example, it was noticed at the beginning of the Russian Revolution of 1917 that the Czar displayed a shocking decline in his health and physical appearance as he saw his power slipping away. When Count

Kokovtsov visited the czar on 19 January 1917, he "hardly recognized the Czar, so much had he aged. His face was thin, his cheeks sunken, his eyes almost without color, the whites yellow and the pupils gray and lifeless. They wandered vaguely from object to object" (Salisbury 1981, 380–81). By contrast, Alexander Kerensky, the initial leader in the revolutionary overthrow of the czar, impressed observers with his energetic appearance. Although we would need direct medical evidence to confirm our speculations, it seems likely that such sudden changes in human dominance ranking among competing males induce physiological changes that cripple the losers and invigorate the winners.

Even if there is some controversy about the exact neuroendocrinological mechanisms associated with sex differences, it is hard to deny Goldberg's claim that the universality of male dominance implies some universal pattern in human biology. Even people inclined to disagree with Goldberg—like Margaret Mead, a feminist anthropologist, and Eleanor Maccoby, a feminist psychologist—have accepted some of his fundamental conclusions. Mead agreed that no society had ever been ruled by women. "As far as we know," she declared, "men everywhere have been in charge of running the show." Even in matrilineal and matrilocal societies—where children inherit through their mother, and where husbands move to live with the family of their wives—"men have been the leaders in public affairs and the final authorities at home" (Mead 1973, 47). Similarly, Maccoby agreed that "the male is, on the average, more aggressive than the female, and this difference does have a biological basis." She also agreed "that males have been dominant in all human societies in recorded history," and this too has some biological basis, because it seems implausible that this universal pattern could emerge by historical accident (Maccoby 1973, 470). A recent survey of the biological and anthropological evidence confirms that male dominance and male violence are human universals rooted in human biology (Wrangham and Peterson 1996).

Against Goldberg, however, Mead and Maccoby asserted that the hitherto universal inclination to male dominance could disappear in the future through social, economic, and technological changes that bring about a social order in which men are not dominant. Goldberg's response was to insist that there is no evidence that such changes reduce the dominance of males in hierarchies. Even the most modern societies today have at least as much male dominance—as measured by the proportion of males in the highest positions of power—as do primitive societies. If there is any difference, it seems that some primitive societies actually have a lower level of male dominance than do modern societies, because modern bureaucratic states tend to be more hierarchical than small hunter-gatherer groups.

Even if male dominance is universal, however, it does not follow from this that all or even most men are more powerful than women. If most men desire dominance, and if most dominance hierarchies necessarily have only a few positions at the top, then most men will fail, and even those who succeed in rising to the top will live in constant fear of losing their dominant position to the many men ambitious to take their place. Male dominance thus brings with it male vulnerability. This is evident in the classic handbook for male dominance behavior, Niccolò Machiavelli's *The Prince:* the man who desires dominance, Machiavelli teaches, must be willing to deceive, coerce, or even kill the many men who are his rivals for power; and once he has achieved dominance, he must anticipate that many others will use the same unscrupulous techniques to replace him. The Machiavellian prince cannot trust anyone, and thus he must live a life based on fear rather than love. As we shall see in chapter 8, most psychopaths are men, which suggests that psychopathic behavior is only a very extreme form of typically male dispositions.

There are many signs of male vulnerability. In the United States today, men on average have a much shorter life expectancy than women, because men are more vulnerable to a wide variety of life-threatening dangers (Farrell 1993). Men die earlier than women from all fifteen leading causes of death. Men have a higher suicide rate. Except for rape, men are far more likely to be victims of violent crime. In every society, most cases of homicidal violence involve men killing men (Daly and Wilson 1988, 1990). In the United States, men suffer 94 percent of the occupational deaths, because the most hazardous jobs are filled mostly by men—jobs such as fire fighting, logging, construction, and mining. In every society, the risks of military combat have been born almost totally by men. In the United States, young men but not young women are required to register for the military draft. Of those who volunteer for military service, the men but not the women are required to be available for combat duty.

As Linda Mealey (1995) has indicated, the connection between male dominance and male vulnerability can be explained by a Darwinian theory of human desires. In evolutionary terms, the male pursuit of dominance is a high-risk strategy with high potential gains but also high potential losses. When males compete aggressively with other males for access to females and other resources that promote reproductive success, the risks of failure—such as being killed by another male—will be great.

Despite the harm that comes to both men and women from the male competition for dominance, it is an essential part of the moral nature of human beings. It is a mistake, therefore, to assume, as is often done, that human life would be better off if we could eliminate male competitiveness or at least subordinate it to female nurturance. The moral order of human nature rests on a rough balance between the predominantly male desire for dominance and the predominantly female desire for nurturance.

THE MORAL COMPLEMENTARITY
OF MALE AND FEMALE NORMS

Darwin gives two conflicting accounts of the relationship between male and female norms in the moral economy of human life. In one account, he defends a moral realism that combines typically male norms such as dominance and courage and typically female norms such as nurturance and sympathy, which he presents as complementary and interdependent inclinations of the human moral constitution. In the other account, he defends a moral utopianism that subordinates the male norms to the female norms, and he expands female sympathy into a disinterested sentiment of universal humanitarianism. Like Joseph Carroll (1995), I accept Darwin's moral realism and reject his moral utopianism.

As we have seen, Darwin believes that in human evolutionary history, the aggressive rivalry between men disposed the male to dominance and courage, while the maternal care required for women disposed the female to nurturance and sympathy. These moral dispositions were shaped by natural selection through tribal conflict, in which a tribal group was more likely to prevail over others if its members displayed "patriotism, fidelity, obedience, courage, and sympathy," which combined typically male and typically female dispositions (Darwin 1871, 1:166). In this way, natural selection favored those moral norms that allowed members of a group to cooperate with one another to compete with other groups. Male competitiveness is part of the moral nature of human beings. Male "spiritedness"—as found in both men and women—supports courage and other virtues necessary for group-against-group conflict. In evolutionary history, courage meant that individuals would fight for the interests of their tribal group against other groups. Sympathy meant that individuals would love those who were members of their tribal group and hate those who were not. "It is no argument against savage man being a social animal, that the tribes inhabiting adjacent districts are almost always at war with each other," Darwin explains, "for the social instincts never extend to all the individuals of the same species" (1871, 1:85). This is Darwin's moral realism.

In some parts of his writing, however, Darwin seeks a transcendent moral norm to escape this harsh vision of human moral nature as based on the competition of groups. As we have seen, he worries that male rivalry "leads to ambition which passes too easily into selfishness." So he looks to women's nature for a higher standard of morality that is less selfish and more selfless. A woman typically differs from a man "chiefly in her greater tenderness and less selfishness." Because of her "maternal instincts," a woman is most naturally inclined to show selfless care for her infants, but she will often extend this sympathetic care to her fellow human beings as well (1871, 2:326). Darwin imagines a history of moral progress in which female sympathy could be gradually extended from the family to small tribes, then to large nations, and eventually to all of humanity. "As man advances in civilization, and small tribes are united into larger communities, the simplest reason would tell each individual that he ought to extend his social instincts and sympathies to all the members of the same nation, though personally unknown to him. This point being once reached, there is only an artificial barrier to prevent his sympathies extending to the men of all nations and races." The most recent advance of sympathy extends it even beyond humanity to include the lower animals, so that now we can see "the most noble attribute of man" in the "disinterested love for all living creatures" (1871, 1:100–101, 1:105). This is Darwin's moral utopianism.

Joseph Carroll argues persuasively that Darwin's vacillation between realism and utopianism in his evolutionary theory of morality creates unresolvable contradictions. Darwin's realist view of morality as rooted in group loyalty, in which male and female norms are complementary, is consistent with Darwin's general determination to explain all of human life within the natural order as shared with all other living beings. But his utopian view of morality as rooted in a disinterested sentiment of universal sympathy, in which female norms prevail over male norms, manifests Darwin's yearning for a moral idealism in which human beings transcend nature through culture in developing their uniquely spiritual capacity for selfless altruism. Carroll shows that Darwin's moral utopianism, like that of his British contemporaries such as Matthew Arnold and George Eliot, derives from a tradition of Christian transcendental idealism, in which humanitarian sympathy was the peak of moral progress. Like Carroll, I think Darwin's moral theory would have been more consistent and more cogent if he had adhered strictly to his realist view of morality.

Darwin's moral reasoning shows the impossibility of sustaining, in any reasonable way, a utopian morality of universal sympathy. For example, Darwin felt great sympathy for the suffering of animals. He contributed regularly to the Royal Society for the Prevention of Cruelty to Animals, and he supported legislation to restrict unnecessary suffering in the scientific use of animals. But as a scientist who never hesitated to kill and dissect animals in his research, he criticized the fanatics who called for so restricting animal research that scientific experimentation with animals would be prohibited. In a public letter, he insisted: "I have all my life been a strong advocate for humanity to animals, and have done what I could in my writings to enforce this duty." On the other hand, he explained, "I know that physiology cannot possibly progress except by means of experiments on living animals, and I feel the deepest conviction that he who retards the progress of physiology commits a crime against mankind" (Darwin 1977, 2:226). So although Darwin believed human beings could feel sympathy for nonhuman animals, particularly those that resembled human beings in their mental capacities, and although he promoted such sympathy by showing how closely related human beings were to some other animals, he recognized that when human interests and animal interests were in conflict, human beings might properly prefer human interests (such as scientific experimentation to satisfy the human desire for understanding) over animal interests.

Furthermore, he also recognized—at least implicitly—that promoting humanitarian sympathy and understanding, oddly enough, meant favoring some human groups over others. After all, primitive human beings feel little sympathy for those outside their own tribe; and the very idea of humanity has emerged only recently in modern civilized societies. Throughout his writing, Darwin assumes that the expansion of the "civilized races" at the expense of "barbarians" and "savages" brings both moral and intellectual improvement. When Darwin saw the people of Tierra del Fuego, at the southern tip of South America, he was so shocked by their savage state, that he wondered whether they were fully human. "Viewing such men, one can hardly make oneself believe that they are fellow-creatures, and inhabitants of the same world" (Darwin 1962, 213). His own life as a scientist moved by a sympathetic desire to understand the order of all living beings depends on the international dominance of Western civilization as led by the English. He knows that only his kind of civilized society supports the intellectual leisure class to which he belongs, and without which there could be no life of the mind devoted to understanding for its own sake (Darwin 1871, 1:102, 1:167–69, 1:238–39).

I agree with Darwin that as a product of natural selection, a human being is a social animal inclined to social cooperation based on kinship and reciprocity, and therefore a human being "would from an inherited tendency still be willing to defend, in concert with others, his fellow-men, and would be ready to aid them in any way which did not too greatly interfere with his own welfare or his own strong desires." But as Darwin says, this natural sociality would "never extend to all the individuals of the same species" (Darwin 1871, 1:85). Darwin contradicts, therefore, this evolutionary theory of natural sociality when he asserts that sympathy can be extended "to the men of all nations and races," or that it can become a "disinterested love for all living creatures" (Darwin 1871, 1:101, 1:105). Joseph Carroll is correct, I think, in claiming that "as an adaptive characteristic of a viable species, sympathy can extend no farther than the boundaries set by collective self-interest" (1995, 368). Consequently, the natural sympathy of human beings is limited by their group identification. The natural sociality of human beings expresses itself as a love of one's own.

Darwin is wrong in thinking that female sympathy—as rooted in maternal care—can expand into a disinterested universal sentiment of humanity. After all, even maternal care manifests itself as a love of one's own offspring and a willingness to defend them against strangers. And although sympathy can be expanded to embrace ever-larger groups based on some sense of shared interests, this will always rest on loving one's own group as opposed to other groups. Darwin's appeal to universal humanitarianism can only be explained as a utopian yearning for an ideal moral realm that transcends nature, which contradicts Darwin's general claim that human beings are fully contained within the natural order.

Darwin's utopian expansion of sympathy into a disinterested sentiment of humanitarianism has become a recurrent theme in the Darwinian tradition. Thomas Huxley—in his famous essay, "Evolution and Ethics"—argued for a radical dualism in which the moral selflessness of human beings transcends their natural selfishness (Huxley 1894a). Contemporary sociobiological theorists such as George Williams (1989, 1993) and Richard Dawkins (1976) have adopted a similar view of morality as transcending biological nature. James Q. Wilson develops a purely natural explanation of the human moral sense as founded in human biology, but he also asserts that the fullest expression of morality is a universal sympathy for all of humanity that goes against human nature: "[U]niversalism is not natural, localism is" (Wilson 1993b, 197). Similarly, Dawkins suggests that because of our uniquely human capacity for "genuine, disinterested, true altruism," we can find ways of "deliberately cultivating and nurturing pure, disinterested altruism—something that has no place in nature, something that has never existed before in the whole history of the world" (Dawkins 1976). Like Darwin himself, Dawkins does not explain how this appeal to "something that has no place in nature" can be consistent with a Darwinian naturalism that accounts for human beings in purely natural terms. By contrast, Frans de Waal (1996, 212–16) recognizes that altruism as rooted in human nature must start with an obligation to oneself and one's own. We care first and most strongly for ourselves and those bound to us by ties of kinship and friendship. Our moral concern can expand to ever-wider circles to include our extended kin, our clan, our group, our nation, all of humanity, and perhaps even all life forms. But the expansion to the wider circles will occur only in those cases where our provisioning of the inner circles is secure. In extreme conditions, where we might be living on the edge of starvation, our moral concern is not likely to stretch much beyond ourselves and those closest to us.

The fundamental mistake of Darwinian utopianism is evident among the sociobiological theorists who identify morality with altruism and then define altruism as selfless behavior. As I suggested in chapter 4, this Kantian separation between natural selfishness and moral selflessness shows the influence of Augustinian asceticism. The assumption that morality requires self-denial, because our natural propensities are evil, supports what de Waal calls "Calvinist sociobiology" because it presumes an implicit acceptance of the doctrine of original sin and the natural depravity of human beings (de Waal 1996, 13–20).

Although they do not recognize themselves as part of a Darwinian tradition of moral utopianism, some feminists have argued for a "female ethics" in which an "ethics of caring" rooted in the woman's experience of maternal care would be extended to all of humanity as a disinterested sentiment (Noddings 1990). Yet such feminists must wonder whether there is a natural limit to female sympathy. So, for example, while Susan Okin declares that female sympathy can be expressed as a "universalizable concern for the welfare of humanity," she admits that such sympathy might be limited to a love of one's own: "It is essential that we know how far women's caring and responsibility extend. We must find out whether and to what extent women and men weigh differently the moral significance of the needs of a distant stranger—a 'far other'—and the needs of someone with whom they have a personal relationship—a 'near other'" (Okin 1990, 158–59).

The possibility that female sympathy can be expanded into a universal humanitarianism supports the hope of some people that some day war can be abolished. The historian John Keegan explains war as purely cultural, and suggests that a change in culture could produce perpetual peace through a culture of humanitarianism (Keegan 1993, 3–4, 58–60, 384–85). But I believe Thucydides and Carl von Clausewitz were more realistic in their belief that war could never disappear, because it is rooted in the natural desires of human beings as political animals. War has been a pervasive feature of human history, even among Paleolithic hunter-gatherers (Keeley 1996). Human beings will always be divided into political groups, and consequently, war will always remain a means of pursuing the political ends of conflicting groups. The clash of interests between political groups will induce human beings to go to war out of fear, interest, or honor (Thucydides, *The Peloponnesian War* 1.75; Clausewitz, *On War*, bk. 1, chap. 1; Howard 1983). Such motives include a sense of justice, because human beings will go to war to assert what they regard as just claims (Walzer 1977; Welch 1993).

The evidence of human history and the logic of human biology indicate that we are naturally inclined to feel more sympathy for those nearest to us than for strangers. Darwin's moral utopianism is mistaken, therefore, in assuming a universal humanitarianism. By contrast, Darwin's moral realism is well grounded in human nature. The typically female desire for nurturance promotes a natural human inclination to sympathy that sustains the social instincts. The typically male desire for dominance promotes a natural human inclination to aggressive self-assertion that sustains the spirited defense of one's group against opponents. The complementarity and interdependence of these typically male and female norms constitute a biological basis for morality.

But if I am right about this, if human beings are not bound together by a universal sentiment of disinterested humanitarianism, then deep conflicts of interest between individuals or between groups can create moral tragedies in which there is no universal moral principle or sentiment to resolve the conflict. When individuals or groups compete with one another, we must either find some common ground of shared interests, or we must allow for an appeal to force or fraud to settle the dispute. The only alternative, which I do not regard as a realistic alternative, is to invoke some transcendental norm of impartial justice (such as Christian charity) that is beyond the order of nature.

NATURAL GENITALS AND NATURAL FEET

Some feminists would seem to say that in the conflicts between men and women and between different cultural groups, there is no common ground of shared interests. If that is so, then there can be no resolution of such conflicts except through force or fraud in which one side exploits the other. I would argue, however, that even in the absence of a universal sympathy, there is a universal human nature—a universal pattern of human desires— to which all human beings can appeal in searching for shared interests to settle their disputes.

To illustrate how the prudent reform of patriarchal customs has to respect both nature and history in looking for shared interests between men and women, consider the custom of circumcision. To show the arbitrary power of custom in human life, the ancient historian Herodotus in his *History* (2.35, 2.103, 3.38) noted the many customs of the Egyptians that were contrary to customs elsewhere. One of the peculiar practices of the

Egyptians was the circumcision of the young. He believed this originated in Egypt (or perhaps Ethiopia) and was adopted by other people through diffusion from Egypt. He thought this confirmed the claim of Pindar: "Custom is king of all."

Most of us are familiar with male circumcision, but we are less familiar with female circumcision. In some parts of the world, a young woman at puberty (or earlier) is required by tradition to have someone cut off her clitoris with a knife or razor (clitoridectomy). In many cases, the sides of the vulva are sewn together, leaving only a tiny hole for the flow of urine and menstrual blood (infibulation). When she is married, the penetration of her husband's penis will slowly and painfully rip her open. Then, once she is pregnant, she may be sewn up again. In addition to the pain, many women die from this; and all are deprived of sexual pleasure. Mothers insist that their daughters have this done because otherwise no man will marry them. Men demand it because they think it guards virginity and dampens the sexual appetite that might tempt a wife to infidelity. In parts of Africa, the Middle East, and Southeast Asia, 60 to 100 million women have undergone this experience of clitoridectomy and infibulation (Koso-Thomas 1987; Lightfoot-Klein 1979, 1989; Perlez 1990).

What should we say about this? Two possible responses are suggested by the comments of Dr. Herant Katchadourian (1985, 32): "These practices, like male circumcision, have ancient roots. But while circumcision in no way incapacitates the male, it is a mutilating procedure in the female that seriously interferes with sexual function and poses serious health hazards. Yet the practice is defended on the grounds that cultures have the right to fashion their own rituals." If we call this practice female "mutilation," are we merely expressing an arbitrary value judgment grounded in Western culture? Does cultural diversity deprive us of any universal standards for condemning such practices? If we permit male circumcision, must we also tolerate female circumcision? Or should we argue, as Dr. Katchadourian does, that circumcision does not "incapacitate" the male as it does the female, because clitoridectomy not only threatens her health but also "interferes with sexual function" by removing the only human organ whose sole function is pleasure? Implicitly this argument appeals to biological universals that transcend cultural relativity: because of their biological nature, all women in all cultures have natural desires and capacities that are frustrated by such a practice, which is thus contrary to women's nature. We would expect that feminists would want to argue the second position so that they could condemn this practice as one more manifestation of the patriarchal oppression of women. But those feminists who have adopted cultural relativism, who have scorned appeals to biological nature in considering the meaning of human sexuality, cannot object to such a deeply rooted cultural tradition without contradicting themselves. The United States Congress has passed a law to make female circumcision a crime. But critics of the law regard it as an ethnocentric attack on the cultural values of Africans who have immigrated to the United States (Dugger 1996).

Hanny Lightfoot-Klein spent many years studying female circumcision, mostly in Sudan. She found that when people were asked to justify the practice, they offered four kinds of answers. They claimed it was rooted in (1) the power of custom, (2) the facts of sexual physiology and behavior, (3) tribal myths, (4) or Islamic religion (1989, 38–42). Olayinka Koso-Thomas (1987, 5–14) heard similar arguments in Sierra Leone. (1) The most common justification for female circumcision is that it is simply a custom that is too strong in the cultures where it prevails to be challenged without the punishment of social ostracism. Even when Lightfoot-Klein found a Muslim leader in Sudan who denounced female circumcision as a barbaric ancient custom, she was shocked to discover that he had had all of his daughters circumcised. "How was this possible in view of his stated beliefs? One could not go against custom, he said. Custom was too strong in the people. No one could defy custom" (1989, 14). When British colonial rulers prohibited female circumcision, their laws were ignored. Even after British withdrawal, native laws against the practice are commonly ineffective. When the World Health Organization and other international groups work to abolish the practice, many Africans scorn this as another ethnocentric imposition of Western European values on Africans. (2) Defenders of female circumcision often speak of its benefits for sexual health. The most common belief is that it protects women from their volatile sexual appetite, which would otherwise lead them to promiscuity and sexual madness. Other claims are that it serves as a birth control measure, that it increases female fertility, that it protects the penis from being poisoned by the clitoris, that it protects women from a variety of diseases and disorders (including kleptomania), and that it increases male sexual pleasure. (3) Tribal myths about the clitoris depict it as controlled by an evil power that can be destroyed only by cutting it off. (4) Finally, many of those who endorse female circumcision are Muslims who believe it is required by their religion.

How would the sciences of human biology help us to assess these justifications for female circumcision? Biological anthropologists understand the power of social ostracism in enforcing the customs of a group, and therefore they might appreciate the difficulty of resisting long-established customs (Gruter and Masters 1986). Sociobiological theories about the differences in male and female reproductive strategies might explain why such a custom has been established. Sarah Hrdy (1981, 184) writes:

> From a biological point of view, women can scarcely be said to benefit from this practice. Why, then, does the society subject women to an operation which both pains and endangers them? Why do men in some societies refuse to marry uncircumcised women? The obvious answer, recognized by feminists and sociobiologists alike, is that female circumcision increases the certainty of paternity and reduces the likelihood that a man will be cuckolded and thus tricked into supporting some other man's offspring. In fact, a commonly cited folk rationale for female circumcision is that the operation promotes chastity by reducing sexual desire.

Hrdy's explanation is misleading, however. That men who demand female circumcision *believe* it ensures the sexual fidelity of their wives is true, and this *belief* on the part of men would explain the practice. Yet whether this belief is *true* is unclear. Lightfoot-Klein reports that many young women engage in premarital promiscuity and then have themselves sewn up to look like virgins, and many circumcised wives are driven to extramarital promiscuity because their husbands cannot satisfy their sexual desires. Furthermore, many men become sexually frustrated or even impotent because circumcision makes intercourse a painful experience for their wives. Another problem is that female circumcision can make childbirth dangerous for both the mother and the child. For these and other reasons, this practice would seem, at least in many cases, to reduce the reproductive success and frustrate the natural desires of both men and women.

Moreover, since Hrdy makes much of the clitoris as the only human organ that has no purpose other than pleasure, and since she stresses the importance of clitoral orgasm as a functional adaptation in the evolution of female sexuality, she gives us good reasons to believe that interfering with that part of female nature will frustrate women in ways that can only be harmful to men as well as women. Even if clitoral orgasm is not an evolutionary adaptation for the female but an incidental effect of penile orgasm as a functional adaptation for the male (Symons 1979), this would not change the fact that clitoral organism is now a potential of female nature that cannot be denied without cost. Although Stephen Jay Gould (1991, 124–38) believes clitoral orgasm is not an evolutionary adaptation, he can properly condemn Sigmund Freud for causing "needless pain and anxiety" in advising women that sexual maturity requires a transfer from clitoral orgasm to vaginal orgasm. Lightfoot-Klein found evidence that some circumcised females were capable of vaginal orgasms, but few women would find this to be sufficient compensation for the painful consequences of clitoridectomy.

Scientific knowledge about the sexual nature of women denies most, if not all, the reasons given for female circumcision. The clitoris is not dangerous either to women or to men. Clitoridectomy does not increase fertility, and it is not an effective method of birth control. In fact, Lightfoot-Klein reports that as people become more educated about the scientific facts of sexuality, they reject female circumcision. Even the appeals to custom and religion can be challenged. Customs can be changed, and the practice of female circumcision has been abolished in many countries where it was previously customary. The belief that Islamic religion dictates this practice is incorrect: the Koran says nothing about it, and there is some evidence that the Prophet Mohammed tried to mitigate this custom by abolishing it or suggesting that there should be only minor cuts on the genitals. In most Islamic countries today, few practice any form of female circumcision.

In judging a customary practice like female circumcision, we must understand the intricate interaction of nature and history. We must consider the peculiar historical conditions that would support such a custom and make it difficult to change. Yet we must also consider the universal nature of men and women—the natural constitution of desires and powers—that might be either expressed or frustrated by such a custom. Perhaps the natural desire of males to control the sexuality of women to secure their paternal investment explains why some men would adopt such a practice. Yet the fact that it interferes so severely with the natural desires of women indicates that the human costs are so high for both women and men that its putative benefits do not justify it.

Practices such as female circumcision seem so utterly foolish that it is hard to explain why women would submit to such unnecessary pain. But any practice that has been accepted by many people for a long time probably originated to satisfy some natural desires. Before condemning such practices and seeking to abolish them, prudence would dictate that we understand how they conform to the ecological circumstances of some societies. Understanding the social conditions that make such practices seem reasonable allows us to work for prudent reforms by changing the social conditions.

Jane Lancaster (1997) has shown that in small-scale societies with little social stratification, men compete for sexual access to fertile women. In such social conditions, men will offer various kinds of "bride wealth" to win the chance to mate with young women, a pattern of behavior found in many societies. By contrast, Lancaster explains, in societies with great social stratification, some men will have greater control than others over the resources that women need to provide for their children, and consequently, young women and their families will compete for marriages with the high-status men whose wealth and power would make them the best husbands and fathers. When men are resource holders, women and their families will "pay" for high-quality grooms. Most men will want wives who are fertile. But beyond that, high-status men can demand various kinds of payment in the form of a dowry. Such men can also demand some guarantee of the virginity and chastity of potential wives, because men do not want to invest their wealth and power in supporting other men's offspring. In such circumstances, women will compete with one another in adopting practices that seem to increase a man's confidence in the paternity of his children. Secluding and guarding women seems to make it difficult for men other than their husbands to have access to them. Veiling women in clothing that covers up their bodies seems to make it less likely that they will arouse another man's sexual interest. Women must then submit to such restrictions on their freedom and comfort to win and keep a marriage to a desirable male.

In some societies of this sort, women will engage in painful practices that appear to guarantee their virginity as brides and their fidelity as wives. Footbinding in China made women desirable as mates for high-status men because it impeded the women's movement so that secret acts of sexual infidelity were less likely (Levy 1966). In some cases, the binding of the feet of young girls was so severe in distorting the growth of the feet that the women could not even walk without help.

Female circumcision would seem to have a similar purpose. The cutting off of a woman's clitoris and the sewing up of her vagina seem to reduce her sexual pleasure and thus suppress her inclination to any sexual contact outside of her marriage. Like many other customs that restrict the freedom of women, female circumcision is designed by women and their families to reassure men with resources that a woman's children have been conceived by her husband and not by another man.

Those who condemn female circumcision as a brutal violation of women's rights often fail to see its purpose in the societies where it is practiced. It is certainly a painful custom, but for the women who practice it, there may be no alternative if they want to marry men willing and able to support them and their children. The most common justification for female circumcision is that it curbs the unruly sexual appetite of women and thus reassures their fathers and husbands that they will be faithful wives. In 1996, the Egyptian government banned female circumcision, but many people resisted the law. "Am I supposed to stand around while my daughter chases men?" complained one Egyptian farmer. "So what if some infidel doctor says it is unhealthy? Does that make it true? I would have circumcised my daughter even if they passed a death sentence against it" (MacFarquhar 1996).

The only prudent way to abolish such a deeply rooted custom is to gradually change the social and economic conditions of a society so that women do not have to compete for marriages to high-status males. As the economic development of a society creates new opportunities for women, so that they are less dependent on high-status men, women feel less need to submit to genital mutilation to attract suitable mates.

Clitoridectomy and infibulation are painful to women because they frustrate women's natural desires for sexual pleasure and bodily health. Yet some women will endure such pain—and impose it on their daughters—if they think this is the only way women can satisfy their natural desires for stable mating and successful parenting.

Gradual reform could eventually abolish cultural practices like female circumcision. How this could be done is illustrated by the history of footbinding in China. Until the first decades of the twentieth century, it was a common custom in China for the feet of young girls to be wrapped so tightly that the toes were bent into the sole in such a way that many women were crippled for life (Levy 1966). Men would refuse to marry women whose feet were not bound. Like female circumcision, it seems that the original and fundamental purpose of female footbinding was to increase the husband's confidence in his wife's fidelity, because women with crippled feet could not easily wander from home in the pursuit of sexual affairs. Yet although this custom was traditional for centuries in China, it was abolished within a few decades. The popular campaign against footbinding was based on the argument that footbinding was "unnatural," and that "natural feet" were desirable for both men and women. The Natural Foot Society was founded in 1895. This and similar groups engaged in three kinds of activity (Levy 1966; Mackie 1996). They promoted an educational campaign on the advantages of natural feet and the disadvantages of bound feet. They showed that the rest of the world did not practice footbinding, and that China was losing respect in the world because of it. Finally, following the example of American temperance societies campaigning against alcohol, members of natural foot societies pledged neither to bind their daughters nor to allow their sons to marry women with bound feet.

The moral controversies surrounding female circumcision and footbinding illustrate what I have identified in chapter 2 as the four sources of moral disagreement: fallible beliefs about circumstances, fallible beliefs about desires, variable circumstances, and variable desires. Drawing on the Gerry Mackie's (1996) comparative study of female circumcision and footbinding, I would offer the following analysis. Most human beings have a strong natural desire to care for their biological children. Therefore, they will tend to support the social practices they believe to be conducive to satisfying that parental desire. Since men are often unsure of their paternity, they will support those practices that they believe will promote the fidelity of their wives, because this gives men confidence that the children in their families are really their own. Since women often compete for access to mates with the resources necessary for raising children successfully, women will want to show evidence that they are likely to be faithful wives, because this will attract mates willing and able to invest resources in the women's children. In highly stratified societies with polygynous mating systems, high-status men will demand fidelity from their many wives, and women will compete with one another in offering signs of such fidelity. In ancient China, it was believed that binding the feet of women would reduce the chances of their being unfaithful to their husbands. Similarly, in parts of

Africa, it has been believed that female circumcision would have the same effect. Consequently, high-status Chinese men preferred to mate with women whose feet had been bound, and high-status African men preferred to mate with women who had been circumcised. Women had to accept these painful practices because otherwise they could not satisfy their desire to mate with men with whom they could successfully raise children. Even if these practices originally promoted female fidelity, they were maintained by social custom long after they had ceased to serve this purpose. For most men, and particularly men with only one wife or few wives, footbinding and female circumcision were not necessary to ensure the paternity of their children. On the contrary, these practices probably interfered with the parental desires of most men and women by threatening the health of women in ways that reduced their fertility, productivity, and longevity. Yet the false belief that footbinding and female circumcision promoted parental desires would sustain these practices.

Therefore, to abolish these practices we would have to expose the falsity of the beliefs supporting them. Any prudent reform movement would also have to organize a sufficiently large number of people to accept the change so that the practices would no longer be enforced by social conformity. Following the pattern of the successful campaign in China against footbinding, we could argue that just as natural feet are better than bound feet, natural genitals are better than mutilated genitals, because bound feet and mutilated genitals create unnecessary suffering for both men and women in frustrating their natural desires for mating and parenting. To support this argument, we could show that most human societies do not practice female circumcision. We could then encourage those in societies where this is still a common practice to join associations of people who pledge not to circumcise their daughters nor to allow their sons to marry circumcised women.

Such a reform movement assumes that social customs can be judged by how well they conform to human desires such as mating and parenting that are universal because they belong to human nature. Feminists who are cultural determinists—who assume that mating and parenting are cultural constructions that vary arbitrarily from one culture to another—cannot embrace such moral reform without contradicting themselves. They might say that practices such as female genital mutilation violate the "human rights" of women. But how can there be "human rights" if there is no human nature?

FEMINIST CULTURALISM

I regard ethics as a natural science, because it is a science of factual judgments about human nature. I believe, therefore, that the science of human biology can contribute to ethical debate insofar as it illuminates the facts of human nature. This is illustrated in the debate over feminism, since biology helps us to understand the nature of men and women. In arguing against my position, however, Linda Fedigan (1992) and Barbara Smuts (1992), both of whom are biological anthropologists and feminists, assume that ethics is a cultural construction that dictates normative judgments about what ought to be the case rather than what is the case.

If "men ought to be just in their treatment of women" is an example of a normative judgment, men might ask, "Why should we be just?" Smuts answers: because "the subjugation of one class of people to the will of another is wrong, no matter what." No matter what? "Is it wrong to treat women as domestic servants incapable of thinking for themselves," the men might respond, "if in fact that's what they're best suited for?" "Furthermore, even if it were wrong, why shouldn't we continue to exploit them as long as we have the power to do so?" At this point, feminists might explain that the men's view of women as fitted only for domestic servitude is incorrect, and they might also explain that treating women as the free and intelligent beings that they are ultimately promotes the happiness of men as well as women. These are factual and not normative judgments. The normative judgments without the factual judgments are empty and unconvincing. The factual judgments without the normative judgments are more likely to convince the men to act justly. Of course, if the factual judgments supporting sexual justice are false, if women really are naturally fitted only for domestic service, and if men's happiness depends on treating women as such, then the case for feminist ethics is unpersuasive.

Consider, once more, the example of female circumcision. Stephen Marglin is an economist at Harvard University. Acting as a research advisor to an international institute on development economics sponsored by the United Nations, he suggests that female circumcision might be defended by Africans with the claim that uncircumcised women bear defective offspring. He explains that this reasoning "may be as well-grounded empirically as any proposition of Western science: if parents, uncles, aunts, grandparents—not to mention the larger society—believe that the offspring of uncircumcised women are inferior, these unfortunate children may be reared in just the fashion that confirms their inferiority" (1990, 14). The general principle at work here, he contends, is manifested in every society, modern as well as traditional: "[R]eality is socially constructed, and belief creates its own truth." Therefore, Westerners who condemn female circumcision are being "ethnocentric."

Feminists who are cultural relativists—who argue that sexual identity is constructed by culture, and that there is no standard in human nature for ranking one culture as better or worse than another—cannot condemn the custom of female circumcision without contradicting themselves. When Alice Walker produced a film documentary on female circumcision in Africa, she was told by many African women that this practice was one of their deeply rooted traditional customs. When Walker criticized the practice as "genital mutilation," she was accused of "cultural imperialism," because it seemed that she was imposing a foreign standard from her American culture on an African culture that did not share her standard. Yet Walker rejected this criticism: "This reluctance to interfere with other cultures leaves African children at risk of mutilation. If we do not speak out, we collude in the perpetuation of this violence. There is no virtue in upholding, even unwittingly, the tradition of female genital mutilation" (Walker and Parmar 1993, 95). At the Fourth World Conference on Women, held in Beijing in 1995, there was a spirited debate over whether condemning female circumcision was an "ethnocentric" attack on African culture. One woman declared: "The function of culture and tradition is to provide a framework for human well-being. If they are used against us, we will reject them" (Crossette 1995). Such an appeal to "human well-being" as a universal standard for judging cultures implies a universal human nature, because it assumes a universal pattern of natural human desires that is violated by practices such as female circumcision.

I would agree that prudence dictates respect for customary practices like female circumcision that cannot be immediately changed or abolished without social disorder. Nevertheless, when women learn that the clitoris is not by nature dangerous to their offspring or to anyone else, they can look for ways to change a custom that harms them unnecessarily, although the opportunities for change will depend upon their ecological circumstances. The normative judgment that women ought to follow the custom of circumcision rests on factual beliefs that can be challenged as false.

And yet, what would we say if the men advocating female circumcision admitted that the true reason for this practice is that it allows them to promote their interests by controlling the sexuality of women? Fedigan and Smuts would seem to say this is factually right although normatively wrong. I would agree with Smuts that ethics arises from conflicts of interest in the search for confluences of interest. I would argue, however, that determining these conflicts and confluences of interest is a factual matter. I have suggested that female circumcision is probably not completely successful in controlling female sexuality, and even if it is, it probably frustrates the sexual and familial desires of men as well as women. In fact, many men in societies with female circumcision have found that sexual intercourse is more pleasurable for them if their wives have not been mutilated. Abolishing female circumcision would seem, therefore, to be in the interests of both men and women. If I am wrong, if the conflict of interests here between men and women is so deep that there are no overriding shared interests, then we find ourselves in a tragic dilemma that will be settled not through ethics and persuasion but through force and fraud.

What alternative is there? Fedigan and Smuts seem to say that when there are radical conflicts of interest, we can invoke ethical norms, with no grounding in empirical reality, which transform human beings into selfless creatures who act for the benefit of others with no compensating benefit for themselves. I would argue, by contrast, that a Darwinian view of ethics would teach that human beings are moved by self-love; yet, as social animals, they are also moved, as an extension of their self-love, to love those attached to them by various social bonds. Not only is self-love opposed to selflessness, it is also opposed to selfishness understood as the myopic disregard for one's social needs.

Of course, natural self-love inclines some human beings to exploit their fellow human beings whenever they can get away with it. Some men desire to exploit women, and masters desire to exploit slaves. But if Darwin is right about the natural moral sense, we can predict that the natural desire of some to exploit others will be checked by the natural desire of their victims to resist exploitation.

CHAPTER 7

MASTER AND SLAVE

Children are naturally adapted to elicit parental care from adults, and parents are naturally adapted to provide such care. Men and women are naturally adapted for mating and conjugal bonding. But slaves are not naturally adapted for serving their masters. Parental care and marriage conform to natural right because they satisfy natural desires for social attachment. Slavery violates natural right because it frustrates the natural desire to be free from exploitation.

In this chapter, I extend my argument for Darwinian natural right by applying it to the history of slavery. I begin with a comparison of ant slavery and human slavery, in which I argue that while slavery among ants and human beings manifests a natural inclination to exploitation, the uniquely human opposition to slavery shows a natural moral sense that resists exploitation. I then argue that throughout the history of the debate over slavery—from Aristotle to David Hume, to Thomas Jefferson, to Charles Darwin, to Abraham Lincoln—one can see the natural moral sense expressed as a joint product of emotional capacities for feeling moral passions like sympathy and anger and rational capacities for judging moral principles like kinship and reciprocity.

These emotional and rational capacities have been shaped by natural selection in human evolutionary history. By nature, human beings are social animals who organize their social life around caring for kin and reciprocal exchange with those who are not kin. In their evolutionary past, sympathy—the capacity for being affected by the feelings of others—enabled human beings to survive and reproduce in societies based on kinship and reciprocity. Sympathy inclines human beings to help one another or at least to refrain from cruelty and to punish those who are cruel. Sympathy originated in the natural bonding of parents and children, which was then extended to all close relatives. Beyond kinship, sympathy was extended to unrelated friends and acquaintances who were bound together by relations of reciprocal exchange, in which people do good for others with some expectation of receiving some good in return. The norms of reciprocity are enforced by natural moral passions such as anger, indignation, and gratitude.

Slavery is therefore a moral problem for human beings because it violates those moral sentiments that arise from sympathy and reciprocity.

Wherever slavery has been practiced, people have either recognized the injustice of the practice, or they have felt compelled to justify it by arguing that those enslaved were not fully human. Slavery would be justified if slaves were fitted by nature for slavery—if they were unable to care for themselves and were naturally adapted to become mere extensions of their master's will, if they lacked the minimal emotional and rational capacities necessary for a moral sense that resists exploitation and demands reciprocity. But in fact human beings are not like that. All human beings, or at least all those not suffering from some abnormal deformity in their emotional and rational capacities, are naturally inclined to assert their independence as human beings with a moral sense governed by sympathy and reciprocity. Consequently, the practice of slavery has always displayed the fundamental contradiction of treating some human beings as if they were not human.

ANT SLAVERY AND HUMAN SLAVERY

Colonies of the honeypot ant species *Myrmecocystus mimicus* conduct ritualized tournaments in fighting for territory. If one colony is weaker than the other, the weaker colony will often be enslaved by the stronger colony (Hölldobler 1976; Hölldobler and Wilson 1990, 219–20, 406–15, 453; Hölldobler and Wilson 1994, 67–73, 87, 126). This is unusual in that the slavemakers and the slaves belong to the same species. In most cases of ant slavery, slavemaking ants enslave ants belonging to a different but closely related species. It might seem that calling this more common pattern "slavery" suggests a false comparison to human slavery, since human beings enslave members of their own species. Ants enslaving members of another species might seem more like human domestication of cattle, horses, and other nonhuman animals. Slavery among the honeypot ants, however, conforms to the human definition of slavery: "subjugation and forced labor of members of the same species" (Hölldobler and Wilson 1994, 126).

Considering the similarities and differences between ant slavery and human slavery illuminates the biological nature of slavery. The similarities suggest that slavery among ants and humans is rooted in a natural inclination to exploitation. The differences suggest that the uniquely human opposition to slavery is rooted in a natural moral sense that resists exploitation.

When the foraging territories of two *Myrmecocystus* colonies overlap, workers from both colonies engage in a tournament of ritualized combat. They walk with a stiltlike posture and raise their heads to look larger than they are. They then go through an elaborate ceremony of mutual intimidation. Real fights are usually fatal, but this rarely occurs during these tournaments that test the strength of the competing colonies without actual combat. Scouts repeatedly return to their nests to recruit workers to the tournament. The stronger colonies can bluff their neighbors away from disputed ground and thus expand their territory. If one colony is much smaller than another and cannot recruit enough workers to the battleground, the weaker colony can be overrun and raided by the stronger colony.

In a raid, the ants engage in real fighting, using mandibular teeth and chemical weapons to kill or cripple their opponents. The raiding ants force their way into the opponent's nest. They kill the queen and capture the larvae, pupae, and youngest adult workers. These captives are taken back to the nest of the raiders. Many of the captives are eaten by the victors. Those captives who remain alive become slave laborers in the nest of the captors. The slaves do all the necessary work for the colony such as foraging for food, rearing the brood, and maintaining the nest. Biologists identify slavemaking ants as "social parasites," who live by exploiting the labor of their slaves.

Such behavior might seem to contradict Darwin's theory of evolution by natural selection. Ants who labor as slaves in foreign colonies will produce no offspring, and they are not even related to the brood they feed and rear. One might think that natural selection would eliminate such behavior, since it deprives the slave ants of any reproductive benefits. But then one could see a similar difficulty for Darwin's theory even in ant colonies without slaves, because the female workers are sterile, and the queen is the only female who reproduces. The workers seem to sacrifice their reproductive interests in caring for the queen's offspring rather than producing offspring of their own.

Darwin admitted that the sterility of worker ants was "one special difficulty, which at first appeared to me insuperable, and actually fatal to the whole theory" (1936a, 203). Yet he thought he could overcome the difficulty by arguing that selection can work on the family as well as the individual. If sterile workers enhance the reproductive success of a family as a whole, then the fertile individuals might pass on to their offspring a tendency for some individuals to be sterile workers (1936a, 204–7). Natural selection might thus favor some individuals sacrificing their personal reproduction to advance the reproductive fitness of close relatives.

A hundred years after he first offered this explanation, Darwin's idea was rendered more precise by an insight of William D. Hamilton (1964). Because of the unusual reproductive system of the social insects, sisters tend to share more genes with one another than with their own offspring, so that sterile sisters who promote the production of more sisters by the queen can indirectly increase their reproductive fitness beyond what they could do as fertile individuals producing their own offspring. The apparently self–sacrificial behavior of the sterile workers is therefore an example of what biologists now call "kin selection": animals will be selected to help close relatives because relatives share genes. It is easy to understand how natural selection favors parents who sacrifice for their offspring, because the genes of the parents are passed on through their offspring. The same logic can explain why animals sacrifice for close relatives who are not their direct offspring, because the sharing of genes applies to relatives other than offspring.

This might not appear to explain ant slavery, however, since the slaves sacrifice themselves for ants that are not their close relatives. How could this emerge by natural selection? Darwin knew that some ants that were not slavemakers raided the nests of other species to seize and eat pupae. He speculated that some of the stolen pupae stored for food might develop into adults and then assume the duties normally performed by workers. If this slave labor proved advantageous to the ants that seized the pupae, then natural selection might eventually promote slave-raiding as a permanent instinct (1936a, 193–96). Natural selection would thus favor the inclination of the slavemaking ants to exploit the labor of potential slaves.

Contemporary myrmecologists such as Bert Hölldobler and Edward O. Wilson believe that Darwin's emphasis on predatory raids as the first step toward slavery is only part of the explanation. Hölldobler and Wilson identify territorial behavior as the prime mover leading to slavery, although predatory raids are also important in their story of how slavery could have evolved: "[T]erritorial raids combined with a strong propensity to transport brood lead to the regular retrieval of alien brood back to the raiders' nest; the raiders destroy and eat most of the captives, but a few survive to join the colony as slave workers" (1990, 452).

Yet why do the slave ants allow themselves to be exploited without resistance? Darwin could not answer this question, because only recently have myrmecologists begun to understand the importance of chemical communication in ant societies. If the cooperation of ants in a nest is explained as a form of nepotism, in that the ants are cooperating to help close relatives, this implies that there must be some mechanism for distinguishing relatives and strangers. Ants must be able to recognize their relatives so that they can discriminate against strangers. Recent research indicates that they smell the difference (Hölldobler and Wilson 1990, 197–208; Hölldobler and Wilson 1994, 101–6). Every ant colony has a distinctive odor that must be learned by each ant from an early age through some process of "olfactory imprinting." Consequently, when pupae are seized in a slave raid and taken to the slavemakers' nest, the emerging slaves form social attachments to the slavemakers because the slaves identify the odor of the alien colony as their own (Moli and Mori 1985; Topoff 1990).

The social organization of an ant colony, as based on caring for close relatives, depends on a few simple chemical cues for distinguishing relatives and strangers. Although this system of chemical communication usually works amazingly well, it also exposes some ants to exploitation by social parasites who manipulate the chemical code, as when slave ants are tricked into treating slavemaking ants as if they were kin.

The similarities between ant slavery and human slavery suggest that in both cases slavery arises as a natural form of social parasitism in which slavemakers exploit their slaves through coercion and manipulation. Just as ant slavery emerges from the coercion of territorial warfare in which the stronger colony enslaves some of the ants of the weaker colony, human slavery can often be traced back to the coercion of war in which victors enslave their captives. Orlando Patterson, in his sociological history of slavery, observes: "Archetypically, slavery was a substitute for death in war" (1982, 5). And just as ant slavery depends on the manipulation of the slave ants through deceptive communication so that they adopt the slavemakers as if they were relatives, human masters promote the false conception of human slavery as a paternalistic relationship in which masters rule over slaves as parents rule over their children (Genovese 1976). Such similarities indicate to Patterson that human slavery can best be understood as "human parasitism," which resembles other forms of social parasitism studied by biologists (1982, 334–42).

Yet the differences between ant slavery and human slavery suggest that human beings are naturally inclined to detect and resist exploitation through slavery. Edward O. Wilson believes the failure of human slavery in contrast to ant slavery illustrates how human nature asserts itself against cultural practices that are oppressive. If human slaves could be molded by the culture of slavery to accept their slavery as fully as those ants for which slavery is automatic, then human slavery could become permanent and free of conflict. This does not happen, because "slaves under great stress insist on behaving like human beings instead of slave ants" (Wilson 1978, 81). Human slaves, for example, maintain their bonds of true kinship in opposition to the bonds of fictive kinship promoted by the paternalistic ideology of the masters. Human nepotistic behavior depends on mental capacities— rational capacities for recognizing kin and emotional capacities for feeling attachment to kin—that are not as easily deceived as the ant system of chemical cues for kinship organization.

Furthermore, human sociality, as Darwin recognized, is based not just on nepotism as supporting cooperation among relatives but also on reciprocity as supporting cooperation even among those who are not relatives. As with other animals, the primordial root of social cooperation among human beings is parental care. "The feeling of pleasure from society," Darwin believed, "is probably an extension of the parental or filial affections, since the social instinct seems to be developed by the young remaining for a long time with the parents" (1936b, 478). Darwin also believed that human beings shared with their primate ancestors an inclination to mutual aid in social activities such as hunting and defense against predators (1936b, 473–80, 497–99). As the mental faculties of human ancestors improved, they would see the advantage of social cooperation founded on reciprocal exchange: "[E]ach man would soon learn that if he aided his fellow-men, he would commonly receive aid in return" (1936b, 499). These social inclinations to parental care, mutual aid, and reciprocal exchange require both rational capacities such as recognizing relatives and neighbors as distinguished from strangers and emotional capacities such as sympathy and anger.

Although rooted in social inclinations that human beings share with other animals, the moral sense is uniquely human because it arises from uniquely human mental capacities for reflection and speech applied to certain social passions. "A moral being," Darwin concluded, "is one who is capable of reflecting on his past actions and their motives—of approving of some and disapproving of others; and the fact that man is the one being who certainly deserves this designation is the greatest of all distinctions between him and the lower animals" (1936b, 912).

Contemporary Darwinian theorists argue that the moral sense emerges as the joint product of both rational and emotional capacities (McGuire 1992; Masters 1992). Human beings have the rational capacity to formulate parental care and reciprocity as norms of conduct. They also have the emotional capacity to enforce these norms through moral passions such as love, gratitude, guilt, shame, anger, and indignation. They can feel love and gratitude towards friends who have helped them. They can feel guilt and shame when they betray their friends. And they can feel anger and indignation against friends who betray them. Of course, the same complex mental abilities that support this moral sense can also be used for deceptive exploitation that violates the moral sense. Cheaters will use rational manipulation to hide the true character of their exploitation—not only in deceiving others but also in deceiving themselves so as better to deceive others. At the same time, however, their potential victims will try to detect and punish their manipulative exploitation (Trivers 1971, 1985).

For social animals, social cooperation is the fundamental condition for life. A social parasite can secure the benefits of social cooperation without the costs by becoming a "free rider" in exploiting the cooperative work of others without contributing any work in return. This strategy succeeds, however, only as long as the parasite can coerce or manipulate other animals into being exploited. By contrast, a social animal that bears some of the costs of cooperation to secure the benefits enters into social relationships based on reciprocity: an animal gets what it wants only if others get what they want.

As social animals, human beings face the same choice—exploitation or reciprocity—but they do so in a more reflective or self-conscious way than is possible for other animals. Human beings can rationally formulate reciprocity as a norm for social conduct and then emotionally enforce that norm through social passions that support reciprocity and punish exploitation. Like other social animals, human beings are naturally inclined to exploitation through coercion and manipulation. But human beings are also naturally inclined to detect and punish exploitation. As social animals, we cannot live without social cooperation. To secure the cooperation of others, we must either win their cooperation by being cooperative ourselves, or we must exploit their cooperation without cooperating with them in return. To exploit the cooperative behavior of others, we must either coerce them or manipulate them.

The debate over human slavery illustrates this conflict between the natural inclination to exploitation through coercion and manipulation and the natural inclination to resist exploitation through the moral sense. Consider, for example, the decision of Judge Thomas Ruffin in 1829 in the North Carolina Supreme Court case of *State v Mann*. A lower court had held that a master could be charged with committing "a cruel and unreasonable battery" upon his slave, just as a parent could be charged with abusing a child. In reversing this decision, Judge Ruffin denied that the master's authority could be limited like parental authority:

> There is no likeness between the cases. They are in opposition to each other, and there is an impassable gulf between them—the difference is that which exists between freedom and slavery—and a greater cannot be imagined. In the one the end in view is the happiness of the youth born to equal rights with that governor on whom the duty devolves of training the young to usefulness in a status which he is afterwards to assume among free men.
>
> With slavery it is far otherwise. The end is the profit of the master, his security and public safety; the subject, one doomed in his own person, and his posterity, to live without knowledge, and without the capacity to make anything his own, and to toil that another may reap the fruits. What moral considerations, such as a father might give to a son, shall be addressed to such a being, to convince him what, it is impossible but that the most stupid must feel and know can never be true—that he is thus to labour upon a principle of natural duty, or for the sake of his own personal happiness, such services can only be expected from one who has no will of his own; who surrenders his will in implicit obedience to that of another. Such obedience is the consequence only of uncontrolled authority over the body. There is nothing else which can operate to produce the effect. The power of the master must be absolute to render the submission of the slave perfect. I must freely confess my sense of the harshness of this proposition; I feel it as deeply as any man can. And as a principle of moral right, every man in his retirement must repudiate it. But in the actual condition

of things, it must be so. There is no remedy. The discipline belongs to the state of slavery. (Genovese 1976, 35)

Ruffin's opinion is often quoted by historians of slavery as a remarkably honest statement of the nature of slavery as exploitation based on the rule of force. "Never has the logic of slavery been followed so faithfully," Eugene Genovese (1976, 35) declares. Orlando Patterson believes that Ruffin "articulated better than any other commentator before or after, the view that the master-slave relationship originated in and was maintained by brute force," and the accuracy of this view is confirmed by the fact that "there is no known slaveholding society where the whip was not considered an indispensable instrument" (1982, 3–4).

As exploitation in which the slaves are forced to labor for benefit of the masters, human slavery is like ant slavery. Unlike ants, however, human beings are endowed by nature with a moral sense that detects and resists exploitation. Slave ants can be tricked by deceptive chemical cues into serving their masters as if they were relatives. Unlike ants, human beings rely more on verbal communication than chemical communication in organizing social life. Just as ants use odors to create social bonds, human beings use words. Just as ants use chemical signals to induce one another to join cooperative endeavors, human beings use rhetorical persuasion to set and enforce the norms of social cooperation. Lawyers and judges like Ruffin are experts in the use of such rhetoric. Since human beings regard kinship as a basis for natural rights and duties, human masters employ rhetorical persuasion to justify their authority over slaves as comparable to the authority of parents over children. Yet this can never fully succeed, because human beings can see, as does Judge Ruffin, that such rhetoric is deceptive in that "there is no likeness between the cases."

Human beings like Judge Ruffin can see the exploitative reality of condemning the slave "to toil that another may reap the fruits." This could be justified only if the slave were truly "one who has no will of his own." The emotional constitution of human beings inclines them to feel disgust at such injustice. "I feel it as deeply as any man can. And as a principle of moral right, every person in his retirement must repudiate it."

Human beings like Judge Ruffin can recognize that forcing one person "to toil that another may reap the fruits" could never be adopted as a "principle of moral right," because this would violate the principle of reciprocity that makes it possible for human beings to cooperate for mutual benefit. The demand for reciprocity is so deeply rooted in human nature that someone like Judge Ruffin feels the injustice of slavery even as he upholds the practice of slavery as an institution that supports his way of life.

Of course, many defenders of slavery who lack Ruffin's tragic sense of his moral predicament have tried to deceive themselves as well as others into believing that their slaves are naturally adapted for slavery. But, as I hope to show in my survey of the debate over slavery from Aristotle to Jefferson to Darwin, such deception must fail as long as human beings can see that slavery cannot be morally justified as rooted in kinship or reciprocity, and therefore slavery can only be exploitation rooted in coercion or manipulation.

ARISTOTLE

As a biologist, Aristotle saw a natural continuity between human beings and other animals, not only in their bodies but also in their emotional and intellectual capacities (Arnhart 1990). Like other animals, human beings are adapted for survival and reproduction. And like other social animals, the social bonding of human beings is rooted in parental care for the young. "Consequently, in the household are first found the origins and springs of friendship, of polity, and of justice" (*EE* 1242b1–2).

Kinship, then, is the primordial social bond. Beyond kinship, unrelated individuals develop attachments through a reciprocal exchange of benefits. A sense of affiliation *(philia)* arises among animals when there is a reciprocity of fellow-feeling. The recipient of a benefit is expected to return the equivalent of what he has received. Social conflict arises when people think this reciprocity has not been maintained (*NE* 1155b34, 1162b22–65b37). Not only personal friendships but also political communities are held together by reciprocal relationships. If people cannot repay good for good, they cannot be bound together by relations of exchange. If they cannot repay evil for evil, they resent being treated as slaves (*NE* 1132b33–33a5). Natural moral passions such as gratitude, anger, and indignation express this human sense of justice as reciprocity (*NE* 1125b31–26a8; *Rh* 1374a17–25, 1378a31–80b33, 1386b9–87b21). Every community rests on some sense of affiliation founded on the common advantage of its members. Although the strongest feeling of common advantage is among those who are biologically related, other bonds can arise insofar as there is any reciprocal sense of shared needs.

The human sense of affiliation can even embrace to some extent all of humanity. As a biologist, Aristotle believes all human beings are united by what they share as one species, "simple and having no differentiation" (*HA* 490b18). Nowhere in his biological writings does Aristotle speak of any human beings as natural slaves. As members of the human species, all normal human beings are potentially political animals with the capacity for articulate speech (*HA* 488a7–10; *PA* 653a27–31, 656a3–14, 686a3–14, 686a24–87b25; *GA* 731a24–31b13, 786b20–26; *Pol* 1253a8–19). Among many animals, there is some affiliative behavior among members of the same species; and this is especially true for human beings who are naturally inclined to *philanthropia*—literally, "affection for humanity." "In one's travels, one can see the recognition and affiliation that link every human being to every other human being" (*NE* 1155a15–25).

As a consequence of his biological understanding of animal bonding, Aristotle sees the moral and political obligations of human beings as a series of concentric circles around the individual. As with all social animals, human beings love others as an extension of their self-love (*NE* 1168a27–69b2). Insofar as justice coincides with affiliation, the claims of justice vary in proportion to the nearness of attachments (*NE* 1155a16–29, 1159b25–60a8, 1165a14–36). One's obligations are stronger to closer relatives than to more distant ones, and stronger to close friends and fellow citizens than to strangers, although there is some weak affiliative attachment to all members of one's species based on a shared humanity. A person's humanitarian sympathy for strangers will almost always be weaker than his egoism, his nepotism, and his patriotism.

There is no friendship or affiliation *(philia)* in relationships where there is no common interest between the parties, Aristotle believes, which is why there is little or no friendship possible in a tyrannical relationship.

> In a tyranny there is no friendship at all or very little of it. For in relations in which there is nothing common to the ruler and to the ruled, there is no friendship, as there is nothing just. The relation is like that of an artist to his tool, or that of the soul to its body, or that of a master to his slave, for in each of these the former is benefited by using the latter; and there is no friendship or anything just towards inanimate things. Nor is there friendship

towards a horse or an ox or towards a slave as a slave, for there is nothing common to the two parties; for a slave is a living tool, and a tool is a lifeless slave. Accordingly, there can be no friendship towards a slave as a slave, but there may be friendship towards him as a human being; for there seems to be something just between every human being and every other who can participate in an association where there is law or agreement, and hence in a friendship to the extent that each is a human being. . . . Friendships are most likely to exist in democracies, for where people are equal, they have many things in common. (*NE* 1161a33–b10)

A remarkable point in this passage is that of all the exploitative relationships mentioned by Aristotle, only two show the unjust contradiction of treating human beings as if they were not human—the tyrant's rule over his subject and the master's rule over his slave. In another passage, Aristotle says "the relation between master and slave, whenever they deserve by their nature to be called such, should be one of friendship and of benefit to both; but if their relation is not such but exists by law and is forced, it leads to contrary results" (*Pol* 1255b13–16). This seems odd considering Aristotle's claim that a master can have no friendship with a slave as slave, although he can be a friend with him as a human being. To justify slavery as natural, a master would have to be a friend to his slave, but the very possibility of friendship presupposes the humanity of the slave and therefore the injustice of enslaving him as though he were not human. As human beings, slaves are inclined by their natural moral sense to favor social relationships that are based on kinship and reciprocity and to resist relationships of forced subjugation as exploitation. Consequently, the theory and practice of slavery must deny the humanity of the slave.

Although it is said that Aristotle developed "the most fully elaborated theory of natural slavery" (Garlan 1988, 122), I would suggest that, whether intentionally or not, his putative defense of slavery is self-contradictory in ways that confirm the incoherence of slavery as denying the humanity of the slave. When Aristotle distinguishes natural slavery from conventional slavery in the *Politics*, he thus indicates that slavery as actually practiced is not necessarily natural. Furthermore, his standards for natural slavery seem difficult, if not impossible, to satisfy. If there were natural masters and natural slaves, they would have to differ "as much as the soul differs from the body and the human being from the brute animal" (1254b16–17). On Aristotle's own terms, this could never be the case, because he makes it clear that slaves *do* have souls, and they *are* human beings (1253b33, 1259b29).

Aristotle recommends that in the best regime all the slaves should have their freedom held out to them as a reward (1330a33–34). Commentators who assume Aristotle endorsed slavery as natural cannot understand this recommendation, because surely slaves with the desire and the capacity for freedom cannot be slaves by nature. As one scholar observes, "[I]f men are natural slaves, it cannot be right, or to their benefit or that of their masters, that they should be transferred to the category of free men, for which nature has not fitted them" (Baldry 1965, 100).

Aristotle clarifies the essence of chattel slavery, and in doing so he exposes its fundamental contradiction. In theory, the slave is a "living tool" of the master, a mere extension of the master's will. In theory, therefore, the slave should be as obedient to the master's will as are the master's inanimate tools, his domesticated animals, or even his own body. A natural slave would be as adapted by nature to the master's will as the master's body is to his soul. A conventional slave is not so adapted by nature, because he is a human being with a mind and will of his own who obeys the master only as constrained by external force. The contradiction in slavery becomes clear when one sees that in practice human beings held as slaves are merely conventional slaves: as human beings, slaves can never become the things they are supposed to be. As human beings, they can never accept their enslavement as easily as ant slaves, because human beings will always show their moral sense by resisting exploitation and demanding reciprocity.

Some commentators believe Aristotle wanted his careful readers to see this contradiction in the practice of slavery (Nichols 1983; Ambler 1987; Lear 1988). Even those scholars who believe he wanted to justify slavery have noticed confusion in his remarks on slavery (Davis 1966, 70–72; Garlan 1988, 125). David Brion Davis, one of the leading modern historians of slavery, says that Aristotle's account of the slave as "both an instrument of action and a conscious agent" brings the contradiction of slavery into clear view. "This ambiguous conception raised many problems and did little more than magnify the basic contraction of human bondage" (1966, 70).

Whether Aristotle did this intentionally (as I and some other scholars believe) or unintentionally (as Davis and others believe) is not crucial for my argument. For whether it was intentional or not, the critical point is that the only serious philosophic analysis of slavery "did little more than magnify the basic contradiction of human bondage." Thus did Aristotle demonstrate that any attempt to defend slavery will contain within itself its own refutation, because it will show the contradiction of treating some human beings as if they were not human.

Any attempt to apply Aristotle's standards for natural slavery brings the ambiguity of his remarks into clear view. This became evident, for example, in the debate over the Spanish conquest of the New World in the sixteenth century. Bartolomé de Las Casas condemned the Spanish enslavement of the Indians. Drawing from Aristotle, he insisted that as a matter of natural right, all human beings must be treated with the respect appropriate to their nature as political animals (Carro 1971). Juan Gines de Sepulveda, the most important opponent of Las Casas, could also cite Aristotle, however, in contending that the American Indians were natural slaves. Debating Sepulveda before the Spanish judges of the Royal Council convoked at Valladolid in 1550, Las Casas (1974, 25–53) responded by arguing that, as understood by Aristotle, human beings are by nature rational and political animals, and therefore if there were a natural slave, who lacked this rational and political capacity, he would be a rare freak or mistake of nature that would fall short of the common nature of man. Such a defective human being would be like a man born blind or crippled. Consequently, it is impossible for an entire race or nation to lack those moral and intellectual capacities that distinguish human beings from other animals. In any case, the rich social and political history of the American Indians demonstrates that they could not be natural slaves. To treat them as natural slaves would contradict their nature as human beings.

That contradiction is evident in the entire history of slavery from ancient Greece to the American South. The most comprehensive history of slavery written in modern times is in a series of books by David Brion Davis (1966, 1975, 1984, 1986). The persistent theme of his writing is the "inherent contradiction of slavery," which "lay not in its cruelty or economic exploitation, but in the underlying conception of man as a conveyable possession with no more autonomy of will and consciousness than a domestic animal. This conception raised a host of problems and was seldom acted upon without compromise" (1966, 62). According to Davis, no slave society could escape "the simple and solid fact . . . that a slave was not a piece of property, nor a half-human instrument, but a man held down by force" (1966, 261). "No lawgivers could forget that tools and instruments do not run away, rebel, commit crimes, or help protect the state from external danger" (1975, 40). Throughout the history of slavery, slaveholders have tried to justify slavery by claiming that the degraded ethnic, religious, or racial identity of the slaves made them less than fully human (1966, 47–54). But this ultimately futile attempt to treat some human beings as non-human animals has generated "conflict, fear, and accommodation" (1975, 82). This was also seen by ancient historians like Thucydides *(Peloponnesian War* 4.80).

The same theme appears in M. I. Finley's studies of ancient slavery. The status of the slave as property, Finley explains, meant that he was always a "deracinated outsider," who had no control over his own person, who was totally under the power of his master, and whose lack of moral personality included the denial of kinship bonds (1983, 75). Since Finley denigrates the "old-fashioned belief in an immutable human nature, indifferent to social structure, values and status" (1983, 108), it is remarkable that he cannot avoid speaking of ancient slavery as an absurd denial of the slave's human nature. The ancient slave societies, he notices, could not evade "the ambiguity inherent in slavery, in the reduction of human beings to the category of property" (1983, 97). "If a slave is a property with a soul, a non-person and yet indubitably a biological human being, institutional procedures are to be expected that will degrade and undermine his humanity and so distinguish him from human beings who are not property" (1983, 95). Corporal punishment, torture, and sexual abuse were three ways to dehumanize slaves by handling them as if they were bodies without souls. Calling slaves *andrapoda* ("man-footed beings") and addressing male slaves of any age as "boy" indicated the same attempt at dehumanization. Finley believes, however, that people in the ancient world could not ignore the evident facts of shared humanity: "[I]t was fundamental that a slave could think, could act deliberately, could join others in concerted actions, including rebellion, could carry out confidential or military assignments" (1983, 99).

Although the history of slavery manifests the power of enslavement to brutalize the slaves, and thus to make them look as if they deserved to be enslaved, that history also shows that, since human slaves cannot transform themselves into nonhuman animals with no moral personality, they will deny the justice of their enslavement by simply acting like human beings.

Consequently, any attempt by the masters to ignore the humanity of their slaves is self-defeating. Unlike slave ants, human slaves will resist their enslavement as contrary to their moral sense.

For example, as one of the general causes for the unusually frequent and intense slave revolts in Jamaica, Orlando Patterson refers to the "general smugness" of the slaveholders, who seemed to believe their slaves really were naturally adapted to slavery and therefore disinclined to rebel no matter how brutally they were treated. He quotes from an eighteenth-century observer:

> One would imagine that Planters really think that Negroes are not of the same Species with us, but being of a different Mould and Nature as well as Colour, they were made entirely for our Use, with Instincts proper for the Purpose, having as great a propensity to subjection as we have to command and loving slavery as naturally as we do liberty; and that there is not need for Management, but that of themselves they will go most pleasantly to hard labour, hard Usages of all kinds, Cruelties and Injustices at the Caprice of one white man—such one would image is the Planter's Way of thinking. (Patterson 1967, 276–77)

To justify slavery, slaveholders must pretend slaves are not human, by pretending that they lack the emotional and rational capacities that incline human beings to demand reciprocity and resist exploitation in their social life. Yet the slaveholders cannot manage their slaves properly unless they see through that pretense, and thereby see the necessity for accommodating the natural moral demands of their slaves. Human slaves are not like slave ants that can be tricked by chemical signals into serving their masters without resistance. Human slaves will show the injustice of their enslavement by manifesting that moral sense that distinguishes human beings from ants and other animals.

One clear way that slaves vindicate their humanity, and thus expose the injustice of their enslavement as based on force without right, is through violent rebellion. But while, in the history of slavery in the New World, slave revolts were common in the Caribbean and Latin America, they were much less common in the American South, which could be interpreted by Southern slaveholders as evidence that slaves in the South were happy with their condition and thus deserved it. This seemed to confirm the paternalistic justification for slavery in the American South, by which the slave's obedience was said to be a fair return for the master's supervision and protection of the slave. Slavery as a paternalistic relationship of mutual benefit for both masters and slaves seemed to conform to Aristotle's standards for natural slavery, in which slaves are naturally adapted to obey masters who are naturally adapted to command.

Eugene Genovese (1976) has shown, however, that although paternalism in the American South was accepted by both masters and slaves, this disguised but did not resolve the fundamental contradiction in enslaving human beings as if they were not human. Southern slaveholders justified slavery as a paternalistic relationship of reciprocal obligations in which the obedience of the slave to the master was a moral duty in return for the dutiful protection and supervision provided by the master. Insofar as the slaves accepted this view of slavery as resting on the paternalistic doctrine of reciprocal obligations, the slaveholders interpreted this to mean that the slaves accepted the justice of their enslavement. The slaveholders refused to see, however, that since the slaves had little choice in the matter, they had to find some accommodation with slavery that would allow them to survive with as much living space as possible. The slaveholders also failed to see that the slaves could use the doctrine of reciprocal obligations to defend their humanity against the dehumanizing effects of slavery. As Aristotle indicated, reciprocity implies a relationship of mutuality in which each party has moral claims on the other. If a master has a right to obedience from the slave, the slave also has a right to protection from the master. Yet such reciprocal obligations make no sense if the slave is not a human being with a will of his own but a mere extension of the master's will, which is the definition of a slave. The paternalistic doctrine of reciprocity thereby exposes the contradiction inherent in slavery as denying the humanity of the slave.

The contradiction in the paternalistic justification of slavery was evident in Southern slave law. James Madison noted this in *The Federalist* (Number 54). Insofar as Southern law put the slave under the absolute power of the master, Madison observed, "the slave may appear to be degraded from the human rank, and classed with those irrational animals which fall under the legal denomination of property." But insofar as the law protected the slave from violent attack, even from his master, and insofar as the law punished the slave for violence against others, "the slave is no less evidently regarded by the law as a member of the society, not as part of the

irrational creation; as a moral person, not as a mere article of property."
Southern judges could never resolve this contradiction in the legal status of
the slave (Genovese 1976, 25–49; Nash 1970a, 1970b, 1979). In holding
him legally responsible for his actions, and in protecting him from the
unjustified violence of others, the slave was regarded by the law as a human
being with all the capacities of a "moral person." But in subordinating him
to the arbitrary force of his master, the slave was regarded by the law as a
nonhuman animal with no capacity for moral judgment, who therefore
could be held as property. Although other animals have some powers of
feeling and thinking that justify our respecting them by not injuring them
without justification, human law manifests our perception that because all
human beings as normal adults have a unique capacity for moral deliberation, for deciding what is good and bad for them, they must be granted
their moral freedom in at least the minimal sense that they cannot be owned
as articles of property with no moral responsibility.

As endowed with emotional capacities for feeling moral passions such
as love and anger and with rational capacities for judging moral principles
such as kinship and reciprocity, all human beings will resist slavery as exploitation. Slavery can be established by coercion and manipulation. But
unlike ant slavery, human slavery will always produce moral anguish and
social conflict.

HUME

In their futile attempt to disguise the master's exploitation of his slave as a
relationship of reciprocal obligations, the Southern slaveholders struggled
with the conflict between human slavery as coercive exploitation and human sociality as reciprocal exchange. If Aristotle is right in believing that
the natural social bonding of human beings beyond the family arises from
reciprocity—returning good for good and evil for evil—then slavery sub-
verts social life by denying the reciprocity of human relationships. For this
reason, David Hume believed that a modern society based on hired labor
conformed better to human nature than an ancient society based on slave
labor: "According to ancient practice, all checks were on the inferior, to
restrain him to the duty of submission; none on the superior, to engage
him to the reciprocal duties of gentleness and humanity. In modern times,

a bad servant finds not easily a good master, nor a bad master a good servant; and the checks are mutual, suitably to the inviolable and eternal laws of reason and equity" (Hume 1985, 384). For Hume—and for those like Thomas Jefferson and Charles Darwin who were influenced by him—slavery is wrong because it violates the sense of reciprocity that expresses the natural moral sense of human beings.

In contrast to the "selfish system" of Thomas Hobbes, Hume argues that human beings are by nature social animals, and from that natural sociality arises a moral sense. The natural instincts to sexual union and parental care incline human beings to familial attachments without which human life would be impossible. Those natural inclinations to social bonding can be extended to social groups beyond the family through ties of affiliation based on mutual affection and aid. The natural sentiments of sympathy and fellow-feeling can even be extended to strangers who share only a common humanity, although ties to family and friends tend to be far stronger than concern for strangers. These natural sentiments of social affection support a natural sense of right and wrong, in that people tend to approve what is useful to social life and disapprove what is detrimental. Moral judgment depends on "some internal sense or feeling, which nature has made universal in the whole species" (1888, 362–63, 398, 483–84, 486, 570–73; 1902, 169–73, 206–8, 214–31, 295–302). The impulse to moral action comes not from reason but from passion, Hume insists, yet reason prompts and directs the passions by determining the truth or falsity of the judgments that accompany each passion (1888, 413–18, 457–63; 1902, 172, 286, 294).

Hume believes this natural moral sense manifests itself in the foundation of justice. If we accepted the "poetical fiction of the golden age," which assumes human beings of perfect moderation and humanity living with an extreme abundance of resources for life, then justice would be unnecessary. If we accepted the "philosophical fiction of the state of nature," which assumes human beings of perfect rapaciousness and malice with an extreme scarcity of resources for life, then justice would be impossible. The normal condition of human society, Hume believes, is between these extremes. Human beings are selfish, but they also show limited generosity to family and friends. And although nature does not provide abundantly for their needs, human labor and industry can usually extract more than enough for their needs. In such a condition, justice is both necessary and possible. Rules for the just acquisition and transfer of property are necessary to regulate human selfishness in ways that promote economic productivity. But formulating and enforcing such rules of property is possible only if human beings feel some concern for the public good. Thus, the rules of justice are artificial in the sense that they are conventions of human contrivance that vary somewhat in variable social circumstances. Yet these rules are also natural in that they reflect natural human inclinations. The rules of justice are "stedfast and immutable; at least, as immutable as human nature" (Hume 1888, 620).

This explanation of how justice conforms to human nature also allows Hume to explain how slavery contradicts human nature.

> Were there a species of creatures intermingled with men, which, though rational, were possessed of such inferior strength, both of body and mind, that they were incapable of all resistance, and could never, upon the highest provocation, make us feel the effects of their resentment; the necessary consequence, I think, is that we should be found by the laws of humanity to give gentle usage to these creatures, but should not, properly speaking, lie under any restraint of justice with regard to them, nor could they possess any right or property, exclusive of such arbitrary lords. Our intercourse with them could not be called society, which supposes a degree of equality; but absolute command on the one side, and servile obedience on the other. Whatever we covet, they must instantly resign: Our permission is the only tenure, by which they hold their possessions: Our compassion and kindness the only check, by which they curb our lawless will: And as no inconvenience ever results from the exercise of a power, so firmly established in nature, the restraints of justice and property, being totally useless, would never have place in so unequal a confederacy.
>
> This is plainly the situation of men, with regard to animals; and how far these may be said to possess reason, I leave to others to determine. The great superiority of civilized Europeans above barbarous Indians, tempted us to imagine ourselves on the same footing with regard to them, and made us throw off all restraints of justice, and even of humanity, in our treatment of them. In many nations, the female sex are reduced to like slavery, and are rendered incapable of all property, in opposition to their lordly masters. But though the males, when united, have in all countries bodily force sufficient to maintain this severe tyranny, yet such are the insinuation, address, and charms of their fair companions, that women are commonly able to break the confederacy, and share with the other sex in all the rights and privileges of society. (Hume 1902, 190–91)

Like Aristotle, Hume believes that if there were natural slaves, they would have to be beings so physically and mentally inferior to normal human beings as to be comparable to brute animals. Like other animals, they might possess reason to some degree, but not to the extent of being able to express their resentment at being treated as purely servile beings. Being unable to assert any independence of mind or will, they would submit to slavery without resistance. Their masters would never feel any need to treat them as equals, and consequently the rules of justice would have no application to the master-slave relationship.

Europeans mistakenly believed the American Indians were natural slaves. Although Hume agrees that European civilization is indeed superior to that of the Indians, he also believes the Indians capable of that rational self-assertion that distinguishes human beings from nonhuman animals and that dictates rules of reciprocal justice. Similarly, women have been treated as slaves in many societies, and yet Hume believes women have the mental capacity—through "insinuation, address, and charms"—to assert their rightful claims against male exploitation. And although he suspects that the black race is naturally inferior to the white races, he believes that the enslavement of blacks denies their human nature as beings with such a degree of mental strength that they will not passively accept a condition of absolute servility (Hume 1985, 208, 383–84). In criticizing slavery, therefore, Hume does not presuppose the absolute equality of human beings in their mental capacities. He only presupposes that all normal human beings as adults attain that minimal level of mental ability required to see the advantage of reciprocity in social relationships and to resent their being denied reciprocity.

Slaveholders try to deceive themselves and others into thinking that their slaves are so emotionally and intellectually inferior as to be naturally adapted for servile obedience without any resistance. But this deception is exposed by the fact that slaves will always resent their enslavement and assert their resentment in ways that demand reciprocity. Justice as reciprocity is natural for human beings because they are social animals, and society presupposes reciprocity among its members. The enslavement of human beings is self-defeating, therefore, because while human beings will always demand reciprocity in their social relationships with one another, the logic of slavery denies any reciprocity between master and slave.

Hume suggests, but without elaboration, that this demand for social reciprocity is rooted in natural inclinations of the human mind that are ultimately biological. Hume presents his moral philosophy as part of a science of human nature in which the moral dispositions arise from the "particular fabric and constitution of the human species," and specifically from the properties of the human mind as shaped by the "natural and physical causes" studied by the sciences of anatomy and natural philosophy (1902, 170; 1888, 7, 13, 275–76). Although he does not investigate those natural sciences, he does indicate that his "anatomy of the mind" would assume that the human mind is governed by the same causes that shape the minds of other animals, and he argues that many of the emotional and intellectual capacities of human beings are found among other animals as well (1888, 176–79, 324–28; 1902, 104–8).

Although human beings are superior in their rationality to other animals, this is a difference in degree rather than kind (1888, 610; 1902, 107). This difference in degree is great enough, however, to create a crucial difference in kind, because the greater intellectual capacity of human beings allows them to become the only animals who exercise moral judgment and display moral passions (1888, 326, 397, 468). Due to their capacities for moral judgment and moral passions, human beings cannot properly be treated as domesticated animals, because insofar as human beings demand reciprocity in their social relations, they will never become mere extensions of a master's will. Unlike domesticated animals, human slaves can judge the exploitative character of their enslavement and feel anger in reaction to such exploitation.

JEFFERSON

One can see, then, that the debate over slavery ultimately becomes a debate over the place of human beings in the natural world. The success of human civilization depends on the skill of human beings in harnessing the forces of nature—living as well as nonliving—to the service of human needs. In every civilization it has seemed advantageous to employ domesticated animals for human purposes. In many civilizations it has seemed advantageous to allow a division of labor in which some human beings benefit from the slave labor of other human beings. Is it contrary to the human nature of slaves to treat them like domesticated animals who have been harnessed to the service of their human masters? Or is it the case that some human beings are so mentally inferior to others that the enslavement of the less intelligent to the more intelligent would benefit the slaves as well as the masters? After all, every high civilization requires a social division of labor. Would a system of natural slavery assign people to the classes for which they are suited—the natural slaves to the laboring classes and the natural masters to the leisured classes?

For Thomas Jefferson, these are questions for the science of human nature as part of the science of natural history. Jefferson studied morality and politics within the context of natural history as it was practiced by European naturalists such as Carl Linnaeus and Georges Buffon, who continued the tradition of botanical and zoological inquiry originated by Aristotle (Atran 1990; Boorstin 1948; Greene 1984). Throughout his life Jefferson collected and analyzed fossils (Jefferson 1972, 43–58; 1984, 783–84, 1189–92). He wrote one of the first scientific studies of a fossil mastodon skeleton. He examined the bones of another giant animal that he labeled *Megalonix* ("great-claw"), which was later identified as a giant sloth. He studied neurophysiology for evidence that animal movement, appetite, and cognition were functions of the nervous system (Jefferson 1944, 716–17). And his methodical digging into an Indian burial mound to test some hypotheses about the origins of such mounds has been praised by modern archaeologists as the first stratigraphic excavation (Fagan 1991, 29; Jefferson 1984, 223–26).

Jefferson's *Notes on the State of Virginia*, the only book he ever wrote, would be identified today as a contribution to human ecology (Boyden 1987; Moore 1985). He considers the political history of Virginia within the context of its natural history as encompassing the whole physical and biotic environment of the region. He examines the human inhabitants—the white Europeans, the American Indians, and the blacks—as part of his study of "animals in America" (1972, 143; 1984, 800–801).

Jefferson's appeal to human nature as the universal foundation for political reasoning was an appeal to human biology (Boorstin 1948; Miller 1988). Against Buffon's assertions as to the "degeneracy of animals in America," Jefferson argued for the universal equality of human beings as members of the same species. "Human nature is the same on every side of the Atlantic, and will be alike influenced by the same causes" (1972, 121). He concluded that the Indians, as adapted for life in a hunting society with little agriculture, differed from the whites not in nature but in "manners," "customs," and "circumstances." He was less sure about the natural equality of the blacks, but he suspected that the degrading conditions of slavery had made it impossible for them to express their true nature. "I believe the Indian, then, to be, in body and mind, equal to the white man. I have supposed the black man, in his present state, might not be so; but it would be hazardous to affirm, that, equally cultivated for a few generations, he would not become so" (1984, 801).

The ground of human equality, Jefferson believed, was the shared nature of human beings as moral and social animals. He explicitly denied the claim he attributed to Hobbes "that the sense of justice and injustice is not derived from our natural organization, but founded on convention only" (1907, 15:24–25). In a letter to John Adams, he criticized Destutt Tracy for agreeing with Hobbes that justice is purely a product of human convention: "I believe, on the contrary, that it is instinct and innate, that the moral sense is as much a part of our constitution as that of feeling, seeing, or hearing" (1907, 15:76). In a letter to Thomas Law, he identified man as a "social animal" with "social dispositions" and a "moral instinct." Some people are born without a moral sense, but they are like those born blind, or deaf, or without hands. And again he explained the variations in moral standards across societies as reflecting the same natural moral sense applied to different circumstances: "Nature has constituted *utility* to man the standard and test of virtue. Men living in different countries, under different circumstances, different habits and regimens, may have different utilities; the same act, therefore, may be useful, and consequently virtuous in one country which is injurious and vicious in another differently circumstanced" (1984, 1338).

Although all human beings are thus equal by nature insofar as they share in the same species-specific nature as moral and social animals, Jefferson also believed they are unequal by nature insofar as they differ in their natural talents and dispositions. There is a "natural aristocracy" of "virtue and talents." For not only has nature formed man for social life, nature has also formed some men with the abilities and dispositions for managing the affairs of society. Jefferson hoped that republican institutions would allow the people to select such "natural aristoi" for office. He offered plans for an educational system in which the majority of the citizens would acquire the minimal knowledge necessary for republican citizenship, while the naturally talented few would acquire the more extensive knowledge necessary for political rule. He warned, however, that even these natural aristocrats would be led by their ambition to become despots if their powers were not limited by a republican citizenry qualified "to know ambition under every guise it may assume; and knowing it, to defeat its views" (Jefferson 1972, 146–49; 1984, 1305–10). A society that conforms to the natural desires and capacities of human beings will allow the ambitious few to satisfy their natural desire to rule, while allowing the people to satisfy their natural desire to be free from exploitation.

From the time he first joined the colonial Virginia legislature in 1769, Thomas Jefferson had proposed emancipating the slaves. In his original draft of the Declaration of Independence, he condemned the British slave trade as "cruel war against human nature itself." He was forced to strike out this clause to appease South Carolina and Georgia, where some wanted to continue the slave trade (Jefferson 1944, 5, 21, 25–26). In 1778, he convinced the state legislature of Virginia to prohibit the foreign importation of slaves. This may have been a case of where moral duty and economic interest coincided, because the fertility of Virginia's slaves made that state a net exporter of slaves to other states.

Readers of Jefferson are usually disturbed to see that his proposals for emancipation include plans for colonizing the freed blacks in another country. Why did he not argue for assimilating them into American society as the social equals of whites? In the *Notes on Virginia*, Jefferson warns of the danger of race war.

> Deep-rooted prejudices entertained by the whites; ten thousand recollections, by the blacks, of the injuries they have sustained; new provocations; the real distinctions which nature has made; and many other circumstances, will divide us into parties, and produce convulsions, which will probably never end but in the extermination of the one or the other race. To these objections, which are political, may be added others, which are physical and moral. (1972, 138)

So while Jefferson believed human beings were equal as members of the same species, he did not believe—in contrast to Darwin—that a universal sentiment of humanity was enough to unite people into one community if they belonged to different groups with competing interests.

The factor that is most difficult to assess, to which Jefferson devotes most of his attention, is "the real distinctions which nature has made" in the races. After surveying the physical and moral characteristics of the black race as he has observed them, he hesitates to accept the conclusion that they are naturally inferior to other races (particularly the Indians and the whites), but he offers this as an "opinion," a "conjecture," a "suspicion." He explains his hesitation by indicating how difficult it is in this area of natural history to separate custom from nature. The degrading circumstances of enslavement make it hard for blacks to express their human nature (1972, 143). Nevertheless, he hopes for a "total emancipation" of these people as the only alternative to a bloody slave revolt in which justice will be on the side of the slaves (1972, 162–63). In 1820, he could still see no escape from the moral dilemma of slavery: "[W]e have the wolf by the ears, and we can neither hold him, nor safely let him go. Justice is in one scale, and self-preservation in the other" (1984, 1434).

Throughout his life, Jefferson was interested in any evidence of the natural capacities of blacks. In 1809, he was pleased to receive a book on black literature. To the author he wrote:

> Be assured that no person living wishes more sincerely than I do, to see a complete refutation of the doubts I have myself entertained and expressed on the grade of understanding allotted to them by nature, and to find that in this respect they are on a par with ourselves. My doubts were the result of personal observation on the limited sphere of my own State, where the opportunities for the development of their genius were not favorable, and those of exercising it still less so. I expressed them therefore with great hesitation; but whatsoever be their degree of talent it is no measure of their rights. Because Sir Isaac Newton was superior to others in understanding, he was not therefore lord of the person or property of others. On this subject they are gaining daily in the opinions of nations, and hopeful advances are making towards their re-establishment on an equal footing with the other colors of the human family. I pray you therefore to accept my thanks for the many instances you have enabled me to observe of respectable intelligence in that race of men, which cannot fail to have effect in hastening the day of their relief. (1984, 1202)

We see here an ambiguity that runs through all of Jefferson's writing on slavery and equality. Does equality in natural right require equality in natural capacities? On the one hand, Jefferson looks for evidence of black intelligence comparable to that of other races to justify their equality. On the other hand, he asserts that "whatever be their degree of talent it is no measure of their rights." After all, if natural intellectual talent were the standard, the Newtons of all races would rightfully rule over all other human beings. Commentators like Daniel Boorstin regard this as a fundamental contradiction in Jefferson's thinking.

Can Jefferson's affirmation of natural equality be made consistent with his affirmation of a "natural aristocracy" whose right to rule is based on "virtue and talents" (1984, 1305)? If so, then natural *equality* cannot mean natural *identity* of capacities or achievements. In the *Notes on Virginia*, Jefferson indicated that even if it were shown that blacks were naturally inferior in "the endowments of the head," the blacks were clearly well endowed in "the heart"—that is to say, in that "moral sense" of right and wrong that is as much a part of human nature as tasting and feeling (1972, 93, 143). Although they are unequal in many respects, blacks are equal to whites in their moral sense, Jefferson seems to say, and thereby equal in their natural rights to life, liberty, and the pursuit of happiness (Wills 1978, 218–28).

It was commonly observed, however, that black slaves were utterly shameless in stealing from their masters; and many masters confessed that they took it for granted that a large portion of a plantation's production would be lost to theft by their slaves (Genovese 1976, 599–609). Many slaveholders took this as evidence that the blacks lacked any sense of morality. Jefferson argues just the opposite.

> That disposition to theft with which they have been branded, must be ascribed to their situation, and not to any depravity of the moral sense. The man, in whose favour no laws of property exist, probably feels himself less bound to respect those made in favour of others. When arguing for ourselves, we lay it down as a fundamental, that laws, to be just, must give a reciprocation of right: that, without this, they are mere arbitrary rules of conduct, founded in force, and not in conscience; and it is a problem which I give to the master to solve, whether the religious precepts against the violation of property were not framed for him as well as his slave? And whether the slave may not as justifiably take a little from one, who has taken all from him, as he may slay one who would slay him? (1972, 142)

Jefferson adds: "Notwithstanding these considerations which must weaken their respect for the laws of property, we find among them numerous instances of the most rigid integrity, and as many as among their better instructed masters, of benevolence, gratitude, and unshaken fidelity" (1972, 142–43).

Far from showing their lack of a moral sense, slaves show the clarity of their moral judgment in taking the goods of their masters. The slaveholders themselves recognize that the laws of property, like any social norms that claim moral sanction, must allow "reciprocation of right." Laws that deny reciprocity by promoting the interests of one group at the expense of another are grounded in force, not right. The fundamental purpose of the laws of property, as Aristotle and Hume saw, is to enforce the rights and duties of reciprocal exchange. Therefore, since the master deprives the slave of all property, the slave is justified by the moral logic of reciprocity in taking the master's property for his own use whenever he can.

The impeccable moral logic of the slaves was evident in the fact that they distinguished between "taking" goods from the master, which was permissible, and "stealing" goods from other slaves, which was prohibited. They recognized the importance of respecting property rights among themselves as a condition of social order founded on reciprocity. Yet they reasoned that if slaves were the absolute property of the master, as required by the logic of slavery, then slaves could not be properly said to "steal" from their masters. After all, a slave who eats some of his master's corn is only transforming the master's property from one form to another, just as when a slave feeds the master's corn to the master's chickens (Genovese 1976, 602).

Thus, again, the slaves expose the contradiction of slavery in treating the slave as a mere extension of the master's will, which denies the humanity of the slave and thus also denies that the slave can have any moral duties towards the master. The slaves show that they are not the inferior beings they are supposed to be; they do this by acting according to the principle of reciprocity as the foundation of human social life in which no human being can be the mere extension of another's will.

Although Jefferson correctly recognizes this as an expression of the moral sense, he is mistaken, I believe, in regarding this as purely an act of the "heart" rather than the "head." Certainly, the moral principle of reciprocity does rest upon passions or sentiments such as anger, indignation, and gratitude. But still, as Aristotle and Hume saw, reason prompts and directs those passions. The subtle *logic* of the slaves in distinguishing "taking" from masters and "stealing" from other slaves, for example, manifests an intellectual capacity that is uniquely human. So although all blacks do not have to be absolutely equal to all whites in their rational faculties to be equal in their moral sense, blacks must at least have that minimal ability for rationally judging principles such as reciprocity that distinguishes human beings from other animals. This does not require the intelligence of a Newton, but it does require an intelligence far beyond any nonhuman animal.

If there were human beings—perhaps an entire race—that lacked that minimal level of rational capacity, so that they could not grasp the logic of principles like reciprocity, such people would be natural slaves. Jefferson's argument seems to be that, with the possible exception of those who suffer from some abnormal mental disorder, all human beings have the minimal emotional and intellectual capacities that support a uniquely human moral sense. Human beings recognize the exploitation in slavery as violating the moral principle of reciprocity, and in response to such exploitation, they feel moral passions such as anger and shame.

Jefferson derived all these characteristics of human nature from a science of natural history according to which each species displays a distinctive array of natural traits. Some scientists of his day interpreted the fossil evidence as suggesting that some species had become extinct, with new species taking their place, so that the natural system of species was not permanent. Eventually, Charles Darwin and Alfred Wallace would interpret this and other evidence as indicating that there had been an evolution of new species from ancestral species by natural selection and other mechanisms. Jefferson thought the evidence for extinction was unconvincing, and he never took very seriously the possibility of an evolutionary origin for species, although he was familiar with the idea from reading Lucretius. In at least one letter, however, he acknowledged that some animals had become extinct (1984, 1467). Despite this apparent difference between Jefferson and Darwin on the origin of species, they agreed that there was a moral sense rooted in human nature, and slavery violated that moral sense.

DARWIN

Like Aristotle, Hume, and Jefferson, Darwin believes that the natural sociality of human beings originates in the biological bonding between parents and children that is extended into the social bonds of kinship. The combination of these social instincts with certain uniquely human intellectual capacities produces the moral sense. As among other social animals, some human beings might feel little social concern. And a few individuals deformed by physiological defects or abnormal upbringing might have no social instincts at all. But such a rare individual would be an "unnatural monster" or "essentially a bad man," who would have to be controlled solely by the fear of punishment (Darwin 1936b, 483, 486, 492–93). Like Aristotle and Jefferson, Darwin identifies the social nature of human beings as a range of behavioral dispositions, so that those few individuals who fall outside the normal range must be seen as "unnatural," like people born blind or without hands. Darwin also agrees with Aristotle, Hume, and Jefferson in believing that, although the moral sense is rooted in social instincts shared with other social animals, moral judgment in the strict sense is uniquely human because it depends upon human capacities for speaking and reasoning.

Darwin believed that the opposition to slavery was one manifestation of this moral sense. When he sailed from England in 1831 on the *Beagle*, he was told that once he had seen slavery in South America, his opinion would change. The captain of the ship, Robert FitzRoy, defended slavery, claiming that most slaves were so well treated and so well adapted to their condition that they would not want to be free. Darwin suspected, however, that slaveholders were too blinded by self-interest to see the suffering that slavery caused. His observations during the voyage confirmed this. He was so impressed by the moral and intellectual character of blacks that he could not help feeling kindness and sympathy towards them. He repeatedly described the painful feelings elicited by the sight of their suffering. His high estimate of the black slaves and his feelings of moral indignation at their treatment led him to look forward to the day when they would revolt and win their freedom (Darwin 1934, xvi, 42–43, 76–77; 1962, 20, 24–25, 496–98; 1985, 238, 312–13, 320).

Slavery is so contrary to our moral feelings, Darwin believes, that slaveholders feel compelled to deceive themselves into thinking the slaves are specially adapted to slavery by their inferior nature, which makes them more like domesticated animals than full human beings. Any justification for black slavery depends on the argument that blacks and whites are separate species that are so constituted by nature that blacks are better off under the rule of whites (1987, 228, 286, 343).

Throughout the history of slavery, slaves have been compared with domesticated animals. Just as cattle, horses, dogs, and other animals have been domesticated for the benefit of their human owners, so it might seem that some human races have been domesticated as slaves for the benefit of their human masters. Darwin wrote extensively on the power of human domestication in changing the traits of domesticated animals, because he wanted to argue that the power of evolutionary mechanisms in shaping new species by natural selection was analogous to the power of human breeders in shaping domesticated species of animals and plants by artificial selection (Darwin 1868; 1936a, 15–37). Yet Darwin saw no evidence that any human races were as adapted for slavery as domesticated animals were adapted for serving their human owners. Unlike domesticated animals, Darwin observed, "no race or body of men has been so completely subjugated by other men, that certain individuals have been preserved and thus unconsciously selected, from being in some way more useful to their masters" (1936b, 415). Here, then, was the fundamental contradiction of slavery—treating some human beings as if they were domesticated beasts bred to serve the pleasures of their human owners (Davis 1996).

In *The Descent of Man*, Darwin surveys the evidence and arguments on both sides of the debate over whether the human races should be ranked as distinct species. He concludes that they should not be so ranked, but should rather be considered variations of one human species. Despite the many anatomical differences between the races, Darwin is impressed by the great similarities that identify all human races as belonging to one species. He particularly stresses "the numerous points of mental similarity." "The American aborigines, Negroes and Europeans are as different from each other in mind as any three races that can be named; yet I was incessantly struck, whilst living with the Fuegians on board the 'Beagle,' with the many little traits of character showing how similar their minds were to ours; and so it was with a full-blooded negro with whom I happened to be intimate" (1936b, 539).

Insisting on the mental similarity of the races as manifesting the unity of the human species strengthens Darwin's appeal to the moral sense of his readers in arguing against slavery, because he can call up that sense of fellow-feeling that people have toward those like themselves. At the end of *The Voyage of the Beagle,* he employs emotionally charged language to evoke his reader's sympathy for the slave and indignation toward the master. "On the 19th of August we finally left the shores of Brazil. I thank God, I shall never again visit a slave-country. To this day, if I hear a distant scream, it recalls with painful vividness my feelings, when passing a house near Pernambuco, I heard the most pitiable moans, and could not but suspect that some poor slave was being tortured, yet I knew that I was as powerless as a child even to remonstrate" (1962, 496). He can scorn the hypocrisy of slaveholders who profess to believe in the fairness of reciprocity while denying it to the slave.

> Those who look tenderly at the slave-owner, and with a cold heart at the slave, never seem to put themselves into the position of the latter;—what a cheerless prospect, with not even a hope of change! Picture to yourself the chance, ever hanging over you, of your wife and your little children—those objects which nature urges even the slave to call his own—being torn from you and sold like beasts to the first bidder! And these deeds are done and palliated by men, who profess to love their neighbours as themselves, who believe in God, and pray that his Will be done on earth! It makes one's blood boil, yet heart tremble, to think that we Englishmen and our American descendants, with their boastful cry of liberty, have been and are so guilty. (1962, 497–98)

Darwin's rhetoric appeals to the moral passions of his reader by condemning the cruelty of slavery as violating that principle of reciprocity that supports human social cooperation. Such rhetorical persuasion is not possible among those ants that practice slavery. Ants lack the natural capacities that make such rhetoric effective among human beings—the emotional capacity to feel anger, indignation, and shame and the rational capacity to judge the principle of reciprocity as essential to a social life free of exploitation. Of course, those same rhetorical capacities of human beings can also be used to defend slavery. Those who benefit from the practice of slavery are often not as candid as Judge Ruffin in admitting that slavery is exploitation supported by brute force alone. Defenders of slavery can try to use manipulative rhetoric to conceal the exploitative character of the master-slave relationship. But in making such a rhetorical defense, they invoke moral standards of logic and sentiment that can be easily used by the opponents of slavery. Although it is possible to make the weaker argument appear to be the stronger, it is easier to make the stronger argument appear to be the stronger, especially when the stronger argument is presented by a skillful rhetorician.

LINCOLN

In presenting the case against slavery, there has been no more skillful rhetorician than Abraham Lincoln. But only a few scholars such as Harry Jaffa (1973) have recognized the intellectual depth of Lincoln's thought about slavery. Like Darwin, Lincoln insists that slavery is contrary to the natural moral sense. He employs five kinds of arguments: I will call them the *historical* argument, the *Euclidean* argument, the *biblical* argument, the *intuitionist* argument, and the *biological* argument. Lincoln shows that any attempt to defend slavery as just either contradicts the American political tradition, or contradicts itself, or contradicts the Bible, or contradicts our natural sense of right and wrong, or contradicts our shared humanity as members of the same species. The fifth argument—the biological argument for our shared humanity—is the most fundamental since the other arguments presuppose it.

Lincoln's *historical* argument is his claim that to uphold slavery as just contradicts the principles of the American Founding as expressed in the Declaration of Independence, in the Constitution, and in other records of the views of the Founders (1953, 2:266–83, 2:403–407, 3:522–50). He also maintains that these principles are grounded in standards of reason and nature that transcend American history. In understanding why slavery is unjust, we grasp something about the universal grounds of all morality. "If slavery is not wrong," Lincoln insisted, "nothing is wrong" (1953, 7:281).

Lincoln's *Euclidean* argument arises from his comparison of the Declaration of Independence and Euclid's geometry. Just as Euclid begins with definitions and axioms that are self-evident and then proves his propositions as logical implications of these starting points, so Jefferson begins with the self-evident truth of equality of rights and then deduces from these the requirements of just government. "The principles of Jefferson are the definitions and axioms of free society" (1953, 3:375). It is essential for Americans to accept these principles because without them political argument is impossible. Political persuasion is like geometry or any other form of reasoning in that it depends on agreement on first principles. If everything is doubted, nothing can be proven. If Americans disagree about the fundamental axioms of the Declaration of Independence, their disagreements will be settled not by persuasion but by force.

How can we respond to those who deny the first principles? We cannot prove the truth of first principles because they are themselves the presuppositions of any proof. If we try to prove first principles, we end up begging the question by implicitly assuming them in the process of proving them. If we cannot strictly prove the truth of our premises to those who deny them, we can at least show that those who deny them contradict themselves. Even if we cannot make a demonstrative argument for the truth of first principles, we can make a dialectical argument. To do this, our opponent must say something, he must assert something, and then we must show that his assertion contradicts his denial of our first principles. Plato's Socratic dialogues provide many examples of this kind of argumentation.

Lincoln employs this technique in arguing for the equality of rights as an axiomatic truth. In a note probably written when he was debating Stephen Douglas, Lincoln reasons as follows:

> If A. can prove, however conclusively, that he may, of right, enslave B.—why may not B. snatch the same argument, and prove equally, that he may enslave A?
>
> You say A. is white, and B. is black. It is *color*, then; the lighter, have the right to enslave the darker? Take care. By this rule, you are to be slave to the first man you meet, with a fairer skin than your own. You do not mean *color* exactly?—You mean the whites are *intellectually* the superiors of the blacks, and, therefore have the right to enslave them? Take care again. By this rule, you are to be slave to the first man you meet, with an intellect superior to your own.
>
> But, say you, it is a question of *interest*; and, if you make it your *interest*, you have the right to enslave another. Very well. And if he can make it his interest, he has the right to enslave you. (1953, 2:222–23)

No rational person would argue for his own enslavement. But any person who argues for the enslavement of others must appeal to some human difference that could be the basis for his own enslavement. Therefore, no rational person can endorse slavery without contradicting himself. Human beings differ in an infinite number of ways—color, intellect, interests, and so on—but each person believes that he has a right to liberty simply by virtue of his humanity. Yet if I affirm that I *as a human being* have a right to liberty, then to be consistent I must also affirm that other human beings have a similar right.

In our natural human inclination to secure the benefits of social cooperation while protecting ourselves from being exploited by others, we appeal to reciprocity as the fundamental principle of fairness in social relationships, which makes it impossible for us to justify enslaving others without contradicting ourselves. "As I would not be a *slave*," Lincoln declares, "so I would not be a *master*. This expresses my idea of democracy" (1953, 2:532). Geometry teaches us the importance of consistency; and by adhering to an equally rigorous consistency in our moral reasoning, we can grasp the foundation of justice in the principle of reciprocity.

In the letter in which Lincoln comments on Jefferson's Euclidean logic, he writes: "This is a world of compensation; and he who would *be* no slave, must consent to *have* no slave. Those who deny freedom to others, deserve it not for themselves; and, under a just God, cannot long retain it" (1953, 3:376). We cannot do wrong without suffering wrong. This is so because human social life is a "world of compensation," a world of reciprocal exchange in which exploiters are ultimately punished by the moral aggression of those they exploit.

Lincoln could have learned this Socratic principle from Ralph Waldo Emerson's essay entitled "Compensation": "Crime and punishment grow out of one stem. Punishment is a fruit that unsuspected ripens within the flower of the pleasure which concealed it" (Emerson 1983, 290). Or he could have learned it from the Bible. Lincoln moves easily from the argument of logical consistency to the invocation of divine justice. This "world of compensation" was created by a God who is free of contradictions and who punishes those whose souls are torn by contradictions.

Lincoln's *biblical* argument against slavery depends on three biblical passages (1953, 2:546, 7:368). The first is from the account of creation: "God created man in His own image" (Gen. 1:27). The second is from God's condemnation of Adam after his disobedience: "In the sweat of thy face shalt thou eat bread, till thou return unto the ground; for out of it wast thou taken: for dust thou art, and unto dust shalt thou return" (Gen. 3:19). And finally Lincoln quotes the statement of the Golden Rule in the Sermon on the Mount: "Therefore all things whatsoever ye would that men should do to you, do ye even so to them: for this is the law and the prophets"

(Matt. 7:12). As created in the image of God, and thus set above other animals, no human being can rightfully be enslaved. As admonished to earn his bread by the sweat of his own face, no man can rightfully eat the bread earned by the sweat of *another man's* face. And as taught to obey the simple fairness of reciprocity in the Golden Rule, no man can rightfully impose on another man a slavery that he would not choose for himself. Similarly, as we have already seen, Judge Ruffin believed that to condemn the slave "to toil that another may reap the fruits" is so clearly exploitative that no rational human being would choose to be a slave.

The injustice of slavery is so evident, Lincoln insists, that anyone with "ordinary perceptions of right and wrong" can see it. This is his *intuitionist* argument, which reinforces the historical, the Euclidean, and the biblical arguments. He notes that even in the South slave-traders are despised: it is considered improper for a gentleman to even shake hands with them (1953, 2:264–65). There is a natural sense of justice that condemns the enslavement of human beings as a violation of reciprocity.

Lincoln thought the defense of slavery as a "positive good" was preposterous. Since human beings show what they think is good by what they desire, slavery cannot be good because no human being has ever desired it for himself. "Although volume upon volume is written to prove slavery a very good thing," Lincoln observed, "we never hear of the man who wishes to take the good of it, *by being a slave himself.*" And, at the same time, "the most dumb and stupid slave that ever toiled for a master, does constantly *know* that he is wronged" (1953, 2:222).

Yet while insisting that opposition to slavery is grounded in man's natural moral sense, Lincoln concedes that the promotion of slavery is grounded in another powerful element of human nature—self-interest (1953, 2:271). There is a natural human inclination to exploit others for one's own benefit, just as there is a natural human inclination to resist such exploitation of oneself by others. As we have seen, Lincoln argues that slavery cannot be in the *true* interest of the master. But it sometimes *seems* to be in a man's interest to secure his own freedom while denying freedom to others. In thus exploiting others, however, he contradicts himself. To hide his contradiction from others—and perhaps even from himself—he pretends that those human beings he enslaves are not truly human, that they lack the emotional and rational capacities that incline them to resist enslavement as exploitation.

To show the falsity of this claim, Lincoln must appeal to the facts of experience—to our recognition that human beings differ in degree but not in their species-specific nature, because they are members of the same species. This is the *biological* argument. Without this argument, the other four arguments would fail. If blacks are not human beings because they belong to a nonhuman species of animals, then the Jeffersonian principle of *human* equality does not apply to them because they are not human, it is not self-contradictory to treat them as if they are not human because in fact they are not, they were not created "in the image of God" because they lack the special capacities distinctive to human beings, and it does not violate our natural moral sense to treat them as inferior beings because in fact they are.

In 1854, when Stephen Douglas proposed opening the Kansas and Nebraska territories to slavery if that were the will of the majority of voters in those territories, Lincoln denounced this as an unnecessary compromise with the evil of slavery. Declaring slavery contrary to "the law of nature," he denied the claim "that the slaveholder has the same right to take his negroes to Kansas that a freeman has to take his hogs or his horses." Negroes cannot be "property in the same sense that hogs and horses are," because as members of the human species, Negroes have "mind, feeling, souls, family affections, hopes, joys, sorrows—something that made them more than hogs or horses" (1953, 2:245–46). In 1859, Lincoln continued to warn that Douglas's policy was changing public sentiment to a denial of the Negro's humanity: "a very significant change it is, being no less than changing the negro, in your estimation, from the rank of a man to that of a brute" (1953, 3:424). Repeatedly, Lincoln returned to this issue: either the Negro is human, and therefore to hold him as property is wrong, or the Negro is not human, but more like a domesticated animal, and therefore to hold him as property is not wrong (1953, 2:264–67).

If Negro slaves were like slave ants in easily accepting their enslavement, then enslaving Negroes would be no more wrong than enslaving ants. But if Negroes are human, then we must expect they have the distinctly human emotional and rational dispositions that resist enslavement as exploitation. Those defenders of slavery like Judge Ruffin who see the humanity of the slaves must admit that their enslavement rests purely on brute force and not on moral right.

Nevertheless, the full recognition of the equality of human beings in their humanity cannot be achieved immediately. Lincoln, in his speech on the Dred Scott case in 1857, made it clear that equality was a standard in principle for American political progress that could be approximated gradually even if never fully actualized in practice. He believed that when the authors of the Declaration of Independence stated the principle of equality, they

> intended to include *all* men, but they did not intend to declare all men equal *in all respects*. They did not mean to say all were equal in color, size, intellect, moral developments, or social capacity. They defined with tolerable distinctness, in what respects they did consider all men created equal—equal in "certain inalienable rights, among which are life, liberty, and the pursuit of happiness." This they said, and this they meant. They did not mean to assert the obvious untruth, that all were then actually enjoying that equality, nor yet, that they were about to confer it immediately upon them. In fact they had no power to confer such a boon. They meant simply to declare the *right*, so that the *enforcement* of it might follow as fast as circumstances should permit. They meant to set up a standard maxim for free society, which should be familiar to all, and revered by all; constantly looked to, constantly labored for, and even though never perfectly attained, constantly approximated, and thereby constantly spreading and deepening its influence, and augmenting the happiness and value of life to all people of all colors everywhere. (1953, 2:405–6)

These remarks and many others of Lincoln on slavery and equality show the influence of Henry Clay, who in turn shows the influence of Jefferson (Lincoln 1953, 2:121–32, 3:300–305). Like Lincoln, Clay affirmed the truth of equality in the Declaration of Independence as "an abstract principle" that should always be kept in view as a fundamental standard, although its practical enforcement would be slow. Racial prejudice would be one great obstacle to progress, and "what man, claiming to be a statesman," Clay asked, "will overlook or disregard the deep-seated and unconquerable prejudices of the people" (Clay 1844, 2:598)? Even the black abolitionist leader Frederick Douglass, reviewing Lincoln's career in 1876, could understand Lincoln's need as a statesman to respect the prejudices of his people: "Viewed from the genuine abolition ground, Mr. Lincoln seemed tardy, cold, dull, and indifferent; but measuring him by the sentiment of his country, a sentiment he was bound as a statesman to consult, he was swift, zealous, radical, and determined" (1955, 4:316).

Lincoln's position, like that of many of the American founders, was that, if the immediate abolition of slavery would have disastrous consequences, such as the dissolution of the American Union or racial war springing from racial hatred, we would have to compromise with slavery, at least temporarily, as a necessary evil. But although historical conditions might constrain our political judgments in forcing us to choose the lesser of evils, we must look to the natural justice of human equality as a standard to be constantly approximated, as we work for the "ultimate extinction" of all human bondage as fast as circumstances permit, thus looking to "the progressive improvement in the condition of all men everywhere" (1953, 2:266, 2:274–76, 2:405–7). Similarly, David Hume had spoken of the "natural progress of human sentiments" as human beings learn by historical experience the benefits of expanding the boundaries of justice to embrace ever larger portions of humanity (1902, 192).

This suggests that the statesman should be able, even if only gradually, to act in response to changing historical circumstances to overcome prejudices that previously might have seemed "deep-seated and unconquerable." There is some evidence that Lincoln did this. Up to 1864, he endorsed the position of Jefferson and Clay that since emancipated blacks could not live on equal terms with whites, emancipation should be followed by colonization in a foreign land so that blacks could establish their own societies. During the Civil War it became evident that colonization was impracticable, so that after the war the freed blacks would somehow have to be assimilated into American society as equal citizens. By early 1864, as Lincoln began to think about the conditions for admitting the Confederate States back into the Union, he suggested requiring "universal suffrage, or, at least, suffrage on the basis of intelligence and military service." He wrote of the black soldiers as men "who have so heroically vindicated their manhood on the battle-field, where, in assisting to save the life of the Republic, they have demonstrated in blood their right to the ballot" (1953, 7:101). To Michael Hahn, the first free-state governor of Louisiana, he proposed that the new state constitution should allow at least some of the blacks to vote—"as, for instance, the very intelligent, and especially those who have fought gallantly in our ranks" (1953, 7:243). Here Lincoln is both bold and cautious. It is bold to suggest that a Southern state should allow any of its former slaves to vote immediately after a civil war over slavery. It is cautious to suggest overcoming white prejudices by giving the vote first to those preeminently qualified by intelligence and military service. A very bold move would be to interpret "universal suffrage" as including women. In one of his earliest campaign letters, in 1836, Lincoln advocated just that; never again did he mention this, perhaps as a concession to another prejudice that he thought unlikely to change in his lifetime (1953, 1:48).

We have wondered what would be the distinctive capacities that would identify blacks as equally human with whites and thus deserving equal rights. In 1854, as we have seen, Lincoln spoke of blacks as having the "mind, feeling, souls, family affections, hopes, joys, sorrows" that distinguish human beings from hogs, horses, or other domesticated animals. Now, in 1864, Lincoln speaks of intelligence and military service. Do these signify, to use Aristotle's language, intellectual virtue and moral virtue? In Aristotle's *Nicomachean Ethics*, he begins his account of the specific virtues with the moral virtue of courage as displayed by the citizen-soldier, and he later turns to the intellectual virtues, culminating in the philosophic life. Certainly, Lincoln does not have in mind anything as grand as philosophic talent as a qualification for voting. But he surely implies that despite the important inequalities in natural talents, both moral and intellectual, a certain minimal level of moral character and intellectual ability must arise in normal human adults before we can treat them as equals.

This is made explicit by John Locke in his classic statement of the principle of equality of rights in the *Second Treatise of Government* (par. 54):

> Though I have said . . . *that all men by nature are equal,* I cannot be supposed to understand all sorts of *equality: age* or *virtue* may give men a just precedency: *excellency of parts* and *merit* may place others above the common level: *birth* may subject some, and *alliance* or *benefits* others, to pay an observance to those to whom nature, gratitude, or other respects, may have made it due: and yet all this consists with the *equality,* which all men are in, in respect of jurisdiction or dominion one over another; which was the *equality* I there spoke of, as proper to the business in hand, being that *equal right,* that every man hath, *to his natural freedom,* without being subjected to the will or authority of any other man.

As distinguished from slave ants, human beings will perceive that being subjected to the absolute will or authority of another is exploitation. And although unequal in many respects, they will insist on the equality of reciprocity in social relationships. Understood in this way, natural equality is compatible with the existence of what Jefferson called "the natural aristocracy" based on "virtue and talents." Furthermore, Locke acknowledges that children do not reach the full state of equality until their natural human capacities for free and rational action have matured under the supervision of their parents. Occasionally, "through defects that may happen out of the ordinary course of nature," some people remain mentally retarded even as adults, and they must be put perpetually under the guardianship of their parents or others appointed by the community (*Second Treatise*, par. 60).

By nature young children and some mentally defective adults cannot be fully free moral agents, because they lack the emotional and rational capacities that create the moral sense, and thus in that respect they are inferior to normal adults. Recognizing this does not deny the principle of human equality properly understood. "The general spread of the light of science," Jefferson believed, "has already laid open to every view the palpable truth, that the mass of mankind has not been born with saddles on their backs, nor a favored few booted and spurred, ready to ride them legitimately, by the grace of God" (Jefferson 1984, 1517). But if biology taught us that blacks were like children in their mental inferiority—if their emotional and rational capacities fell below the minimal range of variation found among normal adults of other races—would we not have to conclude, in "the light of science," contrary to Jefferson's expectations, that blacks have been born "with saddles on their backs," and those of other races have been born "booted and spurred, ready to ride them legitimately"?

For this reason, Lincoln, like Jefferson, thought it important to understand the meaning of that "physical difference" between the races. Jefferson looked to the natural history of human nature as it was understood by the best scientists of his day, but his conclusions were ambiguous and hesitant. The proslavery advocates believed that racial science demonstrated the natural inferiority of the blacks. Lincoln did not agree with the racial science of the proslavery people, and he seemed to be even more confident than Jefferson that blacks were not naturally inferior to whites.

RACIAL SCIENCE

In 1831, Nat Turner's slave rebellion in southern Virginia provoked the Virginia Legislature of 1832 into a reconsideration of slavery (Freehling 1990, 178–90). The debate was initiated in the Virginia House of Delegates by Thomas Jefferson's grandson, Thomas Jefferson Randolph, who warned that if slavery were not soon abolished peacefully by the action of the legislators, it would someday be abolished violently by the rebellion of the slaves. He proposed a new version of his grandfather's plan for gradual emancipation. All Virginia slaves born on or after 4 July 1840, would be emancipated when the women reached eighteen and the men twenty-one. Those emancipated would then be sent to Africa. Although the proposal was defeated, it had strong support. The principal objections concerned the impracticability of the plan. Significantly, no one in this long debate spoke of slavery as a good or as something to be preserved forever.

In reaction to this debate, however, some Southern writers began to move toward an unprecedented defense of slavery as a natural good based on the claim that blacks were biologically inferior to whites. Thomas R. Dew, in his influential writings on the Virginia debate, intimated this in 1832 but without elaboration:

> In the free black, the principle of idleness and dissipation triumphs over that of accumulation and the desire to better our condition; the animal part of the man gains the victory over the *moral;* and he consequently prefers sinking down into the listless inglorious repose of the brute creation, to rising to that energetic activity which can only be generated amid the multiplied, refined, and artificial wants of civilized society. . . . the free black will work nowhere except by compulsion. (1981, 52)

In 1837, John C. Calhoun defended slavery on the floor of the United States Senate not as an evil that had to be tolerated to avoid some greater evil, but as a "positive good" (Calhoun 1992, 474). In that same year, William Harper asserted that slavery was "deeply founded in the nature of man and the exigencies of society," and that the degraded condition of the blacks resulted not from the circumstances of slavery but from their natural inferiority. "The African negro is an inferior variety of the human race" (Harper 1981, 80, 113). By 1857, Samuel Cartwright, in "The Natural History of the Prognathous Species of Mankind," could write that "the white species have qualities denied to the black—one with a free and the other with a servile mind—one a thinking and reflective being, the other a creature of feeling and imitation, almost void of reflective faculties, and consequently unable to provide for and take care of himself" (1963, 147).

The scientific support for these claims came from some of the most prominent American scientists of the time, such as Samuel Morton and

Josiah Nott. Morton was famous in the international scientific community for having the world's largest collection of human skulls. In his *Crania Americana* (1839), he reported his meticulous measurements of the cranial sizes of his skulls, which showed that the Caucasian race had the largest brains of any racial group, thus explaining the superior intellectual and moral capacities of that race. The Negroes had the smallest average cranial sizes. In his *Crania Aegyptiaca* (1844), Morton inferred from cranial measurements that the ancient Egyptians were neither Caucasians nor Negroes but some blend of racial types; he also claimed that Negroes were treated as slaves in ancient Egypt. This was interpreted by some proslavery advocates, including Calhoun, as evidence for Negro slavery as a natural institution (Stanton 1960, 54–72, 126–38).

In 1844, Josiah Nott used cranial measurements combined with other kinds of evidence to conclude that the Caucasian and Negro races were actually two distinct species, and mulattoes were hybrids. ("Mulatto" has the same etymological root as "mule.") Because of their small brains, Nott explained, "the Mongol, the Malay, the Indian and the Negro, are now and have been in all ages and all places, inferior to the Caucasian" (1981, 233). Nott's polygenic theory was controversial in the South because it seemed to deny the biblical teaching that all races were derived from the same original pair of human beings—Adam and Eve. Nevertheless, Nott's arguments were influential with many Southern leaders, including the editors of important journals with large circulations such as the *Southern Quarterly Review* and *De Bow's Review*.

Abolitionists like Frederick Douglass recognized that if the racial science of Morton and Nott was valid, the argument against slavery would be weakened if not completely refuted. Fundamental to the critique of slavery, Douglass believed, is the premise that "human rights stand upon a common basis . . . because all mankind have the same wants, arising out a common nature." This premise would be denied by the scientific claim that blacks and whites belong to separate species of unequal abilities. "Let it be once granted that the human race are of multitudinous origin, naturally different in their moral, physical, and intellectual capacities, and at once you make plausible a demand for classes, grades and conditions, for different methods of culture, different moral, political, and religious institutions, and a chance is left for slavery, as a necessary institution" (Douglass 1955, 2:295, 2:307).

One of Nott's close friends was James Henry Hammond, twice elected governor of South Carolina and elected to both houses of the United States Congress. In his famous "mud-sill" speech of 1858, he manifested the influence of Nott's theory.

> In all social systems there must be a class to do the menial duties, to perform the drudgery of life. That is, a class requiring but a low order of intellect and but little skill. Its requisites are vigor, docility, fidelity. Such a class you must have, or you would not have that other class which leads progress, civilization, and refinement. It constitutes the very mud-sill of society and of political government; and you may as well attempt to build a house in the air, as to build either the one or the other, except on this mud-sill. Fortunately for the South, she found a race adapted to that purpose to her hand. A race inferior to her own, but eminently qualified in temper, in vigor, in docility, in capacity to stand the climate, to answer all her purposes. We use them for our purpose, and call them slaves. We found them slaves by the common "consent of mankind," which, according to Cicero, "*lex naturae est.*" The highest proof of what is Nature's law.
>
> We do not think that whites should be slaves either by law or by necessity. Our slaves are black, of another and inferior race. The *status* in which we have placed them is an elevation. They are elevated from the condition in which God first created them, by being made our slaves. None of that race on the whole face of the globe can be compared with the slaves of the South. They are happy, content, unaspiring, and utterly incapable, from intellectual weakness, ever to give us any trouble by their aspirations. Yours are white, of your own race; you are brothers of one blood. They are your equals in natural endowment of intellect, and they feel galled by their degradation. . . . (Hammond 1963, 122–23)

In March of 1861, Alexander Stephens, the new vice-president of the Confederate States of America, insisted that Jefferson's belief in natural equality had been refuted by modern science. "Our new government," he declared, "is founded upon exactly the opposite idea; its foundations are laid, its corner-stone rests upon the great truth, that the negro is not equal to the white man; that slavery—subordination to the superior race—is his natural and normal condition" (Cleveland 1866, 721). Previously, he explained, governments had allowed some people to rule over others of the same race contrary to the laws of nature. Now, the scientific discovery of racial differences, which was comparable to the discoveries of Galileo and Harvey in challenging popular prejudices, would support the Confederacy as "the first government ever instituted upon the principles in strict conformity to nature" (Cleveland 1866, 722).

If ants could speak, slavemaking ants might say something similar: in every social system, there must be a division of labor between classes, in which one class is devoted to menial labor, for which slave ants are so well adapted by their nature that they are perfectly content. Yet if ants could speak, they would have the rational capacity to detect the sophistic deception in such rhetoric in attempting to hide the exploitative reality of slavery.

Although Nott's racial theory was not initially Darwinian, he eventually accepted Darwin's theory of evolution. In 1866, he wrote a letter to the superintendent of the Freedmen's Bureau, explaining that Darwinian science should not be interpreted to suggest that the natural differences between Negroes and whites could be changed by legal or social means. Darwin's theory does show, he conceded, that races have changed and will continue to change over long periods of time; but these organic changes, he insisted, were too gradual to make any difference for politics. The Freedmen's Bureau cannot change the laws of racial differences because "forms that have been permanent for several thousand years, must remain so at least during the life time of a nation" (Stanton 1960, 187).

Even if we dismiss the old racial science of Morton and Nott as unreasonable, we cannot so easily dismiss the new science of Darwin; and we must wonder whether evolutionary science provides new support for the old racism. As we have seen, Darwin concluded that the races were so similar—particularly in their moral and intellectual capacities—that they should be considered mere varieties of a single human species.

Recent biological research provides evidence for Darwin's affirmation of the rough equality of the races. In 1978, Stephen Jay Gould reported that he had reexamined Samuel Morton's measurements of cranial capacity. He found that Morton had fudged his data—probably unintentionally—to support his prejudices. For example, Morton did not take into account the strong correlation between brain size and overall body size, which means that since males tend to have larger bodies than females, the average brain size for males tends to be larger. When Gould corrected for this and other distorting factors and recalculated mean cranial capacities for different races using Morton's raw data, all races appeared approximately equal (Gould 1978, 1981).

Racial differences continue to be a controversial topic for scientists, as indicated by the recent debate provoked by J. Philippe Rushton (Rushton 1994; Zuckerman and Brody 1988; Silverman 1990). Biologists can define races as subspecies. But the concept of subspecies, although sometimes convenient for certain purposes, depends ultimately on subjective and arbitrary classifications (Wilson and Brown 1953). Furthermore, modern laboratory techniques for quantifying genetic differences indicate that very little of the diversity within the human species can be accounted for by racial classification. Richard Lewontin concluded from such research that "based on randomly chosen genetic differences, human races and populations are remarkably similar to each other, with the largest part by far of human variation being accounted for by the differences between individuals" (1972, 397). Nei and Roychoudhury (1972) reached the same conclusion. Studies of this sort allowed Gould to give a lecture in South Africa in 1984 with the title "Human Equality is a Contingent Fact of History" (Gould 1985).

As just indicated, the same biological research that shows only small differences between human races shows great differences between individuals (Lewontin 1982). Scientists in the field of behavioral genetics have shown the intricate diversity of individual differences as arising from the complex interaction of genetic and environmental factors (Bouchard et al. 1990; Eaves, Eysenck, and Martin 1989; Plomin, DeFries, and McClearn 1990). How can we affirm human equality if no two individuals (except for monozygotic twins) are genetically identical? Some biologists deny that equality is a biological concept (Jacob 1982, 65–66). Ernst Mayr has even declared: "Anyone who believes in the genetic uniqueness of every individual thereby believes in the conclusion, 'No two individuals are *created* equal'" (1982, 79). To say this, however, ignores the fact that the *equality* of all humans as possessing a common human nature is fully consistent with the *inequality* of humans in their different natural endowments. Mayr himself states the point clearly: "In spite of the variability caused by the genetic uniqueness of every individual, there is a species-specific unity to the genetic program (DNA) of nearly every species" (1982, 297). This would be the modern biological justification for the claim of Locke, Jefferson, and Lincoln that, although human beings are naturally unequal in many respects, they are equal in those minimal emotional and intellectual capacities that sustain a moral sense and thus identify them as members of the human species. This understanding of human equality requires not equality as identity but equality as reciprocity: although unequal in many respects, all normal human beings will resist exploitation and demand social cooperation based on reciprocal exchange.

Gould might object to my reference to his lecture in South Africa on human equality. In arguing for human equality as a biological *fact*, he was careful to distinguish this from equality as a moral *value*. "I am, emphatically, not talking about ethical precepts," he insisted, "but about information in our best current assessment. . . . I can only view equality of opportunity as inalienable, universal, and unrelated to the biological status of individuals" (1985, 196–97). This separation of facts and values is commonly thought to indicate that human biology (and human nature in general) has no relevance to moral reasoning. But if this fact-value distinction means that what is good for human beings has no relation to human abilities, needs, or desires, then it is implausible. So implausible is it that even Gould cannot adhere to it consistently. He says that if a species of australopithecines *(Australopithecus robustus)* had survived to the present, its existence would have created "all the ethical dilemmas of a human species truly and markedly inferior in intelligence (with its cranial capacity only one-third our own)" (1985, 198). If biological facts have no moral implications, why would the existence of a humanlike species evidently inferior to *Homo sapiens* present us with "ethical dilemmas"? Gould refers to South Africa in 1984 as "the nation most committed to myths of inequality," and he is surely disingenuous in claiming that he lectured the South Africans on the biological fact of equality without intending this to be a moral argument. Gould's lecture illustrates my general point: the debate over equality is one case where biological facts do have moral consequences.

For human slavery, one human being must claim to hold another human being as property. Since claims to property arise from contests over scarce resources, such claims often manifest conflicts of interest. Such conflicts become even more intense and more complex when the resource that is held as property is an animal with interests of its own. When human beings try to exercise proprietary rights over nonhuman animals, there is often a struggle of wills. When human beings try to hold other human beings as property, the struggle of wills becomes more intricate, because this form of property can defend its interests with as much emotional strength and intelligent calculation as its owners do in defending their interests. Organisms often seek to avoid exploitation. Plants have evolved defenses against herbivores. Animals have evolved capacities for detecting and resisting manipulation by other animals. Human animals have evolved the complex capacities for recognizing and escaping exploitation by other human beings. Consequently, the practice of human enslavement has always induced an unremitting contest between the master's desire to exploit the slave and the slave's desire to resist such exploitation.

If the natural differences between the races were such that the people of one race lacked those minimal emotional and rational abilities that support the moral sense among the people of the other races, then those of the inferior race would be as adapted for slavery as domesticated animals are adapted for domestic service, and those of the enslaved race could properly be treated as perpetual children who would benefit from the direction of human masters. The people belonging to such an inferior race would accept enslavement with little resistance.

Human slavery is wrong because there is no inferior human race like this. There are natural differences between human races just as there are natural differences between individuals of the same race. But these natural differences, both racial and individual, do not justify slavery because they fall within the normal range of variation in the emotional and rational capacities that defines the human species. Hume, Jefferson, Lincoln, and Darwin were right. Slavery is wrong because it means treating some human beings as if they were not human. It means treating some human beings as if they were slave ants.

CONCLUSION

I have argued that the history of the debate over slavery manifests a moral sense that is rooted in the biological nature of human beings. I have also argued that in so far as Darwinian conceptions of human nature allow us to explain that natural moral sense, Darwinian science would support a revival of Aristotelian natural right.

Aristotle distinguished between what was right by nature and what was right by convention. Conventional right varies according to the particular customs, traditions, and laws of human groups. Natural right is universal in so far as it reflects an unchanging human nature. By natural right, we can judge that some societies and social practices are better than others because they conform better to human nature. But even in appealing to natural right, judging what should be done in particular cases requires prudential judgment about what is practicable in the concrete circumstances of action.

Aristotle was a biologist who studied human nature by comparing human beings with other animals. When he considered human beings as political animals, for example, he compared them with other political animals such as ants, bees, and wasps. In the spirit of Aristotle, I have compared human slavery and ant slavery. The similarities suggest that both for human beings and for ants, slavery is a form of social parasitism in which slavemakers exploit their slaves through coercion and manipulation. The differences suggest that human beings resist the exploitation of slavery because it violates their natural moral sense. That moral sense arises as a joint product of emotional capacities for feeling social passions such as anger and love and rational capacities for judging social principles such as kinship and reciprocity. Since those emotional and rational capacities are part of human nature for all normal human beings, the moral sense as an expression of those capacities is a human universal. We should expect, therefore, that in every human society where slavery exists, slavery will produce moral conflict. Unlike slave ants, human slaves will resist exploitation and demand social cooperation based on kinship and reciprocity.

My survey of the history of the debate over slavery—from Aristotle to Lincoln—shows that although slavery has often been deeply rooted in the customs and laws of various societies, slavery has always provoked conflict and anguish because it contradicts human nature. Human slaves show the injustice of their enslavement by manifesting the moral sense that identifies them as human beings. Defenders of slavery must either acknowledge the injustice of slavery as based on coercion or hide that injustice by pretending that human slaves are not really human in that they lack the emotional and rational capacities for expressing a human moral sense.

Lincoln was right: "If slavery is not wrong, nothing is wrong." If it were possible through social learning to alter human nature so that some human beings were so adapted to their slavery and others so adapted to their mastery that slavery was never considered wrong, then nothing would be wrong by nature, because perceptions of right and wrong would then be arbitrary social constructions.

Slavery is wrong because it violates a natural moral sense rooted in human biology. Even when slavery is accepted by the customs and laws of a particular society and thus conforms to conventional right, slavery is contrary to natural right. Prudent statesmanship might dictate some compromise with the evil of slavery if its immediate abolition would be socially disastrous. But even when statesmen like Jefferson and Lincoln argue for compromising with an evil like slavery, the appeal to natural right allows them to recognize the evil as an evil, so that they can work for its elimination as fast as circumstances permit.

The arguments of Jefferson and Lincoln against slavery did not appeal to a utopian morality of universal sympathy. They foresaw that it would be difficult for emancipated blacks to be fully integrated into a multiracial democracy as equals because of a natural tendency to tribalism that would promote racial conflict. So although they saw that racially based slavery is wrong, they feared that the abolition of slavery would be followed by new problems of racial separatism. The history of racial strife in the United States since the Civil War shows that their fears were warranted. Social solidarity is naturally easier in racially homogeneous groups. Yet, still, we must hope that the daily integration of people in a racially mixed society can promote feelings of mutual concern even across racial barriers.

The natural sociality of human beings rests on a tense balance between competition (based on conflicting desires) and collaboration (based on complementary desires). Despite the competition between individuals derived from their conflicting interests, much of the behavior of one individual complements that of other individuals of different age or sex. The natural desire of the young to attach themselves to adults complements the natural desire of adults to care for the young. The masculine desires of adult men complement the feminine desires of adult women. By contrast, the coercion of slaves by masters cannot be based on a natural complementarity of desires. The master's desire to exploit the slave clashes with the slave's desire to be free from exploitation. Consequently, slavery is contrary to human nature and thus contrary to natural right.

CHAPTER 8

THE POVERTY OF PSYCHOPATHIC DESIRE

Throughout this book, I have argued that there is a natural moral sense rooted in human biology. Yet some people, even if only a few, seem to have no moral sense. Benjamin Rush, a prominent physician who signed the Declaration of Independence, agreed with many of the American political founders in believing that the natural moral law was founded on a natural moral faculty for distinguishing good and evil; but he recognized that a few human beings totally lacked this moral faculty because of some "unnatural defect" in their brains (Rush 1815). Similarly, Abraham Lincoln observed that a few people were "natural tyrants" who saw nothing wrong with slavery, because they lacked that natural sense of right and wrong felt by most human beings (Lincoln 1953, 2:264).

In the terminology of modern psychology, those who have no moral sense are psychopaths. They are ruthless social predators who, with no feeling of guilt or regret, charm, manipulate, deceive, attack, and sometimes kill other human beings. Harming others, even friends and family members, does not bother them, because they are incapable of feeling the pain of others. Egoistic, deceitful, greedy, and impulsive, they are utterly asocial creatures who restlessly crave whatever capricious pleasure excites them at any moment without regard to any social norms.

The very existence of such people who lack any moral sense might seem to deny my argument that the moral sense is rooted in human nature. If the psychopath is just as much a product of nature as any other human being, then it might seem that the cultural relativist is right in arguing that morality is not natural but cultural, because the psychopath illustrates the amoral character of a human being who has failed to acquire morality through cultural learning. Against my claim that human nature supports morality, some religious believers might say that the psychopath manifests the evil or sinful character of human desires, and thus shows that morality requires a supernatural transcendence of human nature through God's redemptive grace.

In this chapter, I answer these criticisms. I survey the modern research on psychopathy and conclude that psychopaths suffer from an abnormal poverty of desire: they lack the social desires that support the moral sense in normal people. Without that moral sense, psychopaths must be treated by the rest of us as moral strangers whose dangerous conduct can only be restrained by force. Far from denying the reality of the natural moral sense, the existence of psychopaths shows that the normal pattern of natural desires is the ultimate ground for morality, and therefore moral persuasion is impossible with those few human beings who lack the natural desires typical for all other human beings. If psychopaths are not morally obligated to respect social desires that we feel but they do not, neither are the rest of us morally obligated to refrain from protecting ourselves against their predatory behavior.

THE MASK OF SANITY

Although Aristotle and Charles Darwin believed that most human beings were inclined by nature to develop a moral sense, they recognized that some human beings were morally depraved in that they found pleasure in brutal acts that would not be naturally pleasurable to normal people. Aristotle thought such depravity could arise from three possible causes—from injury, from habituation, or from innate temperament (*NE* 1148b15–49a20). A physical injury could cause mental disorder. Bad habituation, as in those abused from childhood, could cause morbid behavior. Or an inborn abnormality of temperament could cause brutal dispositions. Darwin suggested similar causes when he spoke of those who lacked the social emotions that support the moral sense. Such a person would be an "unnatural monster" and "essentially a bad man," for whom "the sole restraining motive left is the fear of punishment" (1936b, 483, 486).

Today we might call such a person a "psychopath." I will adopt this term although different terms are often used for this same condition. In 1952, in the American Psychiatric Association's *Diagnostic and Statistical Manual of Mental Disorders,* the term "psychopathic personality" was replaced with "sociopathic personality"; and in 1968, this was replaced with "antisocial personality" (American Psychiatric Association 1987). Yet despite the disagreement over labels, there is general agreement on the character of the person being labeled. In the words of Robert Hare, a leading researcher in the field, a psychopath is "a self-centered, callous, and remorseless person profoundly lacking in empathy and the ability to form warm emotional relationships with others, a person who functions without the restraints of conscience" (Hare 1993, 2).

Perhaps the most famous psychopath in recent American history is Ted Bundy, who brutally murdered at least thirty-six young women and perhaps over a hundred before he was executed in Florida in 1989. He did that without ever feeling sympathy, guilt, or shame. Ann Rule, a friend of Bundy who wrote a book about his life, describes him as a "shadow man" with a "hollow soul."

> The Ted Bundy the world was allowed to see was handsome, his body honed and cultivated meticulously, a barrier of strength against eyes that might catch a glimpse of the terror inside. He was brilliant, a student of distinction, witty, glib, and persuasive. He loved to ski, sail, and hike. He favored French cuisine, good white wine, and gourmet cooking. He loved Mozart and obscure foreign films. He knew exactly when to send flowers and sentimental cards. His poems of love were tender and romantic.
>
> And yet, in reality, Ted loved *things* more than he loved people. He could find life in an abandoned bicycle or an old car, and feel a kind of compassion for these inanimate objects—more compassion than he could ever feel for another human being.

"Ted has no conscience," she finally concluded. And for that reason he went through life as a moral alien who imitated, without really feeling or understanding, the social emotions of normal human beings. "To live in our world, with thoughts and actions always counter to the flow of your fellow men, must be an awesome handicap. There are no innate guidelines to follow: the psychopath might as well be a visitor from another planet, struggling to mimic the feelings of those he encounters" (Rule 1989, 397).

If we follow the usage of David Lykken (1995) and other psychologists, we should distinguish the *psychopath* from the *sociopath* as two different kinds of antisocial personality. Psychopaths develop antisocial personalities because they have been born with abnormal temperaments that make it difficult for them to be socialized, even when they have been reared by good parents in good social environments. Sociopaths develop antisocial personalities because although they have been born with normal temperaments, they have failed to be socialized properly due to incompetent parents or unusually deprived social environments. Psychopathic children are innately inclined to be more impulsive, aggressive, daring, and fearless than most children. Because of their fearlessness, they cannot easily be trained by fear of punishment to feel guilt or shame when they violate social rules. Behavioral geneticists have used studies of twins and other research to show that temperamental traits such as fearlessness, impulsiveness, and aggressiveness are genetically influenced (Bouchard, Lykken, McGue, Segal, and Tellegen 1990; Lykken 1995). The psychopathic character expresses genetically innate propensities interacting with environmental circumstances.

To live as social animals in complex communities, human beings were shaped by natural selection to be naturally inclined to learn from parents or other social agents the customs, habits, and rules that sustain decent social life. Human society would not be possible if most human beings were not born with an innate propensity to learn moral behavior. Children of normal temperament with normally competent parents in normal environments usually learn their moral lessons well enough to become decent members of society. But some children with normal temperaments inclined to moral learning never learn their social lessons because of bad parenting or a bad environment, and they can become sociopaths. A very small number of children have such abnormal temperaments that they rarely learn their social lessons even with good rearing, and they can become psychopaths (Lykken 1995).

Of course, the scientific study of psychopathy is a product of modern Western culture, and some scholars have argued that the whole idea of abnormal psychology is a social construction of Western science that does not apply to non-Western cultures. But, in fact, psychopathy and other forms of mental abnormality have been recognized as problems in all human societies throughout history (Murphy 1976). We know from the Bible, for example, that Moses taught that the moral law for Israel would have to be instilled in children by their parents. And yet he recognized that a few children with abnormally unruly temperaments would never acquire this moral education, and so the community would have to deal harshly with them.

> If a man has a stubborn and rebellious son who will not listen to the voice either of his father or of his mother and, even when they punish him, still will not pay attention to them, his father and mother must take hold of him and bring him out to the elders of his town at the gate of that place. To the elders of his town, they will say, "This son of ours is stubborn and rebellious and will not listen to us; he is a wastrel and a drunkard." All his

fellow-citizens must then stone him to death. You must banish this evil from among you. All Israel, hearing of this, will be afraid. (Deut. 21:18–21)

Similarly, Jane Murphy, an anthropologist who studies "cross-cultural psychiatry," argues that many non-Western societies have some notion that resembles the concept of psychopathy. One example is found among a group of Eskimos in northwest Alaska:

> [T]he Eskimos have a word, *kunlangeta*, which means "his mind knows what to do but he does not do it." This is an abstract term for the breaking of many rules when awareness of the rules is not in question. It might be applied to a man who, for example, repeatedly lies and cheats and steals things and does not go hunting and, when the other men are out of the village, takes sexual advantage of many women—someone who does not pay attention to reprimands and who is always being brought to the elders for punishment. One Eskimo among the 499 was called *kunlangeta*. When asked what would have happened to such a person traditionally, an Eskimo said that probably "somebody would have pushed him off the ice when nobody else was looking." (Murphy 1976, 1026)

The mystery of the psychopathic character is conveyed in the title of the classic text for the scientific study of psychopathy written by Hervey Cleckley and first published in 1941—*The Mask of Sanity*. The psychopath is clinically and legally sane; he seems to have normal or even superior intelligence, so that he seems to understand what he is doing. He suffers from none of the delusions of those who are neurotic or psychotic. And yet most normal people would regard him as mentally disordered, because he is unable to feel social emotions such as love, empathy, guilt, shame, and remorse, which allows him to manipulate and injure other human beings with no concern for their pain. After interviewing Bundy, Cleckley concluded that he conformed to this pattern in being "an emotional robot, programmed by himself to reflect the responses that he has found society demands" (Rule 1989, 403).

Psychopathy is four to seven times more prevalent among men than among women. Thus, psychopathy might be an extreme manifestation of typically masculine traits. Psychopaths are estimated to comprise less than four percent of the general population. Yet this small portion of the population is thought to commit more than 50 percent of all the serious crimes in the United States (Mealey 1995; Zuckerman 1994).

The fictional character Hannibal Lector, as portrayed in the book and the movie *The Silence of the Lambs*, is a psychopath. But it is a mistake to assume that he is a typical psychopath. Most psychopaths are not serial killers. Indeed, psychopaths would be less troublesome if they were all serial killers, because serial killers are extremely rare (perhaps no more than a hundred people in all of North America), but psychopaths are more common (perhaps two million in North America) (Hare 1993).

Most criminals are not psychopaths. Most criminal behavior is easier to explain than psychopathic behavior, because most criminal activity is a purposive, even if mistaken, effort to satisfy desires that most of us can understand—desires for money, revenge, status, or sexual gratification. But the psychopath seems hardly motivated by any purposive effort to satisfy his desires. The psychopath may become a thief, but he seems to have no strong desire for money. He may seduce hundreds of women, but he seems to have no strong desire for any woman (Cleckley 1976). Behind the mask of sanity, there is a flat soul that is hardly moved by any strong desires.

THE FLAT SOUL BEHIND THE MASK

Robert Hare, one of the leading clinical psychologists studying psychopathy, has developed the standard diagnostic procedure for identifying psychopaths based on a "psychopathy checklist" of twelve character traits: glib and superficial, egocentric and grandiose, lack of remorse or guilt, lack of empathy, deceitful and manipulative, shallow emotions, impulsive, poor behavior controls, need for excitement, lack of responsibility, early behavior problems, and adult antisocial behavior. A similar list of traits can be found in Cleckley's "clinical profile" of the psychopath (Cleckley 1976, 337–64). In sketching these traits, I follow Hare's account closely.

1. Glib and superficial. Psychopaths are often smooth, charming speakers. Their conversations display humor, intelligence, and urbane sophistication. Psychopaths who have never finished high school can convince people that they have doctoral degrees in a variety of subjects from prestigious universities around the world.

2. Egocentric and grandiose. Psychopaths regard themselves as superior beings who cannot be governed by the rules that govern the rest of us. Their boundless confidence that they can do anything can make them appear cocky and arrogant. But it also makes them powerfully charismatic to many people. When they are brought to trial, they often fire their lawyers and take over their own defense, because they are convinced that they have more legal talent than any lawyer.

3. A lack of remorse or guilt. Ted Bundy killed as many as a hundred young women. In a prison interview, he was asked about guilt. "Guilt? It's this mechanism we use to control people. It's an illusion. It's a kind of social control mechanism—and it's very unhealthy. It does terrible things to our bodies. And there are much better ways to control our behavior than that rather extraordinary use of guilt" (Hare 1993, 41).

4. Lack of empathy. Psychopaths are not moved by the feelings of other people. If they understand the emotions of others, it is only at a very abstract level. Some psychopaths like Bundy have read textbooks in psychology to try to understand the ordinary emotions of life that they have never felt. A psychopathic rapist admitted that he could not fathom the emotions of his victims: "They are frightened, right? But, you see, I don't really understand it. I've been scared myself, and it wasn't unpleasant" (Hare 1993, 44).

5. Deceitful and manipulative. Psychopaths enjoy lying, and they do it with no inhibition. If they are caught in a lie, they respond by fabricating more lies and insisting on their honesty. Many people are deceived because they cannot imagine how anyone could construct such elaborate lies with such appearance of sincerity. One psychopathic women explained that she sometimes "salts the mine" with a true statement. "If they think some of what you say is true, they usually think it's all true" (Hare 1993, 47).

6. Shallow emotions. A common phrase in psychological studies of psychopaths is "emotional poverty." They cannot feel the emotions that everyone else feels. One psychopath observed: "There are emotions—a whole spectrum of them—that I know only through words, through reading and in my immature imagination. I can *imagine* I feel these emotions (know, therefore, what they are), but I *do not*." Another psychopath said he did not understand what other people meant by fear. "When I rob a bank, I notice that the teller shakes or becomes tongue-tied. One barfed all over the money. She must have been pretty messed up inside, but I don't know why" (Hare 1993, 53–54).

7. Impulsive. Psychopaths act to satisfy momentary whims without considering the bad consequences for themselves or others. "One of our subjects," Hare reports, "said that while walking to a party he decided to buy a case of beer, but realized that he had left his wallet at home six or seven blocks away. Not wanting to walk back, he picked up a heavy piece of wood and robbed the nearest gas station, seriously injuring the attendant" (Hare 1993, 58–59).

8. Poor behavior controls. Psychopaths respond with violent aggression to any trivial action that they perceive as insulting. "An inmate in line for dinner was accidentally bumped by another inmate, whom he proceeded to beat senseless. The attacker then stepped back into his place in line as if nothing had happened. Despite the fact that he faced solitary confinement as punishment for the infraction, his only comment when asked to explain himself was, 'I was pissed off. He stepped into my space. I did what I had to do'" (Hare 1993, 60).

9. Need for excitement. Psychopaths need constant stimulation, and so they are quickly bored by any routine activity. It is hard for them to keep any job that requires discipline and concentration over long periods. They use drugs to relieve their boredom. They are attracted to crime and other dangerous activities because the risks are exciting.

10. Lack of responsibility. Psychopaths cannot be trusted to fulfill any commitments to anyone. As parents, for example, psychopaths show their indifference to their children by failing to provide for their welfare and even abandoning them without adult care.

11. Early behavior problems. Psychopaths show their disruptive behavior at an early age. As children, they show their brutal callousness by being cruel to other children and animals. Jeffrey Dahmer as a child enjoyed nailing cats and dogs to trees. Parents of psychopathic children are stunned by deceitfulness, disobedience, and brutality that go far beyond the misbehavior that one normally expects of a child. One mother observed: "The shocking things he did to his baby sister's doll felt like warnings, but we brushed them aside. But when he actually tried to smother his sister in her crib and snipped the skin of her neck with a pair of scissors, we realized with horror that we should have trusted our worst intuitions from the start" (Hare 1993, 67).

12. Adult antisocial behavior. Psychopathic children who act as if social norms do not apply to them grow up to become adults who act the same way. Although some become criminals distinguished by the frequency and variety of their criminal acts, many others are never convicted of a crime but pursue lives of disreputable behavior as abusive family members, con artists, unethical businessmen, and unscrupulous politicians. Many are so charmingly deceptive that their victims do not realize what is happening until it is too late. One psychopath sketched this kind of character in an essay signed, "A psychopath in prison": "He will choose you, disarm you with his words, and control you with his presence. He will delight you with his wit and his plans. He will show you a good time, but you will always get the bill. He will smile and deceive you, and he will scare you with his eyes. And when he is through with you, and he will be through with you, he will desert you and take with him your innocence and your pride. For a long time you will wonder what happened, and what you did wrong" (Hare 1993, 21).

AN EVOLUTIONARY NICHE FOR MACHIAVELLIANS

If Darwin was right in concluding that natural selection favored the development of a natural moral sense among human beings, can he explain the appearance of people who lack any moral sense because they are naturally inclined to psychopathy? If natural selection favors a psychopathic temperament in at least a small portion of the human population, does that show that psychopathy is just as natural as the moral sense?

In trying to explain the evolution of social cooperation by natural selection, Darwinian theorists have shown that in determining the evolutionary advantages of different social strategies, the best thing for an animal to do depends on what other animals are doing (Axelrod 1984; Maynard Smith 1982; Sigmund 1993). Under certain conditions, cooperation can emerge even in a population of egoists based on the strategy of tit for tat: "[F]irst do unto others as you wish them to do unto you, but then do unto them as they have just done unto you" (Trivers 1985, 392). In a population of cheaters, however, any individual pursuing the tit-for-tat strategy would suffer, because every time the individual cooperated with someone, the other person would cheat by failing to reciprocate the cooperation. But if small clusters of tit-for-tat strategists could enjoy the benefits of cooperating with one another—perhaps because they are kin—while refusing to cooperate with the cheaters, the cooperative strategists could increase their reproductive fitness, so that in future generations their descendants would be more numerous than the descendants of cheaters. Eventually, most of the population would be individuals genetically inclined to cooperate based on a tit-for-tat strategy.

Still, even in a population that is predominantly cooperative, it would be advantageous for a few individuals to adopt a cheater strategy so that they could exploit the cooperative behavior of the general population. The success of these cheaters would require skillful deception in escaping detection and thus escaping punishment from those they want to cheat. But then as the number of cheaters increased, the costs of cheating would increase as the cheaters interacted with one another and thus lost the benefits of cooperation. We could predict, therefore, that natural selection would promote populations with mixed strategies: most individuals would practice a cooperative strategy based on tit for tat, but a small number of individuals would practice a cheating strategy of deceptive exploitation.

There are various ways that natural selection could promote such mixed strategies. One way would be for natural selection to favor genetic differences between individuals so that most individuals would be genetically inclined to a cooperative strategy, but a few would be genetically inclined to a cheating strategy. Another way would be for natural selection to favor behavioral flexibility in response to changing environments so that most individuals would choose a cooperative strategy in environments where cooperation is advantageous, but a few would choose a cheating strategy in environments where such a strategy is likely to succeed.

Linda Mealey (1995) has argued that this evolutionary theory of cooperation provides an ultimate explanation for psychopathy. Psychopaths are the result of evolutionary pressures that favor the appearance of a few people who adopt the behavioral strategy of a deceptive social predator. Studies of psychopathy often distinguish between "primary" and "secondary" psychopathy (Fagan and Lira 1980). Primary psychopaths engage in more severe and more frequent antisocial behavior than secondary psychopaths. And while primary psychopaths resist all efforts to change their behavior, secondary psychopaths can learn in the proper environments to change their behavior. Mealey argues that primary psychopaths are those who are genetically inclined by an inborn temperament to psychopathic behavior, and therefore they are unresponsive to the social learning that normally supports moral development. Secondary psychopaths are those whose psychopathy depends more on environmental factors than genetic factors, because they are inclined to adopt a cheater strategy only in those environments where such a strategy seems advantageous, and therefore their behavior can be modified by changes in their environment.

Some Darwinian theorists, such as Robert Trivers (1971, 1985) and Robert Frank (1988), have explained the social emotions supporting human morality as evolutionary adaptations to sustain social cooperation. Love, sympathy, and friendship dispose us to cooperate with our friends and relatives. Guilt and remorse punish us when we break our social commitments. Anger and indignation incline us to punish others who break their social commitments. Displaying such emotions communicates to others our reliability as social partners. Thus, our social emotions enforce a moral sense based on kinship and reciprocity, which has been favored by natural selection so far as it has enhanced the reproductive success of our evolutionary ancestors.

Mealey (1995) has argued, however, that since psychopaths are naturally adapted for an evolutionary niche based not on cooperation but on cheating, they are naturally incapable of feeling the social emotions. And, indeed, as we have seen, "emotional poverty"—the absence or weakness of social emotions—is commonly recognized as a fundamental trait of psychopaths. As Mealey sees it, psychopaths—or, at least, "primary" psychopaths—are naturally adapted by their genotype for a life of deceptive social predation, and being uninhibited by social emotions is part of that adaptation.

If Mealey is right, the emergence of psychopathy as an evolutionary adaptation suggests that there is an evolutionary niche for Machiavellians. People who deceptively manipulate others for their own selfish purposes, and who can do this without feeling any moral regrets, are often identified as Machiavellians, because such conduct seems to be endorsed in the writings of Niccolò Machiavelli. Social psychologists have extracted statements from two of Machiavelli's books—*The Prince* and *The Discourses*—to comprise a questionnaire to test for Machiavellian character traits (Christie and Geis 1970). People who score high on the "Mach scales" tend to be more emotionally detached than those who score low. Machiavellians are effective social manipulators because they pursue rational strategies for winning every social competition without being distracted by an emotional, moral commitment to people or principles. Machiavellians can use strategies of unscrupulous opportunism to achieve positions of wealth, power, and prestige. Indeed, ethologists use the term "Machiavellian intelligence" to denote the clever deception and manipulation employed by animals seeking dominance in complex social hierarchies (Byrne and Whiten 1988; Harcourt and de Waal 1992). Since the human beings that psychologists identify as Machiavellians have many of the traits of psychopaths, Mealey suggests that Machiavellianism is a "low-level manifestation" of psychopathy (Mealey 1995, 534).

Hare would identify Machiavellians as "subcriminal psychopaths," who are just as selfishly manipulative as the criminal psychopath, but who are clever enough to get what they want while appearing to be morally normal (Hare 1993, 113–14). He believes that we can find such people in every realm of social life—such as business, schools, churches, the arts, and politics. "They are fast-talking, charming, self-assured, at ease in social situations, cool under pressure, unfazed by the possibility of being found out, and totally ruthless. And even when exposed, they can carry on as if nothing has happened, often leaving their accusers bewildered and uncertain about their positions" (Hare 1993, 120).

I disagree with Mealey and Hare, however, insofar as they suggest that psychopaths can live successful lives. True psychopaths—people who have all twelve of the psychopathic traits identified by Hare—cannot be successful, because their behavior will always be self-defeating. People who are so capriciously impulsive that they cannot direct their behavior to any deliberate goal, because they lack any strong desires to give them any consistent purpose, are not going to be successful in life. One of the primary traits in Cleckley's "clinical profile" of the psychopath is "failure to follow any life plan": "The psychopath shows a striking inability to follow any sort of life plan consistently, whether it be one regarded as good or evil. He does not maintain an effort toward any far goal at all" (Cleckley 1976, 364).

The reckless behavior of psychopaths in responding to momentary impulses with no concern for future consequences makes it impossible for them to act prudently for any long-term good (Moore and Rose 1995). The same emotional poverty that prevents their caring about the feelings of others also prevents their caring about their own future. As psychologist John Barresi (1995) has observed, this confirms William Hazlitt's insight that it is the same sympathetic imagination that "must carry me out of myself into the feelings of others . . . by which I am thrown forward as it were into my future being and interested in it. I could not love myself, if I were not capable of loving others."

Mealey claims that psychopaths could do well in certain kinds of exciting or dangerous occupations: "novelist, screen play writer, stunt man, talk show host, disk jockey, explorer, race car driver, or skydiving exhibitionist" (Mealey 1995, 538). But all of these activities require some self-control and deliberate planning, which the true psychopath lacks. Hare concedes that psychopaths are not even likely to be good terrorists or mobsters, because their impulsiveness and irresponsibility would make them careless and unreliable (Hare 1993, 62).

I agree that people we might identify as Machiavellians, because they employ deception and manipulation for selfish gain, can sometimes attain worldly success. I also agree that because of the success of such people, natural selection might favor some traits of the Machiavellian temperament. But even Machiavellians show self-control and deliberation in the pursuit of their goals—such as wealth, power, and prestige—and therefore they cannot be complete psychopaths.

For Machiavelli himself the highest goal was political glory on a grand scale, which he believed was so difficult to attain that only a few people with extraordinary abilities in extraordinary circumstances could succeed (see Machiavelli, *The Prince*, chapter 8; *The Discourses*, bk. 1, chapters 10 and 27, bk. 3, chap. 41). The Machiavellian prince is deeply moved by the desire for the honor or prestige that comes from being obeyed or admired. By contrast, the psychopath is not moved by any strong desire. And since reason and desire are mutually dependent, the psychopath cannot really know what he is doing, because the poverty of his desires makes it impossible for him to consistently pursue any plan of life.

TO KNOW BUT NOT TO FEEL

What would explain the occurrence of psychopathic personalities who apparently lack any moral sense? Recent scientific research has concentrated on the three possible causes identified by Aristotle—injury, habituation, or innate temperament. As a result of injuries to certain parts of the brain, some people show dramatic changes in their behavior so that they display some of the traits of psychopathy. But although neurological studies of psychopaths have revealed abnormal patterns of brain functioning, no specific damage to the brain has been found. Some psychopaths seem to have been hurt by the unhealthy circumstances of their childhood, but in many cases the early social environment of the psychopath has been normal. Since psychopathic traits appear very early in a child and appear even when the early circumstances of the child's rearing have been normal, it would seem that many if not most psychopaths have an inborn temperament to psychopathy, although the expression of that temperament will vary in response to social circumstances.

In Vermont in 1848, Phineas Gage, at age twenty-five, was the victim of an unusual accident. Working as a railroad construction foreman, Gage accidentally ignited an explosion that propelled an iron bar through his brain. When he regained consciousness, he could speak and walk. His physician could detect no loss of intelligence or general cognitive functioning. But Gage's personality changed radically. Before the accident, his employers considered him the most reliable employee they had. After the accident, he was so unreliable that he was fired and never again had a good job. His former friends were shocked by capricious, impulsive behavior that they had never seen in him before the accident. They reported, "Gage was no longer Gage."

In 1994, Antonio and Hanna Damasio, neurologists at the University of Iowa, reported that careful analysis of Gage's skull revealed that the damage was to the prefrontal cortices of the frontal lobes of the brain. This confirmed the recent evidence that people with damage to this part of the brain lose their capacities for making practical decisions and processing social emotions (H. Damasio et al. 1994). It seems that this part of the brain is responsible for some uniquely human characteristics: "the ability to anticipate the future and plan accordingly within a complex social environment; the sense of responsibility toward self and others; and the ability to orchestrate one's survival deliberately." Consequently, the injury to Gage's brain caused him to lose "his ability to plan for the future, to conduct himself according to the social rules he previously had learned, and to decide on the course of action that ultimately would be most advantageous to his survival." In short, he lost "the ability to plan his future as a social being" (A. Damasio 1994, 19, 33). His brain damage caused him to act like a psychopath.

Elliot is the name given to one of the many patients examined by the Damasios afflicted with damage similar to Gage's. Elliot had a brain tumor that damaged his frontal lobes before it was removed by surgery. Before the tumor, Elliot was a successful businessman, husband, and father. After the tumor and the surgery, his wife, children, and friends saw his behavior change radically. He made such foolish mistakes in business and daily life that he seemed unable to manage his life. His wife divorced him. He then married a prostitute briefly before going through a second divorce. He finally became a drifter with no source of income who depended on the care of relatives.

Elliot had damage in the ventromedial prefrontal cortices of his frontal lobes (A. Damasio 1994). People with such damage show no loss of intellectual capacity, at least at the level of abstract reasoning. They show no impairment of memory or knowledge. Their language is good. They can solve problems in logic and calculation. Yet they are unable to make good practical decisions that are socially acceptable and personally advantageous. This weakness in their practical reason seems to come from their inability to feel the social emotions. The poverty in their feelings impedes their reasoning. They cannot *think* clearly about practical decisions because they cannot *feel* strongly about the consequences of their decisions.

The Damasios and others have shown that the emotional poverty of people like Elliot can be detected by observing the activity of the autonomic nervous system. This can be done, for example, by measuring skin conductance response. As a result of emotional arousal, the autonomic nervous system slightly increases sweating, which reduces the skin's resistance to the passage of electrical currents. Electrodes connected to the skin and to a polygraph can measure the increase in electrical conductance.

Elliot and others were shown a series of pictures. Some of the pictures were of emotionally disturbing scenes such as mutilated bodies, and others were neutral. Normal people or people with brain damage outside the prefrontal cortices showed a skin conductance response indicating emotional arousal when viewing the disturbing pictures. But Elliot and other patients with prefrontal brain damage showed no such emotional reaction. Similarly, when tested for their responses to neutral words like "paper" and emotional words like "death," Elliot and those like him were not emotionally aroused by the words with emotional connotations (A. Damasio 1994; A. Damasio et al. 1990). Some of the patients like Elliot could explain that they understood intellectually that some words had emotional meaning, but nonetheless they could not feel the emotion.

"We might summarize Elliot's predicament," Antonio Damasio suggests, "as *to know but not to feel*" (A. Damasio 1994, 45). Although Elliot can think abstractly and logically about the world, it is hard for him to mentally weigh alternative courses of action because he lacks the emotional capacity to assign different emotional weight to different choices. His decision making is as flat as his emotions. Damasio infers from this that it is wrong to assume, as many philosophers and scientists do, that reason and emotion are radically separate, and that moral rationality requires a suppression of the emotions. "What the experience with patients such as Elliot suggests," Damasio observes, "is that the cool strategy advocated by Kant, among others, has far more to do with the way patients with prefrontal damage go about deciding than with how normals usually operate" (A. Damasio 1994, 172). This confirms Aristotle's position, which I have summarized in chapter 2, that deliberate choice requires the union of reason and desire, because "thought by itself moves nothing."

Psychopaths have been observed to show the same emotionally flat skin-conductance responses as Elliot and other patients with damage to the ventromedial prefrontal cortices (A. Damasio et al. 1990; Hare 1993). There is no clear evidence that psychopaths have suffered brain damage. One can infer, however, that psychopaths are born with a genetic proclivity for developing abnormal brain circuitry and biochemical activity in, or associated with, the prefrontal cortices. This genetically influenced abnormality in the structure and functioning of the psychopath's brain could induce the same mental deficits as are observed in people with damage to the prefrontal regions of the brain (A. Damasio 1994; Duncan 1995; Raine 1993; Zuckerman 1994).

Psychopaths do feel some emotions. If they felt no emotions at all, if they were never moved by any desires or aversions, they would be utterly inert because they would have no motive to act. But while they feel the primitive emotions necessary for living, they do not feel, or do not feel very deeply, the social emotions necessary for living as a social animal.

Some emotions are universal features of human nature— emotions such as anger, fear, love, hatred, joy, sadness, guilt, shame, pity, indignation, and envy. Aristotle thought these emotions were natural to human beings (*Rh* 1378a20–88b30). Darwin thought the universality of these emotions was indicated by their expression in universal patterns of facial and other nonverbal displays (1872).

Contemporary research by ethologists and psychologists suggests four kinds of arguments for these emotions as natural adaptations of human evolution (Eibl-Eibesfeldt 1989; Lazarus and Lazarus 1994; LeDoux 1996).

(1) We are naturally adapted for such emotions because they moved our evolutionary ancestors to respond appropriately to situations important for survival and reproduction. Insults elicited anger. Threats to life elicited fear. Children needing care elicited love. Violation of social mores elicited guilt and shame. Unjustified suffering elicited pity. And so on. (2) Our closest primate ancestors, such as chimpanzees, show some of these same emotions as supporting their adaptation for complex social life. (3) Some of these emotions have characteristic facial expressions that are universal. (4) Finally, some of these emotions are rooted in specific neural circuitry and biochemical activities of the nervous system and the endocrine system.

Although these natural emotions are universal, how they manifest themselves will vary from one individual to another and from one society to another. Individual and social differences influence both the arousal and the expression of emotions (Lazarus and Lazarus 1994). For example, anger as a desire for revenge for an unjust slight is a human universal because it reflects a universal desire for social status. Yet what counts as a slight will vary for different individuals and different societies, so the arousal of anger will be more common for some individuals and some societies than others. And once anger is aroused, its expression will vary for different individuals and different societies. We know that some individuals are more irascible than others in that they are easily aroused to anger and immediately express their anger. Anthropologists report that people in some societies (like Japan and Tahiti) are more inclined to control the arousal and expression of anger than are people in other societies (like the United States).

But despite the normal variability in human emotions across individuals and societies, no human society could survive if most human beings were not naturally inclined to social emotions such as love, pity, guilt, and shame. Psychopaths and those with damage to the prefrontal cortices of the brain are unusual in being abnormally deficient in these social emotions. As a result of this emotional deficiency, these people cannot live successfully as social animals, and we must treat them as moral strangers.

MORAL STRANGERS

The psychopath is a moral stranger because he lacks a moral sense, which makes him a moral stranger both to himself and to others. He is estranged from himself because without a moral sense his behavior becomes so self-

defeating that he cannot pursue any long-term plan of life. He is estranged
from others because without a moral sense he cannot live in a moral community with others.

As we have seen, Darwin believed that "any animal whatever, endowed with well-marked social instincts, the parental and filial affections
being here included, would inevitably acquire a moral sense or conscience,
as soon as its intellectual powers had become as well, or nearly as well
developed, as in man" (1936b, 471–72). The social instincts of the psychopath are weak because he does not feel sympathy and other social emotions
that incline human beings to social cooperation. Anyone without such
social emotions must become, Darwin concluded, an "unnatural monster"
(1936b, 483). And although the psychopath seems to have normal or even
superior intellectual powers, he cannot use his intellect in a practical way to
pursue any deliberate view of what would be a good life for him.

Psychopaths manifest the interdependence of reason and desire. They
cannot reason well about their lives because their desires are too shallow to
move them consistently toward any goal. Without deep desires, they lack
the motive power to make or enforce any practical decisions conforming
to any coherent pattern of life. Reason without desire cannot move us,
because it is only through feeling desire that things matter to us. Insofar as
psychopaths feel no deep desire, nothing much matters to them. Consequently, they act capriciously, because their lives have no purpose.

Cleckley describes the "emotional poverty, the complete lack of strong
or tragic feeling" in all the psychopaths that he saw.

> Vexation, spite, quick and labile flashes of quasi-affection, peevish
> resentment, shallow moods of self-pity, puerile attitudes of vanity, and
> absurd and showy poses of indignation are all within his emotional scale
> and are freely sounded as the circumstances of life play upon him. But
> mature wholehearted anger, true or consistent indignation, honest, solid
> grief, sustaining pride, deep joy, and genuine despair are reactions not
> likely to be found within this scale. (Cleckley 1976, 348–49)

This poverty of desire, Cleckley believes, leads to a loss of insight and poor
judgment, such that psychopaths cannot learn from experience in planning
out their lives. Even if they formulate a practical conclusion about how to
live a more satisfying life, they cannot execute that conclusion because they
have no emotional conviction to move them. The lives of psychopaths

cannot be successful, therefore, because their behavior is ultimately self-defeating. They are neither good nor evil, because they cannot pursue any plan of life consistently. They are estranged from themselves.

They are also estranged from other human beings, because they do not share that pattern of desires, including the social desires, that is typical for the human species. The moral strangeness of psychopaths—their lack of moral feelings such as sympathy, love, and guilt, which are normal for most human beings—is the reason why novels and movies about psychopaths can be thrilling for many of us. Human beings who live without any moral sense are such an unfathomable mystery that we are simultaneously shocked and fascinated by them.

But on what ground can we treat the psychopath as an "unnatural monster"? If morality depends upon a moral sense, and if the moral sense depends on moral emotions that typically arise in most human beings, then it would seem that those few people who happen not to share those moral emotions are not bound to obey that moral sense. Yet, although it is true that psychopaths are under no moral obligation to conform to the moral sense, because they lack the moral emotions that provide the only basis for moral obligation, it does not follow that we cannot protect our moral community against their attack. Since they lack the moral sentiments that make moral persuasion possible, our only appeal with such people is force and fear.

Philosophers like Kant sometimes argue that morality requires a purely rational logic of universal rules free from any emotion or desire. Psychopaths show that that cannot be true. There is no evidence that psychopaths have any deficit in their capacity for abstract rationality or pure logic. Their immorality comes not from any defect of abstract reason, but from their emotional poverty. They cannot be moral, because they lack the social emotions—such as sympathy, guilt, and shame—that sustain moral conduct.

We cannot properly blame psychopaths for lacking the moral sentiments natural to us, but neither must we pardon them when they threaten us. Although they are not bound by our morality, they cannot rightly expect us to refrain from defending ourselves against their predatory behavior. To sustain any social order at all, we must treat psychopaths as defective or dysfunctional deviations from human normalcy. Moses would have had Ted Bundy stoned to death. We had him electrocuted. Psychopaths must be confined or executed to protect their potential victims, even if psychopaths are not, strictly speaking, "responsible" for their behavior. Even Bundy, asked by a television interviewer whether he deserved to die, answered: "Good question. I think society deserves to be protected from me and from people like me" (Hare 1993, 52).

CHAPTER 9

THE ENDS AND KINDS OF LIFE

In defending my notion of Darwinian natural right, I have assumed the reality of natural ends and natural kinds. I have assumed that human beings exist as a distinct species or kind of animal with a characteristic set of traits. I have also assumed that these natural traits of the species include natural desires that incline human beings to certain ends. These assumptions have allowed me to argue that whatever frustrates the natural ends of the human species is contrary to nature, and whatever fulfills those ends is according to nature.

So, for example, I have argued that parent-child bonding is naturally good for human beings because it satisfies a natural desire for parental care that belongs to human beings as one of the primary traits of the human species. And I have argued that slavery is naturally bad for human beings because it frustrates a natural desire to be free from exploitation that distinguishes the human species from other species, such as those ants for whom slavery is natural. I have also argued that psychopaths can be properly treated as moral strangers because they lack the normal capacity for moral emotions that is naturally required for human beings to satisfy their desires as social animals.

As I indicated in chapter 1, someone could challenge my idea of Darwinian natural right by denying the objective reality of natural kinds and natural ends. Darwin denied the eternal existence and eternal fixity of species by claiming that modern species emerged by a contingent process of evolution from ancestral species. Some people have inferred from this that the Darwinian scientist must deny the objective reality of species differences since they are not permanent and fixed. Darwin also denied that living nature was designed by God according to some cosmic purpose or end. Some people have inferred from this that the Darwinian scientist must deny the objective reality of natural ends as anything other than arbitrary projections of human will.

In this chapter, I will contend that, far from denying natural kinds and natural ends, Darwinian biology provides the only scientific explanation for why living beings emerge in the world as distinct kinds with distinct ends.

NATURAL KINDS

In drawing moral conclusions from the facts of human nature, I assume that there is a human nature, that human beings share certain capacities and desires that distinguish the human species from other species. Is this Aristotelian understanding of species still defensible in the light of modern Darwinian biology? We know now that all human beings, even "identical" twins, are genetically and biochemically unique (Lewontin 1982; Williams 1956). We also know that all species are contingent, in the sense that present species have evolved from ancestral species, and those now existing can become extinct. Does this deny the existence of species as stable realities? In fact, many scholars conclude that Darwinian science shows that species classification is a purely arbitrary convention with no basis in nature.

As a man with medical training, Aristotle knew that each patient was unique, and so the meaning of health and disease varied according to the individual. "For the physician does not cure 'man' except in the incidental way, but Callias or Socrates or some other called by some individual name, who happens to be a man" (*Meta* 981a17). He emphasized that human beings differ in their natural desires insofar as they differ in age, sex, and temperament. But he knew that since human beings are *both* unique *and* similar, the relative importance of uniqueness or similarity depends on the circumstances. Although each human being is physically and psychically unique, neither medicine nor psychology would be possible if each human being were *totally* unique. Moreover, human beings could not live together as social and political animals if they were not fundamentally similar in their natural desires and powers (McShea 1990, chap. 3).

Classifying animals into species based on their similarities and differences illustrates a fundamental feature of human knowledge: to make sense of things we must organize our particular sense impressions into general patterns. To recognize a dog I have to view this particular furry creature before me as a member of the class "dog." Even the simplest perceptual knowledge would be impossible without the application of some universal idea to the evanescent data of the senses. Every common noun manifests this universalizing activity of the mind.   Do we invent these universals and impose them on reality? Or do we somehow discover them in reality itself? This was the issue in the medieval philosophic debate between the "essentialists" (or "realists") and the "nominalists." The nominalists argued that universals have no real existence except as names invented by the human mind to organize sense experience: the world consists of atomic facts, so that whatever patterns we see, based on the apparent likenesses and unlikenesses of things, are only the constructions of our minds. Many of the early modern philosophers in the Western world adopted this position. There is "nothing in the world universal but names," Thomas Hobbes declared, "for the things named are every one of them individual and singular" (*Leviathan*, chap. 4). Similarly, David Hume asserted: "[A]ll beings in the universe, considered in themselves, appear entirely loose and independent of each other" (1888, 466).

Although this originated as an issue in logic and metaphysics, it had implications for biology. Until the nineteenth century, most biologists seemed to be essentialists in that they thought the classification of species manifested the fixed order of nature in "the great chain of being" (Lovejoy 1936). A biologist was expected to identify an organism according to the natural essence that it shared with other members of its species. Obviously, this sort of thinking was an obstacle to the theory of evolution, which claims that species are not eternally fixed since they have evolved into their present form and will continue to change in the future. It is understandable, therefore, that Darwin, in *The Origin of Species*, appeared to take a nominalistic position on the concept of species: "We shall have to treat species in the same manner as those naturalists treat genera, who admit that genera are merely combinations made for convenience. This may not be a cheering prospect; but we shall at least be free from the vain search for the undiscovered and undiscoverable essence of the term species" (1936a, 371). Some scholars interpret this Darwinian denial of essentialism to mean that since *Homo sapiens* is a historically contingent entity, like every other species, there is no such thing as human nature (Hull 1978).

I would argue, however, that, despite the impression conveyed by some passages in Darwin's writings, evolutionary biology does not deny the natural reality of species. In fact, evolutionary theory provides the best biological explanation of the existence of species. Yet this evolutionary account of species is neither strictly essentialist nor strictly nominalist.

In the essentialist tradition of biological classification, logical division was used to classify organisms into genera and species. The system of Carl Linnaeus was the high point of this tradition. Contrary to the common view, Aristotle did not originate this method. On the contrary, he criticized the artificiality of applying logical division to biological phenomena (*PA* 642–44b22); and thus, as Ernst Mayr (1982) has indicated, Aristotle anticipated the modern Darwinian criticisms of essentialist classification. Aristotle's biology was misinterpreted in the Middle Ages by those who viewed his logical concept of "species" as a biological concept of fixed kinds conforming to the teaching of biblical creationism. One commentator explains: "The creation of 'kinds' in the Biblical account of creation was identified with the species of Aristotle's logic, and the result 'the creation of fixed species' is assumed in the classificatory scheme of Linnaeus in the eighteenth century" (Buchanan 1972, 141).

Aristotle noticed how slight the differences are between similar species. Sea squirts, for instance,

> differ but slightly in their nature from plants, and yet they are more like animals than are the sponges, for these completely have the character of plants. For nature passes in a continuous sequence from lifeless things to animals, through living things that are not animals, so that the differences between neighboring groups seem very small because they are so close. (*PA* 681a10–15)

He recognized many intermediate species that stand between water animals and land animals (such as dolphins, whales, and seals) or between land animals and birds (such as bats and ostriches) (*PA* 697a15–97b26). After comparing humans as bipeds with the quadrupeds, he observed that apes are intermediate between the two, being like a biped in having no tail but like a quadruped in having no buttocks (*PA* 689b32–34).

We might see this as evidence of evolution, but Aristotle never developed a theory of evolution because of his heavy reliance on direct observation: we can see the similarities and differences between human beings and apes, but we cannot see apes and human beings evolving from common ancestors. With Darwin's help, we can "see" the evolution of species only by inference from indirect evidence such as the fossil record. As Darwin concedes, his arguments depend on plausibility rather than proof (Darwin 1936a, 13, 62, 70, 102, 133–39, 145–46, 151, 248–49, 254, 353; 1936b, 495, 908–9; 1892, 55–56; Ruse 1973, 96–121).

In comparison with Darwinian biology, we could say that Aristotle's biology is concerned with the functional adaptations of species to their environment rather than the evolutionary origin of those adaptations. For example, Aristotle saw that whales and dolphins resembled land mammals more than fish. Modern Darwinian paleontologists see the same resemblances, but they explain them as a phylogenetic consequence of an evolutionary history in which some species of land mammals became adapted to aquatic life and thus became the ancestors of modern cetaceans (Novacek 1994).

Even though Aristotle thought some of the boundaries between species were fuzzy, he clearly regarded the distinct species as real entities of nature (*PA* 644a24–27). Darwin would have to agree. In his criticisms of Linnaeus's "natural system" of classification, Darwin affirmed the natural reality of species by claiming that only evolutionary biology could uncover the natural basis of classification. He insisted that "the characters which naturalists consider as showing true affinity between any two or more species, are those which have been inherited from a common parent." Therefore, "community of descent is the hidden bond which naturalists have been unconsciously seeking, and not some unknown plan of creation, or the enunciation of general propositions, and the mere putting together and separating objects more or less alike." All true classification "must be strictly genealogical in order to be natural" (Darwin 1936a, 323). In thus seeking a "natural system" of classification based on natural affinities of organisms as they are related by phylogenetic descent, Darwin was closer to Aristotle than to the nominalists (Sloan 1972, 1985).

Denying the historical permanence of species, as the Darwinian must, does not deny the reality of species as natural kinds. Although species are not eternally fixed, since they have evolved from ancestral species, that does not make them any less real during the time of their existence. As Gould would say, "Species are stable entities with very brief periods of fuzziness at their origin" (1980, 213). The very practice of biological science presupposes that the distinctions between species are real distinctions in nature. In the twentieth century, biologists have employed different ways of classifying organisms—such as genetic similarity, morphological similarity, common ancestors, and reproductive isolation. But when these various criteria coincide in identifying individual organisms as belonging to one species, it is reasonable to regard this species as a natural kind (Ruse 1987). From the Darwinian view, a species is neither the manifestation of an eternal essence, as the essentialists would claim, nor simply an arbitrary collection of individuals, as the nominalists would claim.

The natural reality of species is confirmed by the remarkable uniformity across cultures in the "folk classifications" of species as studied by biological anthropologists. In contrast to the assumption of the cultural relativist that human beings view the natural world through culturally constructed images that vary arbitrarily from one culture to another, anthropologists such as Scott Atran (1990) and Brent Berlin (1992) have shown that human beings around the world categorize plants and animals according to universal regularities that reflect the natural order of living beings. This supports the wisdom of Aristotle who believed that, in comparison with the abstract logical schemes of theorists, the commonsense classifications of ordinary people were usually closer to the truth because they were usually rooted in direct experience (*PA* 643b10–15). The folk classification of Aristotle's day made some errors—such as classifying bats as birds and whales as fish—but Aristotle could easily correct these errors while accepting the general validity of popular classification.

I would argue, therefore, that a Darwinian view of species sustains Aristotelian naturalism: there really is a human nature, which includes a species-specific repertoire of desires and capacities, and we can judge moral and political practices by how well they conform to those natural desires and capacities.

It might seem that I have just asserted two points in favor of moral relativism (Sorenson 1988). First, if the good is the desirable, and the desirable varies according to the natural desires of each species, the good differs from one species to another: what is good for human beings is not necessarily good for other species and is therefore not *simply* good. Second, if we accept Darwin's theory of evolution, then the human species, like any other species, is not eternal but a contingent result of evolutionary history that can pass away; and therefore the human good as relative to the desires of the human species is also contingent.

The first point—that what is good varies according to the species—should not disturb us unless we believe the objective reality of the *human* good depends on its being a *cosmic* good. It is sensible to recognize, as Aristotle does, that the term "good" has as many senses as the term "being," and "being" has as many senses as "healthy" (*NE* 1003a33–b15, 1096a24). Whatever is befitting to something is good for it, and therefore goodness varies according to the nature of each thing. The goodness of life is rendered no less real by being relative to each species: "The good is not the same for all animals, but is different in the case of each" (*NE* 1141a31–32). We can see that in those respects as to which we differ from other animals, what is good for us is not good for them. Yet this in no way diminishes the objective reality of the good for us as conforming to our nature.

Some contemporary proponents of "environmental ethics" argue for a "biocentric" or "ecocentric" ethics by which nonhuman entities—plants, animals, and even inanimate things—have inherent value regardless of whether or not they have any instrumental value for human beings (Callicott 1994; Des Jardins 1993). But I reject this. All judgments of value are "anthropocentric" in the sense that whatever we believe to be good must ultimately be good *for human beings* as satisfying *human* desires. Following the lead of wildlife ecologist Aldo Leopold, I would argue that the ecological understanding of the complex interdependence in biotic communities helps human beings to strive for a prudent management of nature to satisfy their intellectual, ethical, and aesthetic desires (Arnhart 1998). Because of their intellectual desire for understanding, human beings can take pleasure in perceiving the natural world as a complex mechanism. Because of their ethical desire for community, human beings can take pleasure in respecting the natural world to which they are tied by a biotic web of relationships. And because of their aesthetic desire for beauty, human beings can take pleasure in marveling at the natural world as a cosmic drama.

The second point on which I seem to have supported a moral relativism—that the good of a species exists only as long as the species exists—should not disturb us unless we believe the objective reality of the *human* good depends on its being an *eternal* good. Even if species are not eternally fixed but have evolved from ancestral species, that does not make them any less real for as long as they endure. That human beings came into existence at all and that they came into existence as the kind of beings they are may be contingent outcomes of an evolutionary process that could have turned out differently. But that human beings now exist and exist with the nature they have means that we can judge as good whatever conforms to their nature and as bad whatever does not.

As Aristotle said in response to Plato, "[T]he Idea of the Good will not be any more good because it is eternal, seeing that a white thing that lasts for a long time is not whiter than a white thing that lasts for a day" (*NE* 1096b3–5). Something good for us because it serves a natural human desire is no less good if our species survives for only a few hundred thousand years. If a huge meteorite were to collide with the earth tomorrow and kill us all, wouldn't we still have to say it was good while it lasted?

NATURAL ENDS

To appeal to nature as a source of moral norms implies a teleological conception of nature as having ends, goals, or purposes. When Aristotle claims that man is by nature the most political animal, he explicitly invokes a natural teleology: political life is natural for man because it is the end or goal *(telos)* of his development, and "nature is an end" (*Pol* 1252b28–53a19). Any notion of natural right or natural law depends on a teleological understanding of nature.

According to Leo Strauss, in *Natural Right and History*, "natural right in its classic form is connected with a teleological view of the universe. All natural beings have a natural end, a natural destiny, which determines what kind of operation is good for them" (1953, 7). The crucial problem for natural right, Strauss believes, is that modern natural science seems to have refuted teleology. "The fundamental dilemma, in whose grip we are, is caused by the victory of modern natural science. An adequate solution to the problem of natural right cannot be found before this basic problem has been solved" (1953, 8). I agree with Roger Masters (1987, 1989), however, that Strauss is wrong in suggesting that the question of teleology depends on physics or astronomy, because Aristotle's teleology is primarily biological, and so the question is whether teleology is necessary for explaining *living* nature.

Like every idea in Aristotle's philosophic work, his "four causes" are refinements of commonsense experience. When we examine something made or produced by human beings, we naturally ask four questions. What is it (formal cause)? What is it made of (material cause)? Who or what made it (efficient cause)? And what is it made for (final cause)? We would ask similar questions about the works of nature, although we might wonder about the question of purpose.

Is it reasonable to ask what daisies and dogs are made for? To avoid personifying nature as a conscious being with intentions, we could say that the final cause for plants and animals is tied to the formal cause: the end or purpose for a daisy or a dog is the fullest and most appropriate development of its potential form. The growth of the daisy or the dog to its mature form somehow fulfills nature's goal. Or should we rather say that, since nature is fully governed by the material laws of physics and chemistry, the "forms" and "ends" of nature have no causal force of their own, because they are only the effects of material and efficient causes? This apparently metaphysical issue has implications for our moral and political reasoning, because how we resolve this issue will influence, if not decide, the question of whether human purposefulness can be rooted in nature, which is the critical question for assessing ethical naturalism.

Allan Gotthelf (1975, 1987) has shown that there are at least three interpretations of Aristotle's conception of final causality. First, it is often assumed that Aristotle's final causes presuppose the action of some immaterial, vital force, which modern critics can easily dismiss as mystical nonsense. Yet although Aristotle does sometimes speak of nature as acting like an artisan, he intends this to be taken metaphorically rather than literally. While believing that art imitates nature, he never infers from this that nature's activity requires the conscious, intentional action of some supernatural or cosmic agent. The final cause of a natural object exists in the object itself. Nature works not like a shipbuilder building a ship, Aristotle explains, but like a doctor doctoring himself (*Ph* 199b30–32).

A second interpretation of Aristotle's notion of final causality, advanced by those who want to reconcile Aristotelian teleology and modern reductionist materialism, is that Aristotle's final cause is not really a cause but only a heuristic concept to make certain natural phenomena intelligible to us, although in reality nature is ultimately reducible to material and efficient causes. This view overlooks, however, the many passages in Aristotle's writings where he clearly denies such materialist reductionism.

I think Gotthelf is right in defending a third interpretation, according to which Aristotle's final causality denotes nature's irreducible potential for form. A careful reading of the pertinent texts, particularly the first section of the *Parts of Animals* and the second book of the *Physics*, suggests that the development, structure, and functioning of a living organism manifest the actualization of its potential for organic form, an actualization that depends upon, but is not reducible to, the natural potentialities of its material elements. For example, the growth of a human embryo requires the actualization of certain material constituents (flesh, blood, food, and so on), but the actualization of the potential for human form in the embryo cannot be accounted for completely as a sum of the actualizations of its material elements. Insisting that nature works through formal and final causes as well as material and efficient causes, with each factor being indispensable but insufficient on its own, Aristotle follows the suggestion of Socrates in Plato's *Phaedo* (96a–99d, 103a–e) that natural causality is irreducibly heterogeneous in combining matter and form, necessity and intelligibility, body and mind.

To speak of the causal power of organic form and nature's striving for ends may sound old-fashioned today in an age of neuroscience and biotechnology, when every manifestation of life, including the human soul, seems explicable as an outcome of a purely mechanistic process. Yet, I would argue, far from refuting Aristotle's teleology, modern biology confirms living nature's irreducible potential for form. If Aristotle's teleology is, as one commentator on Aristotle's *Physics* says, "nothing but his claim that all natural beings are self-maintaining wholes" (Sachs 1995, 247), then modern biology supports such teleology.

Does nature work by necessity or for purposes? Aristotle would say, both. "Everything that occurs is done either because it is necessary or because it is better" (*GA* 717a15–16). By "necessary nature" certain things occur by necessity, things that "rational nature" can use for some purpose (*PA* 663b23–24). We can accept Aristotle's biological teleology while still giving material causes their proper weight. In affirming nature as form and purpose, Aristotle also affirms nature as matter and necessity. When by some natural necessity nature's end is not reached, this is contrary to nature in one sense but according to nature in another sense (*GA* 770b10–16). A deformity in the development of an animal is unnatural in that the usual end of such development has not been fulfilled, but it is natural insofar as even a deformity has natural physical causes. "A monstrosity is not necessary with reference to the purposive or final cause, but as an accident it is necessary" (*GA* 767b13–14).

In previous chapters, we have considered some examples of what Aristotle would call natural deformities or monstrosities. When Harry Harlow's monkeys reared in social isolation grew into adults who did not know how to care for their offspring, this was natural in the sense that it had natural causes, but unnatural in the sense that the abnormal environment impeded the natural development of parental care in those monkeys. Similarly, when some human beings emerge as psychopaths with no capacity for social emotions, this is natural in that it has natural causes, but unnatural in that some abnormality in the brain of the psychopath impedes the natural development of the social emotions necessary to live successfully as a social animal. In such cases, nature's ends have not been fulfilled.

Aristotle does not think every variation in nature is perfectly adapted to some purpose. Nature sometimes has to make awkward adjustments (*PA* 648a14–19, 658b26–59a37, 662b23–63a17, 694a14–94b12). For example, elephants are so large and heavy that their feet can serve only as supports, and they must use their trunks to do some things that other animals would do with their forefeet. Here a nose must be used like a foot. Some biological processes and entities arise as necessary effects without serving any definite purpose. The excretions of the stomach and intestines illustrate this. "For although nature sometimes uses even residues for some benefit, yet we ought not for that reason to look for some purpose in all cases" (*PA* 677a15–18). "Hypothetical necessity" is part of a teleological explanation, but "simple necessity" is not. The "hypothetical necessity" by which an eye is formed with the capacity for vision serves a natural end. The "simple necessity" by which the color of a eye is determined need not serve any end (*GA* 778a16–35). Aristotle would agree, therefore, with those Darwinian biologists, like Gould and Lewontin (1979), who warn against the assumption that nature always achieves perfect adaptations.

The wisdom of Aristotle's combination of teleological and mechanistic explanations is confirmed by the success of many of his biological theories. One paramount example is his explanation of how embryonic development follows a potential pattern in the embryo.

> It is clear that there is something that makes the parts of the embryo, but this does not exist as a definite individual, nor does it exist in the semen at first already perfect. But how does each part arise? . . . whatever arises by nature or by art arises by something *actually* existing out of that which is *potentially* such a being. (*GA* 734b17–22)

To explain how parents act as efficient causes in determining the development of an embryo, Aristotle offers an analogy with mechanical puppets (734b9–17). Even at rest the automaton has a potentiality for a pattern of motion fixed by its internal mechanism. Similarly, parents have implanted a potential pattern of development in the embryo.

One of the greatest controversies in the history of embryology was the conflict between the proponents of "preformation" and the proponents of "epigenesis." According to the first theory, a fertilized egg contains a tiny adult that grows in size without any structural changes. According to the other theory, the egg is amorphous at the beginning, and its development is a gradual differentiation of parts leading to the adult. Biologists finally resolved this controversy by finding some truth in both theories. Mayr (1982, 106) explains: "[T]he epigenesists were correct in stating that the egg at its beginning is essentially undifferentiated, and the preformationists were correct that its development is controlled by something preformed, now recognized as the genetic program." So after thousands of years of debate, biologists now agree that Aristotle was essentially correct: we cannot explain the development of unorganized matter into a complex organism unless we see that some potential "form" *(eidos)* is thereby actualized as the "end" *(telos)* of the growth. We can understand why Max Delbrück, a Nobel Prize winner in molecular biology, once gave a lecture with the title "How Aristotle Discovered DNA" (1976).

There are good reasons for separating this *immanent* teleology of living bodies from Aristotle's *cosmic* teleology of the heavenly bodies (Lennox 1992, 1993; Nussbaum 1978, 93–99, 121–42). Of course, modern science has shown that life on earth *does* depend on a complex combination of cosmic events (Barrow and Tipler 1986). The elements of life—such as hydrogen, carbon, nitrogen, oxygen, and phosphorus—had to be generated by a complex cosmic process. Life as we know it continually depends on the energy of the sun as captured in photosynthesis. But that these and many other cosmic events necessary for life were teleologically ordered seems implausible, at least from the perspective of modern science.

Even from Aristotle's point of view, the heavenly spheres cannot completely determine biological generation "because of the indeterminateness of matter and because of the many principles of generation" (*GA* 778a5–9). Moreover, he explains, in contrast to our observational knowledge of the perishable phenomena of plants and animals, we can have little direct knowledge of the heavenly bodies (*PA* 644b21–45a37). He concedes that his account of the eternity and divinity of the celestial spheres depends on traditional religious opinions handed down from ancient times (*DC* 270b1–26, 279b4–12, 283a30–b6, 284b1–5, 291b24–28; *Meta* 1074b1–14). Moses Maimonides inferred that Aristotle knew his arguments for the eternity of the world were not scientific or philosophic demonstrations but rhetorical appeals to popular opinions (*The Guide of the Perplexed* 1.15). In the *Nico-machean Ethics* (1099b8–24), Aristotle quickly rejects the thought that human happiness is a gift of the gods. And in the *Politics* (1252b24–28, 1268b34–69a14), he denigrates ancestral religious beliefs, and recommends that in the best political community, religious activity would be regulated for the sake of its political utility (1322b18–30, 1329a27–34, 1331b4–6). The power of the gods over the generation of life is only indirect: since it is important for pregnant women to exercise daily, legislators should require them to walk every day to the temples of the gods of childbirth (1335b14–16).

Aristotle's biological teleology cannot be cosmic, because to explain a natural occurrence through its final cause is to explain "why it was better in this way—not absolutely, but relative to the substance of each thing" (*Phy* 198b8). The term "good" has as many senses as the term "being," and "being" has as many senses as "healthy" (*NE* 1003a33–b15, 1096a24). The goodness of life, therefore, is relative to each species. "The good is not single for all animals, but is different in the case of each" (*NE* 1141a31–32).

As human beings, we naturally take an "anthropocentric" perspective; but to do this does not dictate a cosmic hierarchy of ends. In ethics and politics, "we must speak about the good, and about what is good not simply, but for us" (*MM* 1182b3–5). From this point of view, plants exist for the sake of animals, and the other animals exist for the good of man (*Pol* 1256b15–27). Similarly, in biology, we start with human biology as paradigmatic for the rest of living nature. "For monetary currencies are reckoned with reference to what is best known to a people, and so in other fields. But man of all animals is by necessity the one best known to us" (*HA* 491a20–23). Yet we can still recognize the many respects in which other animals are naturally superior to us. With respect to sensory powers, for instance, except in the sense of touch, man's senses are inferior to those of many other animals (*HA* 494b15–18).

Those commentators who claim that Darwin refuted teleology (for example, Ghiselin 1984) commonly assume that there are only two forms of teleological reasoning—either natural theology, in which the design in nature is regarded as evidence for a divine creator, or mystical vitalism, in which the purposeful order of nature is explained as the work of some immaterial force or agent. But this ignores the kind of teleological argument developed in the tradition of functional morphology, a tradition that includes Karl Ernst von Baer, E. S. Russell, Adolf Portmann, and Michael

Polanyi (Grene 1968, 1974; Lauder 1982; Lenoir 1989; Russell 1916). The functional morphologists begin with the facts of organic form and function as biological phenomena that depend upon, but are not reducible to, the laws of physics and chemistry. The purposive organization and goal-directedness of organisms require explanatory principles that go beyond the laws of physics and chemistry, although they do not violate those physical laws. For biological science, therefore, teleological explanations and mechanistic explanations do not contradict but rather supplement one another, because they work at different levels of biological reality (Mayr 1996).

For example, to explain the eye, we would need a causal explanation of the physiological mechanisms in the operation of the eye. But this by itself tells us nothing about the function of the eye, which is to see. To account for that function, we need a teleological explanation. To explain the evolution of the human eye or of the different kinds of eyes possessed by other animals, we would need a teleological explanation of how various optical mechanisms were adapted for various forms of vision that would promote the reproductive success of certain organisms (Dawkins 1995, 1996; Goldsmith 1990; Nilsson and Pelger 1994). The physiological account explains *how* an eye operates. The teleological account explains *why* it operates as it does. Indeed, the explanation of such complex functionality of design as the outcome of natural selection is the primary concern of modern Darwinism (Dawkins 1986; Williams 1966). (The success of such explanations is essential to defend Darwinism against the often repeated claim of its critics that it cannot explain the complex design of organs such as the eye.) Thus, we could say that Darwin's explanation of biological adaptation as the result of natural selection established a scientific teleology (Amundson 1996; Ayala 1968, 1970; Binswanger 1990, 1992; Dobzhansky et al., 1977; Lennox 1992, 1993; Mayr 1988).

Although biologists rarely endorse teleology explicitly, because of the concept's association with vitalism and theology, teleological reasoning permeates modern biology. For instance, one of the most important general concepts in biology is homeostasis (Cannon 1932). All organisms have some ability to maintain a stable internal balance despite changes in their surroundings. The homeostasis of the human body includes many factors, such as maintaining an internal temperature within a narrow range of a few degrees despite great changes in external temperature. Homeostasis is a teleological concept because it assumes goal-directed causality. This was made explicit by Hans Selye (1976, 355–66), who used teleological reasoning about homeostasis to develop the physiological concept of stress.

Even when biologists rely on the mechanistic explanations of biochemistry, they must put these within a framework of functional teleology. For instance, the very possibility of animal life evolving depends on the high efficiency of cells in extracting chemical energy from organic molecules by oxidizing them. An essential part of this oxidative respiration is a sequence of chemical reactions known as the citric acid cycle (also called the Krebs cycle), which extracts the energetic electrons that are used to make ATP (adenosine triphosphate), which is the fuel for cell metabolism in all organisms. The chemist can explain to the biologist *how* these reactions occur. But the biologist also needs an explanation for *why* these particular reactions occur in this particular series. This demands a functional explanation in terms of the goals of the organism. In one of the most widely used and respected textbooks in biology, one finds the following comment: "The citric acid cycle represents one of the best examples of how a biochemical pathway can be organized to accomplish a sophisticated goal. It is clever, efficient, and, as chemistry, beautiful" (Raven and Johnson 1992, 170).

Darwinian theory surely does away with any cosmic teleology by which the universe as a whole would be seen as ordered to some end. The principle of natural selection explains the adaptation of species without reference to any forces guiding nature to secure a cosmic scale of perfection. Yet, although the evolutionary process does not serve goals, the organisms emerging from that process do. Darwin's biology does not deny—rather, it reaffirms—the immanent teleology displayed in the striving of each living being to fulfill its specific ends (Lennox 1992, 1993). Some scholars in the history of biology argue that "the only 'teleology' Darwin criticized was that represented in creationist ideas of special divine providence," and therefore his biology does not deny "the empirical teleology of self-organizing beings" (Cornell 1986, 420). The hackneyed examples are still valid: acorns still grow into oak trees and puppies into dogs. Reproduction, growth, feeding, healing, courtship, parental care for the young—these and many other activities of organisms are goal-directed (Russell 1945). Biologists cannot explain such processes unless they ask about their ends or purposes, and thus they must still look for "final causes."

Since the term "teleology" is commonly associated with cosmic purposiveness, some biologists prefer the term "teleonomy" to designate the goal-directed character of living beings (Pittendrigh 1958). "A teleonomic process or behavior," Mayr (1988, 45) explains, "is one which owes its goal-directedness to the operation of a program," and this is one of the pervasive characteristics of life. The modern biological understanding of teleonomy as governed by the genetic program of DNA confirms Aristotle's insights. Adopting Delbrück's idea, Mayr contends that

> it is quite legitimate to employ modern terms like *genetic program* for *eidos* where this helps to elucidate Aristotle's thoughts. . . . Aristotle saw with extraordinary clarity that it made no more sense to describe living organisms in terms of mere matter than to describe a house as a pile of bricks and mortar. Just as the blueprint used by the builder determines the form of a house, so does the *eidos* . . . give the form to the developing organism, and this *eidos* reflects the terminal *telos* of the full-blown individual. (1988, 56)

On the other hand, it might seem that, far from confirming Aristotle's biological teleology, the discovery of DNA—and of the complex mechanisms by which the interaction of DNA, RNA, and other factors guide the assembly of proteins from amino acids—actually refutes Aristotle. After all, doesn't this allow the molecular biologist, at least in principle, to reduce biology to physics and chemistry by explaining life as a mechanism governed by the genetic code of DNA, which itself is reducible to physical and chemical interactions?

This ignores the irreducible hierarchy of biological phenomena, which does in fact sustain Aristotle's conception of teleology (Anderson 1972; Mayr 1996; Salthe 1985). As just indicated, the biological reduction of formal and final causes to material and efficient causes rests on two ideas: nature as a *mechanism* and DNA as conveying *information* through a code. Each of these ideas, as Michael Polanyi (1968; Polanyi and Prosch 1975) has argued, presumes levels of complexity in which the higher levels cannot be fully accounted for in terms of the lower. The biological reductionist assumes that, since organisms are mechanisms, and mechanisms obey physical and chemical laws, organisms must also be fully explained by such laws. This reasoning fails, however, because mechanisms are not fully accountable through physical and chemical laws. The physical and chemical interactions within a machine must obey the laws of physics and chemistry. But at a higher level of organization, the principle of a mechanism's design determines the structure or boundary conditions within which the physical and chemical interactions occur.

Machines are human artifacts by which human beings harness the laws of physics and chemistry to serve human purposes. To understand a machine we must understand not only the interactions of its physical and chemical elements, but also the organization of these elements for achieving a goal. Explaining the physical-chemical laws that govern a clock or an automobile will not explain these objects as machines if we do not understand their functions. A machine can fail to achieve its goal. But when a clock fails to measure time accurately, or a car fails to provide proper transportation, the laws of inanimate nature have not failed to operate. Rather, the failure is in the breaking down of the structure of the machine so that it does not harness the inanimate forces of nature for useful work. The principles of the machine's functional design presuppose, but are not fully reducible to, the principles of the natural forces harnessed by the machine. Mechanistic explanations must include teleological explanations that refer to the goals or functions of machines, by which we judge their success or failure. We thereby invoke principles of organization that transcend inanimate nature.

The same kind of hierarchy holds true for DNA as conveying information. If DNA were completely determined by physical-chemical laws, it could not function as a code. This must be so, because the material carrier of a code must be physically and chemically neutral (more or less) to the code it carries. For example, as I write this book, I must harness the physical and chemical properties of paper and ink to convey my ideas symbolically; but the syntax and the semantics of the symbols on the page are not governed by the chemistry of ink blots on paper. A chemist who did not understand English would not be able to interpret my writing just by doing a chemical analysis of the ink on the paper. Similarly, the sequence of nucleotide bases in a DNA chain can convey information only if the sequence has not been simply determined by physical-chemical laws. If the patterns of ink blots on my paper or the patterns of a DNA series were fully explainable by physical-chemical laws, such patterns could not carry information. The success of a living organism, like the success of a piece of writing, requires the organization of meaningless matter into meaningful form.

Teleological reasoning is necessary at all levels of the organization of a living being. But for ethical naturalism the primary concern is at the level of animal movement. As I have argued in chapter 2, animals move to satisfy their natural desires based on some information about the threats and opportunities in their environment. Any complete explanation of animal movement must include some notion of relative success or failure of the animal in satisfying its desires in different environments.

The same is true for human movement, except that the human cognitive capacity for gathering and assessing information through abstract social symbols intensifies the social evolution of human beings, and consequently any reasonable explanation of human movement includes some judgment of the relative success or failure of different societies in satisfying human desires in different environments. We cannot explain social practices such as slavery, familial attachments, or female circumcision without some prudential judgment of moral achievement or failure. If we defend these practices, we must argue that, in the circumstances in which they occur, they conform better to human desires and capacities than their alternatives. If we condemn these practices, we must argue that since they frustrate human desires, either they should be immediately changed, or they should be changed as soon as circumstances permit. If we tried to avoid either defending or condemning, we could not understand these or any other social practices, because every social practice is a pattern of thought and action that has some end, goal, or purpose, so that any explanation necessarily includes some assessment of its success in attaining its purpose in harmony with the purposes of other social practices.

In previous chapters, I have argued that parent-child bonding and male-female bonding are natural because they satisfy natural human desires. Any attempt to abolish such social bonding is contrary to nature because it prevents human beings from fulfilling their natural ends. Female circumcision and slavery, by contrast, are unnatural because they frustrate natural human desires. Therefore, abolishing female circumcision and slavery is according to nature because this helps human beings to fulfill their natural ends. In this way, Darwinian natural right rests on a teleological conception of animal movement as a striving for natural ends.

CHAPTER 10

NATURE AND NATURE'S GOD

Darwinian natural right does not require any religious beliefs. All of my reasoning in this book rests on assertions about human nature as adapted by natural selection for life on earth. Whatever evidence and arguments I have presented for my assertions depend on the examination of natural human experience by natural reason. I have not invoked any religious beliefs about a supernatural reality, such as the beliefs that the world was created by God, that human beings were created in the image of God, or that God legislated a moral law for his human creatures. But some religious believers would object that morality must collapse if it has no transcendent support from the will of God.

For example, in a review of James Q. Wilson's book, *The Moral Sense*, Father Richard John Neuhaus, a conservative Catholic theologian, complained: "The treatment of religion—or, more accurately, the non-treatment of religion—is the most unsatisfactory part of the book. . . . Wilson dramatically breaks from the tradition that he would champion by relegating the transcendent to the category of the irrelevant" (Neuhaus 1993, 56). Religious believers like Neuhaus would argue that natural moral sentiments by themselves cannot sustain morality. Human beings will not be moral unless they believe that God provides the transcendent ground of morality (Neuhaus 1996, 17). Without such divine sanction, the sentiments, feelings, or passions supporting morality are merely arbitrary preferences. If we cannot appeal to some divine standard of goodness, they insist, then we have no reason to prefer good sentiments over bad sentiments. If the bad man is just as strongly inclined to his badness as the good man is to his goodness, how can we praise the good and blame the bad, if we cannot invoke any divinely ordained standards of good and bad? Or, to put the question in the more dramatic language of Dostoevsky, must we not conclude that if God is dead, everything is permitted?

In response to this objection, I will argue in this chapter that insofar as the moral sense is natural, it does not *require* religious belief, although religious belief can *reinforce* the moral sense by confirming the lessons of nature, which is the work of "natural religion." In developing that argument, I will begin by surveying the comments on religion by Wilson, Roger Masters, and Robert McShea. I will trace their view of morality and religion back to Aristotle, Hume, and Darwin as belonging to the tradition of ethical naturalism in moral philosophy. I will suggest that the idea of a natural moral sense supported by natural religion is implicit in the Mosaic law of the Bible and in the account of the Mosaic law given by Thomas Aquinas. Finally, I will argue that religious longings for transcendent meaning express a natural desire to understand that can be explained as a purely natural outcome of natural evolutionary causes.

McSHEA, MASTERS, AND WILSON

As I have suggested previously in this book, Wilson, Masters, and McShea are political scientists who defend a notion of natural right similar to what I have offered. McShea does not think that belief in God or any other transcendent authority provides any solid support for human morality (McShea 1990, 49–63). Any appeal to God as the supernatural source of morality creates more controversy than it resolves, McShea suggests, for at least three reasons. First, we would have to agree on the existence and benevolence of God, but that raises issues that are even more controversial than morality. Second, even if we agree on God's existence and benevolence, we would have to communicate with him to determine his will, but human beings have never found any authoritative way to choose between contradictory claims to divine communication. Third, even if God's communication of his will were clear, we would have to be properly motivated to obey his will, but it is not evident that either the love of God or the anticipation of rewards and punishments in the afterlife moves most human beings so strongly that they would obey his moral law without any natural sanctions: after all, one of the paramount themes of religious texts such as the Bible is the stubborn immorality of those who profess religious belief.

Masters and Wilson show more respect for religion than does McShea, yet they agree with McShea's claim that morality finds sufficient support in human nature without any appeal to religious doctrines. Masters believes that religious faith and natural reason provide alternative foundations for moral obligation, so that neither side of the great debate between reason and faith can refute the other (Masters 1993, 6–11, 152–53).

Wilson believes that morality cannot depend on the fear of eternal damnation propagated by revealed religions. He points to modern China and Japan as examples of societies with stable moral orders but without any pervasive religious beliefs about divine rewards and punishments. The moral conduct of most people most of the time, he concludes, arises not from religious convictions but from "the instincts and habits of a lifetime, founded in nature, developed in the family, and reinforced by quite secular fears of earthly punishment and social ostracism" (Wilson 1993b, 220).

ARISTOTLE AND AUGUSTINE

Like Wilson, McShea, and Masters, Aristotle says so little about religion in the *Nicomachean Ethics* that one could easily infer that it contributes nothing essential to the ethical life of human beings. As we have seen earlier, the aim of ethics for Aristotle is happiness or the fullest satisfaction of human desires over a complete life. The attainment of happiness requires goods of the body (such as health), external goods (such as wealth), and the goods of the soul (the moral and intellectual virtues). The virtues of the soul arise from natural dispositions cultivated through habituation and learning. Most of the *Ethics* is devoted to the virtues, which are mostly products of human activity. So the ethical pursuit of happiness might seem to be a purely human endeavor that does not require divine aid.

And yet, Aristotle acknowledges in the *Ethics* that conceptions of the divine might influence our moral conduct or thought in four possible ways. First, happiness is thought by many people to be a gift of the gods, because the bodily goods and external goods necessary for happiness depend on good fortune, which appears to be determined by divine fate or providence (*NE* 1099a32–1100a9). Although Aristotle recognizes that fortunate circumstances provide the indispensable conditions of happiness, he insists that we should be primarily concerned with shaping the virtues of character, while assuming that good character allows us to bear most misfortunes with nobility. He also doubts the truth of the popular belief in divine providence, by reasoning that if divinity means perfection, divine beings cannot care for human beings, because such care would show their dependence on human beings and thus their imperfection. The perfect activity of divinity must be so utterly self-sufficient as to be indifferent to human affairs (*NE* 1154b21–31, 1178b7–24).

But while Aristotle gives arguments against divine providence, he also suggests that the popular belief in such providential care can be used to enforce the behavior required by nature. Many of the traditional myths about the gods can be employed "as a means of persuading the many and as something useful for the laws and for matters of expediency" (*Meta* 1074b4–7). For example, from his biological studies of gestation and childbirth, Aristotle concludes that women who become too sedentary during gestation have trouble during delivery (*HA* 587a1–5; *GA* 775a30–35). So, in the *Politics*, when he prescribes for the superintendence of childbirth in his sketch of the best regime, he indicates that pregnant women need daily exercise, and one way to ensure this is to require that they walk every day to worship at the temples of the goddesses of childbirth (*NE* 1145a7–11; *Pol* 1322b19–30, 1335b11–19).

Aristotle indicates that a second link between ethics and divinity arises when one identifies the natural causes of innate temperament as divine causes. Some people are naturally disposed from birth to virtue, while others are naturally disposed to depravity (*NE* 1148b15–49a20). Human beings cannot become morally or intellectually virtuous, and cannot therefore attain the goods of the soul, if they are not inclined from birth with passionate dispositions to acquire the virtues. Aristotle identifies the innate propensities to moral passions—such as anger, pity, love, and shame—as praiseworthy states of character. These passions manifest a natural moral sense. These innate dispositions to the moral passions are not much under human control, because they depend on those natural biological causes that determine the inherited traits of temperament (*GA* 767b24–69b31). If one identifies those natural causes as divine causes, then divine power determines whether we are innately inclined to virtue. "It is clear that nature's part is not in our power to do anything about but is present in those who are truly fortunate through some divine cause" (*NE* 1179b22–24).

A third way in which Aristotle connects ethics to the divine is through the idea that happiness, or the activity that most fully constitutes happiness, is "divine" in the sense of being highest or perfect (*NE* 1099b10–17). In this sense, God and the Good are synonymous; and the best human beings are godlike (*NE* 1101b10–1102a4, 1123b13–24, 1145a15–35). In this sense, furthermore, the intellect is the most divine part of human nature, which separates human beings from other animals, and the contemplative activity of the intellect constitutes the most divine life for human beings (*NE*

1177a12–79a32; *DA* 430a17–26; *Meta* 982b29–83a12). Therefore, if the gods did exercise providential care over human life, they would love the intellect and intellectual human beings most (*NE* 1179a25–32). God himself might be best conceived as pure Intellect thinking itself (*Meta* 1074b15–75a11).

Finally, as a fourth way in which ethics and religion might be related, Aristotle speaks of traditional myths in which the eternity of the highest heavenly bodies is seen as the ultimate manifestation of divine order. He invokes this mythic belief in support of his argument that "the primary substance of bodies" is eternal in that it has neither origin nor end. "All human beings have some conception of gods, and all assign the highest place to the divine, both barbarians and Greeks, as many as believe in gods, supposing that immortal is linked with immortal" (*DC* 270b6–10). "The ancients of very early times passed on to posterity in the form of a myth a tradition that the heavenly bodies are gods and that the divinity encompasses the whole of nature" (*Meta* 1074b1–4). But while the fundamental order of the physical universe is eternal, all other natural beings—including all plants and animals—are mortal in that they come into being and pass away (*DC* 283b26–84b5, 298b6–30; *PA* 644b23–45a24). As mortal animals, human beings can grasp the eternal only in the mind's momentary contemplation of nature's eternal order (*NE* 1141a30–41b15, 1177a12–79a32). Thus, Aristotle denies two central tenets of biblical religion—the divine creation of the world out of nothing and the immortality of the soul in an afterlife (*NE* 1111b23).

Aristotle's natural religion—the religion in which "the divinity encompasses the whole of nature"—supports his ethical naturalism. Human beings strive for happiness by satisfying their natural desires, which requires bodily goods, external goods, and the moral and intellectual virtues that constitute the goods of the soul. None of these goods require religious belief. Nevertheless, "all human beings have some conceptions of gods," and Aristotle believes that those religious conceptions that are rooted in natural human experience can reinforce the natural moral inclinations of human beings.

Because of the natural contingency of the human condition, the goods of life depend to some degree on chance or luck. Human beings exert only partial control over the physical and social conditions necessary for the bodily and external goods of life. And they have little control over the innate temperaments necessary for the goods of the soul. This lack of complete power over chance will lead some human beings to worship gods that are believed to have providential care over these goods. Aristotle suggests that such beliefs in divine providence can be used to enforce the dictates of human prudence in managing the contingencies of life.

Aristotle observes that human beings naturally long for perfection, for the full satisfaction of their desires. As social animals, they desire to live in communion with others. As rational animals, they desire to understand the order of things. Yet as mortal animals, they can know only momentary and incomplete satisfaction of these social and rational desires. Although Aristotle respects human conceptions of the divine as manifesting human longings for perfection, he suggests that such longings become unreasonable if they ignore the eternal limits of nature.

Augustine and other biblical theologians have argued, however, that the transcendent longings of human beings point beyond the limits of nature to God as the Creator of nature (Arnhart 1993, 77–100; Walker 1990, 79–112). While pagan philosophers like Aristotle think human beings as mortal animals can be happy, Augustine insists that human beings can never be truly happy as long as they are mortal, because their deepest natural desires can only be satisfied through an immortal union with their Creator. "God has instilled naturally in us that we desire to be happy and immortal" (*City of God*, bk. 9, chaps. 14–15; bk. 10, chaps. 1, 29).

Since nature depends for its existence on a supernatural cause, Augustine believes, nature is not fully intelligible on its own terms. The contingencies of nature's allocation of the goods of earthly life—bodily goods, external goods, and the goods of innate temperament—do not conform to any intelligible standard of excellence. Sometimes the good suffer, and the bad prosper. And even if the good prosper, their earthly prosperity is ruined by the prospect of death.

Nature becomes intelligible only if we see it as created out of nothing by God, with human beings created in the image of God but fallen into a sinful state that separates them from their Creator. We can then understand why human beings yearn for a satisfaction that no natural goods can give them, because we can see that human beings yearn for a redemption from their fallen condition in the natural world, a heavenly redemption in which they can enjoy eternal union with their Creator.

As corrupted by original sin, human beings cannot rely on a natural moral sense rooted in their natural desires, Augustine believes, because their sinful bodily desires rebel against the rule of their rational will, which creates conflict in their souls and in their social life. They will have neither individual nor social peace until their redemption in heaven, when they will finally attain the eternal happiness of the City of God (*City of God*, bk. 13, chaps. 1–3; bk. 14, chaps. 1, 15; bk. 19, chap. 21; bk. 22, chap. 30). As I have indicated earlier, Augustinian asceticism supports a Kantian view of morality that I reject.

Augustine believes that morality cannot be secure without belief in a providential God who provides for the immortality of the soul in an afterlife where the good are rewarded and the bad punished. How then was it possible for Aristotle, who denied divine providence and the immortality of the soul, to sustain his belief in morality as founded on human nature? Was he deluded? Or could his purely naturalistic ethics be defended against Augustine's attack?

HUME AND DARWIN

Like Aristotle, David Hume denied divine providence and the immortality of the soul. Also like Aristotle, Hume believed that morality could be rooted in the natural experience of human beings without any necessity for appealing to God as Moral Legislator. Therefore, in defending his position against the criticisms of biblical believers, Hume showed how an Aristotelian naturalism in ethics might be defended in a world shaped by the moral tradition of biblical religion.

How can we know by reason alone the existence and attributes of God? From Aristotle to the present, the most common, if not the most plausible answer, has been that we can reason to God from the order of nature by moving from effects to causes until we infer God as the First Cause. For many people, the design of nature implies a Divine Designer. In his *Dialogues Concerning Natural Religion*, Hume suggests that this design argument for God's existence fails because it assumes a false analogy between the causes of order in nature and the human mind (Hume 1992, 100–103, 203–18). From the existence of a house, we can infer the existence of a human architect, because of our natural experience in seeing how houses can emerge as products of human minds. But it would be a false

analogy to see any fundamental similarity in inferring the existence of a
Divine Architect from the observed existence of the world, because we
have no natural experience in seeing how the world could emerge as a
product of a Divine Mind. We do have experience, however, in seeing
how natural order emerges in plants and animals through natural processes
of reproduction and growth, and therefore we might well assume that the
order of the world as a whole emerged in a similar way by purely natural
causes. He doubts that by reason and experience alone we can know a
divine cause only by its effects if the cause bears no resemblance to any
causes we have ever observed.

Even if the design argument did prove God's existence, Hume argues
in the *Enquiry Concerning Human Understanding* (section 11), this would not
add anything to our moral knowledge. In reasoning from the effect to the
cause, the cause must be exactly proportioned to the effect, so that we
cannot logically attribute to the cause any quality not exactly required to
produce the effect. Any cause as inferred only by its observable effects
cannot be known to produce any new effects that are not observable. Therefore, in reasoning from the order of nature to God as First Cause, we
cannot infer God to have any moral quality beyond the moral dispositions
that we now experience as part of our nature. Consequently, it adds nothing to our natural moral inclinations to invoke God as the cause of those
inclinations. We cannot infer from our natural moral experience that God
will reward the good and punish the bad in an afterlife, because these new
effects go beyond the ordinary course of nature as we now experience it.
Since we have no natural experience of rewards and punishments in Heaven,
we cannot infer such rewards and punishments from our world.

Hume summarizes his argument in the following passage.

> I deny a providence, you say, and supreme governor of the world,
> who guides the course of events, and punishes the vicious with infamy
> and disappointment, and rewards the virtuous with honour and success, in
> all their undertakings. But surely, I deny not the course itself of events,
> which lies open to every one's inquiry and examination. I acknowledge,
> that, in the present order of things, virtue is attended with more peace of
> mind than vice, and meets with a more favourable reception from the
> world. I am sensible, that, according to the past experience of mankind,
> friendship is the chief joy of human life, and moderation the only source
> of tranquillity and happiness. I never balance between the virtuous and
> the vicious course of life; but am sensible that, to a well-disposed mind,

every advantage is on the side of the former. And what can you say more, allowing all your suppositions and reasonings? You tell me, indeed, that this disposition of things proceeds from intelligence and design. But whatever it proceeds from, the disposition itself, on which depends our happiness or misery, and consequently our conduct and deportment in life is still the same. It is still open for me, as well as you, to regulate my behaviour, by my experience of past events. And if you affirm, that, while a divine providence is allowed, and a supreme distributive justice in the universe, I ought to expect some more particular reward of the good, and punishment of the bad, beyond the ordinary course of events, I here find the same fallacy which I have before endeavoured to detect. You persist in imagining, that, if we grant that divine existence, for which you so earnestly contend, you may safely infer consequences from it, and add something to the experienced order of nature, by arguing from the attributes which you ascribe to your gods. You seem not to remember, that all your reasonings on this subject can only be drawn from effects to causes; and that every argument, deduced from causes to effects, must of necessity be a gross sophism; since it is impossible for you to know anything of the cause, but what you have antecedently, not inferred, but discovered to the full, in the effect. (Hume 1902, 140–41)

If "a well-disposed mind" can infer from "the experienced order of nature" that virtue, friendship, and moderation are required for human happiness, then inferring that God created this order of nature adds nothing necessary for moral knowledge and moral conduct. Hume concedes, however, that some human beings might not have such a "well-disposed mind" that they can see that virtue is better than vice from reasoning about natural experience; and for such people, beliefs about divine rewards and punishments in an afterlife beyond the order of nature might provide their only motivation for moral conduct (Hume 1902, 147). So while religious beliefs about divine providence and immortality of the soul are not a requirement for the morality of those who reason well about natural experience, such beliefs might be a necessary reinforcement for the morality of those who do not reason so well about nature. Hume would insist, however, that judging the truth of such beliefs is a matter of faith rather than reason. Theology "has a foundation in *reason*, so far as it is supported by experience. But its best and most solid foundation is *faith* and divine revelation" (Hume 1902, 165).

By reasoning about human nature, Hume argues, we can see that morality depends on a moral sense—"some internal sense or feeling, which nature has made universal in the whole species" (1902, 173). And although other animals do not have a moral sense, because they lack the human capacity for moral judgment, human morality is rooted in social instincts (such as parental care of the young) that are manifested in other animals (1888, 176–79, 324–28, 397–98; 1902, 104–8). "The lives of men depend upon the same laws as the lives of all other animals" (1985, 582). Hume anticipates Darwin's theory of evolution by natural selection, because Hume suggests that the order that we see in the moral nature of human beings, like the order in all of living nature, might be the product of natural forces that favor those adaptations to the world that enhance survival and reproduction (1992, 228–29, 240–42, 246–47, 261, 268, 270, 277–78). "All the *sentiments* of the human mind, gratitude, resentment, love, friendship, approbation, blame, pity, emulation, envy, have a plain reference to the state and situation of man, and are calculated for preserving the existence, and promoting the activity of such a being in such circumstances" (1902, 217).

Under the influence of Hume and other moral-sense philosophers, Darwin developed his biological theory of the moral sense as the evolutionary product of natural selection (Darwin 1871, 1:70–106, 2:390–94; 1987, 619–29). Some religious believers feared that an evolutionary account of human origins would deny divine providence and the immortality of the soul, and thus deprive morality of its transcendent foundations. Darwin was disturbed by the complaint of Adam Sedgwick, an influential professor of geology at Cambridge University, that if any theory of evolution were correct, "morality is moonshine" (Browne 1995, 468). Darwin suggested, however, that morality as rooted in a natural moral sense did not require religious belief in divine providence or immortality, although such beliefs could reinforce the dictates of nature (1871, 1:65–69, 1:104–106, 1:165–66, 2:394–96; 1936b, 473). His wife worried that he did not share her deeply felt religious beliefs, but he reassured her that despite his doubts about religion, "luckily there were no doubts as to how one ought to act" (Browne 1995, 396–99; Darwin 1987, 123, 169, 171–73).

MOSES AND AQUINAS

To affirm that there is a natural moral law that does not require religious belief should not be seen as an attack upon religion, because religious teachers like Moses and Thomas Aquinas would agree that natural morality as rooted in human nature can be known by natural reason without divine revelation.

When Moses presented his laws to the Jews, he declared that the practical wisdom of those laws would become evident to all human beings, even those who did not worship the true God. "Keep them, put them into practice, and other peoples will admire your wisdom and prudence. Once they know what all these laws are, they will exclaim, 'No other people is as wise and prudent as this great nation'" (Deut. 4:6). Moses thus implied that all human beings in principle could recognize the prudential goodness of those moral laws that were adapted to the natural human condition.

To justify his laws, Moses repeatedly insisted that if the Jews obeyed his laws, they and their children would survive and prosper in their new land (Deut. 30:15–20). He made no claims about immortality of the soul or about rewards and punishments in an afterlife. Instead, like Darwin, he argued that the purpose of morality was to secure the earthly survival and prosperity of oneself and one's progeny. The first commandment of God in the Bible is "Be fruitful and multiply" (Gen. 1:28). For Moses, promoting the survival and reproduction of the Jews required social norms that led individuals to cooperate within their group to compete with other groups (Deut. 4:40, 6:1–3, 11:8–9, 20, 23:9–14, 25:11–16, 30:15–20). Moses taught that "whoever obeys the law will find life in it" (Lev. 18:5). Saint Paul cited this as the fundamental aim of the Mosaic Law (Rom. 10:5). It should not be surprising, therefore, that Darwinian theorists can explain the Mosaic law as promoting the reproductive interests of the Jews (Hartung 1995; MacDonald 1994, 35–55). As a product of natural human experience, not only Judaism but all religious beliefs and practices serve the natural desires of human beings in diverse social and physical environments, and consequently we would explain religion as an adaptation of human ecology (Burkert 1996; Reynolds and Tanner 1995).

Aquinas concluded that the "moral" precepts of the Mosaic law, as distinguished from the "ceremonial" and "judicial" precepts, belonged to natural law, and therefore they did not depend on divine revelation (*Summa Theologica* I–II, q. 100, a. 1). Quoting Justinian's *Institutes*, Aquinas recognized natural law or natural right *(ius naturale)* as "that which nature has taught to all animals," because it corresponds to natural biological desires such as self-preservation, sexual union, parental care of the young, and living in social groups (*Summa Theologica* I–II, q. 94, a. 2). The Mosaic law is natural, therefore, insofar as it satisfies these natural desires by securing the conditions for life, sexuality, familial bonding, and social order generally. The practical wisdom of this natural moral law can be recognized by any human being who uses natural reason to reflect on the lessons of natural human experience. The natural requirements of social order—such as prohibitions against murder, stealing, lying, and adultery—are typically part of the ethical teaching of any durable religious tradition (Smart 1996, 196–214). The ultimate concurrence of natural morality and religious morality is affirmed in the famous reference of Thomas Jefferson at the beginning of the Declaration of Independence to "the Laws of Nature and of Nature's God."

Even that principle of the Mosaic law that might seem to demand an idealistic selflessness—"love your neighbor as yourself" (Lev. 19:18)—actually conforms to the natural self-love and tribalism of human beings. As the biblical context makes clear, and as Aquinas insists, "your neighbor" refers only to one's kin and those of one's own group. The Hebrew word *reya*, which is translated into English as "neighbor," means "companion" or "friend." Consequently, as Jesus indicated, the Mosaic teaching "love your neighbor" means "love your neighbor and hate your enemy" (Matt. 5:43). In contrast to the Kantian view of morality as utterly selfless, Aquinas argues that the Mosaic law follows Aristotle's teaching that by nature our love of others is an extension of our self-love, and therefore we should love those nearest to us—our family, friends, and fellow citizens—more than strangers (*Summa Theologica* II–II, q. 26, aa. 4–8; q. 31, a. 3). Consequently, the Mosaic law prescribes a tough-minded military policy, because human survival requires that human beings fight for their group against competing groups (Deuteronomy 20; Numbers 31). The Old Testament teaches the Silver Rule: "Do not to another what you would not have done to yourself" (Tob. 4:15). If the desire for revenge is natural for human beings, then the Silver Rule is a rule of prudence. The prohibition of murder, for example, is enforced by the fear of punishment from those who would revenge a murder. "He who sheds the blood of man, by man shall his blood be shed" (Gen. 9:6).

It is sometimes asserted that in the modern world the moral universalism of political statements like the Declaration of Independence shows that human beings have transcended the moral tribalism of the past. But even

Jefferson's Declaration is a declaration of war in asserting the separate existence of the American people against British rule. Jefferson concludes that document by declaring that the Americans will defend their independence by treating the British and all of mankind in the same way—"Enemies in War, in Peace Friends" (Jefferson 1984, 23). So while human beings can feel some philanthropic sentiment for all of their fellow human beings, the conditions of human life on earth dictate a natural tribalism in group-against-group conflict that makes perpetual peace on earth impossible.

Aquinas believes, however, that unlike other animals, human beings are inclined not only to the natural end of earthly happiness, but also to the supernatural end of eternal happiness, which will bring perpetual peace. And while the natural law as known by natural reason can secure the natural end, only divine law as revealed to faith can secure the supernatural end (*Summa Theologica* I–II, q. 91, a. 4; q. 98, a. 1). Therefore, not only does the divine law of the Bible prescribe the moral and intellectual virtues necessary for earthly happiness, which can be understood by natural human experience even without the Bible, the divine law also prescribes the theological virtues (faith, hope, and charity), which could not be understood without the supernatural revelation of the Bible (I–II, q. 62, aa. 1–2).

Aquinas agrees with Hume, therefore, in his claim that morality as serving the earthly happiness of human beings conforms to the "ordinary course of nature," which does not depend on religious belief, while any conception of the eternal happiness of human beings in an afterlife must depend on faith and revelation rather than reason and experience. Of course, if one believes in the existence of God as the omnipotent creator of the universe, as Aquinas does, then the ultimate source of natural law—and everything else—is God. Natural law has been instilled in the human soul by God. And yet Aquinas can still argue that those who are not believers in God can know the natural law by natural reason, although they are ignorant of its divine origin.

Like Hume and Darwin, Aquinas thinks that human morality arises from natural inclinations that human beings share with other animals. "Something is good insofar as it is desirable," Aquinas believes (*Summa Theologica* I, q. 5, a. 6). Therefore, all animals seek their natural good in seeking to satisfy their natural desires. Under the influence of Aristotle's biology, Aquinas concludes that, although only human beings act from "free" judgment in satisfying their desires, other animals act from an "estimative" judgment about what will satisfy their desires. All animals have a natural capacity for practical judgment that shows a "participation in prudence and reason" and a "likeness of moral good" (I, q. 83, a. 1; q. 96, a. 1; I–II, q. 11, a. 2; q. 24, a. 4; q. 40, a. 3).

To illustrate the importance of this biological psychology for Aquinas's understanding of the natural moral law, consider his remarks on the nature of monogamous and polygamous marriages (*Summa Theologica,* suppl., q. 41, a. 1). Of the moral precepts of the Mosaic law that Aquinas regards as natural, many pertain to marriage and familial bonding. Marriage is a natural institution insofar as it serves two natural ends. As its first natural end, marriage provides for the natural good of the offspring, because human children derive their existence, their nourishment, and their education from parents, and this is best achieved by the joint care of the mother and the father. As its second natural end, marriage provides for the cooperative division of labor in the household between a man and a woman who naturally desire to live together because they are not separately self-sufficient.

Nature does not incline all animals to such familial bonding. Aquinas observes that among animals whose offspring can care for themselves or can be cared for sufficiently by the mother, there is no enduring bond between mothers and fathers. But among animals such as some birds whose offspring require the care of both parents, there is some enduring bond between male and female. Among human beings, the offspring need the care of both parents for a long time, and consequently the bond between human mothers and fathers is typically strong.

Aquinas argues that marriage belongs to natural law in conforming to three levels of human nature: the generic nature that human beings share with other animals, the specific nature that is distinctively human, and the temperamental nature that distinguishes individual human beings (*Summa Theologica* I–II, q. 46, a. 5). Marriage is generically natural insofar as the dependence of offspring on the care of both parents is characteristic of other animals as well as human beings. Marriage is specifically natural insofar as it satisfies a desire for lifelong conjugal bonding that may be uniquely human. And marriage is temperamentally natural insofar as the desire for conjugal union is common to most human beings but not all (suppl. q. 41, a. 2, ad 4).

To the question of whether having several wives is against natural law, Aquinas's answer is that "it is in some manner against natural law, and in some manner not against it" (*Summa Theologica*, suppl., q. 65, a. 1). For a man to have several wives can conform to the first natural end of marriage—procreation and parental care—because one man can impregnate several wives and help care for the children they produce. This is clearly natural for those animal species in which males impregnate many females. But although polygyny does not completely frustrate the second natural end of marriage—the cooperative division of labor between spouses—it does tend to make this more difficult, because jealousy between the co-wives disrupts the household. Therefore, polygyny is partially natural but not completely natural: it is unnatural to the extent that several wives will naturally find it hard to cooperate in sharing a husband because of their sexual jealousy.

Aquinas indicates that some people, appealing to the Golden Rule as a principle of natural law, would claim that if polygyny (one husband with multiple wives) is natural, then polyandry (one wife with multiple husbands) should also be natural. That we should do to others what we would want done to ourselves is a natural precept. But husbands would not want their wives to have other husbands. Therefore, it is argued, husbands violate the natural principle of reciprocity in wanting to have more than one wife. Aquinas rejects this reasoning, however. The reciprocity of the Golden Rule, he insists, assumes a natural sameness between the parties, but this is not true between men and women in their marital relationships. By nature it is easier for wives to share a husband than it is for husbands to share a wife. In a polyandrous marriage, the husbands would never be sure which children were theirs, and consequently they would not give the children the care they needed. For human beings as well as other animals, the male is more jealous of the female than the female is of the male. For this reason, Aquinas declares, polygyny but not polyandry has been sanctioned by law and custom in some societies. So while monogamy is natural, and polygyny is somewhat natural but somewhat unnatural, polyandry is utterly unnatural.

As we have seen in chapters 5 and 6, Darwinian theory and contemporary research in biological anthropology confirm Aquinas's position. Despite great variation in the details of marital and familial institutions, marriage and the family are universal to all human societies (Ember and Ember 1993; Murdock 1949; Stephens 1963). They are universal because they solve some universal human problems: how to care for infants who are dependent on adult care for a long time, how to share the products of a sexual division of labor in the household, and how to prevent or mitigate sexual competition. Although mothers tend to be more extensively devoted to child-care than are fathers, human beings rely far more than other mammals on the parental care of both mother and father. Monogamy is the predominant form of marriage. Even in societies where polygyny is permitted, most marriages are monogamous: there are not enough women to allow most men to have more than one wife, and most men lack the social and economic resources to support polygamous families. Furthermore, polygynous families are often disrupted by the jealousy among the wives. Consequently, polygyny requires elaborate rules to mediate conflicts over the competing claims of the co-wives. Sororal polygyny—where the wives are sisters—is one way to mitigate conflict.

While monogamy is universal, and polygyny is at least permitted in many societies, polyandry is extremely rare. Because women become jealous when they think their mate is diverting time and resources to another woman, it is difficult for women to live together as co-wives in polygynous marriages. Because men become jealous when they think their mate is diverting sexual favors to another man, it is almost impossible for men to live together as co-husbands in polyandrous marriages. Contemporary research in evolutionary psychology confirms the importance of male and female jealousy in setting these limits on marital relationships. Sexual jealousy is found in every human society. Nowhere do people share mates without becoming jealous (Buss 1994, 125–41, 178–79).

Some anthropologists have suggested that polyandry is so unusual among human beings as to be "unnatural" (Stephens 1963, 34). In the few cases where it does occur, polyandry is fraternal: a wife of one brother becomes the wife of all, even brothers born after the wedding. This fraternal arrangement moderates the jealousy of the males and ensures that the offspring are related to them. In Tibet, where it has been extensively studied, polyandry seems to be an adaptation to unusual ecological circumstances (Crook and Crook 1988; Levine 1988). There is a shortage of women and of good land. Polyandry in Tibet is limited to former serfs who were given fixed amounts of land by their lords, and polyandry seems to be a way of keeping these small parcels of land in the same family.

This kind of evidence from the natural experience of human beings suggests that Aquinas was right about marriage and the family as part of the natural law. The moral inclinations and moral precepts that support the family are natural because they satisfy two natural desires—the parental care of children and conjugal bonding. This illustrates how a natural moral sense can be founded on natural reason and natural experience without any need for religious belief.

Aquinas believes, however, that marriage also serves a supernatural end that goes beyond its natural ends. As a sacrament, marriage is one of the seven sacraments of the Catholic Church. A sacrament is a sign or symbol of a spiritual mystery that surpasses natural understanding, a mystery that foreshadows the perfect holiness that human beings will achieve in Heaven by the grace of Christ. The sacrament of marriage symbolizes the supernatural mystery of Christ's union with the Church (*Summa Theologica*, III, q. 60, a. 2; suppl., q. 42). If this religious doctrine strengthens the marital commitment of those who believe it, then it reinforces the natural moral sense associated with marital bonding and thereby promotes the earthly happiness of human beings. But the sacred meaning of the doctrine points beyond nature to the eternal happiness that Aquinas believes to be the final end of human longing.

Although the religious doctrine of marriage as a sacrament can support the natural morality of marital bonding, this religious view of marriage can also promote an imprudent dogmatism that goes against human nature. The Catholic Church's prohibition of divorce, for example, is contrary to the natural pattern of human mating. Once children have reached a certain age, there is no natural need for the parents to remain together forever. In some ecological circumstances, even mothers with young children might have enough economic independence to raise their children without the help of the fathers. While Aquinas concedes this, he tries to argue that permanent monogamy is required by nature to ensure the children's inheritance (*Summa Theologica*, suppl., q. 67). But securing the inheritance of familial property is important only in certain social and economic circumstances. In agrarian societies, like those that prevailed in medieval Europe, the rate of divorce is low, because an agrarian economy makes husbands, wives, and children permanently dependent on one another and on the land they farm. But in hunting-gathering societies, and in industrialized and urbanized societies, husbands and wives have enough economic independence to pursue the natural human inclination to serial monogamy, in which human beings marry, divorce, and then remarry (Fisher 1992).

Belief in marriage as a sacrament that symbolizes an eternal mystery is an act of faith rather than reason. The existence of an eternal realm of happiness beyond nature rests on the belief that the natural universe is not a self-sufficient whole, because it was created miraculously out of nothing by God, and Aquinas concedes that this doctrine of creation is "an object of faith, but not of demonstration or science" (*Summa Theologica* I, q. 46, a. 2).

This illustrates the natural relationship between the moral sense and religious belief. Insofar as the moral sense is rooted in human nature, it can be understood by reflection on the lessons of natural human experience without any need for religious doctrine. That is what Aquinas means when he separates natural law and divine law. By natural law, human beings need the moral and intellectual virtues to satisfy their natural desires as they strive for earthly happiness. The need for these virtues becomes evident to any- one who thinks clearly about the conditions of human life on earth. This natural understanding of morality does not require religious belief. Never- theless, belief in divine law can reinforce this natural morality by strength- ening the religious believer's devotion to the natural virtues. The ultimate purpose of divine law, however, is not to strengthen the natural virtues but to instill the supernatural virtues, because the aim of divine law is not the temporal happiness of human beings as mortal creatures adapted for life on earth, but the eternal happiness of human beings as spiritual creatures who long for union with their Creator.

If we really do yearn to transcend the limits of our natural mortality and attain a perfect happiness beyond death, the pursuit of that happiness must be by faith in some revealed religion. But however that may be, we can rest assured that our earthly happiness is securely founded in our nature as mortal animals endowed with a moral sense that serves our natural desires.

Still, the religious believer would insist that even if human beings could secure the moral conditions of life without religious belief, that would not fully satisfy them. Human beings, unlike any other animals, cannot live unless they believe they know *why* they live. They desire to understand the meaning of life within the cosmos, and that intellectual desire manifests a spiritual longing that reaches beyond nature to some supernatural realm that can only by grasped by religious faith.

THE DESIRE TO UNDERSTAND

"All human beings by nature desire to understand." This first sentence of Aristotle's *Metaphysics* states one of our fundamental beliefs about our nature and our place in the natural world. Although other animals have some awareness of their surroundings, we seem to be the only beings with fully conscious self-awareness and the capacity to reflect on the meaning of things. As human beings, we yearn to know not only the facts of how things are in the world but also the reasons why they are as they are. As an expression of this desire to understand, we wonder how we should understand our desire to understand. Can we explain this as a product of purely natural causes? Or is it the miraculous work of a divine Creator?

As we have seen, Darwin maintained that even the highest moral and intellectual faculties of the human mind could be understood as the work of the same natural evolutionary causes that shaped the rest of the living world. Yet Alfred Russel Wallace, who developed his own theory of natural selection at the same time that Darwin formulated his, insisted that while evolution by natural selection could account for the "animal nature" of human beings, the "spiritual nature" of human beings as manifested in their moral and intellectual powers could only be explained as the work of a divine cause. Wallace reasoned that the human mind's capacity for the abstract ideas of art, science, and religion would have had no practical use for survival and reproduction in evolutionary history, and therefore such a power could not have been favored by natural selection. The only adequate cause for such a spiritual power must be in "the unseen universe of Spirit" (Cronin 1991, 353–67; Wallace 1891, 473–78). Some biologists today, such as John Eccles, a Nobel Prize–winning neurologist, continue to defend Wallace's position. Eccles insists that the uniquely human propensity for pondering the mystery of the universe shows the human soul to be "a supernatural spiritual creation" and therefore "a miracle forever beyond science" (1989, 236–37). Similarly, while Pope John Paul II has accepted the scientific evidence for the evolution of the human body from living matter, he still insists that "the spiritual soul is immediately created by God" (John Paul II 1997, 29).

In defense of Darwin's position, however, I would argue that the natural human desire to understand—which sustains art, science, and religion—

has emerged by purely natural causes. The mental capacities that sustain the intellectual desires of human beings can be explained as natural products of human evolutionary history. And while these mental capacities evolved originally because of their practical benefits for human survival and reproduction, these capacities allow modern human beings in civilized societies to assume a theoretical attitude in seeking understanding for its own sake.

A common indication that we do have a natural desire to understand, Aristotle observes, is the pleasure we take in our senses (*Meta* 980a21–27). Although much of the time we seek out sensory knowledge of the world because of its usefulness in managing our practical affairs, we also delight in sensory experience for its own sake even when there is no practical benefit. We find touching, smelling, tasting, hearing, or seeing things in the world intrinsically pleasurable.

All animals, Aristotle indicates, have some capacity for sensation, and some can develop their sensory knowledge into memory, which gives them a greater capacity for learning than those animals without memory. But even the animals with perceptual memory lack the human capacity for organizing memories into reflective experience, which is the basis for art and science. Yet despite these intellectual differences between human beings and other animals, we can see in some other animals the tendency to curiosity or playful exploration that is the natural root of the human desire to understand (Eibl-Eibesfeldt 1989, 580–93).

Through art and science, human beings draw universal conclusions about the regularities in their sensory experience. Unlike other animals, human beings seek to understand the causes or principles of sensory experience. For example, the earliest human beings not only observed the motions of the stars and planets, but they also developed mythic explanations for why these motions had to be they way they were. Initially, such thinking was directed to providing for the necessities of life. But in the most civilized societies, some people—such as the priestly class in ancient Egypt— had the leisure to pursue the arts and sciences as good in themselves. The philosophic life is the peak of this development, as a few people find the quest for theoretical understanding to be the highest life for a human being (*Meta* 980a27–983a23).

The theoretical life, as devoted to understanding for its own sake, is manifested not only in the life of Aristotle himself, but also in the life of Darwin. In 1842, Darwin and his wife bought a house outside of London in the village of Down. He called it Down House, and he lived and wrote there for forty years. On the grounds of his property, he designed a path covered with sand that started at the house, wound through his fields and garden, and then returned to the house (Milner 1990, 144–45, 393–94). He called it his "Sandwalk" or "thinking path," because every morning and afternoon, he would walk around the path while thinking through some problem in his scientific research. At the beginning of the path, he would pile up some flints, so that as he completed a circuit, he could knock off a flint with his walking stick. This allowed him to measure the difficulty of the problem he was pondering by the number of circuits around the path required to solve it. He might have a "three-flint problem" one day, and a "four-flint problem" another.

These are the habits of a man for whom thinking about the deepest questions is the highest pleasure of life. And, of course, he thought his theory of evolution by natural selection answered many of those questions. But can Darwin's theory explain the origins of people like himself? Can the intense curiosity of a scientist like Darwin, which manifests the human desire to understand, be accounted for by the purely natural causes of evolutionary history? Is there any reason to believe that natural selection favored the evolution of brains capable of debating the theory of evolution? Or should we agree with Wallace and Eccles that the intellectual yearning to probe the mysteries of the universe identifies human beings as spiritual creatures of a supernatural Creator?

Wallace contended that the highest powers of the human brain could not be products of evolution by natural selection, because the survival and reproduction of the earliest human ancestors in the primitive conditions of evolutionary history would have required intellectual capacities not much greater than those of apes. Therefore, the complex mental abilities necessary for art, science, and religion, which human beings now display, cannot be explained as evolutionary adaptations favored by natural selection.

In response to Wallace, Darwin argued that the mental powers of human beings could be explained by the same logic that supports any explanation by the theory of natural selection. Inferring that some trait has emerged by natural selection requires three premises. First, there must be natural variation in the trait. Second, those variations must be to some great degree inherited. Finally, those inherited variations must be subject to selective pressure such that those enhancing survival and reproduction are favored over those that do not. Darwin thought the development of human mental capacities satisfied all three premises (Darwin 1936b, 430–32, 445–70, 496–98, 909–15). The mental capacities of animals are highly variable both within and between species. To a large degree, those mental capacities are inherited. And in the circumstances of evolutionary history, natural selection would have favored those mental capacities that increased the chances of survival and reproduction.

The evolutionary success of human beings in becoming the dominant animal on earth has depended on human intelligence. The technical intelligence of human ancestors allowed them to understand and manipulate the physical and organic world in which they found themselves. Their social intelligence combined with social tools such as language allowed them to cooperate in large groups for competition against other groups. The practical benefits of such technical and social inventions could not be secured without the development of the human powers for "observation, memory, curiosity, imagination, and reason" (Darwin 1936b, 432).

Once such intellectual powers had been fashioned by natural selection because of their practical benefits, they could then be used for formulating abstract ideas of art, religion, and science that might go beyond the needs of practical life. "As soon as the important faculties of the imagination, wonder, and curiosity, together with some power of reasoning, had become partially developed, man would naturally crave to understand what was passing around him, and would have vaguely speculated on his own existence" (Darwin 1936b, 469). This natural desire to understand human existence might then lead some human beings to religious belief in the power of spiritual agencies to explain natural phenomena. Or it might lead others, like Darwin, to formulate scientific theories of the natural origins of life. This Darwinian theory of the origins of the human mind provides an evolutionary basis for Aristotle's view of the natural desire to understand: mental capacities and dispositions that originally served the practical necessities of life can become intrinsically pleasurable for those people with the inclination and leisure to pursue a purely theoretical life. Religious faith might dictate the belief that God's will stands behind this natural process. But natural reason can explain this history of the human mind—at least in principle—without appeal to supernatural causes.

Still, even if this Darwinian account of the human mind is plausible in principle, the exact details of how the mind emerged in evolutionary history is unclear. In the century since Darwin's death, research in many fields—such as archaeology, biology, psychology, and neurology—has begun to clarify some of the details in the history of the mind. The best survey of this research is Merlin Donald's *Origins of the Modern Mind* (1991). Although there have been criticisms of his theory, Donald has been remarkably persuasive in defending his position (Donald 1993; Mithen 1996).

Donald argues that human beings share "episodic" cognition with other primates such as chimpanzees. The sensory knowledge of apes includes the ability to store in memory their perceptions of specific episodes and to retrieve these memories in response to environmental cues, but they have only limited ability to represent or reflect on their episodic memories. So, for example, human trainers might teach chimpanzees to use an equal sign according to some rule for associating events in their environment, but the chimpanzees would never understand the concept of "equivalence." This confirms Aristotle's claim that although many animals have memory of their sensations and can be taught, only human beings can recollect and deliberate about their memories (*Mem* 453a7–14; *HA* 488b24–27).

Donald believes that the first stage in the cognitive evolution of human ancestors beyond the episodic capacities of other primates came with the "mimetic" cognition of *Homo erectus*, from about 1.5 million years ago. Mimetic skill is the ability to use the body for the nonverbal representation of stored memories. Ritual, dance, nonverbal gesturing, and toolmaking would have been expressions of mimetic representation.

The second stage in our cognitive evolution, Donald believes, was the development of language about one hundred thousand years ago with *Homo sapiens sapiens*. Language made possible a mythic culture of narrative thought in which human ancestors could represent and reflect on reality through storytelling. Through the oral traditions of myth, human beings could explain and predict the entire universe as represented in metaphorical thought. The cognitive complexity of mythic thought became most evident in the art and artifacts of the Upper Paleolithic period (forty thousand to ten thousand years ago).

The third and final stage in the evolution of the uniquely human mind, according to Donald, came with the emergence of "theoretic" cognition, in which symbolic thought was brought under the control of analytic reasoning through formal logic and systematic reflection. The theoretic collection and analysis of ideas and data was facilitated by the development of

writing and other devices for the external storage of memories. Early cal-
endars and megalithic monuments (such as Stonehenge) for astronomical
observation are perhaps the first evidence of theoretic reasoning. But the
full development of theoretic civilization, Donald argues, occurred first in
ancient Greece. Greek society was the first to foster speculative philosophy
and science as a way of life in which reflective understanding was pursued
for its own sake.

It would seem, then, that Darwin's true "thinking path"—the path of
thought that led to the kind of theoretical life he lived—did not begin at
Down House. It began in Aristotle's Greece where the human desire to
understand was first fully expressed. But perhaps it really began with that
first Paleolithic ancestor who looked into the night sky, shuddered in awe,
and wondered how to make sense of it all.

Our natural desire to understand leads us to search for ultimate explanations. And as suggested in Jefferson's appeal to "the Laws of Nature and
of Nature's God," that search for ultimate causes that would explain the
universe culminates in a fundamental alternative: either we take nature as
the ultimate source of order, or we look beyond nature to God as the
ultimate source of nature's order. Our desire to understand is satisfied ultimately either by an intellectual understanding of nature or by a religious
understanding of God as the creator of nature.

Religion is any system of beliefs and practices that assumes that the
natural world depends on a supernatural power, and that the satisfaction of
human desires requires the support of that supernatural power. Despite the
great variability in religious experience, every human society has manifested this religious understanding of the world in some form.

As indicated by Richard Swinburne (1979, 1996, 1997) in his philosophic argument for the existence of God, there are at least three possible
ultimate explanations of the universe: materialism, humanism, and theism.
According to the materialist, everything can be explained as caused by the
physical activity of material objects. According to the humanist, the mental
experience—the soul or mind—of human beings exerts its own causal activity
that cannot be fully explained through the physical activity of material objects
(such as the neuronal activity of the human brain). But according to the theist,
to fully explain the material order of physical events or the immaterial
order of mental events, one must assume that God is the source of all order
as the omnipotent creator of both the physical world and the human mind.

In his defense of theism, Swinburne contends that we can reason to the existence of God as the simplest way of explaining the order in the natural world that is presupposed in all scientific explanations. Science explains physical events by postulating the simplest causal laws of nature that would explain those events, and science explains mental events as emerging somehow from the physical events in the brain. So, for example, Darwinian theory might explain the organic order in plants and animals as produced in evolutionary history by the causal laws of evolution (such as reproduction with slight variation and natural selection of the fittest variations). Darwinian theory might also explain mental events as products of complex brains adapted by natural selection for survival and reproduction. These are true scientific explanations, Swinburne argues, but they are not ultimate explanations. Why are there laws of evolution at all? And why are mental events associated with physical events in the brain in just the way they are? Why is nature orderly rather than chaotic? And why is nature ordered the way it is and not differently? To answer these questions, Swinburne insists, we must reason to the existence of God as the ultimate cause of nature's order, as the omnipotent power that created everything out of nothing and continues to sustain everything that exists. To explain why the laws of nature are the way they are, we must appeal to nature's God. Many contemporary scientists would agree with this (Margenau and Varghese 1992).

This kind of reasoning shows the natural root of religious belief in the human mind. Human beings have a natural desire to understand that will not rest until they explain everything. So, when they see the wonderful order in nature, many human beings are inclined to interpret this as evidence of a supernatural power that is the ultimate source of that order.

Many human beings have acquired a need for redemption from the world that will not be satisfied by a scientific understanding of nature (Nietzsche, *Human, All Too Human*, secs. 27, 34, 132, 150, 251, 272, 476). They feel a transcendent longing that manifests itself not as philosophic wonder before nature but as religious awe in the face of a mysterious Being that is the ungrounded ground of everything that exists. The continuing appeal of this religious yearning for supernatural transcendence is evident in the work of some of the most influential artists and thinkers of the twentieth century—such as Martin Heidegger (1959, 1993), who proclaims: "Only a god can save us" (Wolin 1993, 107).

Other human beings, by contrast, will be satisfied with a purely intel-

lectual understanding of nature's order that does not require religious belief. All explanation depends on some ultimate reality that is unexplained.
As argued by Hume (1992) and recent exponents of Hume's position like
J. L. Mackie (1982), all explanation presupposes the observable order of the
world as the final ground of explanation that cannot itself be explained. To
the question of why nature has the kind of order that it has, the only
reasonable answer is that we must accept this as a brute fact of our experience. That's just the way it is. In response to Swinburne, Hume and others
would insist that there is nothing in our experience of the world that would
make it likely, or even comprehensible, that something would have the
power to create everything in the world out of nothing. Therefore, if we
are reasoning from our ordinary experience of the world, the existence of
an omnipotent God is highly improbable.

Moreover, the Humean philosophers would contend, even if we appeal to the existence of God as the ultimate cause of nature's order, we still
could not explain the ultimate cause of God. Indeed, Swinburne concedes
that the religious believer cannot explain why God is the way he is. "It is
very unlikely," Swinburne insists, "that a universe would exist uncaused,
but rather more likely that God would exist uncaused" (1979, 131). The
Humean, however, would say just the opposite. Since we have never directly observed God creating everything out of nothing, but every day we
observe the causal regularities of nature, the existence of an uncaused nature is far more probable than the existence of an uncaused God. Consequently, in our search for ultimate explanations, we must appeal either to
nature or to God as the unexplained ground of all explanation (Arnhart
1997).

Thus does the natural desire to understand lead us to this most fundamental of choices—nature or God, reason or revelation. The Humean
philosophers can claim to refute revelation by showing that reasoning from
our ordinary experience of the world makes the existence of God highly
improbable. But even if philosophers can show that revelation is improbable, they cannot show that it is impossible; and therefore, as Leo Strauss
(1979, 1983) argued, reason cannot completely refute revelation (Sorenson
1997). Philosophy cannot refute revelation, and theology cannot refute
philosophy, because any attempted refutation would have to beg the question at issue. "All alleged refutations of revelation presuppose unbelief in
revelation, and all alleged refutations of philosophy presuppose already faith

in revelation. There seems to be no ground common to both, and therefore superior to both" (Strauss 1979, 11).

But even if this choice between reason and revelation is left open, this would not weaken the arguments I have made for Darwinian natural right. For as we have seen, the moral teaching of revelation—at least as conveyed in the Hebrew Bible—conforms to the natural desires of human beings as rooted in human biology. As Strauss suggests, the Bible can be understood by natural human reason as a solution to natural human problems (Strauss 1979, 116). Religion does not change human nature. Rather, it reinforces with divine authority the teachings of natural reason as to the conditions for securing the fullest satisfaction of human longings.

Moved by their desire to understand, human beings will seek the uncaused ground of all causes. This will lead some human beings to a religious understanding of God. It will lead others to an intellectual understanding of nature. Yet, in either case, the good is the desirable. And perhaps the greatest human good, which would satisfy the deepest human desire, would be to understand human nature within the natural order of the whole.

The idea of Darwinian natural right offers us one way of understanding our human place in nature. We are neither mindless machines nor disembodied spirits. We are animals. As animals we display the animate powers of nature for movement, desire, and awareness. We move to satisfy our desires in the light of our awareness of the world. We are a unique species of animal, but our distinctively human traits—such as symbolic speech, practical deliberation, and conceptual thought—are elaborations of powers shared in some form with other animals. Our powers for habituation and learning allow us to alter our natural environments, but even these powers are extensions of the behavioral flexibility shown by other animals. So even if the natural world was not made for us, we were made for it, because we are adapted to live in it. We have not been thrown into nature from some place far away. We come from nature. It is our home.

References

Able, Kenneth P., and Verner P. Bingman. 1987. "The Development of Orientation and Navigation Behavior in Birds." *Quarterly Review of Biology* 62:1–47.

Adair, Douglass. 1974. *Fame and the Founding Fathers.* New York: Norton.

Adler, Mortimer. 1967. *The Difference in Man and the Difference It Makes.* New York: Holt, Rinehart, Winston.

———. 1971. *The Common Sense of Politics.* New York: Holt, Rinehart, Winston.

———. 1991. *Desires, Right and Wrong.* New York: Macmillan.

Adler, Mortimer, and Charles Van Doren, eds. 1977. *Great Treasury of Western Thought.* New York: R. R. Bowker.

Alexander, Richard. 1979. *Darwinism and Human Affairs.* Seattle: University of Washington Press.

———. 1987. *The Biology of Moral Systems.* Hawthorne, N.Y.: Aldine de Gruyter.

———. 1989. "Evolution of the Human Psyche." In Paul Mellars and Christopher Stringer, eds., *The Human Revolution: Behavioral and Biological Perspectives on the Origins of Modern Humans*, 455–513. Princeton: Princeton University Press.

———. 1990. "How Did Humans Evolve? Reflections on the Uniquely Unique Species." Special Publications, No. 1, Museum of Zoology, The University of Michigan.

Allen, E., et al. 1978. "Sociobiology—Another Biological Determinism." In Arthur L. Caplan, ed., *The Sociobiology Debate*, 280–90. New York: Harper and Row.

Altmann, Jeanne. 1980. *Baboon Mothers and Infants.* Cambridge: Harvard University Press.

Ambler, Wayne. 1987. "Aristotle on Nature and Politics: The Case of Slavery." *Political Theory* 15:390–410.

American Psychiatric Association. 1987. *Diagnostic and Statistical Manual of Mental Disorders*. 3d rev. ed. Washington, D.C.: American Psychiatric Association.

Amundson, Ron. 1996. "Historical Development of the Concept of Adaptation." In Michael R. Rose and George V. Lauder, eds., *Adaptation*, 11–53. San Diego: Academic Press.

Anastaplo, George. 1975. "Citizens and Human Beings: Thoreau, Socrates, and Civil Disobedience." In *Human Being and Citizen*, 203–13. Chicago: Swallow Press.

———. 1980. "Abraham Lincoln's Emancipation Proclamation." In Ronald Collins, eds., *Constitutional Government in America*, 421–26. Durham, N.C.: Carolina Academic Press.

Anderson, P. W. 1972. "More Is Different." *Science* 177:393–96.

Andrewartha, H. G., and L. C. Birch. 1984. *The Ecological Web*. Chicago: University of Chicago Press.

Angier, Natalie. 1997. "Sexual Identity Not Pliable After All, Report Says." *New York Times*, 14 March.

Aoki, Chiye, and Philip Siekevitz. 1988. "Plasticity in Brain Development." *Scientific American* 259 (December): 56–67.

Aquinas, Thomas. 1961. *Summa Theologiae*. 5 vols. Madrid: Biblioteca de Autores Christianos.

Arendt, Hannah. 1978. *The Life of the Mind*. San Diego: Harcourt Brace Jovanovich.

Aristotle. 1984. *The Complete Works of Aristotle*. Edited by Jonathan Barnes. Princeton: Princeton University Press.

Arnhart, Larry. 1981. *Aristotle on Political Reasoning: A Commentary on the "Rhetoric."* DeKalb: Northern Illinois University Press.

———. 1984. "Darwin, Aristotle, and the Biology of Human Rights." *Social Science Information* 23:493–521.

———. 1985. "Abraham Lincoln's Biblical Liberalism." *The St. John's Review* 36:25–39.

———. 1987. *Political Questions: Political Philosophy from Plato to Rawls*. New York: Macmillan.

———. 1988. "Aristotle's Biopolitics: A Defense of Biological Teleology against Biological Nihilism." *Politics and the Life Sciences* 6:173–229, with nine commentaries (192–222) and the author's response (223–25).

———. 1990. "Aristotle, Chimpanzees, and Other Political Animals." *Social Science Information* 29:479–559.

———. 1992. "Feminism, Primatology, and Ethical Naturalism." *Politics and the Life Sciences* 11:157–70, 177–78.

———. 1993. *Political Questions: Political Philosophy from Plato to Rawls*. 2d ed. Prospect Heights, Ill.: Waveland Press.

———. 1994a. "The Darwinian Biology of Aristotle's Political Animals." *American Journal of Political Science* 38:464–85.

———. 1994b. "A Sociobiological Defense of Aristotle's Sexual Politics." *International Political Science Review* 15:69–95.

———. 1994c. "The Biology of Natural Right." A review of *The Nature of Politics* and *Beyond Relativism*, by Roger Masters. *The Review of Politics* 56:762–65.

———. 1995. "The New Darwinian Naturalism in Political Theory." *American Political Science Review* 89:389–400.

———. 1997. "George Anastaplo on Non-Western Thought." *The Political Science Reviewer* 26:214–47.

———. 1998. "Aldo Leopold's Land Ethic as Human Ecology." In Charles Rubin, ed., *Restoring Conservationism*. Lawrence: University Press of Kansas.

Atran, Scott. 1985. "Pre-theoretical Aspects of Aristotelian Definition and Classification of Animals: The Case for Common Sense." *Studies in the History and Philosophy of Science* 16:113–63.

———. 1987. "Origin of the Species and Genus Concepts: An Anthropological Perspective." *Journal of the History of Biology* 20:195–279.

———. 1990. *Cognitive Foundations of Natural History*. Cambridge: Cambridge University Press.

Augustine. 1950. *The City of God*. Translated by Marcus Dod. New York: Random House, Modern Library.

———. 1964. *On Free Choice of the Will*. Translated by Anna S. Benjamin and L. H. Hackstaff. New York: Macmillan.

Axelrod, Robert. 1984. *The Evolution of Cooperation*. New York: Basic Books.

Ayala, Francisco J. 1968. "Biology as an Autonomous Science." *American Scientist* 56:207–21.

———. 1970. "Teleological Explanations in Evolutionary Biology." *Philosophy of Science* 37:1–15.

———. 1987. "The Biological Roots of Morality." *Biology and Philosophy* 2:235–52.

Baker, Myron Charles, and Michael A. Cunningham. 1985. "The Biology of Bird-Song Dialects." *Behavioral and Brain Sciences* 8:85–133.

Baldry, H. C. 1965. *The Unity of Mankind in Greek Thought*. Cambridge: Cambridge University Press.

Barkow, Jerome H. 1989. *Darwin, Sex and Status*. Toronto: University of Toronto Press.

Barkow, Jerome, Leda Cosmides, and John Tooby, eds. 1992. *The Adapted Mind: Evolutionary Psychology and the Generation of Culture*. New York: Oxford University Press.

Barnouw, Victor. 1978. *An Introduction to Anthropology: Ethnology*. 3d ed. Homewood, Ill.: Dorsey Press.

Barratt, Alfred. 1869. *Physical Ethics; or, The Science of Action.* London: Williams & Norgate.

Barres, John. 1995. "You Can Cheat People, But Not Nature!" *Behavioral and Brain Sciences* 18:544–45.

Barrow, John D., and Frank J. Tipler. 1986. *The Anthropic Cosmological Principle.* New York: Oxford University Press.

Bazerman, Charles. 1993. "Intertextual Self-Fashioning: Gould and Lewontin's Representations of the Literature." In Jack Selzer, ed., *Understanding Scientific Prose.* Madison: University of Wisconsin Press.

Beare, John A. 1906. *Greek Theories of Elementary Cognition.* Oxford: Oxford University Press.

Becker, Gary S. 1981. *A Treatise on the Family.* Cambridge: Harvard University Press.

———. 1991. "Family." In John Eatwell, Murray Milgate, and Peter Newman, eds., *The World of Economics,* 248–60. New York: Norton.

Becker, Jill B., S. Marc Breedlove, and David Crews, eds. 1992. *Behavioral Endocrinology.* Cambridge: MIT Press.

Beer, Colin G. 1991. "From Folk Psychology to Cognitive Ethology." In Carolyn A. Ristau, ed., *Cognitive Ethology,* 19–33. Hillsdale, N.J.: Lawrence Erlbaum.

Beit-Hallahmi, Benjamin. 1981. "The Kibbutz: Revival or Survival?" *Journal of Family Issues* 2:259–74.

Benedict, Ruth. 1936. *Patterns of Culture.* Boston: Houghton Mifflin.

Bennett, Jonathan. 1991. "How is Cognitive Ethology Possible?" In Carolyn A. Ristau, ed., *Cognitive Ethology,* 35–49. Hillsdale, N.J.: Lawrence Erlbaum.

Berlin, Brent. 1992. *Ethnobiological Classification: Principles of Categorization of Plants and Animals in Traditional Societies.* Princeton: Princeton University Press.

Berlin, Brent. 1992. *Ethnobiological Classification: Principles of Categorization of Plants and Animals in Traditional Societies.* Princeton: Princeton University Press.

Berlin, B., D. E. Breedlove, and P. H. Raven. 1974. *Principles of Tzeltal Plant Classification.* New York: Academic Press.

Berns. Laurence. 1994. "Aristotle and Adam Smith on Justice: Cooperation Between Ancients and Moderns?" *Review of Metaphysics* 48:71–90.

Betzig, Laura. 1989. "Causes of Conjugal Dissolution: A Cross-Cultural Study." *Current Anthropology* 30:654–76.

Bigelow, Robert. 1969. *The Dawn Warriors.* Boston: Little, Brown.

Binswanger, Harry. 1990. *The Biological Basis of Teleological Concepts.* Los Angeles: Ayn Rand Institute Press.

———. 1992. "Life-based Teleology and the Foundations of Ethics." *The Monist* 75:84–103.

Black, Ira B. 1991. *Information in the Brain: A Molecular Perspective.* Cambridge: MIT Press.

Blackwell, Antoinette Brown. 1875. *The Sexes Throughout Nature.* New York: Putnam & Sons.

Bloom, Allan. 1987. *The Closing of the American Mind.* New York: Simon and Schuster.

Bloom, Howard. 1995. *The Lucifer Principle.* New York: Atlantic Monthly Press.

Bluestone, Natalie Harris. 1987. *Women and the Ideal Society: Plato's "Republic" and Modern Myths of Gender.* Amherst: University of Massachusetts Press.

Bock, Kenneth. 1980. *Human Nature and History.* New York: Columbia University Press.

Boehm, Christopher. 1983. "The Evolutionary Development of Morality as an Effect of Dominance Behavior and Conflict Interference." In Margaret Gruter and Paul Bohannan, eds., *Law, Biology and Culture,* 134–47. Santa Barbara, Calif.: Ross-Erikson.

———. 1992. "Segmentary 'Warfare' and the Management of Conflict: Comparison of East African Chimpanzees and Patrilineal-Patrilocal Humans." In Alexander H. Harcourt and Frans de Waal, eds., *Coalitions and Alliances in Humans and Other Animals,* 137–73. Oxford: Oxford University Press.

———. 1997. "Impact of the Human Egalitarian Syndrome on Darwinian Selection Mechanics." *American Naturalist* 150:S100–S121.

Boesch, Christophe. 1991. "Teaching among Wild Chimpanzees." *Animal Behaviour* 41:530–32.

———. 1994. "Hunting Strategies of Gombe and Tai Chimpanzees." In Richard W. Wrangham, W.C. McGrew, Frans de Waal, and Paul G. Heltne, eds., *Chimpanzee Cultures,* 77–91. Cambridge: Harvard University Press.

Boesch, Christophe, and Hedwige Boesch. 1989. "Hunting Behavior of Wild Chimpanzees in the Tai National Park." *American Journal of Physical Anthropology* 78:547–73.

Bogin, Barry. 1988. *Patterns of Human Growth.* Cambridge: Cambridge University Press.

———. 1990. "The Evolution of Human Childhood." *Bioscience* 40:16–25.

Bonner, John T. 1980. *The Evolution of Culture in Animals.* Princeton: Princeton University Press.

———. 1993. *Life Cycles.* Princeton: Princeton University Press.

Boorstin, Daniel. 1948. *The Lost World of Thomas Jefferson.* New York: Henry Holt.

Borgerhoff Mulder, Monique. 1991. "Human Behavioural Ecology." In J. R. Krebs and N. B. Davies, eds., *Behavioural Ecology: An Evolutionary Approach.* Oxford: Blackwell Scientific.

Borgia, Gerald. 1994. "The Scandals of San Marco." *Quarterly Review of Biology* 69:373–75.

Bouchard, Thomas J., David T. Lykken, Matthew McGue, Nancy L. Segal, and Auke Tellegen. 1990. "Sources of Human Psychological Differences: The Minnesota Study of Twins Reared Apart." *Science* 250:223–28.

Bourke, Andrew F. G., and Nigel R. Franks. 1995. *Social Evolution in Ants.* Princeton: Princeton University Press.

Bower, Bruce. 1988a. "Alcoholism's Elusive Genes." *Science News* 134 (30 July):74–75.

———. 1988b. "Intoxicating Habits." *Science News* 134 (6 August):88–89.

Bowlby, John. 1982. *Attachment.* 2d ed. New York: Basic Books.

Boyden, Stephen. 1987. *Western Civilization in Biological Perspective: Patterns in Biohistory.* Oxford: Oxford University Press.

Brandow, S. K. 1979. "Illusion of Equality: Kibbutz Women and the Ideology of the 'New Jew.'" *International Journal of Women's Studies* 2:268–86.

Brauth, Steven E., William S. Hall, and Robert J. Dooling. 1991. *Plasticity of Development.* Cambridge: MIT Press.

Brecht, Arnold. 1959. *Political Theory.* Princeton: Princeton University Press.

Breedlove, S. Marc. 1992. "Sexual Differentiation of the Brain and Behavior." In J. B. Becker, S. M. Breedlove, and D. Crews, eds., *Behavioral Endocrinology*, 30–70. Cambridge: MIT Press.

Bricke, John. 1996. *Mind and Morality: An Examination of Hume's Moral Psychology.* New York: Oxford University Press.

Brockmann, H. Jane. 1984. "The Evolution of Social Behaviour in Insects." In J. R. Krebs and N. B. Davies, eds., *Behavioural Ecology: An Evolutionary Approach*, 340–61. Oxford: Blackwell Scientific Publications.

Brown, Donald E. 1991. *Human Universals.* Philadelphia: Temple University Press.

Brown, Kevin L. 1992. "On Human Nature: Utilitarianism and Darwin." *Social Science Information* 31:239–65.

Brown, Richard E. 1985. "Hormones and Paternal Behavior in Vertebrates." *American Zoologist* 25:895–910.

Browne, Janet. 1995. *Charles Darwin: Voyaging.* New York: Alfred A. Knopf.

Buchanan, Scott. 1972. *Truth in the Sciences.* Charlottesville: University Press of Virginia.

Buckle, Stephen. 1991. *Natural Law and the Theory of Property: Grotius to Hume.* Oxford: Oxford University Press.

Bunge, M. 1977. "Emergence and the Mind." *Neuroscience* 2:501–9.

Burke, Edmund. 1955. *Reflections on the Revolution in France.* Indianapolis: Bobbs-Merrill, The Library of Liberal Arts.

Burkert, Walter. 1996. *Creation of the Sacred: Tracks of Biology in Early Religions.* Cambridge: Harvard University Press.

Buss, David M. 1989. "Sex Differences in Human Mate Preferences: Evolutionary Hypotheses Tested in 37 Cultures." *Behavioral and Brain Sciences* 12:1–49.

————. 1994a. *The Evolution of Desire: Strategies of Human Mating*. New York: Basic Books.

————. 1994b. "The Strategies of Human Mating." *American Scientist* 82:338–49.

Byrne, Richard W., and Andrew Whiten, eds. 1988. *Machiavellian Intelligence: Social Expertise and the Evolution of Intellect in Monkeys, Apes, and Humans*. Oxford: Clarendon Press.

Calhoun, John C. 1992. *Union and Liberty: The Political Philosophy of John C. Calhoun*. Edited by Ross M. Lence. Indianapolis: Liberty Fund.

Callicott, J. Baird. 1994. "Conservation Values and Ethics." In Gary K. Meffe and C. Ronald Carroll, eds., *Principles of Conservation Biology*, 24–49. Sunderland, Mass.: Sinauer.

Campbell, Anne. 1993. *Men, Women, and Aggression*. New York: Basic Books.

————. 1995. "A Few Good Men: Evolutionary Psychology and Female Adolescent Aggression." *Ethology and Sociobiology* 16:99–123.

Campbell, Bernard. 1985. *Human Evolution*. 3d ed. New York: Aldine.

Campbell, Donald T. 1980. "Social Morality Norms as Evidence of Conflict Between Biological Human Nature and Social System Requirements." In Gunther Stent, ed., *Morality as a Biological Phenomenon*, 67–82. Berkeley: University of California Press.

Campbell, Joseph. 1968. *The Hero with a Thousand Faces*. Princeton: Princeton University Press.

Cannon, Walter B. 1939. *The Wisdom of the Body*. 2d ed. New York: Norton.

Capaldi, Nicholas. 1966. "Hume's Rejection of 'Ought' as a Moral Category." *Journal of Philosophy* 63:126–37.

————. 1989. *Hume's Place in Moral Philosophy*. New York: Peter Lang.

Carlson, Mary, and Felton Earls. 1997. "Psychological and Neuroendocrinological Sequelae of Early Social Deprivation in Institutionalized Children in Romania." In C. Sue Carter, I. Izja Lederhendler, and Brian Kirkpatrick, eds., *The Integrative Neurobiology of Affiliation*, 419–28. New York: The New York Academy of Sciences.

Carlson, Neil. 1991. *Physiology of Behavior*. 4th ed. Boston: Allyn and Bacon.

Caro, T. M., and M. D. Hauser. 1992. "Is There Teaching in Nonhuman Animals?" *The Quarterly Review of Biology* 67:151–74.

Carro, Venancio. 1974. "The Spanish Theological-Juridical Renaissance and the Ideology of Bartolomé de Las Casas." In Juan Friede and Benjamin Keen, eds., *Bartolomé de Las Casas in History*, 237–77. DeKalb: Northern Illinois University.

Carroll, Joseph. 1995. *Evolution and Literary Theory*. Columbia: University of Missouri Press.

Carter, C. Sue, A. Courtney DeVries, Susan E. Taymans, R. Lucille Roberts, Jessie R.

Williams, and Lowell L. Getz. 1997. "Peptides, Steroids, and Pair Bonding." In C. Sue Carter, I. Izja Lederhendler, and Brian Kirkpatrick, eds., *The Integrative Neurobiology of Affiliation*, 260–72. New York: The New York Academy of Sciences.

Carter, C. Sue, and Lowell L. Getz. 1993. "Monogamy and the Prairie Vole." *Scientific American* 268 (June): 100–106.

Carter, C. Sue, I. Izja Lederhendler, and Brian Kirkpatrick, eds. 1997. *The Integrative Neurobiology of Affiliation*. New York: The New York Academy of Sciences.

Carter, C. Sue, Jessie R. Williams, Diane M. Witt, and Thomas R. Insel. 1992. "Oxytocin and Social Bonding." *Annals of the New York Academy of Sciences* 652:204–11.

Cartwright, Samuel. 1963. "The Natural History of the Prognathous Species of Mankind." In Eric L. McKitrick, ed., *Slavery Defended*, 139–47. Englewood Cliffs, N.J.: Prentice-Hall.

Catchpole, Clive K. 1986. "The Biology and Evolution of Bird Songs." *Perspectives in Biology and Medicine* 30:47–62.

Catchpole, Clive K., and P. J. B. Slater. 1995. *Bird Song: Biological Themes and Variations*. Cambridge: Cambridge University Press.

Chagnon, Napoleon. 1983. *Yanomamo: The Fierce People*. New York: Holt, Rinehart and Winston.

———. 1988. "Life Histories, Blood Revenge, and Warfare in a Tribal Population." *Science* 239:985–92.

Chambers, Robert. 1844. *Vestiges of the Natural History of Creation*. London: John Churchill.

Chandler, John. 1991. "Ethical Philosophy." In Mary Maxwell, ed., *The Sociobiological Imagination*, 157–69. Albany: State University of New York Press.

Charney, Davida. 1993. "A Study in Rhetorical Reading: How Evolutionists Read 'The Spandrels of San Marco.'" In Jack Selzer, ed., *Understanding Scientific Prose*. Madison: University of Wisconsin Press.

Chase, Ivan D. 1991. "Vacancy Chains." *Annual Review of Sociology* 17:133–54.

Chase, Ivan D., and Theodore H. DeWitt. 1988. "Vacancy Chains: A Process of Mobility to New Resources in Humans and Other Animals." *Social Science Information* 27:83–98.

Cheney, Dorothy, Robert Seyfarth, and Barbara Smuts. 1986. "Social Relationships and Social Cognition in Nonhuman Primates." *Science* 234:1361–66.

Cheney, Dorothy L., and Robert M. Seyfarth. 1990. *How Monkeys See the World*. Chicago: University of Chicago Press.

Christie, Richard, and Florence Geis, eds. 1970. *Studies in Machiavellianism*. New York: Academic Press.

Churchland, Paul. 1995. *The Engine of Reason, the Seat of the Soul: A Philosophical Journey into the Brain*. Cambridge: MIT Press.

————. 1996. "Flanagan on Moral Knowledge." In Robert N. McCauley, ed., *The Churchlands and their Critics*, 302–10. Cambridge, Mass.: Blackwell Publishers.

Cicero, Marcus Tullius. 1931. *De finibus bonorum et malorum*. Translated by H. Rackham. Cambridge: Harvard University Press.

Clark, Stephen R. L. 1975. *Aristotle's Man*. Oxford: Oxford University Press.

Clausewitz, Carl von. 1976. *On War*. Translated by Michael Howard and Peter Paret. Princeton: Princeton University Press.

Clay, Henry. 1844. *The Life and Speeches of Henry Clay*. Edited by Daniel Mallory. 2 vols. New York: Van Amringe and Bixby.

Cleckley, Hervey. 1976. *The Mask of Sanity*. 5th ed. St. Louis: C. V. Mosby.

Cleveland, Henry. 1866. *Alexander H. Stephens in Public and Private, with Letters and Speeches*. Philadelphia: National Publishing Company.

Clutton-Brock, T. H. 1991. *The Evolution of Parental Care*. Princeton: Princeton University Press.

Cole, Blaine. 1988. "Individual Differences in Social Insect Behavior: Movement and Space Use in *Leptothorax allardycei*." In Robert L. Jeanne, ed., *Interindividual Behavioral Variability in Social Insects*, 113–45. Boulder: Westview Press.

Cooper, John M. 1989. "Political Animals and Civic Friendship." In Gunther Patzig, ed., *Aristoteles' "Politik."* Göttingen: Vandenhoeck & Ruprecht.

Cornell, John F. 1986. "Newton of the Grassblade? Darwin and the Problem of Organic Teleology." *Isis* 77:405–21.

Corning, Peter. 1983. *The Synergism Hypothesis*. New York: McGraw-Hill.

Coyne, Jerry A., and Brian Charlesworth. 1997. Letter. *Science* 276:337–41.

Cronin, Helena. 1991. *The Ant and the Peacock*. Cambridge: Cambridge University Press.

Cronk, Lee. 1991. "Human Behavioral Ecology." *Annual Review of Anthropology* 20:25–53.

Crook, John H. 1989. "Socioecological Paradigms, Evolution, and History." In V. Standen and R. A. Foley, eds., *Comparative Socioecology: The Behavioural Ecology of Humans and Other Animals*. Oxford: Blackwell Scientific.

Crook, John H., and Stamati J. Crook. 1988. "Tibetan Polyandry: Problems of Adaptation and Fitness." In Laura Betzig, Monique Borgerhoff Mulder, and Paul Turke, eds., *Human Reproductive Behaviour: A Darwinian Perspective*, 97–114. Cambridge: Cambridge University Press.

Cropsey, Joseph. 1977. "Political Life and a Natural Order." In *Political Philosophy and the Issues of Politics*, 221–30. Chicago: University of Chicago Press.

Crossette, Barbara. 1995. "Female Genital Mutilation by Immigrants is Becoming Cause for Concern in the U.S." *New York Times*, 10 December.

Cumberland, Richard. 1727. *A Treatise of the Laws of Nature*. Translated by John Maxwell. London: R. Phillips.

Daly, Martin, and Margo Wilson. 1983. *Sex, Evolution, and Behavior*. Belmont, Calif.: Wadsworth.

———. 1988. *Homicide*. Hawthorne, N.Y.: Aldine de Gruyter.

———. 1990. "Killing the Competition: Female/female and Male/male Homicide." *Human Nature* 1:81–107.

———. 1995. "Discriminative Parental Solicitude and the Relevance of Evolutionary Models to the Analysis of Motivational Systems." In Michael Gazzaniga, ed., *The Cognitive Neurosciences*, 1269–86. Cambridge: MIT Press.

Damasio, Antonio R. 1994. *Descartes' Error: Emotion, Reason, and the Human Brain*. New York: G. P. Putnam's Sons.

Damasio, Antonio R., and Hanna Damasio. 1992. "Brain and Language." *Scientific American* 267(September):88–95.

Damasio, Antonio R., Daniel Tranel, and Hanna Damasio. 1990. "Individuals with Sociopathic Behavior Caused by Frontal Damage Fail to Respond Autonomically to Social Stimuli." *Behavioural Brain Research*. 41:81–94.

Damasio, Hanna, Thomas Grabowski, Randall Frank, Albert Galaburda, and Antonio R. Damasio. 1994. "The Return of Phineas Gage: Clues about the Brain from the Skull of a Famous Patient." *Science* 264:1102–5.

Damon, William. 1988. *The Moral Child: Nurturing Children's Natural Moral Growth*. New York: Free Press.

Darwin, Charles. 1859. *The Origin of Species*. London: John Murray. Facsimile of first edition, with introduction by Ernst Mayr. Cambridge: Harvard University Press, 1964.

———. 1868. *The Variation of Animals and Plants Under Domestication*. 2 vols. London: John Murray.

———. 1871. *The Descent of Man*. 2 vols. London: John Murray. Facsimile of first edition, with introduction by John T. Bonner and Robert M. May. Princeton: Princeton University Press, 1981.

———. 1872. *The Expression of the Emotions in Man and Animals*. New York: D. Appleton. Facsimile of the first edition, with introduction by Konrad Lorenz. Chicago: University of Chicago Press, 1965.

———. 1892. *The Various Contrivances by Which Orchids Are Fertilized by Insects*. New York: D. Appleton. Facsimile of second edition, with a foreword by Michael Ghiselin. Chicago: University of Chicago Press, 1984.

———. 1881a. *The Formation of Vegetable Mold, through the Action of Worms*. Facsimile, with foreword by Stephen Jay Gould. Chicago: University of Chicago Press, 1985.

———. 1881b. *The Power of Movement in Plants*. New York: D. Appleton. Facsimile, with preface by Barbara G. Pickard. New York: Da Capo Press, 1966.

———. 1888. *The Different Forms of Flowers on Plants of the Same Species*. London: John Murray. Facsimile, with foreword by Herbert G. Baker. Chicago: University of Chicago Press, 1986.

———. 1892. *The Autobiography of Charles Darwin and Selected Letters*. Edited by Francis Darwin. New York: D. Appleton. Facsimile. New York: Dover Publications, 1958.

———. 1936a. *The Origin of Species*. 6th ed. In *The Origin of Species and the Descent of Man*. New York: Random House, Modern Library.

———. 1936b. *The Descent of Man*. 2d ed. In *The Origin of Species and the Descent of Man*. New York: Random House, Modern Library.

———. 1962. *The Voyage of the Beagle*. Edited by Leonard Engel. Garden City, N.Y.: Doubleday Anchor Books.

———. 1977a. "A Biographical Sketch of an Infant." In Paul H. Barrett, ed., *The Collected Papers of Charles Darwin*, 2:191–200. Chicago: University of Chicago Press.

———. 1977b. *The Collected Papers of Charles Darwin*. Edited by Paul H. Barrett. 2 vols. Chicago: University of Chicago Press.

———. 1986. *The Correspondence of Charles Darwin*. Vol. 2: *1837–43*. Edited by Frederick Burkhardt and Sydney Smith. Cambridge: Cambridge University Press.

———. 1987. *Charles Darwin's Notebooks, 1836–1844*. Edited by Paul H. Barrett, Peter J. Gautrey, Sandra Herbert, David Kohn, and Sydney Smith. Ithaca: Cornell University Press.

Davis, David Brion. 1966. *The Problem of Slavery in Western Culture*. Ithaca: Cornell University Press.

———. 1975. *The Problem of Slavery in the Age of Revolution, 1770–1823*. Ithaca: Cornell University Press.

———. 1984. *Slavery and Human Progress*. New York: Oxford University Press.

———. 1986. *From Homicide to Slavery*. New York: Oxford University Press.

———. 1996. "At the Heart of Slavery." *New York Review of Books* 43 (17 October): 51–54.

Davitt, Thomas E. 1978. *The Basic Values in Law*. Milwaukee: Marquette University Press.

Dawkins, Richard. 1976. *The Selfish Gene*. Oxford: Oxford University Press.

———. 1986. *The Blind Watchmaker*. New York: Norton.

———. 1989. *The Selfish Gene*. 2d ed. Oxford: Oxford University Press.

———. 1995. *River Out of Eden: A Darwinian View of Life*. New York: Basic Books.

————. 1996. *Climbing Mount Improbable.* New York: Norton.

Deely, John N. 1971. "Animal Intelligence and Concept-Formation." *The Thomist* 35:43–93.

————. 1982. *Introducing Semiotic.* Bloomington: Indiana University Press.

Degler, Carl N. 1991. *In Search of Human Nature: The Decline and Revival of Darwinism in American Social Thought.* New York: Oxford University Press.

Delbrück, Max. 1976. "How Aristotle Discovered DNA." In K. Huang, ed., *Physics and Our World,* 123–30. New York: American Institute of Physics.

Depew, David J. 1995. "Humans and Other Political Animals in Aristotle's *History of Animals.*" *Phronesis* 40:156–81.

Depew, David J., and Bruce H. Weber. 1995. *Darwinism Evolving: Systems Dynamics and the Genealogy of Natural Selection.* Cambridge: MIT Press.

Des Jardins, Joseph. 1993. *Environmental Ethics: An Introduction to Environmental Philosophy.* Belmont, Calif.: Wadsworth.

Dew, Thomas R. 1981. "Abolition of Negro Slavery." In Drew Gilpin Faust, ed., *The Ideology of Slavery,* 23–77. Baton Rouge: Louisiana State University Press.

de Waal, Frans. 1982. *Chimpanzee Politics: Power and Sex Among Apes.* New York: Harper and Row.

————. 1986. "Integration of Dominance and Social Bonding in Primates." *Quarterly Review of Biology* 61:459–79.

————. 1989a. *Peacemaking Among Primates.* Cambridge: Harvard University Press.

————. 1989b. "Food Sharing and Reciprocal Obligations among Chimpanzees." *Journal of Human Evolution* 18:433–59.

————. 1992. "The Chimpanzee's Sense of Social Regularity and Its Relation to the Human Sense of Justice." In Roger D. Masters and Margaret Gruter, eds., *The Sense of Justice: Biological Foundations of Law,* 241–55. Newbury Park, Calif.: Sage.

————. 1996. *Good Natured: The Origins of Right and Wrong in Humans and Other Animals.* Cambridge: Harvard University Press.

de Waal, Frans, and Frans Lanting. 1997. *Bonobo: The Forgotten Ape.* Berkeley: University of California Press.

Diamond, Marian C. 1988. *Enriching Heredity: The Impact of the Environment on the Anatomy of the Brain.* New York: Free Press.

Diamond, Milton, and H. Keith Sigmundson. 1997. "Sex Reassignment at Birth." *The Archives of Pediatric and Adolescent Medicine* 151:298–304.

Dobzhansky, Theodosius, F. J. Ayala, G. L. Stebbins, and J. W. Valentine. 1977. *Evolution.* San Francisco: W. H. Freeman.

Donald, Merlin. 1991. *Origins of the Modern Mind: Three Stages in the Evolution of Culture and Cognition.* Cambridge: Harvard University Press.

————. 1993. "Précis of *Origins of the Modern Mind.*" *Behavioral and Brain Sciences* 16:737–91.

Donnelly, Jack. 1982. "Human Rights as Natural Rights." *Human Rights Quarterly* 4:391–405.

Douglass, Frederick. 1955. *The Life and Writings of Frederick Douglass.* Edited by Philip S. Foner. 5 vols. New York: International Publishers.

Dugger, Celia. 1996. "Tug of Taboos: African Genital Rite vs. U.S. Law." *New York Times,* 28 December.

Dunbar, Robin I.M. 1988. *Primate Social Systems.* Ithaca: Cornell University Press.

————. 1993. "Coevolution of Neocortical Size, Group Size and Language in Humans." *Behavioral and Brain Sciences* 16:681–735.

Duncan, John. 1995. "Attention, Intelligence, and the Frontal Lobes." In Michael Gazzaniga, ed., *The Cognitive Neurosciences,* 721–33. Cambridge: MIT Press.

Dupre, John. 1987. "Human Kinds." In John Dupre, ed., *The Latest on the Best: Essays on Evolution and Optimality,* 327–48. Cambridge: MIT Press.

————. 1990. "Global versus Local Perspectives on Sexual Difference." In Deborah Rhode, ed., *Theoretical Perspectives on Sexual Difference,* 47–62. New Haven: Yale University Press.

Durham, William. 1976. "Resource Competition and Human Aggression, Part I: A Review of Primitive War." *Quarterly Review of Biology* 51:385–415.

Eaves, L. J., H. J. Eysenck, and N. G. Martin. 1989. *Genes, Culture and Personality.* New York: Academic Press.

Eccles, John. 1989. *Evolution of the Brain: Creation of the Self.* London: Routledge.

Eccles, John, and Daniel Robinson. 1984. *The Wonder of Being Human.* New York: Free Press.

Edwards, Carolyn Pope. 1993. "Behavioral Sex Differences in Children of Diverse Cultures: The Case of Nurturance to Infants." In Michael E. Pereira and Lynn A. Fairbanks, eds., *Juvenile Primates: Life History, Development, and Behavior,* 327–38. New York: Oxford University Press.

Eibl-Eibesfeldt, Irenäus. 1974. *Love and Hate: The Natural History of Behavior Patterns.* New York: Schocken Books.

————. 1989. *Human Ethology.* Hawthorne, N.Y.: Aldine de Gruyter.

Eimas, Peter D. 1985. "The Perception of Speech in Early Infancy." *Scientific American* 252 (January): 46–52.

Einstein, Gillian. 1997. "Sex, Sexuality, and the Brain." In Dale Purves, George J. Augustine, David Fitzpatrick, Lawrence C. Katz, Anthony-Samuel LaMantia, and James O. McNamara, eds., *Neuroscience: Molecules to Mind,* 529–48. Sunderland, Mass.: Sinauer Associates.

Eldredge, Niles, and Stephen Jay Gould. 1972. "Punctuated Equilibria: An Alternative to Phyletic Gradualism." In T. J. M. Schopf, ed., *Models in Paleobiology*, 83–115. San Francisco: Freeman, Cooper and Company. Reprinted in Niles Eldredge, *Time Frames: The Rethinking of Darwinian Evolution and the Theory of Punctuated Equilibria* (New York: Simon and Schuster, 1985).

Ellickson, Robert C. 1991. *Order without Law: How Neighbors Settle Disputes.* Cambridge: Harvard University Press.

Elshtain, Jean Bethke. 1987. "Against Androgyny." In Anne Phillips, ed., *Feminism and Equality*, 139–59. New York: New York University Press.

———. 1992. "Battered Reason." *The New Republic* 207 (5 October): 25–29.

Elwood, R. W., and S. J. Neil. 1992. *Assessments and Decisions: A Study of Information Gathering by Hermit Crabs.* London: Chapman and Hall.

Ember, Carol, and Melvin Ember. 1992. "Resource Unpredictability, Mistrust, and War." *Journal of Conflict Resolution* 36:242–62.

———. 1993. *Anthropology.* 7th ed. Englewood Cliffs, N.J.: Prentice-Hall.

Emerson, Ralph Waldo. 1983. *Essays and Lectures.* New York: The Library of America.

Emlen, Stephen T. 1995. "An Evolutionary Theory of the Family." *Proceedings of the National Academy of Science* 92:36–47.

Emlen, Stephen T., and Peter H. Wrege. 1994. "Gender, Status, and Family Fortunes in the White-fronted Bee-Eater." *Nature* 367:129–32.

Espinas, Alfred. 1878. *De Sociétés animales.* Paris: Librairie Germer Bailliere.

Fagan, Brian M. 1984. *Clash of Cultures.* New York: W. H. Freeman.

———. 1991. *Ancient North America: The Archaeology of a Continent.* New York: Thames and Hudson.

Fagan, Thomas J., and Frank T. Lira. 1980. "The Primary and Secondary Sociopathic Personality: Differences in Frequency and Severity of Antisocial Behaviors." *Journal of Abnormal Psychology* 89:493–96.

Fagen, Robert. 1993. "Primate Juveniles and Primate Play." In Michael E. Pereira and Lynn A. Fairbanks, eds., *Juvenile Primates: Life History, Development, and Behavior*, 182–96. New York: Oxford University Press.

Farrell, Warren. 1993. *The Myth of Male Power: Why Men Are the Disposable Sex.* New York: Simon and Schuster.

Fedigan, Linda Marie. 1986. "The Changing Role of Women in Models of Human Evolution." *Annual Review of Anthropology* 15:25–66.

———. 1992. "Neither a Genre of Feminism nor of Ethical Naturalism: Primatology as a Source of Naturalistic Truth and Fallacy." *Politics and the Life Sciences* 11:172–74.

Field, Tiffany. 1990. *Infancy.* Cambridge: Harvard University Press.

Fingarette, Herbert. 1988a. "Alcoholism: The Mythical Disease." *The Public Interest*, no. 91:3–22.

———. 1988b. *Heavy Drinking: The Myth of Alcoholism as a Disease.* Berkeley: University of California Press.

Finley, M. I. 1983. *Ancient Slavery and Modern Ideology.* New York: Penguin Books.

Finnis, John. 1979. *Natural Law and Natural Rights.* Oxford: Clarendon Press.

Fisher, Helen E. 1992. *Anatomy of Love: The Natural History of Monogamy, Adultery, and Divorce.* New York: Norton.

———. 1995. "The Nature and Evolution of Romantic Love." In William Jankowiak, ed., *Romantic Passion: A Universal Experience?*, 23–41. New York: Columbia University Press.

Flanagan, Owen. 1996. "Ethics Naturalized: Ethics as Human Ecology." In Larry May, Marilyn Friedman, and Andy Clark, eds., *Mind and Morals: Essays on Ethics and Cognitive Science*, 19–43. Cambridge: MIT Press.

Fox, Robin, ed. 1975. *Biosocial Anthropology.* New York: John Wiley.

———. 1983. *Kinship & Marriage: An Anthropological Perspective.* Cambridge: Cambridge University Press.

———. 1989. *The Search for Society: Quest for a Biosocial Science and Morality.* New Brunswick, N.J.: Rutgers University Press.

Frank, Robert. 1988. *Passions within Reason.* New York: Norton.

Freehling, William W. 1990. *The Road to Disunion.* New York: Oxford University Press.

Freeman, Derek. 1983. *Margaret Mead and Samoa: The Making and Unmaking of an Anthropological Myth.* Cambridge: Harvard University Press.

Futuyma, Douglas. 1983. *Science on Trial: The Case for Evolution.* New York: Pantheon.

Galdikas, Biruté, and Paul Vasey. 1991. "Primatology." In Mary Maxwell, ed., *The Sociobiological Imagination*, 111–29. Albany: State University of New York Press.

Gardner, R. Allen, and Beatrix T. Gardner. 1969. "Teaching Sign Language to a Chimpanzee." *Science* 165:664–72.

Gardner, R. Allen, Beatrix T. Gardner, and Thomas E. Van Cantfort, eds. 1989. *Teaching Sign Language to Chimpanzees.* Albany: State University of New York Press.

Garlan, Yvon. 1988. *Slavery in Ancient Greece.* Translated Janet Lloyd. Ithaca: Cornell University Press.

Geertz, Clifford. 1973. *The Interpretation of Cultures.* New York: Basic Books.

———. 1984. "Anti Anti-Relativism." *American Anthropologist* 86 (March): 263–78.

Genovese, Eugene D. 1976. *Roll, Jordan, Roll: The World the Slaves Made.* New York: Random House, Vintage Books.

Ghiselin, Michael. 1984. Foreword to *The Various Contrivances by which Orchids are Fertilized by Insects*, by Charles Darwin. Chicago: University of Chicago Press.

Gibbons, Ann. 1992a. "Chimps: More Diverse Than a Barrel of Monkeys." *Science* 255:287–88.

———. 1992b. "Plants of the Apes." *Science* 255:921.

Gilligan, Carol. 1982. *In a Different Voice.* Cambridge: Harvard University Press.

Goldberg, Steven. 1973. *The Inevitability of Patriarchy.* New York: William Morrow.

———. 1993. *Why Men Rule: A Theory of Male Dominance.* LaSalle, Ill.: Open Court.

Goldsmith, Timothy H. 1990. "Optimization, Constraint, and History in the Evolution of Eyes." *Quarterly Review of Biology* 65:281–322.

———. 1991. *The Biological Roots of Human Nature.* New York: Oxford University Press.

Gomperz, Theodor. 1905. *Greek Thinkers.* 4 vols. London: Macmillan.

Goodall, Jane. 1983. "Order without Law." In Margaret Gruter and Paul Bohannan, eds., *Law, Biology, and Culture*, 50–62. Santa Barbara, Calif.: Ross-Erikson.

———. 1986. *The Chimpanzees of Gombe.* Cambridge: Harvard University Press.

———. 1990. *Through a Window: My Thirty Years with the Chimpanzees of Gombe.* Boston: Houghton Mifflin.

Gordon, Deborah M. 1991. "Behavioral Flexibility and the Foraging Ecology of Seed-eating Ants." *American Naturalist* 138:379–411.

———. 1992. "Phenotypic Plasticity." In Evelyn Fox Keller and Elisabeth A. Lloyd, eds., *Keywords in Evolutionary Biology*, 355–62. Cambridge: Harvard University Press.

Gotthelf, Allan. 1975. *Aristotle's Conception of Final Causality.* Columbia University dissertation. Ann Arbor, Mich.: University Microfilms.

———, ed. 1985. *Aristotle on Nature and Living Things.* Pittsburgh: Mathesis Publications.

———. 1987. "Aristotle's Conception of Final Causality." In Allan Gotthelf and James G. Lennox, eds., *Philosophical Issues in Aristotle's Biology*, 204–42. Cambridge: Cambridge University Press.

Gotthelf, Allan, and James G. Lennox, eds. 1987. *Philosophical Issues in Aristotle's Biology.* Cambridge: Cambridge University Press.

Gottlieb, Gilbert. 1984. "Evolutionary Trends and Evolutionary Origins: Relevance to Theory in Comparative Psychology." *Psychological Review* 91:448–56.

Gould, James L. 1984. "Natural History of Honey Bee Learning." In Peter Marler and Herbert S. Terrace, eds., *The Biology of Learning*, 47–74. New York: Springer-Verlag.

———. 1993. "Ethological and Comparative Perspectives on Honey Bee Learning." In D. R. Papaj and A. C. Lewis, eds., *Insect Learning*, 18–50. New York: Chapman and Hall.

Gould, James L., and Carol Grant Gould. 1988. *The Honey Bee*. New York: Scientific American Library.

Gould, James L., and Peter Marler. 1984. "Ethology and the Natural History of Learning." In Peter Marler and H. S. Terrace, eds., *The Biology of Learning*, 149–80. Berlin: Springer-Verlag.

———. 1987. "Learning by Instinct." *Scientific American* 256 (January): 74–85.

Gould, Stephen Jay. 1977. *Ever Since Darwin: Reflections in Natural History*. New York: Norton.

———. 1978. "Morton's Ranking of Races by Cranial Capacity." *Science* 200:503–9.

———. 1980. *The Panda's Thumb*. New York: Norton.

———. 1981. *The Mismeasure of Man*. New York: Norton.

———. 1985. *The Flamingo's Smile*. New York: Norton.

———. 1989. *Wonderful Life: The Burgess Shale and the Nature of History*. New York: Norton.

———. 1991. *Bully for Brontosaurus*. New York: Norton.

———. 1997a. "Darwinian Fundamentalism." *New York Review of Books* 44 (12 June): 34–37.

———. 1997b. "Evolution: The Pleasures of Pluralism." *New York Review of Books* 44 (26 June): 47–52.

Gould, Stephen Jay, and Richard Lewontin. 1979. "The Spandrels of San Marco and the Panglossian Paradigm—A Critique of the Adaptationist Programme." *Proceedings of the Royal Society of London B* 205:581–98. Reprinted in Elliott Sober, ed., *Conceptual Issues in Evolutionary Biology*, 2d ed. (Cambridge: MIT Press, 1994).

Gray, J. Glenn. 1970. *The Warriors: Reflections on Men in Battle*. New York: Harper & Row.

Greene, John C. 1984. *American Science in the Age of Jefferson*. Ames: Iowa State University Press.

Grene, Marjorie. 1968. *Approaches to a Philosophical Biology*. New York: Basic Books.

———. 1974. "Aristotle and Modern Biology." In *The Understanding of Nature*, 74–107. Boston: D. Reidel.

Griffin, Donald. 1984. *Animal Thinking*. Cambridge: Harvard University Press.

———. 1992. *Animal Minds*. Chicago: University of Chicago Press.

Griffiths, P. E., and R. D. Gray. 1994. "Developmental Systems and Evolutionary Explanation." *The Journal of Philosophy* 91:277–304.

Grossman, James B., Alice Carter, and Fred R. Volkmar. 1997. "Social Behavior in Autism." In C. Sue Carter, I. Izja Lederhendler, and Brian Kirkpatrick, eds., *The Integrative Neurobiology of Affiliation*, 440–54. New York: The New York Academy of Sciences.

Grotius, Hugo. 1925. *The Law of War and Peace*. Translated by Francis W. Kelsey. Oxford: Clarendon Press.

Gruter, Margaret, and Roger D. Masters, eds. 1986. *Ostracism: A Social and Biological Phenomenon*. New York: Elsevier.

Hamilton, Alexander, James Madison, and John Jay. 1961. *The Federalist Papers*. Edited by Clinton Rossiter. New York: The New American Library.

Hamilton, W. D. 1964. "The Genetical Evolution of Social Behavior." *Journal of Theoretical Biology* 7:1–52. Reprinted in W. D. Hamilton, *The Narrow Roads of Gene Land*. Vol. 1 of *The Collected Works of W. D. Hamilton*, 11–82. New York: W. H. Freeman, 1996.

Hammond, John Henry. 1963. "Speech on the Admission of Kansas." In Eric McKitrick, ed., *Slavery Defended*, 122–23. Englewood Cliffs, N.J.: Prentice-Hall.

Hampson, Elizabeth, and Doreen Kimura. 1992. "Sex Differences and Hormonal Influences on Cognitive Function in Humans." In Jill B. Becker, S. Marc Breedlove, and David Crews, eds., *Behavioral Endocrinology*, 357–98. Cambridge: MIT Press.

Hanke, Lewis. 1974. *All Mankind is One*. DeKalb: Northern Illinois University Press.

Haraway, Donna. 1989. *Primate Visions: Gender, Race, and Nature in the World of Modern Science*. New York: Routledge.

Harcourt, Alexander H. 1992. "Cooperation in Conflicts: Commonalities Between Humans and Other Animals." *Politics and the Life Sciences* 11:251–59.

Harcourt, Alexander H., and de Waal, Frans, eds. 1992. *Coalitions and Alliances in Humans and Other Animals*. Oxford: Oxford University Press.

Hare, Robert D. 1993. *Without Conscience: The Disturbing World of the Psychopaths Among Us*. New York: Pocket Books.

Harlow, Harry. 1986. *From Learning to Love: The Selected Papers of H. F. Harlow*. New York: Praeger.

Harper, William. 1981. "Memoir on Slavery." In Drew Gilpin Faust, ed., *The Ideology of Slavery*, 79–135. Baton Rouge: Louisiana State University Press.

Hartung, John. 1995. "Love Thy Neighbor: The Evolution of In-Group Morality." *The Skeptic* 3:86–99.

Hatch, Elvin. 1983. *Culture and Morality: The Relativity of Values in Anthropology*. New York: Columbia University Press.

Hauser, Marc D. 1996. *The Evolution of Communication*. Cambridge: MIT Press.

Hausfater, Glenn, and Sarah B. Hrdy, eds. 1984. *Infanticide: Comparative and Evolutionary Perspectives*. Hawthorne, N.Y.: Aldine de Gruyter.

Heidegger, Martin. 1959. *An Introduction to Metaphysics*. Translated by Ralph Manheim. New Haven: Yale University Press.

————. 1993. "What is Metaphysics?" In David Farrell Krell, ed., *Martin Heidegger: Basic Writings*, 90–110. New York: HarperCollins Publishers.

Herodotus. 1987. *The History*. Translated by David Greene. Chicago: University of Chicago Press.

Herrick, C. Judson. 1956. *The Evolution of Human Nature*. Austin: University of Texas Press.

Hewlett, Barry S. 1992. "Husband-Wife Reciprocity and the Father-Infant Relationship among Aka Pygmies." In Barry S. Hewlett, ed., *Father-Child Relations: Cultural and Biosocial Contexts*, 153–76. Hawthorne, N.Y.: Aldine de Gruyter.

Hill, K. 1993. "Life History Theory and Evolutionary Anthropology." *Evolutionary Anthropology* 2:78–88.

Hiraiwa-Hasegawa, Mariko. 1989. "Sex Differences in the Behavioral Development of Chimpanzees at Mahale." In Paul G. Heltne and Linda A. Marquardt, eds., *Understanding Chimpanzees*, 104–15. Cambridge: Harvard University Press.

Hirschi, T., and M. Gottfredson. 1983. "Age and the Explanation of Crime." *American Journal of Sociology* 89:552–84.

Hobbes, Thomas. 1957. *The Leviathan*. Michael Oakeshott, ed. Oxford: Basil Blackwell.

————. 1949. *De Cive or The Citizen*. Edited by Sterling P. Lamprecht. New York: Appleton-Century-Crofts.

————. 1991. *De Homine*, chapters 10–15. In Bernard Gert, ed., *Man and Citizen*. Indianapolis: Hackett Publishing Company.

Holcomb, Harmon R. 1993. *Sociobiology, Sex, and Science*. Albany: State University of New York Press.

Hölldobler, Bert. 1976. "Tournaments and Slavery in a Desert Ant." *Science* 192:912–14.

Hölldobler, Bert, and Edward O. Wilson. 1990. *The Ants*. Cambridge: Harvard University Press.

————. 1994. *Journey to the Ants*. Cambridge: Harvard University Press.

Horgan, John. 1988. "Why Warfare?" *Scientific American* 259 (November): 20–22.

Horowitz, Maryanne C. 1976. "Aristotle and Woman." *Journal of the History of Biology* 9:183–213.

House, James S., Karl R. Landis, and Debra Umberson. 1988. "Social Relationships and Health." *Science* 241:540–45.

Howard, Michael. 1983. *The Causes of War*. Cambridge: Harvard University Press.

Hrdy, Sarah Blaffer. 1981. *The Woman That Never Evolved*. Cambridge: Harvard University Press.

————. 1986. "Empathy, Polyandry, and the Myth of the Coy Female." In Ruth Bleier, ed., *Feminist Approaches to Science*, 119–46. New York: Pergamon.

Hubbard, Ruth. 1990. *The Politics of Women's Biology.* New Brunswick, N.J.: Rutgers University Press.

Hull, David. 1978. "A Matter of Individuality." *Philosophy of Science* 45:335–60.

———. 1983. *Darwin and His Critics.* Chicago: University of Chicago Press.

Hume, David. 1888. *A Treatise of Human Nature.* Edited by L. A. Selby-Bigge. Oxford: Oxford University Press.

———. 1902. *Enquiries Concerning the Human Understanding and Concerning the Principles of Morals.* 2d ed. Oxford: Clarendon Press.

———. 1985. *Essays.* Edited by Eugene F. Miller. Indianapolis: Liberty Classics.

———. 1992. *Writings on Religion.* Edited by Antony Flew. Peru, Ill.: Open Court.

Humphrey, Nicholas. 1976. "The Social Function of Intellect." In P. P. G. Bateson and R. A. Hinde, eds., *Growing Points in Ethology.* Cambridge: Cambridge University Press.

Hunter, R. H. F. 1995. *Sex Determination, Differentiation and Intersexuality in Placental Mammals.* Cambridge: Cambridge University Press.

Huxley, Thomas H. 1871. "Mr. Darwin's Critics." *Contemporary Review* 18:443–76.

———. 1894a. *Evolution and Ethics.* London: Macmillan.

———. 1894b. *Collected Essays.* 9 vols. London: Macmillan.

Insel, Thomas R. 1992a. "Oxytocin and the Neurobiology of Attachment." *Behavioral and Brain Sciences* 15:515–16.

———. 1992b. "Oxytocin—A Neuropeptide for Affiliation: Evidence from Behavioral, Receptor Autoradiographic, and Comparative Studies." *Psychoneuroendocrinology* 17:3–35.

Insel, Thomas R., and C. Sue Carter. 1995. "The Monogamous Brain." *Natural History* 104 (August): 12–14.

Insel, Thomas R., and Terrence J. Hulihan. 1995. "A Gender-Specific Mechanism for Pair-Bonding: Oxytocin and Partner Preference Formation in Monogamous Voles." *Behavioral Neuroscience* 109:782–89.

Insel, Thomas R., Larry Young, and Zuoxin Wang. 1997. "Molecular Aspects of Monogamy." In C. Sue Carter, I. Izja Lederhendler, and Brian Kirkpatrick, eds., *The Integrative Neurobiology of Affiliation*, 302–16. New York: The New York Academy of Sciences.

Itani, Junichiro. 1988. "The Origin of Human Equality." In Michael Chance, ed., *Social Fabrics of the Mind*, 137–56. Hillsdale, N.J.: Lawrence Erlbaum.

Jacob, François. 1982. *The Possible and the Actual.* New York: Pantheon.

Jacobs, Barry L. 1994. "Serotonin, Motor Activity and Depression-related Disorders." *American Scientist* 82:456–63.

Jacobs, Bob, and Michael Raleigh. 1992. "Attachment: How Early, How Far?" *Behavioral and Brain Sciences* 15:517.

Jaffa, Harry V. 1965. *Equality and Liberty: Theory and Practice in American Politics.* New York: Oxford University Press.

———. 1973. *Crisis of the House Divided.* 2d ed. Seattle: University of Washington Press.

———. 1975. *The Conditions of Freedom: Essays in Political Philosophy.* Baltimore: The Johns Hopkins University Press.

Jaggar, Alison. 1983. *Feminist Politics and Human Nature.* Totowa, N.J.: Rowman and Allanheld.

———. 1990. "Sexual Difference and Sexual Equality." In Deborah Rhode, ed., *Theoretical Perspectives on Sexual Difference,* 239–55. New Haven: Yale University Press.

Jaisson, Pierre, Dominique Fresneau, and Jean-Paul Lauchard. 1988. "Individual Traits of Social Behavior in Ants." In Robert L. Jeanne, ed., *Interindividual Behavioral Variability in Social Insects,* 1–52. Boulder: Westview Press.

Jankowiak, William R., and Edward F. Fischer. 1992. "A Cross-Cultural Perspective on Romantic Love." *Ethnology* 31:149–55.

Jeanne, Robert L. 1991. "Polyethism." In Kenneth G. Ross and Robert W. Matthews, eds., *The Social Biology of Wasps,* 389–425. Ithaca: Cornell University Press.

Jefferson, Thomas. 1907. *The Writings of Thomas Jefferson.* 20 vols. Albert Ellery Bergh, ed. Washington, D.C.: Thomas Jefferson Memorial Association.

———. 1944. *The Life and Selected Writings of Thomas Jefferson.* Edited by Adrienne Koch and William Peden. New York: Random House, The Modern Library.

———. 1972. *Notes on the State of Virginia.* Edited by William Peden. New York: Norton.

———. 1984. *Writings.* Edited by Merrill D. Peterson. New York: The Library of America.

Jeffrey, C. Ray. 1994. "The Brain, the Law, and the Medicalization of Crime." In Roger D. Masters and Michael T. McGuire, eds., *The Neurotransmitter Revolution: Serotonin, Social Behavior, and the Law,* 161–78. Carbondale: Southern Illinois University Press.

Jerison, Harry J. 1970. "Brain Evolution: New Light on Old Principles." *Science* 170:1224–25.

———. 1973. *Evolution of the Brain and Intelligence.* New York: Academic Press.

———. 1985. "On the Evolution of Mind." In David A. Oakley, ed., *Brain and Mind,* 1–31. London: Methuen.

Johansen, Donald, and Maitland Edey. 1981. *Lucy: The Beginnings of Humankind.* New York: Warner Books.

John Paul II. 1997. "Theories of Evolution." *First Things,* no. 69 (March): 28–29.

Johnsgard, Paul A. 1983. *Cranes of the World.* Bloomington: Indiana University Press.

Johnson, Gary. 1995. "The Evolutionary Origins of Government and Politics." In Joseph Losco and Albert Somit, eds., *Human Nature and Politics*, 243–305. Greenwich, Conn.: JAI Press.

Johnson, Philip. 1991. *Darwin on Trial*. Downers Grove, Ill.: Intervarsity Press.

Johnston, Timothy D. 1988. "Developmental Explanation and the Ontogeny of Birdsong: Nature/Nurture Redux." *Behavioral and Brain Sciences* 11:617–63.

Jolly, Alison. 1985. *The Evolution of Primate Behavior*. 2d ed. New York: Macmillan.

Jonas, Hans. 1966. *The Phenomenon of Life*. New York: Dell.

———. 1984. *The Imperative of Responsibility*. Chicago: University of Chicago Press.

Justinian. 1987. *Justinian's Institutes*. Translated by P. Burks and G. McLeod. Ithaca: Cornell University Press.

Kagan, Jerome. 1981. *The Second Year*. Cambridge: Harvard University Press.

———. 1984. *The Nature of the Child*. New York: Basic Books.

———. 1994. *Galen's Prophecy: Temperament in Human Nature*. New York: Basic Books.

Kandel, Eric R. 1991. "Cellular Mechanisms of Learning and the Biological Basis of Individuality." In Eric R. Kandel, James H. Schwartz, and Thomas M. Jessell, eds., *Principles of Neural Science*, 1009–31. New York: Elsevier.

Kandel, Eric R., and Robert D. Hawkins. 1992. "The Biological Basis of Learning and Individuality." *Scientific American* 267 (September): 78–86.

Kandel, Eric R., and Thomas Jessell. 1991. "Early Experience and the Fine Tuning of Synaptic Connections." In Eric R. Kandel, James H. Schwartz, and Thomas M. Jessell, eds., *Principles of Neural Science*, 945–58. 3d ed. New York: Elsevier.

Kano, Takayoshi. 1992. *The Last Ape: Pygmy Chimpanzee Behavior and Ecology*. Translated by Evelyn Ono Vineberg. Stanford, Calif.: Stanford University Press.

Kant, Immanuel. 1956. *Critique of Practical Reason*. Translated by Lewis W. Beck. Indianapolis: Bobbs-Merrill.

———. 1959. *Foundations of the Metaphysics of Morals*. Translated by Lewis White Beck. Indianapolis: Bobbs-Merrill.

———. 1965. *Critique of Pure Reason*. Translated by Norman Kemp Smith. New York: St. Martin's Press.

———. 1970. *Kant's Political Writings*. Translated by H. B. Nisbet. Cambridge: Cambridge University Press.

———. 1983. "Speculative Beginning of Human History." In *"Perpetual Peace" and Other Essays*. Translated by Ted Humphrey. Indianapolis: Hackett.

———. 1987. *Critique of Judgment*. Translated by Werner S. Pluhar. Indianapolis: Hackett.

Katchadourian, Herant. 1985. *Fundamentals of Human Sexuality*. New York: Holt, Rinehart and Winston.

Keegan, John. 1976. *The Face of Battle*. New York: Penguin Books.

———. 1993. *A History of War*. New York: Alfred A. Knopf.

Keeley, Lawrence H. 1996. *War Before Civilization: The Myth of the Peaceful Savage*. New York: Oxford University Press.

Keyt, David. 1991. "Three Basic Theorems in Aristotle's *Politics*." In David Keyt and Fred D. Miller, Jr., eds., *A Companion to Aristotle's "Politics"*, 118–41. Oxford: Basil Blackwell.

Kimura, Doreen. 1992. "Sex Differences in the Brain." *Scientific American* 267 (September): 118–25.

———. 1996. "Sex, Sexual Orientation and Sex Hormones Influence Human Cognitive Function." *Current Opinion in Neurobiology* 6:259–63.

Kitcher, Philip. 1982. *Abusing Science: The Case Against Creationism*. Cambridge: MIT Press.

———. 1985. *Vaulting Ambition: Sociobiology and the Quest for Human Nature*. Cambridge: MIT Press.

———. 1990. "Developmental Decomposition and the Future of Human Behavioral Ecology." *Philosophy of Science* 57:96–117.

Klaw, Spencer. 1993. *Without Sin: The Life and Death of the Oneida Community*. New York: Penguin.

Kleiman, Devra. 1977. "Monogamy in Mammals." *Quarterly Review of Biology* 52:39–69.

Klein, Jacob. 1985. "On the Nature of Nature." In Robert B. Williamshon and Elliott Zuckerman, eds., *Lectures and Essays*, 219–39. Annapolis, Md.: St. John's College Press.

Klein, Richard. 1989. *The Human Career: Human Biological and Cultural Origins*. Chicago: University of Chicago Press.

Kohler, Wolfgang. 1927. *The Mentality of Apes*. London: Routledge & Kegan Paul.

Kojève, Alexandre. 1969. *Introduction to the Reading of Hegel*. Translated by James H. Nichols Jr. New York: Basic Books.

Konner, Melvin. 1982. *The Tangled Wing: Biological Constraints on the Human Spirit*. New York: Holt, Rinehart, Winston.

Koso-Thomas, O. 1987. *The Circumcision of Women*. London: Zed Books.

Kraemer, Gary W. 1992. "A Psychobiological Theory of Attachment." *Behavioral and Brain Sciences* 15:493–541.

Kramer, Peter D. 1993. *Listening to Prozac*. New York: Viking.

Kroeber, Alfred. 1917. "The Superorganic." *American Anthropologist* 19:163–213.

———. 1928. "Sub-Human Culture Beginnings." *The Quarterly Review of Biology* 3:325–42.

Kuhl, Patricia J. 1991. "Perception, Cognition, and the Ontogenetic and Phylogenetic Emergence of Human Speech." In Steven E. Brauth, William S. Hall, and Robert J. Dooling, eds., *Plasticity of Development*, 73–106. Cambridge: Cambridge University Press.

Kullman, Wolfgang. 1980. "Der Mensch als politisches Lebewesen bei Aristoteles." *Hermes* 108:419–43.

———. 1991. "Man as a Political Animal in Aristotle." In David Keyt and Fred D. Miller Jr., eds., *A Companion to Aristotle's Politics*, 94–117. Oxford: Basil Blackwell.

Kummer, Hans. 1968. *Social Organization of Hamadryas Baboons*. Chicago: University of Chicago Press.

———. 1982. "Social Knowledge in Free-ranging Primates." In D. R. Griffin, ed., *Animal Mind-Human Mind*, 113–30. New York: Springer-Verlag.

Kummer, Hans, W. Gotz, and W. Angst. 1974. "Triadic Differentiation: An Inhibitory Process Protecting Pair Bonds in Baboons." *Behaviour* 49:62–87.

Lack, David. 1957. *Evolutionary Theory and Christian Belief*. London: Methuen.

Lamb, Michael E., Joseph H. Pleck, Eric L. Charnov, and James A. Levine. 1985. "Paternal Behavior in Humans." *American Zoologist* 25:883–94.

———. 1987. "A Biosocial Perspective on Paternal Behavior and Involvement." In Jane B. Lancaster, Jeanne Altmann, Alice S. Rossi, and Lonnie R. Sherrod, eds., *Parenting Across the Life Span*, 111–42. New York: Aldine de Gruyter.

Lancaster, Jane. 1994. "Human Sexuality, Life Histories, and Evolutionary Ecology." In Alice S. Rossi, ed., *Sexuality Across the Life Course*. Chicago: University of Chicago Press.

———. 1997. "The Evolutionary History of Human Parental Investment in Relation to Population Growth and Social Stratification." In Patricia A. Gowaty, ed., *Feminism and Evolutionary Biology*, 466–88. New York: Chapman and Hall.

Lancaster, Jane, and Chet Lancaster. 1983. "Parental Investment: The Hominid Adaptation." In David J. Ortner, ed., *How Humans Adapt*, 33–65. Washington, D.C.: Smithsonian Institution Press.

Las Casas, Bartolomé de. 1974a. *In Defense of the Indians*. Translated by Stafford Poole. DeKalb: Northern Illinois University Press.

———. 1974b. *The Devastation of the Indies*. Translated by Herme Briffault. New York: Seabury Press.

.Lauder, George. 1982. Introduction to *Form and Function*, by E. S. Russell. Chicago: University of Chicago Press.

Lazarus, Richard S., and Bernice N. Lazarus. 1994. *Passion and Reason*. New York: Oxford University Press.

Lear, Jonathan. 1988. *Aristotle: The Desire to Understand.* Cambridge: Cambridge University Press.

LeDoux, Joseph E. 1995. "In Search of an Emotional System in the Brain: Leaping from Fear to Emotion and Consciousness." In Michael Gazzaniga, ed., *The Cognitive Neurosciences*, 1049–61. Cambridge: MIT Press.

———. 1996. *The Emotional Brain.* New York: Simon and Schuster.

Lennox, James G. 1992. "Teleology." In Evelyn Fox Keller and Elisabeth A. Lloyd, eds., *Keywords in Evolutionary Biology*, 324–33. Cambridge: Harvard University Press.

———. 1993. "Darwin *Was* a Teleologist." *Biology and Philosophy* 8:409–21.

Lenoir, Timothy. 1989. *The Strategy of Life: Teleology and Mechanics in Nineteenth-Century German Biology.* Chicago: University of Chicago Press.

Leopold, Aldo. 1949. *A Sand County Almanac.* New York: Oxford University Press.

Lerner, Gerda. 1986. *The Creation of Patriarchy.* New York: Oxford University Press.

Lerner, Ralph. 1987. *The Thinking Revolutionary: Principle and Practice in the New Republic.* Ithaca: Cornell University Press.

LeVay, Simon. 1993. *The Sexual Brain.* Cambridge: MIT Press.

———. 1996. *Queer Science: The Use and Abuse of Research into Homosexuality.* Cambridge: MIT Press.

Levine, Nancy E. 1988. *The Dynamics of Polyandry: Kinship, Domesticity and Population on the Tibetan Border.* Chicago: University of Chicago Press.

Levy, Howard S. 1966. *Chinese Footbinding.* New York: Walton Rawls.

Lewin, Roger. 1993. *The Origin of Modern Humans.* New York: Scientific American Library.

Lewis, C. S. 1967. "Nature." In *Studies in Words*, 24–74. Cambridge: Cambridge University Press.

Lewontin, Richard. 1972. "The Apportionment of Human Diversity." *Evolutionary Biology* 6:381–98.

———. 1982. *Human Diversity.* San Francisco: W. H. Freeman.

———. 1992. "Genotype and Phenotype." In Evelyn Fox Keller and Elisabeth A. Lloyd, eds., *Keywords in Evolutionary Biology*, 137–44. Cambridge: Harvard University Press.

Lieberman, Philip. 1984. *The Biology and Evolution of Language.* Cambridge: Harvard University Press.

———. 1991. *Uniquely Human: The Evolution of Speech, Thought, and Selfless Behavior.* Cambridge: Harvard University Press.

Lightfoot-Klein, Hanny. 1989. *Prisoners of Ritual: An Odyssey into Female Genital Circumcision in Africa.* Binghamton, N.Y.: Harrington Park Press.

Lincoln, Abraham. 1953. *Collected Works of Abraham Lincoln.* Edited by Roy Basler. 8 vols. New Brunswick, N.J.: Rutgers University Press.

Linton, Ralph. 1952. "Universal Ethical Principles: An Anthropological View." In Ruth Anshen, ed., *Moral Principles of Action,* 645–60. New York: Harper.

——. 1954. "The Problem of Universal Values." In R. Spencer, ed., *Method and Perspective in Anthropology,* 145–68. Minneapolis: University of Minnesota Press.

Lloyd, G. E. R. 1983. *Science, Folklore and Ideology.* Cambridge: Cambridge University Press.

Locke, John. 1959. *An Essay Concerning Human Understanding.* 2 vols. New York: Dover.

——. 1970. *Two Treatises of Government.* Edited by Peter Laslett. Cambridge: Cambridge University Press.

Locke, John L. 1993. *The Child's Path to Spoken Language.* Cambridge: Harvard University Press.

Lopreato, Joseph. 1984. *Human Nature and Biocultural Evolution.* Boston: Allen & Unwin.

Lorenz, Konrad. 1952. *King Solomon's Ring.* New York: Thomas Y. Crowell.

——. 1971. "Do Animals Undergo Subjective Experience?" In *Studies in Animal and Human Behavior,* 2:323–37. Cambridge: Harvard University Press.

Lovejoy, Arthur. 1936. *The Great Chain of Being.* Cambridge: Harvard University Press.

Luria, A. R. 1980. *Higher Cortical Functions in Man.* 2d ed. New York: Basic Books.

Lykken, David. 1995. *The Antisocial Personalities.* Hillsdale, N.J.: Lawrence Erlbaum.

Maccoby, Eleanor E. 1973. Review of *The Inevitability of Patriarchy,* by Steven Goldberg. *Science* 182:469–71.

——. 1980. *Social Development: Psychological Growth and the Parent-Child Relationship.* San Diego: Harcourt Brace Jovanovich.

MacDonald, Kevin. 1994. *A People That Shall Dwell Alone: Judaism and Group Evolutionary Strategy.* Westport, Conn.: Praeger.

MacFarquhar, Neil. 1996. "Mutilation of Egyptian Girls: Despite Bans, It Goes On." *New York Times,* 8 August.

Machiavelli, Niccolò. 1940. *The Prince & The Discourses.* New York: Random House, Modern Library.

MacIntyre, Alaisdair. 1959. "Hume on 'Is' and 'Ought.'" *Philosophical Review* 68:451–68.

MacKay, D. M. 1978. "Selves and Brains." *Neuroscience* 3:599–606.

Mackie, Gerry. 1996. "Ending Footbinding and Infibulation: A Convention Account." *American Sociological Review* 61:999–1017.

Mackie, J. L. 1982. *The Miracle of Theism: Arguments for and against the Existence of God.* Oxford: Oxford University Press.

Mackintosh, James. 1836. *Dissertation on the Progress of Ethical Philosophy*. Edinburgh: Adam and Charles Black.

MacLean, Paul D. 1990. *The Triune Brain in Evolution: Role in Paleocerebral Functions*. New York: Plenum.

Madsen, Douglas. 1985. "A Biochemical Property Relating to Power Seeking in Humans." *American Political Science Review* 79:448–57.

———. 1986. "Power Seekers Are Different: Further Biochemical Evidence." *American Political Science Review* 80:261–69.

Maimonides, Moses. 1963. *The Guide of the Perplexed*. Translated by Shlomo Pines. Chicago: University of Chicago Press.

Manin, Bernard. 1985. "Montesquieu et la Politique Moderne." *Cahiers de Philosophe Politique* 2:157–229.

Mansbridge, Jane J., ed. 1990. *Beyond Self-Interest*. Chicago: University of Chicago Press.

Margenau, Henry, and Roy A. Varghese, eds. 1992. *Cosmos, Bios, Theos*. LaSalle, Ill.: Open Court.

Marglin, Stephen. 1990. "Towards the Decolonization of the Mind." In F. A. Marglin and S. A. Marglin, eds., *Dominating Knowledge: Development, Culture, and Resistance*, 1–28. Oxford: Oxford University Press.

Maritain, Jacques. 1941. "Human Equality." In *Ransoming the Time*, 1–32. New York: Scribner's.

Marler, Peter. 1970. "Birdsong and Speech Development: Could There Be Parallels?" *American Scientist* 58:669–73.

———. 1976. "On Animal Aggression: The Roles of Strangeness and Familiarity." *American Psychologist* 31:239–46.

———. 1991a. "Differences in Behavioural Development in Closely Related Species: Birdsong." In Patrick Bateson, ed., *The Development and Integration of Behaviour*, 41–70. Cambridge: Cambridge University Press.

———. 1991b. "The Instinct for Vocal Learning: Songbirds." In Steven E. Brauth, William S. Hall, and Robert J. Dooling, eds., *Plasticity of Development*, 107–25. Cambridge: MIT Press.

Marler, Peter, and Herbert S. Terrace, eds. 1984. *The Biology of Learning*. New York: Springer-Verlag.

Marler, Peter, and Mirawko Timura. 1964. "Culturally Transmitted Patterns of Vocal Behavior in Sparrows." *Science* 146:1483–86.

Martin, Marie A. 1991. "Hutcheson and Hume on Explaining the Nature of Morality: Why It is Mistaken To Suppose Hume Ever Raised the 'Is-Ought' Question." *History of Philosophy Quarterly* 8:277–89.

Maryanski, Alexandra, and Jonathan H. Turner. 1992. *The Social Cage: Human Nature and the Evolution of Society*. Stanford, Calif.: Stanford University Press.

Mason, William A. 1982. "Primate Social Intelligence." In Donald R. Griffin, ed., *Animal Mind-Human Mind*, 131–43. New York: Springer-Verlag.

Masters, Roger D. 1987. "Evolutionary Biology and Natural Right." In Kenneth L. Deutsch and Walter Soffer, eds., *The Crisis of Liberal Democracy: A Straussian Perspective*, 48–67. Albany: State University of New York Press.

———. 1989a. "Obligation and the New Naturalism." *Biology and Philosophy* 4:17–32.

———. 1989b. *The Nature of Politics*. New Haven: Yale University Press.

———. 1990. "Evolutionary Biology and Political Theory." *American Political Science Review* 84:195–210.

———. 1992a. "Naturalistic Approaches to Justice in Political Philosophy and the Life Sciences." In Roger D. Masters and Margaret Gruter, eds., *The Sense of Justice: Biological Foundations of Law*, 67–92. Newbury Park, Calif.: Sage.

———. 1992b. "Toward a More Coherent Theory of Justice." In Roger D. Masters and Margaret Gruter, eds., *The Sense of Justice: Biological Foundations of Law*, 290–306. Newbury Park, Calif.: Sage.

———. 1993. *Beyond Relativism: Science and Human Values*. Hanover, N.H.: University Press of New England.

———. 1994a. "Why Study Serotonin, Social Behavior, and Law?" In Roger D. Masters and Michael T. McGuire, eds., *The Neurotransmitter Revolution: Serotonin, Social Behavior, and the Law*, 3–16. Carbondale: Southern Illinois University Press.

———. 1994b. "Conclusions for Public Policy: Early Intervention, Special Education, and the Law." In Roger D. Masters and Michael T. McGuire, eds., *The Neurotransmitter Revolution: Serotonin, Social Behavior, and the Law*, 227–41. Carbondale: Southern Illinois University Press.

———. 1994c. "Primate Politics and Political Theory." In Glendon Schubert and Roger D. Masters, eds., *Primate Politics*, 221–50. Lanham, Md.: University Press of America.

Masters, Roger D., and Margaret Gruter, eds. 1992. *The Sense of Justice: Biological Foundations of Law*. Newbury Park, Calif.: Sage.

Maxwell, Mary, ed. 1991. *The Sociobiological Imagination*. Albany: State University of New York Press.

Maynard Smith, John. 1964. "Group Selection and Kin Selection." *Nature* 201:1145–47.

———. 1982. *Evolution and the Theory of Games*. Cambridge: Cambridge University Press.

Mayr, Ernst. 1982. *The Growth of Biological Thought*. Cambridge: Harvard University Press.

———. 1988. *Toward a New Philosophy of Biology*. Cambridge: Harvard University Press.

————., 1996. "The Autonomy of Biology: The Position of Biology among the Sciences." *Quarterly Review of Biology* 71:97–106.

Mazur, Allan, and Alan Booth. 1997. "Testosterone and Dominance in Men." *Behavioral and Brain Sciences*, in press.

McClelland, David C. 1985. *Human Motivation*. Glenview, Ill.: Scott, Foresman.

McGrew, W.C. 1991. "Apes Cast Out of Eden?" *Nature* 354:324.

————. 1992. *Chimpanzee Material Culture*. Cambridge: Cambridge University Press.

McGuire, Michael T. 1992. "Moralistic Aggression, Processing Mechanisms, and the Brain: The Biological Foundations of the Sense of Justice." In Roger D. Masters and Margaret Gruter, eds., *The Sense of Justice: Biological Foundations of Law*, 31–46. Newbury Park, Calif.: Sage.

McShea, Robert J. 1978. "Human Nature Theory and Political Philosophy." *American Journal of Political Science* 22:656–79.

————. 1990. *Morality and Human Nature: A New Route to Ethical Theory*. Philadelphia: Temple University Press.

Mead, Margaret. 1928. *Coming of Age in Samoa*. New York: Morrow.

————. 1935. *Sex and Temperament in Three Primitive Societies*. New York: Morrow.

————. 1949. *Male and Female: A Study of the Sexes in a Changing World*. New York: Morrow.

————. 1973. "Does the World Belong to Men—Or to Women?" *Redbook* 141 (October): 46–52.

Mealey, Linda. 1995. "The Sociobiology of Sociopathy." *Behavioral and Brain Sciences* 18:523–99.

Midgley, Mary. 1978. *Beast and Man: The Roots of Human Nature*. Ithaca: Cornell University Press.

Mill, John Stuart. 1959. *On Liberty*. Indianapolis: Bobbs-Merrill.

————. 1964. *Autobiography*. New York: New American Library.

————. 1970. *The Subjection of Women*. In Alice S. Rossi, ed., *Essays on Sex Equality*. Chicago: University of Chicago Press.

Miller, Charles A. 1988. *Jefferson and Nature*. Baltimore: Johns Hopkins University Press.

Miller, Fred D., Jr. 1995. *Nature, Justice, and Rights in Aristotle's "Politics"*. Oxford: Clarendon Press.

Milton, Katherine. 1988. "Foraging Behaviour and the Evolution of Primate Intelligence." In Richard W. Byrne and Andrew Whiten, eds., *Machiavellian Intelligence: Social Expertise and the Evolution of Intellect in Monkeys, Apes, and Humans*, 285–305. Oxford: Clarendon Press.

————. 1993. "Diet and Primate Evolution." *Scientific American* 269 (August): 86–93.

Mithen, Steven. 1996. *The Prehistory of the Mind.* New York: Thames and Hudson.

Mivart, St. George Jackson. 1973. "Darwin's *Descent of Man.*" In David Hull, ed., *Darwin and His Critics*, 354–84. Chicago: University of Chicago Press.

———. 1893. "Evolution in Professor Huxley." *The Popular Science Monthly* 44:319–33.

Miyadi, Denzaburo. 1964. "Social Life of Japanese Monkeys." *Science* 143:783–86.

Moli, Francesco, and Alessandra Mori. 1985. "The Influence of the Early Experience of Worker Ants on Enslavement." *Animal Behaviour* 33:1384–87.

Monaghan, Edward P., and Stephen E. Glickman. 1992. "Hormones and Aggressive Behavior." In J. B. Becker, S. M. Breedlove, and D. Crews, eds., *Behavioral Endocrinology*, 261–85. Cambridge: MIT Press.

Montesquieu, Baron de. 1989. *The Spirit of the Laws.* Translated by Anne M. Cohler, Basia Carolyn Miller, and Harold Samuel Stone. Cambridge: Cambridge University Press.

Montgomery, Sy. 1991. *Walking with the Great Apes: Jane Goodall, Dian Fossey, Birute Galdikas.* Boston: Houghton Mifflin.

Moore, Chris, and Michael R. Rose. 1995. "Adaptive and Nonadaptive Explanations of Sociopathy." *Behavioral and Brain Sciences* 18:566–67.

Moore, Frank L. 1992. "Evolutionary Precedents for Behavioral Actions of Oxytocin and Vasopressin." *Annals of the New York Academy of Sciences* 652:156–65.

Moore, G. E. 1968. *Principia Ethica.* Cambridge: Cambridge University Press.

Moore, John A. 1985. "Human Ecology." *American Zoologist* 25:483–637.

———. 1988. "Understanding Nature—Form and Function." *American Zoologist* 28:449–584.

———. 1993. *Science as a Way of Knowing: The Foundations of Modern Biology.* Cambridge: Harvard University Press.

Morgan, Lewis Henry. 1851. *League of the Ho-de-no-sau-nee, or Iroquois.* Rochester: Sage & Brother. Reprint, New York: Citadel Press, 1962.

Morris, Desmond. 1982. Foreword to *Chimpanzee Politics*, by Frans de Waal. New York: Harper & Row.

Morris, Henry. 1985. *Scientific Creationism.* 2d ed. El Cajon, Calif.: Master Books.

Morton, Samuel G. 1839. *Crania Americana.* Philadelphia: John Pennington.

———. 1844. *Crania Aegyptiaca. Transactions of the American Philosophical Society* 9:93–159.

Mount, Ferdinand. 1982. *The Subversive Family: An Alternative History of Love and Marriage.* London: Jonathan Cape.

Mulhern, J. J. 1972. "Mia monon pantachou kata physin he arete." *Phronesis* 17:260–68.

Muncy, Raymond. 1974. *Sex and Marriage in Utopian Communities: Nineteenth-Century America.* Baltimore: Penguin.

Murdock, George P. 1945. "The Common Denominator of Cultures." In Ralph Linton, ed., *The Science of Man in the World Crisis*, 123–42. New York: Columbia University Press.

———. 1949. *Social Structure*. New York: Free Press.

Murphy, Jane M. 1976. "Psychiatric Labeling in Cross-Cultural Perspective." *Science* 191:1019–28.

Naroll, Raoull. 1983. *The Moral Order*. Beverly Hills, Calif.: Sage Publications.

Nash, A. E. K. 1970a. "Fairness and Formalism in the Trials of Blacks in the State Supreme Courts of the South." *Virginia Law Review* 56:64–100.

———. 1970b. "A More Equitable Past? Southern Supreme Courts and the Protection of the Antebellum Negro." *North Carolina Law Review* 48:197–242.

———. 1979. "Reason of Slavery: Understanding the Judicial Role in the Peculiar Institution." *Vanderbilt Law Review* 32:7–218.

Nei, Masatoshi, and Arum K. Roychoudhury. 1972. "Gene Differences between Caucasian, Negro, and Japanese Populations." *Science* 177:534–36.

Neuhaus, Richard John. 1993. Review of James Q. Wilson, *The Moral Sense*. *National Review*, 23 August, 55–57.

———. 1996. "Religion and the Shifting Center in American Politics." *The Long-Term View* 3:73–77.

Newman, S.A. 1988a. "Idealist Biology." *Perspectives in Biology and Medicine* 31:353–68.

———. 1988b. "Does Human Genetic Engineering Have a Scientific Basis?" *Report from the Institute for Philosophy and Public Policy* 8 (Winter): 6–8.

Nichols, Mary P. 1983. "The Good Life, Slavery, and Acquisition: Aristotle's Introduction to Politics." *Interpretation* 11:171–83.

Nietzsche, Friedrich. 1986. *Human, All Too Human*. Translated by R. J. Hollingdale. Cambridge: Cambridge University Press.

Nilsson, Dan, and Susanne Pelger. 1994. "A Pessimistic Estimate of the Time Required for an Eye to Evolve." *Proceedings of the Royal Society of London* B2561:53–58.

Nishida, Toshisada. 1979. "The Social Structure of Chimpanzees of the Mahale Mountains." In David A. Hamburg and Elizabeth R. McCown, eds., *The Great Apes*, 73–121. Menlo Park, Calif.: Benjamin/Cummins.

———. 1987. "Local Traditions and Cultural Transmission." In Barbara Smuts, Dorothy L. Cheney, Robert M. Seyfarth, Richard W. Wrangham, and Thomas T. Struhsaker, eds., *Primate Societies*, 462–74. Chicago: University of Chicago Press.

———. 1990. "A Quarter Century of Research in the Mahale Mountains: An Overview." In Toshisada Nishida, ed., *The Chimpanzees of the Mahale Mountains*, 3–35. Tokyo: University of Tokyo Press.

Nitecki, Matthew H., ed. 1988. *Evolutionary Progress*. Chicago: University of Chicago Press.

Noble, William, and Iain Davidson. 1991. "The Evolutionary Emergence of Modern Human Behaviour: Language and its Archaeology." *Man* 26:223–53.

Noddings, Nel. 1990. "Ethics from the Standpoint of a Woman." In Deborah Rhode, ed., *Theoretical Perspectives on Sexual Difference*, 160–73. New Haven: Yale University Press.

Nott, Josiah. 1981. "Two Lectures on the Natural History of the Caucasian and Negro Races." In Drew Gilpin Faust, ed., *The Ideology of Slavery*, 206–38. Baton Rouge: Louisiana State University.

Novacek, Michael. 1994. "Paleontology: Whales Leave the Beach." *Nature* 368:807.

Noyes, John Humphrey. 1853. *Bible Communism*. Brooklyn, N.Y.: Published at the Office of the *Circular*.

———. 1870. *History of American Socialisms*. Philadelphia: Lippincott.

———. 1875. *Home-Talks*. Oneida, N.Y.: Published by the Oneida Community.

Noyes, Pierrepont. 1937. *My Father's House: An Oneida Boyhood*. New York: Farrar & Rinehart.

Numbers, Ronald L. 1992. *The Creationists: The Evolution of Scientific Creationism*. New York: Alfred A. Knopf.

Nussbaum, Martha. 1978. *Aristotle's "De Motu Animalium"*. Princeton: Princeton University Press.

———. 1986. *The Fragility of Goodness*. Cambridge: Cambridge University Press.

———. 1990. "Aristotelian Social Democracy." In R. Bruce Douglass, Gerald M. Mara, and Henry S. Richardson, eds., *Liberalism and the Good*, 203–52. New York: Routledge.

———. 1992a. "Human Functioning and Social Justice: In Defense of Aristotelian Essentialism." *Political Theory* 20:202–46.

———. 1992b. "Justice for Women." *New York Review of Books* 39 (8 October): 43–48.

———. 1993. "Non-Relative Virtues: An Aristotelian Approach." In Martha Nussbaum and Amartya Sen, eds., *The Quality of Life*, 242–69. New York: Oxford University Press.

Okin, Susan M. 1989. *Justice, Gender, and the Family*. New York: Basic.

———. 1990. "Thinking Like a Woman." In Deborah Rhode, ed., *Theoretical Perspectives on Sexual Difference*, 145–59. New Haven: Yale University Press.

Ornstein, Robert, and David Sobel. 1987. *The Healing Brain*. New York: Simon and Schuster.

Owens, Joseph. 1988. "The Self in Aristotle." *Review of Metaphysics* 41 (June): 707–22.

Oyama, Susan. 1985. *The Ontogeny of Information*. Cambridge: Cambridge University Press.

Pagden, Anthony. 1982. *The Fall of Natural Man: The American Indian and the Origins of Comparative Ethnology.* Cambridge: Cambridge University Press.

Panksepp, Jaak. 1992. "Oxytocin Effects on Emotional Processes: Separation Distress, Social Bonding, and Relationships to Psychiatric Disorders." *Annals of the New York Academy of Sciences* 652:243–52.

Panksepp, Jaak, Stephen M. Siviy, and Lawrence A. Normansell. 1985. "Brain Opioids and Social Emotions." In Martin Reite and Tiffany Field, eds., *The Psychology of Attachment and Separation*, 3–49. Orlando, Fla.: Academic Press.

Paradis, James. 1989. "*Evolution and Ethics* in its Victorian Context." In James Paradis and George C. Williams, *Evolution and Ethics*, 3–55. Princeton: Princeton University Press.

Passingham, Richard. 1982. *The Human Primate.* San Francisco: W. H. Freeman.

———. 1993. *The Frontal Lobes and Voluntary Action.* Oxford: Oxford University Press.

Patterson, Orlando. 1967. *The Sociology of Slavery.* Rutherford, N.J.: Fairleigh Dickinson University Press.

———. 1982. *Slavery and Social Death.* Cambridge: Harvard University Press.

Pelikan, Jaroslav. 1993. *Christianity and Classical Culture: The Metamorphosis of Natural Theology in the Christian Encounter with Hellenism.* New Haven: Yale University Press.

Percy, Walker. 1975. *The Message in the Bottle.* New York: Farrar, Straus and Giroux.

Pereira, Michael E., and Lynn A. Fairbanks, eds. 1993. *Juvenile Primates: Life History, Development, and Behavior.* New York: Oxford University Press.

Perlez, J. 1990. "Puberty Rite for Girls is Bitter Issue Across Africa." *New York Times*, 15 January.

Peterson, Dale, and Jane Goodall. 1993. *Visions of Caliban: On Chimpanzees and People.* New York: Houghton Mifflin.

Pianka, E. R. 1970. "On 'r' and 'K' Selection." *American Naturalist* 104:592–97.

Pinker, Steven. 1994. *The Language Instinct.* New York: William Morrow.

Pinker, Steven, and Paul Bloom. 1990. "Natural Language and Natural Selection." *Behavioral and Brain Sciences* 13:707–84.

Pitt, Roger. 1978. "Warfare and Hominid Brain Evolution." *Journal of Theoretical Biology* 72:551–75.

Pittendrigh, Colin. S. 1958. "Adaptation, Natural Selection, and Behavior." In Anne Roe and George Gaylord Simpson, eds., *Behavior and Evolution*, 390–416. New Haven: Yale University Press.

Plato. 1961. *The Collected Dialogues of Plato.* Edited by Edith Hamilton and Huntington Cairns. Princeton: Princeton University Press.

Plomin, Robert, and C. S. Bergeman. 1991. "The Nature of Nurture: Genetic Influence on 'Environmental' Measures." *Behavioral and Brain Sciences* 14:373–86.

Plomin, Robert, J. C. DeFries, and G. E. McClearn. 1990. *Behavioral Genetics*. 2d ed. New York: W. H. Freeman.

Plomin, Robert, Michael J. Owen, and Peter McGuffin. 1994. "The Genetic Basis of Complex Human Behaviors." *Science* 264:1733–39.

Plutchik, Robert. 1994. *The Psychology and Biology of Emotion*. New York: Harper Collins.

Poinsot, John. 1985. *Tractatus de Signis*. Translated by John Deely. Berkeley: University of California Press.

Polanyi, Michael. 1968. "Life's Irreducible Structure." *Science* 160:1308–12. Reprinted in Michael Polanyi, *Knowing and Being*, Marjorie Grene, ed., 225–39. Chicago: University of Chicago Press, 1969.

Polanyi, Michael, and Harry Prosch. 1975. *Meaning*. Chicago: University of Chicago Press.

Pollock, Linda A. 1983. *Forgotten Children: Parent-Child Relations from 1500 to 1900*. Cambridge: Cambridge University Press.

Popper, Karl, and John Eccles. 1977. *The Self and Its Brain*. London: Routledge & Kegan Paul.

Portmann, Adolf. 1967. *Animal Forms and Patterns*. Translated by Hella Czech. New York: Schocken Books.

Power, Margaret. 1991. *The Egalitarians—Human and Chimpanzee*. Cambridge: Cambridge University Press.

Premack, David, and Ann James Premack. 1983. *The Mind of an Ape*. New York: Norton.

Pufendorf, Samuel. 1964. *De Jure Naturae et Gentium Libri Octo*. Translated by C. H. Oldfather and W. A. Oldfather. New York: Oceana Publications.

Quiatt, Duane, and Vernon Reynolds. 1993. *Primate Behaviour: Information, Social Knowledge, and the Evolution of Culture*. Cambridge: Cambridge University Press.

Raine, Adrian. 1993. *The Psychopathology of Crime: Criminal Behavior as a Clinical Disorder*. San Diego: Academic Press.

Rakic, Pasko. 1991. "Plasticity of Cortical Development." In Steven E. Brauth, William S. Hall, and Robert J. Dooling, eds., *Plasticity of Development*, 127–61. Cambridge: MIT Press.

Raleigh, Michael J., and Michael T. McGuire. 1994. "Serotonin, Aggression, and Violence in Vervet Monkeys." In Roger D. Masters and Michael T. McGuire, eds., *The Neurotransmitter Revolution: Serotonin, Social Behavior, and the Law*, 129–45. Carbondale: Southern Illinois University Press.

Raven, Peter H., and George B. Johnson. 1989. *Biology*. 2d ed. St. Louis: Times Mirror/Mosby College Publishing.

Real, Leslie. 1991. "Animal Choice Behavior and the Evolution of Cognitive Architecture." *Science* 253:980–86.

————, ed. 1994. *Behavioral Mechanisms in Evolutionary Ecology*. Chicago: University of Chicago Press.

Redfield, Robert. 1962. *Human Nature and the Study of Society*. Chicago: University of Chicago Press.

Reeve, Hudson K. 1991. "*Polistes*." In Kenneth G. Ross and Robert W. Matthews, eds., *The Social Biology of Wasps*, 99–148. Ithaca: Cornell University Press.

Reynolds, Vernon. 1980. *The Biology of Human Action*. San Francisco: W. H. Freeman.

Reynolds, Vernon, and Ralph Tanner. 1995. *The Social Ecology of Religion*. New York: Oxford University Press.

Richards, Robert. 1987. *Darwin and the Emergence of Evolutionary Theories of Mind and Behavior*. Chicago: University of Chicago Press.

Richardson, Henry S. 1992. "Desire and the Good in *De Anima*." In Martha C. Nussbaum and Amélie O. Rorty, eds., *Essays on Aristotle's "De Anima,"* 381–99. Oxford: Oxford University Press.

Ricklefs, Robert E., and Caleb E. Finch. 1995. *Aging: A Natural History*. New York: Scientific American Library.

Ricoeur, Paul. 1966. *Freedom and Nature: The Voluntary and the Involuntary*. Evanston, Ill.: Northwestern University Press.

Ridley, Matt. 1997. *The Origins of Virtue: Human Instincts and the Evolution of Cooperation*. New York: Viking.

Ristau, Carolyn A., and Donald Robbins. 1982. "Language in the Great Apes: A Critical Review." *Advances in the Study of Behavior* 12:141–255.

Robertson, Constance Noyes. 1970. *Oneida Community: An Autobiography, 1851–76*. Syracuse: Syracuse University Press.

————. 1972. *Oneida Community: The Breakup, 1876–1881*. Syracuse, N.Y.: Syracuse University Press.

Rodseth, Lars, Richard W. Wrangham, Alisa M. Harrigan, and Barbara Smuts. 1991. "The Human Community as a Primate Society." *Current Anthropology* 32:221–54.

Rorty, Richard. 1983. "Post-Modernist Bourgeois Liberalism." *Journal of Philosophy* 80:583–89.

————. 1989. *Contingency, Irony, and Solidarity*. Cambridge: Cambridge University Press.

Rose, Michael R. 1991. *Evolutionary Biology of Aging*. New York: Oxford University Press.

Roseler, Peter-Frank. 1991. "Reproductive Competition during Colony Establishment." In Kenneth G. Ross and Robert W. Matthews, eds., *The Social Biology of Wasps*, 309–35. Ithaca: Cornell University Press.

Rosenberg, Alexander. 1985. *The Structure of Biological Science*. Cambridge: Cambridge University Press.

————. 1992. *Economics—Mathematical Politics or Science of Diminishing Returns?* Chicago: University of Chicago Press.

Rosenblatt, Jay S. 1992. "Hormone-Behavior Relations in the Regulation of Parental Behavior." In Jill B. Becker, S. Marc Breedlove, and David Crews, eds., *Behavioral Endocrinology*, 219–59. Cambridge: MIT Press.

Ruddick, Sara. 1980. "Maternal Thinking." *Feminist Studies* 6:342–67.

————. 1989. *Maternal Thinking.* New York: Ballantine Books.

Rule, Ann. 1989. *The Stranger Beside Me.* Revised and updated edition. New York: Signet.

Ruse, Michael. 1973. *The Philosophy of Biology.* Atlantic Highlands, N.J.: Humanities Press.

————. 1986. *Taking Darwin Seriously.* New York: Basil Blackwell.

————. 1987. "Biological Species: Natural Kinds, Individuals, or What?" *British Journal for the Philosophy of Science* 38:225–42.

Rush, Benjamin. 1815. "An Inquiry into the Influence of Physical Causes upon the Moral Faculty." In *Medical Inquiries and Observations*, 1:93–124. 4 vols. Philadelphia: M. Carey.

Rushton, J. Philippe. 1994. *Race, Evolution, and Behavior.* New Brunswick, N.J.: Transaction Publishers.

Russell, E. S. 1916. *Form and Function.* London: John Murray. Facsimile, with Introduction by George V. Lauder. Chicago: University of Chicago Press, 1982.

————. 1945. *The Directiveness of Organic Activity.* Cambridge: Cambridge University Press.

Rusting, Rick. 1993. "Why Do We Age?" *Scientific American.* 267(December):130–41.

Sachs, Joe. 1995. *Aristotle's "Physics": A Guided Study.* New Brunswick, N.J.: Rutgers University Press.

Sacks, Oliver. 1985. *The Man Who Mistook His Wife for a Hat.* New York: Summit Books.

Sahlins, Marshall. 1976. *The Use and Abuse of Biology: An Anthropological Critique of Sociobiology.* Ann Arbor: University of Michigan Press.

Salisbury, Harrison. 1981. *Black Night, White Snow: Russia's Revolutions, 1905–1917.* New York: Da Capo.

Salkever, Stephen G. 1990. *Finding the Mean: Theory and Practice in Aristotelian Political Philosophy.* Princeton: Princeton University Press.

Salthe, Stanley N. 1985. *Evolving Hierarchical Systems.* New York: Columbia University Press.

Sapolsky, Robert. 1988. "Lessons of the Serengeti: Why Some of Us Are More Susceptible to Stress." *The Sciences*, May/June, 38–42.

————. 1992. "Neuroendrocrinology of the Stress Response." In Jill B. Becker, S. Marc

Breedlove, and David Crews, eds., *Behavioral Endocrinology*, 287–324. Cambridge: MIT Press.

Scarr, Sandra. 1992. "Developmental Theories for the 1990s: Development and Individual Differences." *Child Development* 63:1–19.

Schubert, Glendon, and Roger D. Masters, eds. 1991. *Primate Politics*. Carbondale: Southern Illinois University Press.

Scott, John Paul. 1989. *The Evolution of Social Systems*. New York: Gordon and Breach.

Scott, John Paul, and John L. Fuller. 1965. *Genetics and the Social Behavior of the Dog*. Chicago: University of Chicago Press.

Scrimshaw, Susan C. 1984. "Infanticide in Human Populations." In Glenn Hausfater and Sarah Blaffer Hrdy, eds., *Infanticide: Comparative and Evolutionary Perspectives*. Hawthorne, N.Y.: Aldine.

Scull, A. and D. Favreau. 1986. "The Clitoridectomy Craze." *Social Research* 53:243–60.

Seeley, Thomas D. 1985. *Honeybee Ecology*. Princeton: Princeton University Press.

———. 1989. "The Honey Bee Colony as a Superorganism." *American Scientist* 77:546–53.

———. 1995. *The Wisdom of the Hive: The Social Physiology of Honey Bee Colonies*. Cambridge: Harvard University Press.

Seger, Jon. 1991. "Sisters in Arms." *Nature* 353:804.

———. 1996. "Exoskeletons Out of the Closet." *Science* 274:941.

Selye, Hans. 1976. *The Stress of Life*. 2d ed. New York: McGraw-Hill.

Serpell, James, and J. A. Jagoe. 1995. "Early Experience and the Development of Behaviour." In James Serpell, ed., *The Domestic Dog: Its Evolution, Behaviour, and Interactions with People*, 79–102. Cambridge: Cambridge University Press.

Seyfarth, Robert M., and Dorothy L. Cheney. 1994. "The Evolution of Social Cognition in Primates." In Leslie A. Real, ed., *Behavioral Mechanisms in Evolutionary Ecology*, 371–89. Chicago: University of Chicago Press.

Shanley, Mary Lyndon. 1989. *Feminism, Marriage, and the Law in Victorian England, 1850–1895*. Princeton: Princeton University Press.

Shepard, Roger N. 1987. "Evolution of a Mesh between Principles of the Mind and Regularities of the World." In John Dupre, ed., *The Latest on the Best: Essays on Evolution and Optimality*, 251–75. Cambridge: MIT Press.

Showalter, E. 1985. *The Female Malady: Women, Madness, and English Culture, 1850–1980*. Princeton: Princeton University Press.

Sigmund, Karl. 1993. *Games of Life: Explorations in Ecology, Evolution, and Behavior*. Oxford: Oxford University Press.

Silk, Joan B. 1990. "Human Adoption in Evolutionary Perspective." *Human Nature* 1:25–52.

Silverman, Irwin. 1990. "The r/K Theory of Human Individual Differences." *Ethology and Sociobiology* 11:1–9.

Simon, Yves R. 1951. *Philosophy of Democratic Government*. Chicago: University of Chicago Press.

Simpson, Peter. 1986. "Autonomous Morality and the Idea of the Noble." *Interpretation* 14:353–70.

Slater, P. J. B. 1983. "The Study of Communication." In T. R. Halliday and P. J. B. Slater, eds., *Animal Behaviour: Communication*, 9–42. New York: W. H. Freeman.

Sloan, Phillip R. 1972. "John Locke, John Ray, and the Problem of the Natural System." *Journal of the History of Biology* 5:1–53.

———. 1985. "Essay Review: Mayr on the History of Biology." *Journal of the History of Biology* 18:145–53.

Smart, Ninian. 1996. *Dimensions of the Sacred: An Anatomy of the World's Beliefs*. Berkeley: University of California Press.

Smith, Adam. 1982. *The Theory of Moral Sentiments*. Indianapolis: Liberty Classics.

Smith, Eric Alden, and Bruce Winterhalder, eds. 1992. *Evolutionary Biology and Human Behavior*. New York: Aldine de Gruyter.

Smuts, Barbara. 1985. *Sex and Friendship in Baboons*. Hawthorne, N.Y.: Aldine.

———. 1992a. "Male Aggression against Women: An Evolutionary Perspective." *Human Nature* 3:1–44.

———. 1992b. "Feminism, the Naturalistic Fallacy, and Evolutionary Biology." *Politics and the Life Sciences* 11:174–76.

Smuts, Barbara, and David J. Gubernick. 1992. "Male-Infant Relationships in Nonhuman Primates: Paternal Investment or Mating Effort?" In Barry S. Hewlett, ed., *Father-Child Relations: Cultural and Biosocial Contexts*, 1–30. Hawthorne, NY: Aldine de Gruyter.

Sober, Elliott. 1984. *The Nature of Selection*. Cambridge: MIT Press.

———. 1993. *Philosophy of Biology*. Boulder: Westview Press.

Sorenson, Leonard R. 1988. "On the Problematic Dimensions of Bioethics and the Preconditions of Natural Right." *Politics and the Life Sciences* 6:215–20.

———. 1997. "On Strauss's 'On the Mutual Influence of Theology and Philosophy.'" An unpublished paper.

Spiro, Melford E. 1954. "Is the Family Universal?" *American Anthropologist* 56:839–46.

———. 1979. *Gender and Culture: Kibbutz Women Revisited*. Durham, N.C.: Duke University Press.

Spitz, Rene. 1952. "Authority and Masturbation." *Psychoanalytic Quarterly* 21:490–514.

———. 1965. *The First Year of Life*. New York: International Universities Press.

Springer, Sally, and Georg Deutsch. 1985. *Left Brain, Right Brain.* New York: W. H. Freeman.

Spuhler, John N. 1959. "Somatic Paths to Culture." In John Spuhler, ed., *The Evolution of Man's Capacity for Culture,* 1–13. Detroit: Wayne State University Press.

Stacey, P. B., and C. E. Bock. 1978. "Social Plasticity in the Acorn Woodpecker." *Science* 202:1298–1300.

Stanton, William. 1960. *The Leopard's Spots: Scientific Attitudes Toward Race in America, 1815–59.* Chicago: University of Chicago Press.

Stearns, Stephen C. 1992. *The Evolution of Life Histories.* New York: Oxford University Press.

Stent, Gunther S. 1978a. *Paradoxes of Progress.* San Francisco: W. H. Freeman.

———. 1978b. "Introduction." In Gunther S. Stent, ed., *Morality as a Biological Phenomenon,* 1–18. Berkeley: University of California Press.

———. 1985. "Thinking in One Dimension: The Impact of Molecular Biology on Development." *Cell* 40:1–2.

Stephens, William N. 1963. *The Family in Cross-Cultural Perspective.* New York: Holt, Rinehart and Winston.

Storing, Herbert J., ed. 1981. *The Complete Anti-Federalist.* 7 vols. Chicago: University of Chicago Press.

Strauss, Leo. 1952. *The Political Philosophy of Hobbes.* Translated by Elsa M. Sinclair. Chicago: University of Chicago Press.

———. 1953. *Natural Right and History.* Chicago: University of Chicago Press.

———. 1958. *Thoughts on Machiavelli.* Glencoe, Ill.: Free Press.

———. 1977. *The City and Man.* Chicago: University of Chicago Press.

———. 1979. "The Mutual Influence of Theology and Philosophy." *The Independent Journal of Philosophy* 3 (1979):111–18.

———. 1983. "Jerusalem and Athens: Some Preliminary Reflections." In Leo Straus, *Studies in Platonic Political Philosophy,* 147–73. Chicago: University of Chicago Press.

———. 1991. *On Tyranny.* Victor Gourevitch and Michael S. Roth, eds. New York: The Free Press.

Strickberger, Monroe W. 1996. *Evolution.* 2d ed. Boston: Jones and Bartlett.

Strum, Shirley. 1987. *Almost Human: A Journey into the World of Baboons.* New York: Random House.

Strum, Shirley and Bruno Latour. 1991. "Redefining the Social Link: From Baboons to Humans." In Glendon Schubert and Roger D. Masters, eds., *Primate Politics,* 73–85. Carbondale: Southern Illinois University Press.

Sullivan, Andrew. 1995. *Virtually Normal: An Argument About Homosexuality.* New York: Alfred A. Knopf.

Sumner, William Graham. 1907. *Folkways.* Lexington, Mass.: Ginn and Company.

Sundstrom, Liselotte, Michel Chapuisat, and Laurent Keller. 1996. "Conditional Manipulation of Sex Ratios By Ant Workers: A Test of Kin Selection Theory." *Science* 274:993–95.

Swinburne, Richard. 1979. *The Existence of God.* Oxford: Oxford University Press.

———. 1996. *Does God Exist?* Oxford: Oxford University Press.

———. 1997. *The Evolution of the Soul.* Rev. ed. Oxford: Oxford University Press.

Symons, Donald. 1979. *The Evolution of Human Sexuality.* New York: Oxford University Press.

Tannen, Deborah. 1990. *You Just Don't Understand: Women and Men in Conversation.* New York: William Morrow.

Tanner, Nancy. 1987. "The Chimpanzee Model Revisited and the Gathering Hypothesis." In Warren G. Kinzey, ed., *The Evolution of Human Behavior: Primate Models,* 3–27. Albany: State University of New York Press.

Terrace, H. S., et al. 1979. "Can an Ape Create a Sentence?" *Science* 206:891–902.

Thompson, Richard F. 1985. *The Brain: An Introduction to Neuroscience.* New York: W. H. Freeman.

Thucydides. 1982. *The Peloponnesian War.* Translated by Richard Crawley. New York: Random House, Modern Library.

Tiger, Lionel. 1992. *The Pursuit of Pleasure.* Boston: Little, Brown.

Tiger, Lionel, and Joseph Shepher. 1975. *Women in the Kibbutz.* New York: Harcourt Brace Jovanovich.

Tiger, Lionel, and Robin Fox. 1971. *The Imperial Animal.* New York: Dell.

Tinbergen, Niko. 1963. "On Aims and Methods of Ethology." *Zeitschrift für Tierpsychologie* 20:410–33. Reprinted in Lynne D. Houck and Lee C. Drickamer, eds., *Foundations of Animal Behavior,* 114–37. Chicago: University of Chicago Press, 1996.

———. 1968. "On War and Peace in Animals and Man." *Science* 160:1411–18.

Tork, Istvan. 1990. "Anatomy of the Serotonergic System." *Annals of the New York Academy of Sciences* 600:9–34.

Tooby, John, and Irven DeVore. 1987. "The Reconstruction of Hominid Behavioral Evolution through Strategic Modeling." In Warren G. Kinzey, ed., *The Evolution of Human Behavior: Primate Models,* 183–237. Albany: State University of New York Press.

Topoff, Howard. 1990. "Slave-making Ants." *American Scientist* 78:520–28.

Towne, William F., and Wolfgang H. Kirchner. 1989. "Hearing in Honey Bees: Detection of Air-Particle Oscillations." *Science* 244:686–88.

Trevarthen, Colwyn. 1992. "Emotions of Human Infants and Mothers and Development of the Brain." *Behavioral and Brain Sciences* 15:524–25.

Trevathan, Wenda R. 1987. *Human Birth: An Evolutionary Perspective*. Hawthorne, N.Y.: Aldine de Gruyter.

Trigger, Bruce G. 1985. *Natives and Newcomers: Canada's "Heroic Age" Reconsidered*. Kingston, Ont.: McGill-Queens University Press.

Trivers, Robert. 1971. "The Evolution of Reciprocal Altruism." *Quarterly Review of Biology* 46:35–57.

―――. 1972. "Parental Investment and Sexual Selection." In Bernard Campbell, ed., *Sexual Selection and The Descent of Man, 1871–1971*, 136–79. Chicago: Aldine. Reprinted in Lynne D. Houck and Lee C. Drickamer, eds., *Foundations of Animal Behavior*, 795–838. Chicago: University of Chicago Press, 1996.

―――. 1985. *Social Evolution*. Menlo Park, Calif.: Benjamin/Cummings.

Turnbull, Colin. 1983. *The Human Cycle*. New York: Simon and Schuster.

Tylor, Edward. 1871. *Primitive Culture*. 2 vols. London: John Murray.

Tyson, Edward. 1699. *Orang-outang, sive Homo Sylvestris; or the Anatomy of a Pygmie compared with that of a Monkey, an Ape, and a Man*. London: The Royal Society.

Virkkunen, Matti, Judith DeJong, John Bartko, Frederick K. Goodwin, Markku Linnoila. 1989. "Relationship of Psychobiological Variables to Recidivism in Violent Offenders and Impulsive Fire Setters: A Follow-up Study." *Archives of General Psychiatry* 46:600–603.

Voland, E. 1988. "Differential Infant and Child Mortality in Evolutionary Perspective: Data from the Late 17th to 19th Century Ostfriesland (Germany)." In Laura L. Betzig, M. Borgerhoff Mulder, and Paul Turke, eds., *Human Reproductive Behaviour: A Darwinian Perspective*, 253–62. Cambridge: Cambridge University Press.

―――. 1989. "Differential Parental Investment: Some Ideas on the Contact Area of European Social History and Evolutionary Biology." In V. Standen and R. A. Foley, eds., *Comparative Socioecology: The Behavioural Ecology of Humans and Other Animals*. Oxford: Blackwell Scientific.

von Frisch, Karl. 1967. *The Dance Language and Orientation of Bees*. Cambridge: Harvard University Press.

von Uexkull, Jakob. 1957. *A Stroll Through the World of Animals and Men*. Translated by Claire H. Schiller. In Claire H. Schiller, ed., *Instinctive Behavior*, 5–80. New York: International Universities Press.

Walker, Alice, and Pratibha Parmar. 1993. *Warrior Marks: Female Genital Mutilation and the Sexual Blinding of Women*. New York: Harcourt Brace.

Walker, Graham. 1990. *Moral Foundations of Constitutional Thought: Current Problems, Augustinian Prospects*. Princeton: Princeton University Press.

Wallace, Alfred Russel. 1891. *Darwinism: An Exposition of the Theory of Natural Selection*. London: Macmillan.

Walters, Jeffrey R., and Robert M. Seyfarth. 1987. "Conflict and Cooperation." In *Primate Societies*, ed. Barbara B. Smuts et al., 306–17. Chicago: University of Chicago Press.

Walzer, Michael. 1977. *Just and Unjust Wars*. New York: Basic Books.

Welch, David A. 1993. *Justice and the Genesis of War*. New York: Cambridge University Press.

Wenke, Robert J. 1984. *Patterns in Prehistory*. 2d ed. Oxford: Oxford University Press.

West, Mary Maxwell, and Melvin Konner. 1976. "The Role of the Father: An Anthropological Perspective." In Michael E. Lamb, ed., *The Role of the Father in Child Development*, 185–217. New York: Wiley.

Wheeler, William Morton. 1910. *Ants: Their Structure, Development and Behavior*. New York: Columbia University Press.

———. 1928. *The Social Insects*. New York: Harcourt, Brace.

———. 1939. "The Ant-Colony as an Organism." In *Essays in Philosophical Biology*, 3–27. Cambridge: Harvard University Press.

Whiting, Beatrice B., and John W. M. Whiting. 1975. *Children of Six Cultures*. Cambridge: Harvard University Press.

Wickler, Wolfgang. 1972. *The Biology of the Ten Commandments*. New York: McGraw-Hill.

Wiener, Linda. 1990. "Of Lice and Men: Aristotle's Biological Treatises." *The St. John's Review* 40, no. 1:39–52.

Willhoite, Fred. 1976. "Primates and Political Authority: A Biobehavioral Perspective." *American Political Science Review* 70:1110–26.

Williams, George C. 1966. *Adaptation and Natural Selection*. Princeton: Princeton University Press.

———. 1989a. "A Sociobiological Expansion of *Evolution and Ethics*." In James Paradis and George C. Williams, *Evolution and Ethics*, 179–214. Princeton: Princeton University Press.

———. 1993. "Mother Nature is a Wicked Old Witch." In Matthew Nitecki and Doris V. Nitecki, eds., *Evolutionary Ethics*, 217–32. Albany: State University of New York Press.

Williams, Roger J. 1956. *Biochemical Individuality*. Austin: University of Texas Press.

Wills, Garry. 1978. *Inventing America: Jefferson's Declaration of Independence*. New York: Doubleday.

Wilson, David Sloan. 1994. "Adaptive Genetic Variation and Human Evolutionary Psychology." *Ethology and Sociobiology* 15:219–35.

Wilson, David Sloan, and Elliott Sober. 1994. "Reintroducing Group Selection to the Human Behavioral Sciences." *Behavioral and Brain Sciences* 17:585–654.

Wilson, Edward O. 1971. *The Insect Societies*. Cambridge: Harvard University Press.

———. 1975. *Sociobiology*. Cambridge: Harvard University Press.

———. 1978. *On Human Nature*. Cambridge: Harvard University Press.

———. 1984. *Biophilia*. Cambridge: Harvard University Press.

———. 1994. *Naturalist*. Washington, D.C.: Island Press.

Wilson, Edward O., and William L. Brown. 1953. "The Subspecies Concept and Its Taxonomic Application." *Systematic Zoology* 2:97–111.

Wilson, James Q. 1991. *On Character*. Washington, D.C.: AEI Press.

———. 1993a. "The Moral Sense." *American Political Science Review* 87:1–11.

———. 1993b. *The Moral Sense*. New York: Free Press.

———. 1993c. "The Family-Values Debate." *Commentary* 95:24–31.

Wilson, James Q., and Richard J. Herrnstein. 1985. *Crime and Human Nature*. New York: Simon and Schuster.

Winslow, James T., Nick Hastings, C. Sue Carter, Carroll R. Harbough, and Thomas R. Insel. 1993. "A Role for Central Vasopressin in Pair Bonding in Monogamous Prairie Voles." *Nature* 365:545–47.

Winston, Mark L. 1987. *The Biology of the Honey Bee*. Cambridge: Harvard University Press.

Witt, Diane M. 1997. "Regulatory Mechanisms of Oxytocin-Mediated Sociosexual Behavior." In C. Sue Carter, I. Izja Lederhendler, and Brian Kirkpatrick, eds., *The Integrative Neurobiology of Affiliation*, 287–301. New York: The New York Academy of Sciences.

Wolin, Richard, ed. 1993. *The Heidegger Controversy: A Critical Reader*. Cambridge: MIT Press.

Wollstonecraft, Mary. 1983. *Vindication of the Rights of Woman*. New York: Penguin Books.

Wrangham, Richard W. 1993. "The Evolution of Sexuality in Chimpanzees and Bonobos." *Human Nature* 4:47–79.

Wrangham, Richard W., and Dale Peterson. 1996. *Demonic Males: Apes and the Origins of Human Violence*. Boston: Houghton Mifflin.

Wrangham, Richard W., W. C. McGrew, Frans de Waal, and Paul G. Heltne, eds. 1994. *Chimpanzee Cultures*. Cambridge: Harvard University Press.

Wright, Robert. 1990. "The Intelligence Test." *The New Republic*, 29 January.

———. 1994. *The Moral Animal: The New Science of Evolutionary Psychology*. New York: Pantheon.

Yuwiler, Arthur, Gary L. Brammer, and K. C. Yuwiler. 1994. "The Basics of Serotonin Neurochemistry." In Roger D. Masters and Michael T. McGuire, eds., *The Neurotransmitter Revolution: Serotonin, Social Behavior, and the Law*, 37–46. Carbondale: Southern Illinois University Press.

Zuckerman, Marvin. 1994. "Impulsive Unsocialized Sensation Seeking: The Biological Foundations of a Basic Dimension of Personality." In John E. Bates and Theodore D. Wachs, eds., *Temperament: Individual Differences at the Interface of Biology and Behavior*, 219–55. Washington, D.C.: American Psychological Association.

Zuckerman, Marvin, and Nathan Brody. 1988. "Oysters, Rabbits, and People: A Critique of 'Race Differences in Behavior.'" *Personality and Individual Differences* 9:1025–33.

Zuckerman, Solly. 1932. *The Social Life of Monkeys and Apes*. London: Kegan Paul, Trench, Trubner.

Index